The Antichrist

Vincent P. Miceli, S.J.

The Antichrist

The Final Campaign Against the Savior

SOPHIA INSTITUTE PRESS
Manchester, New Hampshire

Nihil Obstat
Rev. William B. Smith, S.T.D.
Censor Librorum

Imprimatur
Rev. Joseph T. O'Keefe
Vicar-General, Archdiocese of New York
January 24, 1981, New York, N.Y.

Sophia Institute Press
Box 5284, Manchester, NH 03108
1-800-888-9344

www.SophiaInstitute.com

Sophia Institute Press® is a registered trademark of Sophia Institute.

paperback ISBN 978-1-64413-644-7
ebook ISBN 978-1-64413-645-4
Library of Congress Control Number: 2022930170
First printing

*To the millions of crowned and uncrowned martyrs who have suffered
and still suffer courageously for the Faith at the hands of militant
organized atheists, this book is dedicated with admiration and
thanksgiving. May they be inspired to persevere in their heroic struggle
by the fortitude and fidelity of their spiritual leaders and confreres,
Aleksandr Solzhenitsyn and Karol Wojtyla, Pope John Paul II.*

Foreword

And every spirit that dissolves Jesus is not of God,
but is of Antichrist, of whom you have heard that
he is coming, and now is already in the world.

I John 4:3

As G. K. Chesterton once remarked, the cleverest thing the devil ever did was to induce people to believe that he did not exist. It was truly a masterstroke, enabling him to carry on his nefarious operations, not just with the tolerance of so-called enlightened opinion; but with the active cooperation of well-meaning, charitable people like Eleanor Roosevelt, not to mention a large body of clergy of all denominations. Thus, for instance, the devil has been able to gain access to such organizations as the World Council of Churches, inducing them to foster the setting up of Marxist regimes in Africa and elsewhere, and generally to advance the cause of atheism and materialism. In the nether regions, I feel sure, to this day they speak with awe of all their lord and master, in his nonexistent capacity, has been able to achieve at the Vatican Councils, and after, in the way of demoralizing and disbanding the religious orders just when they were most needed, disrupting all accepted liturgical arrangements, including the Mass, and involving Catholic schools and colleges in the same Gadarene rush to moral vacuity as secular institutions—all ostensibly brought about under the auspices of the good Pope John.

With the devil, in consensus terms, abolished, but seemingly achieving an ascendency everywhere, it is easy to fall into a mood of hopelessness and inertia. In his latest book, *The Antichrist*, Fr. Miceli offers a powerful challenge to so defeatist an attitude. He looks back on the long record of the devil's activities as, in the words of the book of Job, he has gone to and fro in the earth and up and down in it, everywhere making mischief and creating chaos; yet always ultimately, as Fr. Miceli shows, frustrated in the working out of his devilish purposes by his chief adversary, Christ and His Church Militant. As for the existing situation—the chief danger now, Fr. Miceli insists, is not so much the devil's own malign operations as the distortions he has been able to induce, as a nonperson, in the words and teaching of the gospels, and the consequent devastating loss of faith among Christians and in Christian institutions resulting therefrom. In other words, we are witnessing today the exact fulfillment of the apostle Paul's prophecy just before he died that a time would come when professing Christians would not tolerate sound doctrine, but follow after their own lusts, preferring fantasy to truth.

It was John Henry Newman who foresaw with unique clarity how in our time, in the twentieth century, some two thousand years after St. Paul's prophecy was uttered, every particular would come to pass, down to the smallest detail. Fr. Miceli quotes Newman again and again in this sense—true words beautifully expressed, marvelous in their force, insight, and elegance. Truly, God never leaves us in unrelieved darkness; always throughout history somewhere a voice is raised, confuting the devil's false assumptions and deceiving hopes—for instance, today Solzhenitsyn's. All we need is ears to hear, a mind to understand, and a heart to believe, for which our prayers must endlessly be addressed to God, asking of Him ultimately only: "Thy will be done."

The havoc that has been made on the devil's behalf among Catholics and in their Church is so drastic and widespread as to leave an outsider like myself baffled and bewildered. How can it possibly be that priests and religious should allow themselves to get involved in the squalid power struggles that now, as always, characterize every variety of government and regime whatever its particular ideology may be, as well as revolutionary and insurrectionary movements, thereby implying that when our Lord said that His kingdom was not of this world, He meant that it was? Who would ever have envisaged nuns joining in, and even promoting, the wicked corruption of children through what is called sex education, but in practice amounts to an invitation to early debauchery? What an appalling scandal that young students with vocations should run the greatest risk of losing their faith, not in Vanity Fair where the world's pleasures and prizes, such as they are, continue to be on offer, but in the very seminaries where they receive their training for the priesthood! Some of the examples given in this vein by Fr. Miceli are hair-raising and it is greatly to his credit that he has the courage and integrity to cite them, without, I may add, sparing misguided Christian intellectual leaders, painful as this criticism must be to him.

No one who has lived at all perceptively can possibly doubt the devil's presence and scurvy practices in the world. As Judas had an essential role in the great drama of the Incarnation, so has the devil in all our history, as well as in each individual life. Milton could never have written *Paradise Lost* without a leading role for Satan; and in nature itself there is a force of gravity pulling all dead matter downward, as a counterpoise to the force of growth and creativity pushing all live matter upward. I have to believe in the devil because I have met him in all sort of disguises;

most terrifyingly on looking into a mirror and seeing there a face—my own, full of the passions and appetites of this world, "with slavering mouth and itching ears," as St. Bernard of Clairvaux puts it. Again, the devil infallibly crops up in all egotistic pursuits—in the quest for power, money, celebrity, as well as in ostensibly disinterested ones, for a kingdom of heaven on earth in all its various models—GNP-affluent, Marxist-apocalyptic, workaday-welfare, Gulag-special, and many another.

To a discerning nose he smells like a muskrat, and to a discerning eye glows with a feverish flush. As a fallen angel, he can readily simulate virtue, and find persuasive words to recommend murdering babies by the million in abortion operations to enhance the quality of life; likewise killing off the old and infirm, also in millions, to ensure that they die with dignity, the two operations amounting to a nonstop humane holocaust exceeding in scale and callousness anything of the kind hitherto mounted, not excepting the much-publicized Nazi holocaust.

The devil's most effective work in our time, however, has been done in the media, especially television, which he has more or less taken over. What a triumph for him to be able, for instance, to transmit scenes of depravity and violence into millions of homes, and generally to spread confusion as to what is real and what is fantasy, what is good and what is evil, thereby achieving, on a scale hitherto undreamt of, his most cherished purpose—making the words chanted by the Horrid Sisters in Shakespeare's play *Macbeth*: "Fair is foul, and foul is fair," the consensus, or orthodoxy, of a godless world. What a moment that must have been for the devil, too, when the ravings of a sick mind—Nietzsche's—were echoed in the seminaries of the West, and nominal successors of St. Thomas Aquinas solemnly announced that God was dead, the announcement naturally being taken up avidly by the media, and appearing on what must be one of the devil's favorite placards, the cover of *Time* magazine.

In war it is necessary, not just to have adequate forces for attack and defense, but also to study the enemy's past and present strategy and tactics. This is staff work, for which, in the everlasting Holy War against the devil, *The Antichrist* is a masterly textbook, telling us the order of the battle in past campaigns, briefing us on the disposition of forces and the terrain in the present line-up, and preparing us for the forays and battles that lie ahead. That a crucial campaign is already upon us cannot be doubted. I thank God that there are priests and teachers like Fr. Miceli to act as His intelligence officer, and ensure that the soldiers of Christ may know who are their enemies, however camouflaged, and where are the booby-traps and ambushes, and take heart in the knowledge that, seemingly out-numbered and out-gunned as they may be, with God on their side victory at last is certain.

Malcolm Muggeridge

Contents

Introduction

Pope John Paul II, about two years before he was elected supreme Pontiff, emphasized the tragic moral destitution into which the entire world – Christian and non-Christian – had fallen before the all-out assault of Satan and his demonic legions. At the end of his visit to the United States in 1976, Karol Cardinal Wojtyla made a short farewell speech that received very little coverage in the press. On the occasion of his being elected Pope John Paul II, *The Wall Street Journal* resurrected and published his U.S. valedictory on November 9, 1978. Here is his assessment of the advance of the powers of darkness:

> We are now standing in the face of the greatest historical confrontation humanity has gone through. I do not think the wide circle of the American society or the wide circles of the Christian community realize this fully. We are now facing the final confrontation between the Church and the Anti-Church, of the Gospel versus the anti-Gospel. This confrontation lies within the plans of divine providence; it is a trial which the whole Church, and the Polish Church in particular, must take up.
>
> It is a trial not only of our nation and the Church, but in a sense, it is a test of 2000 years of culture and Christian civilization with all its consequences for human dignity, individual rights, human rights and the rights of nations.[1]

---

[1]   *The Wall Street Journal*, November 9, 1978.

In this book our aim is to examine this growing crisis of Christianity. Our exposition is meant to alert Christians to the growing struggle, to the mounting intensity and savagery of this confrontation. Our second aim is not meant to produce doom or despair, but, using the words of Christ, to exhort Christians to courage and zeal in the fight for God's cause. Our Lord, speaking of the final confrontation, encouraged His followers thus: "And when you hear of wars and tumults, do not be afraid.. . . This will be a time for you to bear testimony. . . . By your endurance you will gain your souls.... Now when these things begin to take place, look up and raise your heads, because your redemption is drawing near.[2] ... Have confidence; I have overcome the world."[3]

In a previous book, *The Gods of Atheism*, I had a three-pronged purpose: 1) to hunt out the philosophical and theological origins of atheism over the last two hundred years, 2) to trace the alarming social escalation of atheism in modern times, 3) to indicate a Christian counterattack to atheism's international organization and militarization in its politico-moral crusade against Christianity. That book was written ten years ago.[4] Today atheism, flushed with many more victories over the intellectual and moral fiber of the West, and territorially over nations in Asia, Africa, South America, Central America, Cuba, and elsewhere, declares more boldly than ever that the main task of its messianic inundation of the nations is the total, final defeat of Christ and His Church.

Another purpose of this book is to indicate how far down the road from atheism to nihilism the world has traveled in its

---

[2] Luke 21:9, 13, 19, 28.
[3] John 16:33.
[4] Vincent P. Miceli, S.J., introduction to *The Gods of Atheism* (New Rochelle, NY: Arlington House Publishers, 1971).

death-wish to be dominated by the Antichrist. The signs of our times are very similar to, though on a more wicked, much vaster scale, those that preceded the coming of "the day of the Lord" in the times of Noah, of Sodom and Gomorrah, and of Christ. To be sure the name and time of the Antichrist are known only to God. But the portents of his nearness are evident everywhere in the general desertion of the Faith and the worldwide escalation of moral turpitude.

Of course, agnostic and atheistic sophisticates will smile patronizingly at the prophecy of the Antichrist's coming in a pestilence of heresies, preternatural heroics, and world wars. Progressist Christians will join the intellectual scoffers. Indeed these latter will act as catalysts for the coming of the Antichrist. They are in the forefront of the great apostasy. They have promulgated to the four winds the insidious theory that one actually damages the case for Christ and His Church by openly, intelligently, and courageously stating it. Of such Christians who have lost their faith and their nerve Dr. Austin Farrer wrote:

> There are frontiersmen and frontiersmen of course. There is what one might call the Munich school, who will always sell the pass in the belief that their position can be more happily defended from the foothills to the rear. Such people are not commonly seen as apologists. They are reckoned to be New Theologians. They are too busy learning from their enemies to do much in defense of their friends.[5]

But the secularist scoffers are always with us. Unfortunately, they have increased alarmingly within the Church. Yet it was thus

[5] Dr. Austin Farrer, from his chapter "The Christian Apologist," in *Light on C. S. Lewis* (London: Geoffrey Bles, 1965), p. 23.

3

in the days of Noah who was laughed to scorn as he built his ark of salvation.[6] It was thus in the days of Abraham as he pleaded fruitlessly with Sodom and Gomorrah. It was thus in the days of Christ as he wept over the city of Jerusalem. All these skeptics, however, were wiped out violently for their incredulity and licentiousness. It will be thus at the end of time. For wicked men and societies are too proud to accept and understand the ways of God.

But perhaps my main ambition in this book is to counteract a mood of defeatism that is infecting all the Churches. For in a thoroughly secularized society, such as we have today, Christians are tempted to be "with it," to regard their faith as a purely private, if not secret, affair, and to rationalize their refusal to influence their non-Christian neighbors openly by such false slogans as, "Arguments never convert anyone; only example converts."[7] If the doctrine of the Antichrist proves anything, it demonstrates that Christians are willy-nilly engaged in all-out spiritual war for eternal survival with the followers of Satan. If they are to be true to Christ, and to themselves, Christians must energetically conquer through words of truth and deeds of holiness the widespread will at large to disbelieve in the supernatural; they must rout with intelligent vigor avant-garde clerics and all appeasers who attempt to compromise Christian dogma and morals. Only such an uncompromising counterattack on the forces of atheism, admitted or camouflaged, will turn back the assaults of Satan and prepare Christians to confront the Antichrist successfully.

Christians must develop the courage to defy the tyranny of dogmatic atheism. They must become apologists for the Faith

6 See Matt. 24:36–39 on the comparison between the coming of the Antichrist and the flood.
7 Sir Arnold Lunn, "Apologetics without Apology," *Triumph*, November 1966, pp. 15–17.

and there should be nothing "apologetic" about their presentation of the case for Christianity.[8] Again Dr. Austin Farrer gives
us a full picture of the competent Christian apologist who will
not be intimidated by any evil forces: "The typical apologist is a
man whose every dyke is his last ditch. He will carry the war into
the enemy's country; he will yield not an inch of his own."[9] St.
John wrote his Apocalypse, which is full of horrendous plagues,
persecutions, and demonic assaults on the faithful, in order to
console the Christians of his day who were suffering under the
severe persecution of Nero. He depicts for them the victory of
the Lamb slain to save mankind, but risen in power and glory to
destroy Satan and the Antichrist in the final confrontation. That
Lamb that was slain is now alive, glorified and ruling forever at
the right hand of the Father. So, too, the fighting faithful must
suffer for a while. But they too will be eternally glorified in the
company of the Lamb. "Resist the devil and he will flee you,"[10]
Holy Scripture advises us. Resist the Antichrist and he will fall
together with his master Satan. This book aims to develop a
competent, successful, courageous, holy Resistance Movement
among Christians against the devil, and all his works and pomps,
especially, though, against Satan's commander-in-chief on earth,
the Antichrist.

[8] Ibid.
[9] Farrer, op. cit., p. 23.
[10] James 4:7.

Chapter 1

The Antichrist Revisited

Another book on the Antichrist? Why? As long as time and history last, the fortunes of Christ and the Antichrist will be a topic of absorbing interest to all men. But especially in our age of global, political upheaval, religious convulsions, the rapid spread of militantly organized atheism, and the flight from God into secularism, it should not at all be surprising that a new spate of books treating of the Antichrist, the end of the world and its day of wrath has inundated the reading market. Some of these books and many articles are written in a somewhat scholarly manner, but the vast majority of them are popular, journalistic, even novelistic creations. As for the run of movies treating this subject, there is such a morbid preoccupation with depicting bizarre violence, sensational sex, and perverted religions that millions watch fascinated with mankind's virtuosity in performing and experimenting with wickedness.

To mention but a few of the books recently published, Hal Lindsey has written *The Late Great Planet Earth* and *There's a New World Coming*, stressing the impending end of the earth and the imminency of the millennium. Boice has written *The Last and the Future World*; Willington has produced *The King Is Coming*. And J. Dwight Pentecost's creation is entitled *Things to Come*. Then, too, a recent work co-authored by two Catholic priests, the Rev.

John M. Tombler and the Rev. Hubert J. Funk, *The Raptured,* has joined the flood of modern apocalyptic writings.

Though I have read some of these books and skimmed through many others, I have no intention here of giving a critique of them. I admire the authors' attempt to update and apply these prophecies to the collapsing Christianity of our tragic times, but I do have a serious reservation about all of these books, and it is this: good intentions about and honest efforts at explaining difficult prophecies cannot justify the creation of theology-fiction in explaining them and, least of all, the presentation of personal speculations as *facts* found in these prophecies.

All of the above-mentioned books, and many others I have scanned, are full of personal speculations presented as historical facts. For example, it is stated categorically that the Antichrist will be Satan incarnate. This is a metaphysical impossibility, for only God, or one of the divine persons, can possess two natures in one person. An incarnation of Satan whereby he would possess two natures—human and angelic—in one angelic person would call for infinite power, something a mere creature cannot have. Or again, it is said that an Antipope will be the Second Beast arising from the earth and acting as the Antichrist's false Prophet, aiding him to destroy Rome and the Catholic Church. Even historical events are predicted with bold assurance, for example, that the Russians will invade the Middle East and be defeated by Israel. So it goes on and on, with a timetable of coming apocalyptic events so detailed that, if it is true what Christ told us about only the Father knowing the time and details of the Antichrist's coming, one can only conclude that the leakage of top secrets from the councils of the Holy Trinity is as bad as that from the councils of the State Department.

The thing wrong with such "facts" is that they are not revelations from God; they are not found in the prophecies of Scripture.

How can we explain this rush to chart with exactitude the details of the last days? Leaving aside the motive of calculated deception, for the authors seem very sincere, the fault has to be a combination of curiosity and impatience. We see the proclivity to this same fault in the millions of readers who buy and avidly read these books without critical thought. The authors are impatient with the obscurity, the mystery, the complexity of these prophecies. And so they attempt to read specifics into them, thinking that thereby they are helping their fellowmen. But, in attempting to prove things ahead of their time, they prove too much, fall into error and create a theology-fiction that trivializes the word of God. Christ told men to look for the signs of the times; the specifics would be given man when he needed them, when he could bear them. Man must wait on God's hour. At the Last Supper, Christ said to His apostles: "Many things I have yet to say to you, but you cannot bear them now. But when he, the Spirit of truth has come, he will teach you all the truth."[11] Clearly then, in order to prevent the faithful from falling into erroneous predictions it is appropriate today to review briefly and update the Church's teaching on the Antichrist.

But questions persist about the advisability of another book on the Antichrist. Have saints and scholars finally decided whether the word *Antichrist* is merely a generic term comprising in its meaning all evil movements of heretics, schismatics, apostates, and impious empires? Is it now definitely proved that the Antichrist is not a mere evil ethical spirit, or political system, or racial dynasty, or succession of rulers, or some cosmic power? Or have we now further proof that the Antichrist will be, according to the universal tradition of the Church, one man, an individual of extraordinary powers who will with genius

[11] John 16:12, 13.

organize and lead all evil persons and movements in a total war against Christ and His Church?

St. John the Evangelist distinguishes the Antichrist from all other adversaries of Christ. Moreover, Sacred Scripture imprints upon the mind, even after allowing for the figurative character of prophetic language, the strong impression that the Antichrist is to be an individual man. Consider this passage:

> Let no man deceive you by any means unless there come a revolt first, and the man of sin be revealed, the son of perdition, who opposeth, and is lifted up above all that is called God, or that is worshipped so that he sitteth in the temple of God, showing himself as if he were God. And then that wicked one shall be revealed whom the Lord Jesus shall kill with the spirit of His mouth; and shall destroy with the brightness of His coming, him, whose coming is according to the working of Satan, in all power, and signs, and lying wonders.[12]

Now consider this passage from Daniel:

Another shall rise after them, and he shall be diverse from the first, and he shall subdue three kings. And he shall speak great words against the Most High, and shall wear out the saints of the Most High, and think to change times and laws: and they shall be given into his hand until a time and times and the dividing of time. But the judgment shall sit, and they shall take away his domination, to consume and destroy it unto the end.[13]

And Daniel once more:

---

[12] Paul, 2 Thess. 2:3, 4, 8, 9.
[13] Dan. 7:24-26.

And there shall stand up in his place, one most vile, and unworthy of kingly honour: and in a few days he shall be destroyed, not in rage nor in battle. And there shall stand up in his place one despised, and the kingly honour shall not be given hi: and he shall come privately, and shall obtain the kingdom by fraud. And such as deal wickedly against the covenant shall deceitfully dissemble, but the people that know their God shall prevail and succeed. And they that are learned among the people shall teach man: and they shall fall by the sword, and by fire, and by captivity, and by spoil for many days.[14]

And in much the same vein St. John the Evangelist writes:

There was given him a mouth speaking great things and blasphemies; and power was given unto him to continue forty-two months. And he opened his mouth in blasphemy against God, to blaspheme His name and His tabernacle and them that dwell in heaven. And it was given unto him to make war with the saints, and to overcome them; and power was given him over all kindreds and tongues and nations. And all that dwell upon the earth shall worship him, whose names are not written in the book of the life of the Lamb slain from the foundation of the world.[15]

Such specific personal titles and characteristics cannot refer to an abstract ethical force for evil, or to a collective body or to movements of evil. An individual is specifically pointed out and identified by his supreme capacity and stunningly unique career in the pursuit of evil. He is the ultimate culmination of all

[14] Dan. 11:20, 21, 32, 36.
[15] John, Apoc. 13:5-7.

wicked precursors in the perpetration of evil against God and Christ. This man of sin will combine in himself all the malice and wicked art found in all previous evil persons. All the Fathers and theologians unanimously concur in this belief that the Antichrist will be an individual person. In fact Bellarmine and Suarez, two famous Jesuit theologians—Bellarmine being also a saint and doctor of the Church—teach that the personal existence of the Antichrist must be considered an object of divine faith.

But the questions remain. Granted that the Antichrist is to be a person, have exegetes and mystics revealed new, specific facts about his origin, personality, career, times, and deeds? Up to the present the Antichrist has appeared in a cloud of vague, conjectural, uncertain, enigmatic, complex, perplexing—at times even apparently contradictory—prophecies. Perhaps this book will unravel the riddle of the Antichrist?

Scripture tells us that "secret things belong to the Lord, our God." And God reveals his secrets through chosen prophets in the revelations He gives them. But it is the nature of prophetical language to present revelations in allegorical, figurative terms, indiscriminately mingling the past, present, and future, conveying only some accidental circumstances of facts, saying a minimum of what they substantially are and leaving to time the office of specifying, classifying, and inserting them into their circumstantial historical datelines. As John Henry Cardinal Newman notes in his "Advent Sermons on Antichrist," "It is not ordinarily the course of Divine Providence to interpret prophecy before the event."[16] Moreover, revelation does not intend to provide us with complete answers in all details, but

---

[16] John Henry Newman, *Tracts for the Times*, Vol. 5, "The Times of Antichrist" (London: J.G F. & J. Rivington, 1840), p. 3.

purposely leaves truths revealed with some aura of mystery, the better to purify man's faith in the fires of trial and expectation, the better to keep him alert, fighting, faithful, and persevering in the certainty of the main truth of the Lord's Second Coming, as well as in the uncertainty of the precise time of his arrival.

Historical events alone will give the answers to many difficulties we cannot solve concerning the Antichrist and the last times. How often did the events in our Lord's life sweep away the clouds of obscurity darkening many passages of the Old Testament that prophesied about the life, times, and deeds of the Messiah? This phenomenon of later clarification by the event of prophecies contained in the Old Testament led St. Augustine to construct this lapidary truth: *Novum Testamentum in Vetere latet, et Vetus in Novo patet.* "While the New Testament lies hidden in the Old, the Old Testament becomes clarified in the New."[17] We can safely say, then, that the prophecies of both testaments not yet fulfilled, concerning the arrival of the Antichrist and the Second Coming of Christ, are for us what prophecies concerning the Messiah were for the Jews before His coming. They are partially open and partially sealed books. They present us with several certain expectations now: (1) the Antichrist, whoever he may be or whatever he may do, is sure to come; (2) miracles are to be wrought by the Antichrist and the Two Witnesses of God; (3) Satan, if bound, is bound only for a short time and will certainly be released; (4) the war between good and evil is not over, but is building daily to an explosion of global, satanic dimensions; (5) the victory of Christ and His followers is assured. On the other hand, the time of the end of the world, the full identity of the

---

[17]   Quoted by Rev. P. Huchede in *History of Antichrist* (Rockford, IL: Tan Books and Publishers, 1969), p. 8.

Antichrist, his national and international allies, the details of his life—all these events and many others are presently shrouded in the aura of the unknown and we will have full clarification of them only when they are fulfilled in history.

Still, with so many truths about the Antichrist very obscure, doubtful, and problematic, what practical use is there to be found in speaking and writing about this "man of lawlessness"? Cardinal Newman states that it is never unprofitable for Christians to bear in mind that they live under a miraculous economy of salvation. Man's salvation began in a hidden, silent, mysterious miracle—the Incarnation—and will be consummated in a glorious global miracle—the Parousia. Moreover, in an age of unbelief in the transcendent and the total secularization of the sacred, it is a necessary divine grace to reflect on the supernatural saga of the Antichrist as a salutary counterpoise to the corrupt tendencies of the times. Then, too, it is always profitable to reflect on the whole economy of salvation from beginning to end—from the Creation and Fall to the First Coming of Christ, from the First to the Second Coming of Christ, from His cross to His crowning. Such meditations help Christians reawaken in themselves the truth that they share a solidarity with the holy prophets and ancient people of God. Apocalyptic studies can remind Christians that they participate in the same New Covenant, priesthood, sacraments, rights, duties, and glorious destiny won for all by Christ. Rumination on the Antichrist must perforce lead Christians to realize that they live in a sinful world, that they are called to be witnesses to Christ in this wicked world, that reproach and suffering are to be their normal lot, not some strange happening. Inquiry into the epic of the Antichrist can awaken men's hearts and expand their vision to see the divine meaning of history, to appreciate fully the indispensable place of Christ in mankind's salvation. Searchings into the tragedy of the Antichrist will help men make saving acts of faith, hope, and contrition, and perform deeds of charity in order to avoid the dismal destiny of that son of perdition. Then, too, in the words of St. Thomas Aquinas: "The knowledge of the simplest truth in the superior order gives us more pleasure than a perfect knowledge of the sublimest truths of an inferior order."[18] Thus, the knowledge of the Antichrist, like "all Scripture inspired by God, is profitable to teach, to reprove, to correct, and to instruct in justice."[19] Nothing can so strengthen our religious convictions and order our lives toward God and righteousness as a deep appreciation of the tragedy of eternal damnation. Nothing can so inspire and console us in our trials as the realization that God intends to conquer Satan, the Antichrist and their evil forces through our puny cooperation and suffering fidelity to his cause. Needless to say, knowledge of the Antichrist also enables us to analyze and baffle the designs of Satan as they appear in the desires and plottings of evil men. We are forewarned of his snares and learn how to resist him. We learn how to correct our impatience and presumption in the face of temptations. We learn how to distrust ourselves as we advance in confidence in Christ. In a word, sober meditations on the fortunes of the Antichrist are a spiritual investment against the forces of hell, an insurance of our triumph over them.

Furthermore, every generation is called upon to relate the spiritual conditions of its times to the conditions that will prevail during the age of the Antichrist. The comparison of the

[18] St. Thomas, *Summa Contra Gentiles*, book 1, chapter VIII.
[19] Paul, 2 Tim. 3:16.

iniquitous deeds of the Antichrist with the degenerate evils of our day could be a salutary grace. Recognition of the evil similarity between these two perverse generations could help remove the veil of self-righteous deception from our hypocritical generation. Knowledge of the frightful chastisements that must fall upon the generation of the Antichrist could help dissolve the dishonest rationalizations of our age that attempt to justify apostasy and immorality under the slogans of progress and liberation. In the light of the severe judgments visited on the Antichrist, our age's secularization of society, desacralization of liturgy, demythologization of the Bible, organization of militant atheism in the East, of materialistic atheism in the West, and proliferation of revolutionary heresy and immorality everywhere should arouse the modern world to fear that God will visit it with punishments similar in severity to those to be inflicted on the rebellious age of the Antichrist.

Finally, a word on what we hope to accomplish in this work. In a study that attempts to clarify and conduct apocalyptic prophecies to the port of truth, the author must avoid shipwreck by steering a wise course between the Scylla of extravagant interpretations and the Charybdis of foolish, credulous conclusions. The intelligent and clear must be presented with discernment; the mysterious left for explanation by the events. Such is the purpose of this study and its updating of the problem of the Antichrist to our times. Naturally, recourse will be had to the Fathers of the early Church who often treated of the Antichrist. Indeed, they helped form the consistent oral tradition on the subject. The Fathers assert that they received certain scriptural explanations, certain details of the history of the Antichrist, certain unanimous agreements on his personality, career, and destiny from the apostles or from their immediate successors. Hence, when the

Fathers agree in their reporting about the Antichrist, they ought to be considered trustworthy witnesses, claiming our unqualified credence. For it would be unreasonable, even for the severest critic, not to accept the unanimous testimony of such enlightened, virtuous, prudent men, many of whom died as martyrs in defense of the truths they lived and taught. Of course, when the teaching of the Fathers is founded on their personal opinions, or on uncertain testimony, our esteem for their persons will not prevent us from accepting more probable opinions, or even of abandoning their conclusions, with deference to their authority, when the constant dogmatic or moral truths of the Church require it.

We hope not to be impelled by excessive curiosity, nor to plunge impetuously into the marvelous and sensational. Such a morbid craving for precise details before the events has led many to produce extravagant claims to the prophetic gift and to the power of communicating with the world of spirits. This fall into false prophecy is the nemesis God allows to afflict nations and persons who lose their faith, patience, and trust in Him. True, man as a provident animal must have truths to cling to now and others to strive for in the future. But as his faith in the God-given partial, yet adequate, revelations for his present and future salvation fades from his heart, man moves inevitably to substitute miserable mythologies that can only be sponsored by the father of lies and his human agents. Alfred Plummer comments sagaciously on this spiritual tragedy:

> Man is never content with merely forsaking the fountains
> of living waters: he ever goes on to hew for himself cisterns,
> broken cisterns, that can hold no water. Israel, having
> cast off Jehovah and slain the prophets, took to idols,

soothsayers and necromancers. Greece and Rome, having learnt from Epicurus to banish the gods, and from Lucian to laugh at them, became the eager dupes of the miracle-monger, the augur and the astrologer. Julian discarded Christianity and believed in magic. The freethinkers of the French Revolution, who followed in his footsteps, rejected the Prophets and the Apostles as liars and fools, and accepted without question the impostures of Cagliostro and the Rosicrucians. Nor can our age afford to throw stones.[20]

[20] Alfred Plummer, introduction to John J. von Dollinger, *Prophecies and the Prophetic Spirit in the Christian Era* (London: Rivingtons, 1873) pp. xix, xx.

Chapter 2

Is The Antichrist Theology-Fiction?

Some scholars claim that the person and feats of the Antichrist are theology-fiction. The whole legend is meant to teach mankind a moral and religious lesson. Moreover, despite the entangled and fantastic nature of this myth of the Antichrist or, better still, because of these very characteristics, the legend of the Antichrist has lent itself to literary developments of supreme power, imagination, charm, and tragedy. Mirrored in this masterpiece of fiction a demonic-human adversary, arising from the depths of the sea or from the darkness of the underworld, rebels against the gods above and wages all-out war to establish the kingdom of the wicked as the eternal conqueror of the kingdom of the good. In this apocalyptic fantasy are to be found the hopes, sufferings, aspirations, fears, and despairs of the masses of humanity throughout the ages. These are felt and surface in an especially poignant manner in times of political upheavals and religious convulsions. For the Antichrist's feats excite the popular imagination as much as, indeed even more than, dogmatic wranglings. Man will never exhaust in time the full interpretation of the Antichrist epic.

W. Bousset in his book *The Antichrist Legend* insists that the origin of the Pauline picture of the Antichrist is to be found in the Babylonian or Persian chaos myths, which narrate the cosmic combat that took place at the beginning of time between the gods and the mythological monsters that symbolized the dark forces of nature. According to the Babylonian myth, Tiamat, ruler of the depths of darkness, attacked the gods but was defeated by Marduk, son of the god Ea.[21] In the Persian saga Ahura-Mazda rebelled against the god Angre-Mainyu but was also vanquished by the forces of the deity.[22] Gunkel and Reitzenstein agree with the theory of Bousset. Other scholars, however, have found the beginnings of the adventures of the Antichrist in the dualism of the opposing supernatural forces of good and evil as narrated in Iranian mythology. Jewish eschatology, assert these scholars, took up this religious fable, accommodated it to its own monotheistic history, projected it into a future showdown struggle and predicted the final victory of Yahweh and Israel who would then both rule the nations forever with a rod of iron.

Prophecy versus Mythology

In order to refute the theory that the Antichrist legend arose from Eastern pagan mythologies, we must explain the radical differences between true and false prophets, between true and false predictions.[23] For the Jews, the Chosen People of God, prophecy first and foremost consisted in a special kind of knowledge. It was primarily a revelation of things far off, of future events pertaining to man's temporal and eternal destiny in his relationships

[21] Wilhelm Bousset, *The Antichrist Legend* (London: Hutchinson, 1896).

[22] Emory Stevens Bucke, ed., *The Interpreter's Dictionary of the Bible*, Vol. 1, A--D (New York: Abingdon Press, 1962), p. 141.

[23] Arthur Devine, "Prophecy," in *The Catholic Encyclopedia*, Vol. XII, ed. Charles George Herbermann (New York: Robert Appleton, 1911), pp. 473-476.

to God, angels, devils, and his fellowmen. The prophetic revelation, which was removed from man's normal way of knowing things, treated of God, of matters of faith, of morality, of mysteries, of spiritual substances urging men to good or evil, and of the direction of man's freely undertaken human acts. Early in the Old Testament, prophets are called seers because they see what others do not and they unveil things hidden in mystery. In order for this knowledge to be communicated to others, it was incarnated in the spoken and written word. Isaiah could say: "That which I have heard from the Lord of hosts, the God of Israel, I have declared to you."[24] But since God alone can confirm the truth of prophetic pronouncements that are beyond the scope of human reason, prophecy was also intertwined necessarily with the working of miracles. Scripture relates: "There arose no more a prophet in Israel like unto Moses, whom the Lord knew face to face, in all signs and wonders."[25]

On the other hand, for pagan peoples prophecy was mythological. Though steeped in spiritualism and sorcery, such mythologies were oriented chiefly toward national and political purposes. In them gods, semi-gods, titans, and monsters acted out such a fantastic epic that its puerile, and often degrading, deeds provide irrefragable proof that such nonsense could never have been revealed by an infinitely holy and intelligent God, nor could it ever be worthy of human persons made in his image and likeness. Hosea, referring to the pagan prophet, warned the Jews: "Know ye, O Israel, that the prophet was foolish, the spiritual man was mad."[26] Why did he say this? Because the pagan prophet

[24] Isa. 21:10.
[25] Deut. 34:10, 11.
[26] Hos. 9:7.

was known as a false prophet. He was recognized as fraudulent because he was inspired not by God but by his own imagination, emotions, and desires stimulated by spirits of the underworld during ceremonies of sorcery. Jeremiah cautioned Israel: "Harken not to the words of the prophets that prophesy to you, and deceive you; they speak a vision of their own heart, and not out of the mouth of the Lord."[27] And Ezekiel adds: "Woe to the foolish prophets that follow their own spirit and see nothing."[28]

A true prophet is called by God; a false prophet comes in his own name or in that of his ruler. St. Peter wrote: "For prophecy came not by the will of man at any time: but the holy men of God spoke, inspired by the Holy Spirit."[29] Thus the recipient of the gift of prophecy should, as a rule, be good and virtuous. Mystical writers agree that this gift is granted by God for the most part to holy persons. For the gift of prophecy is an extraordinary grace bestowed directly by God, similar to the vocation to the priesthood. But in the case of the grace of prophecy there is this difference: the gift of prophecy is never confined to any particular tribe, family, or class of persons. There was never any external rite by which the office of prophet was inaugurated. Rather its exercise is always extraordinary and depends on the immediate call of God. Though moral goodness is more profitable to a prophet, it is not necessary in order to obtain the gift of prophecy. God used Balaam, an idolatrous soothsayer, and his donkey to predict the destruction of the Moabites at the hands of the Jews. Then, too, Caiaphas, the high priest, conspirator with the other chief priests and Pharisees to kill Christ,

---

[27] Jer. 23:16.
[28] Ezek. 13:3.
[29] 2 Pet. 1:21.

prophesied truly that Christ would die to save the nation. And the children who sang the praises of Christ on His triumphal entry into Jerusalem revealed Him as the Messiah. At the time, Christ answered the irate high priests who objected to the children's praise of Him as the Messiah by reminding them that if God could not find human voices through which to prophesy the truth about His Son, He could make the very stones cry out His message to mankind.

The message of the true prophet always conforms to Christian truth and piety for the Spirit of Truth speaks through him. But the false prophet often proposes predictions that are against faith and morals. True prophets make predictions that concern events outside the reach of all natural knowledge, and have for their objects contingent realities that God alone could know. The predictions of true prophets always concern something of a grave and important nature—i.e., something for the good of the Church and the salvation of souls. These rules help to distinguish true prophets and their predictions from false prophets and the puerile, senseless fables of fortune-tellers, crystal-gazers, spiritualists, and charlatans. At best the merely human oracle may produce poetical mythologies of great literary value after the fashion of Homer and Virgil, who immortalized the heroes of their countrymen. But the oracles of the true God, though concerned with this life, by far transcend it. They are concerned with a second life and glory or a second death and damnation for all eternity beyond the grave. The prophecies of merely human oracles lack supranatural, supratemporal, and, *a fortiori*, supernatural vision; their events are imprisoned in the unraveling reel of sense and time.

Moreover, true prophets are certain in their own minds of what they see and are predicting. They fearlessly oppose their own oracles to the preaching and predictions of false prophets. They insist their oracles come from heaven, not from themselves, and compel acceptance of their oracles under penalty of revolt against God.[30] On the other hand, merely human oracles are often uncertain, indeed devious in their predictions. Like the Delphic Oracle, they give ambiguous answers that can be interpreted as correct however the predicted event turns out. Jeremiah could say: "In truth the Lord sent me to you, to speak all these words in your hearing."[31] A sign of the prophet's certitude may be gathered from the way he conducts himself in fulfilling the command of God. Often he gives up his most precious possessions and even his life to fulfill God's charge. Abraham prepared to sacrifice his son, which he would never have done had he not been most certain of the divine request for this sacrifice. When God reveals events to prophets, He also gives them the surety of the truth of His message. For true prophets do not make themselves prophets; they do not come forth from a professional school of prophets. "I am not a professional or voluntary prophet," Amos told King Amasias, who wished to prevent him from prophesying at Bethel. "I am a herdsman, plucking wild figs. And the Lord took me when I followed the flock and said to me: 'Go, prophesy to my people Israel.'"[32] David was a shepherd and boy-harpist, but when seized by the Holy Spirit he became a prophet-psalmist. Isaiah, a member of the aristocracy in the Kingdom of Judah, was given the vision of the Lord sitting on a throne of glory; an angel purified his lips with a burning coal and God said to him: "Go, preach to My people the

[30] Jean Cales, "Prophecy, Prophet and Prophetess," in *The Catholic Encyclopedia*, Vol. XII, op. cit., pp. 473–476.
[31] Jer. 26:15.
[32] Amos 7:14, 15.

terrible judgments of the Lord."[33] Jeremiah was consecrated from his mother's womb as a prophet, but when called in a vision to proclaim the wrath of God against the nations, he endeavored to be excused from a duty so dangerous and painful. All to no avail, for God so inflamed his heart that, despite his effort to conceal the oracles entrusted to him, he zealously fulfilled his office—even unto suffering martyrdom for doing so. "Ah, ah, ah, Lord God! Behold I cannot speak for I am a child."[34] Ezekiel, of the priestly race, prophesied as a Jewish captive in Babylonia. He saw the glory of God on a fiery chariot drawn by celestial beings. He heard a voice commanding him to go and find the children of Israel, that rebellious nation with hardened heart and brazen face. Without equivocation he is commanded to deliver to that wicked people the divine threats revealed to him. "And he said to me: Son of man, receive in thy heart, and hear with thy ears, all the words that I speak to thee: And go get thee in to them of the captivity, to the children of thy people, and thou shalt speak to them, and shalt say to them: Thus saith the Lord: If so be they will hear and will forbear."[35] Moreover, the manifest sanctity of their lives, the miracles they wrought, and the prophecies they accomplished demonstrated to their contemporaries, and to all mankind, the truth of the claims of the genuine prophets.

Even St. Paul, who clearly predicts the coming of the Antichrist, did not become a prophet by his own choice. Persecutor and ravisher of the infant Church, he was struck from his horse at the Damascus gate by a vision of Christ and converted almost

[33] Isa. 6:9.
[34] Jer. 1:6.
[35] Ezek. 3:10–11.

instantly into God's prophet to the Gentiles. The apostles were nearly all fishermen with no aspirations of being much more until Christ came into their lives and called them to be prophets. Such also was the case with Levi, the tax collector. In an instant, at the call of Christ, he left his monies to become Matthew, prophet of the New Testament. All these simple men were called to predict truths far beyond the capacities of the wisest sages.

We have already seen in Chapter One that St. Paul's delineation of the Antichrist has an entirely satisfactory origin in the revelations of the Old Testament, especially in the major prophets and particularly in Ezekiel, who reports Yahweh's victory against the combined forces of evil. These forces are represented as historical persons, spiritual and human; they are individuals and nations united under the Archenemy to destroy the kingdom of God. The revelations of the Old and New Testaments, unlike pagan mythologies, are not man-made predictions. St. Paul insists on this truth with the Galatians: "For I give you to understand, Brethren, that the gospel which was preached by me is not of man. For I did not receive it of man, nor was I taught it, but I received it by a revelation of Jesus Christ."[36] And while writing to the Thessalonians to explain the circumstances surrounding the coming of the Antichrist and the day of the Lord, St. Paul recalls to them some important details of his revelation:

> Let no man deceive you by any means unless there come a revolt first, and the man of sin be revealed, the son of perdition, who opposeth, and is lifted up above all that is called God, or that is worshipped so that he sitteth in the

[36] St. Paul, Gal. 1:11, 12.

temple of God, showing himself as if he were God. And then that wicked one shall be revealed whom the Lord Jesus shall kill with the spirit of His mouth; and shall destroy with the brightness of His coming, him, whose coming is according to the working of Satan, in all power, and signs, and lying wonders.[37]

St. John the Apostle also testifies that his revelations of the last days came to him suddenly from the Lord:

And I was in the spirit on the Lord's day, and I heard behind me a great voice, as of a trumpet, saying: "What you see write in a book and send it to the seven churches." ... And when I saw I fell at His feet as one dead.... And He said to me: "These words are trustworthy and true"; and the Lord, the God of the spirits of the prophets, sent His angel to show His servants what must shortly come to pass.... And he said to me: "Do not seal up the words of the prophecy of this book; for the time is at hand." ... I testify to everyone who hears the words of the prophecy of this book. If anyone shall add to them, God will add unto him the plagues that are written in this book. And if anyone shall take away from the words of the book of this prophecy, God will take away His portion from the tree of life, and from the holy city, and from the things that are written in this book. He who testifies to these things says: "It is true, I come quickly."[38]

Finally there is the test of ascertaining whether prophecies made by the seers have been fulfilled in the way foretold. Now

---

[37] St. Paul, 2 Thess. 2:3-6.
[38] St. John, Apoc. 1:10, 11; 22:6, 10, 18-20.

the true prophets have already had many of their predictions literally fulfilled by the events of history. Their predictions about the Messiah, His birth, trials, preaching, betrayal, sufferings, death, and triumph have been marvelously accomplished. Then, too, their predictions about the fate of the Chosen People, the call of the Gentiles, the creation of the Church, and many, many other salvation events have come to be realized in history with startling accuracy. It is only reasonable then to conclude that such reliable prophets, when predicting other events as yet not realized in history, cannot be deceived about the veracity of those events. We who are separated from the true prophets by thousands of years should be convinced of their veracity by two incontrovertible proofs: 1) the sublime phenomenon of Messianism that they predicted and that culminated in Christ, the God-Man, and His Church, 2) the excellence of the religious and moral teaching that they revealed, a teaching worthy of the holiness of God and the destiny of God's children. Moreover, their prophecies, even those as yet not realized in history, remain living realities in the consciences of men today and will be so until the end of time. The Church always looks forward and prepares herself for the return of her Savior in the final showdown between Him and the forces of the Antichrist. Her prayers, liturgy, exhortations, penances, and writings continue to warn her children to watch, pray, and be vigilant for the final assault and victory.

None of these signs of true prophecy are to be found in the authors of pagan mythologies. Dumb, nonexistent gods, products of their own dreams, are the sources of their prophecies. Such magicians never perform true miracles to prove their predictions. Such seers are not willing to suffer or die to testify to the truth of their predictions. More often than not, true prophets have suffered and died to testify to the truth of their oracles.

As a matter of fact, Babylonian and Persian myths, even as their Roman and Greek counterparts, have long been discarded by enlightened humanity as interesting fantasies. Science, history, anthropology, and, above all, the revelations of Christianity have totally discredited them as events of history. It is quite the reverse with the predictions of the Bible. As history and science advance more evidence is found to strengthen the truths of the Bible. We can conclude then, without fear of falling into error, that the prediction of the Antichrist is not theology-fiction. The Antichrist is not a development from mythological fables. His origin is not to be found in man's imagination. But the truth about the Antichrist comes to us from God revealing it to His prophets, His apostles, to His Church throughout the whole of salvation history. Hence, the Antichrist is not a legend of man's fantasy. The tragic truth is that the Antichrist is the final legacy of Satan's rebellion against and man's fall from the friendship of God. The Antichrist is the final fulfillment of the mystery of iniquity that is at work among men in their time of trial and temptation. For in truth, as St. Paul tells us, when he comes the Antichrist will be "the man of sin" and "the son of perdition."[39]

---

[39] 2 Thess. 2:3.

Chapter 3

The Antichrist in Scripture

Who is the Antichrist? What does the notion of the Antichrist signify? Where do we first hear about the Antichrist? These important questions must be given reasonable, if not adequate, answers if Christians are to understand and cooperate with the fulfillment of God's judgments in the apocalyptic history of their own times.

We will begin with the third question and work back to the first. The word *Antichrist* occurs only in the Epistles of St. John the Evangelist. In his first Epistle, when warning the faithful against false teachers, St. John wrote:

> Dear children, it is the last hour; and you have heard that Antichrist is coming, so now many antichrists have arisen; whence we know that it is the last hour. They have gone forth from us, but they were not of us. For if they had been of us, they would surely have continued with us; but they were to be made manifest, that not one of them is of us.... He is the Antichrist who denies the Father and the Son.[40]

---

[40] 1 John 2:18–23.

31

And every spirit that severs Jesus is not of God, but is of Antichrist, of whom you have heard that he is coming and now is already in the world.[41]

For many deceivers have gone forth into the world who do not confess Jesus as the Christ coming in the flesh. This is the deceiver and the Antichrist.[42]

It is evident from the above quotations that St. John supposes that the early Christians are already acquainted with the doctrine concerning the coming of the Antichrist. "You have heard that Antichrist is coming." "And every spirit that severs Jesus ... is of Antichrist, of whom you have heard that he is coming." Now St. John speaks of several Antichrists and he carefully distinguishes between the many and the one principal agent. "Antichrist is coming, so even now many antichrists have arisen." There are so-called real parallelisms to these occurrences in the Apocalypse, in the Pauline Epistles, in the Gospels, and in the book of Daniel. The scriptural references to the coming of the Antichrist are clearer, more explicit in the Apocalypse and the Pauline Epistles; such references in the Gospels and the book of Daniel are less explicit and are reasonably derived from prophecies and a theology of typology. Let us briefly explore these sources.

The Antichrist in the Pauline Epistles

From the writings of St. Paul, the readers of St. John's letters would already have known about the doctrine of the coming of the Antichrist before the end of the world. St. John himself

[41] 1 John 4:3.
[42] 2 John 1:7.

described the heretics of his day who kept denying the Incarnation as faint images of the future great Antichrist. St. Paul had already, in equally vivid language, described more fully that future Super-Antichrist. The occasion for his description was as follows. In the Church of Thessalonica disturbances of the Faith had erupted on account of the belief that the Second Coming of Christ was imminent. This false impression had arisen partly because of a misunderstanding of Paul's first letter to this church and partly because of the machinations of deceivers. It was with a view to clearing up false impressions and restoring serenity in the Faith that St. Paul wrote his second Epistle to the Thessalonians in which he explains the necessary connection between the coming of the Antichrist and the Second Coming of Christ.

> Let no man deceive you by any means unless there come a revolt first, and the man of sin be revealed, the son of perdition, who opposeth, and is lifted up above all that is called God, or that is worshipped so that he sitteth in the temple of God, showing himself as if he were God. And then that wicked one shall be revealed whom the Lord Jesus shall kill with the spirit of His mouth; and shall destroy with the brightness of His coming, him, whose coming is according to the working of Satan, in all power, and signs, and lying wonders.[43]

St. Paul's doctrine is clearly expounded. "The day of the Lord" will be preceded by "a revolt," and the revelation of the "man of sin." The "man of sin" will sit in the temple of God, showing himself as if he were God; he will work signs and lying

[43] Paul, 2 Thess. 2:3–10.

wonders by the power of Satan. Thus the "man of sin" will be in the service of Satan, will be Satan's prophet and wonder-worker; through the "man of sin" Satan will make his final, all-out assault against mankind and the kingdom of Christ, His Church. The "man of sin" will seduce those who received not the love of truth, that they might be saved. But the Lord Jesus shall kill this man of sin with the spirit of His mouth and destroy him with the brightness of His coming. As to the time of the "man of sin's" coming, St. John places that arrival at "the last hour." But we know that for St. John "the last times," "the last hour" of salvation history is the time extending from the Resurrection of Christ to His Second Coming. That is why St. John also mentions that already many antichrists have arisen letting us know that it *is* the last hour. In a sense "he (the great Antichrist) is already in the world" in the persons of his types, his precursors.

St. Paul tells us that "the mystery of iniquity is already at work, provided only that he who is at present restraining it, does still restrain, until he is gotten out of the way." Later we will consider the restraining force that is obstructing the arrival of the Antichrist. Briefly, then, the "day of the Lord" will be preceded by the "man of sin" identified in St. John's Epistles as the Antichrist; the "man of sin" is preceded by a "revolt" or a great apostasy; this apostasy is the evil fruit of "the mystery of iniquity which is already at work," and which, according to St. John, shows itself here and there in the faint types and forerunners of *the* Antichrist. St. Paul also gives three stages in the evolution of evil as it prepares mankind for the coming of the Antichrist: the leaven of iniquity, the great apostasy, the arrival of the "man of sin." He then adds a clause calculated to determine the time of the main event—the arrival in power of the

Antichrist. "Provided only that he who is at present restraining it, does still restrain, until he is gotten out of the way." This clause indicates something that is blocking the Antichrist's arrival first by referring to it as a thing, and then as a person. Here we will, for the present, merely enumerate the principal opinions as to the meaning of the mysterious "restrainer" of the Antichrist's coming to world power. We prescind from discussing their value at this point. The scholars Grimm and Simar hold that the impediment of the main event is the "man of sin"; the main event is the Second Coming of Christ. Now most Latin Fathers and later interpreters hold that the great impediment to the Antichrist's coming to power is the Roman Empire. For them the main event being impeded is the coming of the "man of sin," the seizing of the world power by the Antichrist. Protestant theologians living after the seventeenth century held that St. Paul, while prophesying about the future, was also referring to persons and events of his own times that were times of great persecution for the Church. Thus the *thing* and the *person* impeding the arrival of the "man of sin" are variously identified by these theologians with the Emperors Caligula, Titus, Nero, Claudius, Domitian, etc. Dollinger thinks that St. Paul is referring immediately to contemporary events that are, however, types of the eschatological person. The destruction of Jerusalem under Titus, for example, is a type of the Lord's Second Coming.

The further question has been asked and discussed through the centuries. From what source or sources did St. Paul receive his teaching on the Antichrist? Here again we meet with a variety of explanations. Several Protestant writers have advanced the view that St. Paul was expressing his own personal convictions based on the Jewish tradition and the imagery of the prophets

Daniel and Ezekiel. Dollinger's opinion is that St. Paul is expressing the impression produced on the early Church by the eschatological teaching of Jesus Christ. However, Catholic writers
throughout the ages have generally taught that St. Paul uttered a
prophecy concerning the "man of sin" which he received from
the inspiration of the Holy Spirit. The Church has traditionally
adhered to this interpretation.

The Antichrist in the Apocalypse

Nearly all reputable scriptural commentators find the Antichrist
mentioned in the Apocalypse of St. John the Evangelist, but they
do not agree as to the particular chapter and verse of the book in
which he is depicted. Some point to the "beast" of chapter 11
who will kill the two witnesses, Elias and Enoch, when they return to the earth in the last days for their final testimony in
honor of God and His Son, Jesus Christ:

> And I will grant unto my two witnesses to prophesy for a
> thousand two hundred and sixty days, clothed in sackcloth.
> These are the two olive trees and the two lamp stands that
> stand before the Lord of the earth. ... These have power to
> shut heaven, so that it will not rain during the days of their
> prophesying; and they have power over the waters to turn
> them into blood and to smite the earth with every plague
> as often as they desire.
>
> And when they have finished their testimony, the beast
> that comes up out of the abyss will wage war against them,
> and will conquer them and will kill them. And their dead
> bodies will lie in the streets of the great city, which is
> called mystically Sodom and Egypt where their Lord was
> also crucified. And men from the tribes and peoples and

tongues and nations will look upon their bodies three days and a half; and they will not allow their dead bodies to be laid in tombs. And the inhabitants of the earth will rejoice over them and make merry; and they will send gifts to one another because these two prophets tormented the inhabitants of the earth.

And after the three days and a half, the breath of life from God entered into them. And they stood up on their feet, and a great fear fell upon those who saw them. And they heard a great voice from heaven saying to them, "Come up hither." And they went up to heaven in a cloud and their enemies saw them.[44]

Others think the "red dragon" of chapter 12 is the Antichrist. The great red dragon makes his appearance suddenly, without anything further having been said of the "beast" just announced in chapter 11. Is St. John here progressing from particularities to generalities? Is he revealing in the red dragon the mystery of evil centered in Satan through a sort of flashback to the very beginning of all creation, spiritual as well as temporal? Is he now trying to explain to the faithful of the first century the deeper meaning of the Antichrist by exposing the machinations of Satan acting through the red dragon to destroy the elect of Christ? It seems that with the announcement of the beast the ultimate peak of prophetic explanation was reached. Now the red dragon is introduced so as to portray more of the activities of the Antichrist in his fight against the woman, who symbolizes at the same time Mary, the Mother of God, and the Church. Satan's influence over men and nations is being exerted through the beast and the red dragon.

[44] Apoc. 11:3–12.

And a great sign appeared in heaven : a woman clothed with the sun, and the moon was under her feet, and upon her head a crown of twelve stars. And being with child, she cried out in her travail and was in the anguish of delivery. And another sign was seen in heaven, and behold, a great red dragon having seven heads and ten horns, and upon his head seven diadems. And his tail was dragging along the third part of the stars of heaven, and it dashed them to the earth; and the dragon stood before the woman who was about to bring forth, that, when she had brought forth, he might devour her son. And she brought forth a male child, who is to rule ... all nations with a rod of iron; and her child was caught ... up to God and to his throne. And the woman fled into the wilderness where she has a place prepared by God, and there they may nourish her a thousand two hundred and sixty days.

... And I heard a loud voice in heaven saying, "Now has come the salvation, and the power and the kingdom of our God, and the authority of his Christ; for the accuser of our brethren has been cast down, he who accused them before our God day and night." ...

And when the dragon saw that he was cast down to the earth, he pursued the woman who had brought forth the male child.

... And the dragon was angered at the woman and went away to wage war with the rest of her offspring, who keep the commandments of God, and hold fast the testimony of Jesus.[45]

[45] Apoc. 12:1–17.

But St. John tells us that "there was a battle in heaven; Michael and his angels battled with the dragon, and the dragon fought and his angels. And they did not prevail, neither was their place found anymore in heaven. And the great dragon was cast down, the ancient serpent, he who is called the devil and Satan, who leads astray the whole world; and he was cast down to the earth and with him his angels were cast down." Michael, in the angelology of Daniel and St. John, is the angel who leads people to God and defends them against his enemies. The role he plays is characterized by these two circumstances and, although this scene takes place in heaven before the beginning of time, he already appears in the perspective of the earthly struggle the people of God must pursue with Satan, as well as the struggle of the Church against impious nations. Thus the red dragon seems to be rather Satan than the Antichrist, though both Satan and the Antichrist will use all impious nations and all human forces of evil to destroy the Church.

We have seen that Satan as the great red dragon was defeated by Michael the Archangel, expelled forever from the realm of the pure spirits and allowed to remain on earth as the Prince of Darkness continuing his revolt against God by seducing men. In accordance with his crafty nature, Satan remains in the background and uses human agents to snare human victims, individuals as well as nations. Some scholars saw Satan incarnate, as it were, in the beast that destroyed Elias and Enoch. This human person they identified as the Antichrist. But in chapter 13 St. John introduces his readers to two more beasts. One rises from the sea—that is to say, taking into account the location of the prophet on the island of Patmos—from the West. This beast has seven heads and ten horns. Possessing the red dragon's own authority and might, the beast from the West wages war on the saints, overcomes them, and draws the nations into the trap of its seductions. Some scholars hold that this beast of the sea is the Antichrist. Then there arrives a second beast, the beast of the earth, that is, from the East. This beast is an assistant to the beast from the sea, aiding him to triumph over men in a Sodom of pleasure and corruption, in an Egypt of servitude. The beast from the East has two horns like those of a lamb, but it speaks as does a dragon. It possesses all the authority and might of the beast from the sea and leads nations to the worship of its master, the beast from the sea. Performing marvelous deeds, even drawing down fire from heaven, the beast of the earth leads the inhabitants of the earth astray into blasphemy and moral corruption, branding them on the forehead or on the right hand with the mark of the Prince of Darkness. Some exegetes hold that the beast of the earth is the Antichrist.

Then there are many scholars who identify the Antichrist with the scarlet-colored beast "having seven heads and ten horns" unveiled in chapter 17.

> And I saw a woman sitting upon a scarlet-colored beast, full of names of blasphemy, having seven heads and ten horns. And the woman was clothed in purple and scarlet, and covered with gold and precious stones and pearls, having in her hand a golden cup full of abominations and the uncleanness of her immorality. And upon her forehead a name written—a mystery—Babylon the great, the mother of harlotries and of the abominations of the earth. And I saw the woman drunk with the blood of the saints and with the blood of the martyrs of Jesus. And when I saw her, I wondered with a great wonder.[46]

[46] Apoc. 17:3-6.

The woman seen sitting on the scarlet beast is interpreted by nearly all the scholars as Rome or the Roman Empire.[47] Here pagan Rome is closely linked with the scarlet beast, bearing his names of blasphemy, wallowing in his luxury, sharing his idolatrous prostitutions, his inebriation with the blood of the martyrs. Pagan Rome, seated as queen of the world on seven hills, ruled by seven kings of whom five have fallen, one is and the other is not yet come, is the kingdom of Satan. St. John is referring to a definite fragment of contemporary history in this graphic image. Are we able to name the seven kings or emperors, these seven auxiliaries of the scarlet beast who either persecuted Christians or allowed them to be persecuted? There seems to be no doubt that we can. Domitian, the first emperor to claim divine honors during his lifetime, was in power at the time the Apocalypse was written. The five emperors before him were truly incarnations of the beast scarlet with the blood of martyrs. Running through the rulers that preceded Domitian we can enumerate: Titus (79–81), Vespasian (69–79), the interregnum with Galba, Otho, and Vitellius (68–69), Nero (54–68), and Claudius (41–54). Claudius would be the first to have persecuted Christians according to St. John at the end of the first century. Through the evil works of these emperors one truth stands forth unmistakably. Again and again throughout history Satan ignites impious, blasphemous political powers in order to lead mankind astray and destroy the kingdom of God among men. But the scarlet beast, representing the diabolical power that seduces men, is doomed to final destruction. Roman power, the incarnation of this scarlet beast, is the first to be destroyed. Other political powers arising from this

---

[47] Henri Marie Feret, O.P., *The Apocalypse of St. John* (Westminster, MD: The Newman Press, 1958), p. 188.

same source will likewise be destroyed by the Lamb and the saints. "These shall fight with the Lamb and the Lamb will overcome them. Because he is the Lord of lords and the King of kings. And they that are with him are called, the Elect and faithful."[48]

Finally, some exegetes identify the Antichrist with Satan himself, loosed out of his prison during the last days to make his ultimate, desperate, curtain-falling assault on the Church.

> And when the thousand years are finished, Satan will be released from his prison, and will go forth and deceive the nations which are in the four corners of the earth, Gog and Magog, and will gather them together for the battle; the number of whom is as the sand of the sea. And they went over the breadth of the earth and encompassed the camp of the saints and the beloved city. And the fire from God came down out of heaven and devoured them. And the devil who deceived them was cast into the pool of fire and brimstone, where are also the beast and the false prophet; and they will be tormented day and night forever and ever.[49]

The false prophet seen in the pool of fire together with the beast is the second wild beast, the beast from the earth, from the East. Gog and Magog signify the nations which Satan and his human assistants will corrupt and direct in their attack on the Church, here identified as "the camp of the saints, and the beloved city." Taken from the prophet Ezekiel, Gog and Magog were understood by him to be the nations that would rise against the promised Messiah. Thus, used figuratively here, Gog and Magog are the earthly powers, corrupted by Satan, his Antichrist,

[48] Apoc. 17:14.
[49] Apoc. 20:7–10.

and their human agents, that will make the history-closing, apocalyptic, but futile, onslaught against the Church.

The Antichrist in the Old Testament

When one has studied the image of the Antichrist in St. Paul's second Epistle to the Thessalonians, one easily recognizes the "man of sin" in the "little horn" that the prophet Daniel describes as a great power arising from a "fourth beast, terrible and wonderful and exceedingly strong," which he saw in a vision at night.

> And behold eyes like the eyes of a man were in this horn, and a mouth speaking great things. I beheld till thrones were placed and the Ancient of days sat.... The judgment sat and the books were opened. I beheld because of the voice of the great words which that horn spoke.... And that horn was greater than the rest of the horns. I beheld and lo, that horn made war against the saints, and prevailed over them.... And he shall speak words against the High One, and shall crush the saints of the Most High; and he shall think himself able to change times and laws, and they shall be delivered into his hands until a time, and times and half a time. And the judgment shall sit that *his* power may be taken away, and be broken into pieces, and perish even to the end.[50]

Now scriptural exegetes are agreed that the ten horns on the head of the fourth beast seen by the prophet Daniel represent ten kingdoms, idolatrous successors of Alexander the Great's empire who persecuted the Chosen People of God. The angel in the Apocalypse explains a similar vision to St. John thus: "And

[50] Dan. 7:8–26.

the ten horns that you saw are ten kings who ... will receive authority as kings for one hour with the beast. They will fight against the Lamb."[51]

But the "little horn" that brings down three of the other kingdoms is commonly understood to be the Antichrist. Moreover, since Daniel was prophesying about the present and the future, this figure of the "little horn" also applied to the great, contemporary persecutor of the people of God, Antiochus Epiphanes, who is a true type of the Antichrist. The ten kings who parcelled out the empire of Alexander are also figures and types of political powers that shall be persecuting the Church about the time of the Antichrist. As for "a time, and times, and half a time," we have here universal agreement that the reign and persecution of the Antichrist will last three and one-half years. This is in harmony with St. John's prediction of the Antichrist's reign, one thousand two hundred and sixty days.

Another rather satisfying preview and explanation of St. Paul's concept of the Antichrist is to be found in the prophet Ezekiel who depicts Yahweh's war against the forces of evil and the definite victory of Yahweh over Gog and the evil political allies known as Magog.

> And you, son of man, prophesy against Gog and say:
> Thus says the Lord God: Behold I come against you, O
> Gog.... And I will break your bow in your left hand, and
> I will cause your arrows to fall out of your right hand.
> You shall fall upon the mountains of Israel, you and all
> your bands, and your nations that are with you.... And
> I will send a fire on Magog.... And they shall know that

---

[51] Apoc. 17:12, 14.

I am the Lord. And I will make my holy name known in the midst of my people Israel, and my holy name shall be profaned no longer. And the Gentiles shall know that I am the Lord, the Holy One of Israel. Behold, it comes, and it is done, says the Lord God: this is the day whereof I have spoken.[52]

In the prophet Isaiah we also find a great thrust and influence on apocalyptic writings that indicate the Antichrist. In his prediction of the Fall of the king of Babylon, who had vanquished and oppressed the people of Israel, some scholars find a clear foretoken of the Antichrist. Moreover, others see in the king of Babylon, who aspired to dominate the nations and to become like unto Yahweh, the figure of Satan whose ape the human Antichrist must ever be in evil desires, deeds, and final destiny. Though the prophet's words, according to the letter, are spoken of the wicked king of Babylon, yet in a deeper spiritual sense they apply to the Antichrist and, above all, to his master Lucifer, the prince of devils, who was created a bright angel, but fell through pride and rebellion against God.

How are you fallen from heaven, O Lucifer, who did rise in the morning! How are you fallen to the earth, that did wound the nations? And you said in your heart: I will ascend unto heaven, I will exalt my throne above the stars of God. I will sit in the mountain of the covenant, in the sides of the north. I will ascend above the height of the clouds. I will be like the Most High. But yet you shall be brought down to hell, into the depths of the pit.[53]

[52] Ezek. 39:1–8.
[53] Isa. 14:12–15.

One who studies carefully finds a wondrous correspondence between the historical situations treated in the revelation of Isaiah and that of the seer of Patmos. In chapters 13 and 14 Isaiah encourages the Israelite captives by prophesying to them, in the name of God, the fall of the Babylonian king, "destroyer of nations," who aspires to raise his throne on an equality with God. To strengthen and enlighten the Christians persecuted by Rome, the new Babylon, St. John permits the faithful to watch the fall of another brilliant star, like unto the king of Babylon and, like him, responsible for the agonies of the Chosen People of God. Here the revelation of St. John pursues its course. The brilliant falling star in the Apocalypse that is flung into the pit can only signify the emperor of Rome who is full of mysterious power for evil and thus must be subjected to a dramatic natural and supernatural fall. The king of Babylon in Isaiah is also a great power for evil and must suffer a similar fall "into the depths of the pit." In both situations the picture conjured up obviously portrays personages of the highest rank possessing spiritual orbits that can almost be described as cosmic. Thus, starting from the prophecy of Isaiah, but filling out and by far surpassing it, St. John makes it clear that another, greater Antichrist is to be found in Rome and its emperor. Moreover, this more brilliant star is also destined to be thrown into the pit after it has tormented the Church for three and one-half years. As active a destroyer of nations and usurper of divinity as the king of Babylon was, yet even more avid than he will Rome and the ultimate Antichrist be in political destruction and the appropriation to themselves of the honors of the most High in the last days. When Christian tradition formally identifies Satan with the text of Isaiah, it follows the line laid down by St. John in his Apocalypse, which Isaiah himself forecast by his own extraordinary revelation. The intimate relationship between Satan and the Antichrist and their political influence on salvation history are brought into focus as their roles in God's plan for salvation are revealed by both prophets.

Aspects of the Antichrist are also found in the apocalyptic visions of the prophet Joel. We should stress here that the apocalyptic genre of writing contained revelations that concerned themselves primarily with the eschatological future of the persecuted people of God. Whereas the prophets addressed their oracles to the people of their own times, using symbols and visions to encourage and instruct them, the apocalyptic writers emphasized the end of the world, the destruction of the cosmic agents of evil and the final justification of the ways of God toward men. Thus the apocalyptic writers addressed not only their contemporaries but people and nations of all times. They were universalists; they formed a link between the Old and New Testaments, between the Chosen and the Baptized people of God, between the Synagogue and the Church, the saints fighting on earth and the saints triumphant in heaven. The Chaldeans and other enemies had invaded Israel and wreaked havoc upon the unfaithful Chosen People. Most Catholic scholars place the prophesying of Joel before the destruction of Jerusalem around 586 BC.

> Blow you the trumpet in Sion, sound an alarm in my holy mountain, let all the inhabitants of the land tremble, because the day of the Lord comes ... a day of darkness and of gloominess, a day of clouds and whirlwinds. A numerous and strong people as the morning spread upon the mountains: the like to it has not been seen from the beginning, nor shall be after it even to the years of generation and

generation.... For the day of the Lord is great and very terrible, and who can stand it?

And I will show wonders in heaven; and in earth, blood and fire and vapor of smoke. The sun shall be turned into darkness and the moon into blood, before the great and dreadful day of the Lord does come. And it shall come to pass that everyone that shall call upon the name of the Lord shall be saved; for in Mount Sion and in Jerusalem shall be salvation and in the residue whom the Lord shall call.[54]

In this attack of "the northern enemy" against the Chosen People, many interpreters saw Holofernes as a precursor of the Antichrist. God destroyed him through the strategy and courage of the valiant woman Judith, herself a type of Mary, the Mother of God through whom God also crushes the Serpent's head.

Now many of the apocalyptic elements of history are also found in the prophecy of Zechariah who prophesied during the second year of King Cyrus when the Jews were returning home from their captivity in Babylon. His prophecy is full of mysterious figures and promises partly applicable to the synagogue and the rebuilding of the temple, partly relating to the Church of Christ and the last times. In the days of the Babylonian captivity, Zechariah speaks of two witnesses or "sons of oil"—anointed ones of the Lord—who testify to the Lord before the whole earth. These two witnesses, the high priest Josue or Jesus and Zorobabel, Prince of Judah, are types of the two witnesses found in St. John, Elias and Enoch, who will appear in the last days to testify by shedding their blood for the glory of God, His Son, and their Church. This day of the Lord is also described by Zechariah:

[54] Joel 2:1-3, 30-33.

Behold the days of the Lord shall come, and your spoils shall be divided in the midst of you. And I will gather all nations to Jerusalem to battle, and the city shall be taken, and the woman shall be defiled.... And you shall flee into the valley of those mountains over against Jerusalem towards the East.... And the Lord my God shall come and all the saints with him.[55]

But before God rescues Jerusalem and his people from the forces of the Antichrist, the prophet Malachi predicts the second coming of Elias: "Behold, I will send you Elias the prophet, before the coming of the great and dreadful day of the Lord . . . lest I come and strike the earth with anathema."[56] It is certain that the testimony of these two witnesses for a thousand two hundred and sixty days will stir up the hostility of "the inhabitants of the earth," those who cling to the kingdom of Satan and reject the kingdom of Christ. And the Antichrist, symbolized by the persecution of Antiochus and the Babylonians who set fire to the temple of Jerusalem and demolished it completely in 587 BC, will be the leader of the coordinated powers of evil in the last days.

The Antichrist in the Gospels

Many commentators have found more or less clear allusions to the Antichrist in the coming of the false Christs and false prophets predicted by Christ himself in the Gospels. In Matthew chapter 24 we read of the great seducers arising at the end of time in order to destroy the elect.

---

[55] Zech. 14:1–5.
[56] Mal. 4:5–6.

And in answer Jesus said to them, "Take care that no one leads you astray. For many will come in my name saying, 'I am the Christ,' and they will lead many astray.... And many false prophets will arise and lead many astray. And because iniquity will abound, the charity of many will grow cold.... And if anyone say to you, 'Behold, here is the Christ,' or 'There he is,' do not believe it. For false Christs and false prophets will arise and will show great signs and wonders so as to lead astray, if possible, even the elect."[57]

In Mark's account of the end of the world we have much the same allusions to auxiliary antichrists preparing the way for the Archantichrist who may well be the director of the "abomination of desolation."

For many will come in my name saying, "I am he"; and they will lead many astray.... And when you see the abomination of desolation, standing where it ought not—let him who reads, understand.... For false Christs and false prophets will arise and show signs and wonders so as to lead astray, if possible, even the elect.[58]

Here "the abomination of desolation standing where it ought not" is understood by some to be the Antichrist who has set up his throne in the very temple of God and is demanding from his followers acts of adoration and sacrifice.

In Luke's narration of the end of the world we read the same warning against false Christs and prophets.

[57] Matt. 24:4–5, 23–24.
[58] Mark 13:6, 14, 22.

And he said, "Take care not to be led astray. For many will
come in my name saying, 'I am he,' and 'The time is at
hand.' Do not, therefore, go after them.... And Jerusalem
will be trodden down by the Gentiles, until the times of
the nations be fulfilled."[59]

The Gentiles here are seen by many as the militant allies of
"the man of sin," the Antichrist who will fulfill his mission in
"the times of the nations," i.e., three and one-half years of assault
on the Church.

In St. John's Gospel, the Antichrist is seen by some in the
one Christ is speaking about when he upbraids the Jews for their
incredulity.

I do not receive glory from men. But I know that you have
not the love of God in you. I have come in the name of my
Father, and you do not receive me. If another come in his
own name, him you will receive.[60]

The Antichrist will come in his own name, having no credentials from God but only power from Satan, and the wicked who
reject Christ will follow the Antichrist in his war against Christ
and the community of the saints on earth.

The Scriptural Portrait of the Antichrist

The Scriptures reveal that many different prophets predicted
diverse details about the Messiah. Some prophets predicted His
miraculous and divine origin from a virgin and the power of
the Holy Spirit, another predicted His birthplace, another the
flight into Egypt, another the town of His youth, another His

[59] Luke 21:8, 24.
[60] John 5:41–43.

miraculous powers, some others details of His public life and Passion, still others His resurrection and glory. But all these details, and many others, about the Messiah remained disparate and mysterious to the Jews throughout the ages during which the Chosen People awaited the coming of the Christ. Only when He finally arrived, lived, taught His sublime doctrine, performed His miracles and mission, died on the cross, rose again after three days, founded His Church, ascended into heaven, and sent His Holy Spirit on the young Church were His followers, through many flashbacks and comparisons with the historical reality before their eyes, able to put together the full composite portrait of the true Christ, Son of Man and Son of God, the sole unique Redeemer of the human race.

In a similar way we have had to consult the Scriptures in order to get some kind of portrait of the Antichrist. And this procedure is quite reasonable for, after all, the Antichrist exists only because Christ exists. The Antichrist is the archenemy of Christ, a sort of demonic-human adversary of Christ who will appear before the Second Coming of Christ as the last and worst oppressor and persecutor of the Church of Christ, only in turn to be defeated and overcome by Christ when the Savior returns to the earth as the universal Judge in power and glory. Naturally, we are at a disadvantage in attempting the composite portrait of the Antichrist because he has not yet arrived, as far as we know, nor have we seen him in action. We cannot give concrete details of his life and mission the way we can of the life of Christ who has already come and initiated the last times of salvation and glory. Yet we do have many inspired predictions about the Antichrist and, moreover, we can discover many truths about the Antichrist by researching the spiritual analogies, the opposite parallelisms, and the contradictory missions of the Christ and the Antichrist.

The Christ is the Son of God sent by His Father as the Son of Man to redeem and sanctify men. The Antichrist is, in a metaphorical, spiritual sense, the son of Satan sent by his Prince of Darkness to destroy and corrupt men. Christ is the suffering Servant of the Lord, obedient unto death, observing the Law of God and raising it to the perfection of the New Law of Love. The Antichrist, on the other hand, surpasses all others in hostility to God; he is the leader of a final revolt against God, "the man of sin," a kind of incarnation of the Archrebel Satan, "the man of lawlessness," "the son of perdition." Motivated by hatred of God and man, he opposes every aspect of true religion and takes his seat, as the abomination of desolation, in the holy place in the temple of God, proclaiming that he himself is God. Christ is the Lamb of God who saves and nurtures the elect. The Antichrist is the Beast of Satan, the red dragon, who with other beasts makes plans and raises armies to persecute the faithful and mount the final conflict against the Church. Christ is the source of the truth, being the Son of God. The Antichrist is the channel of falsity for his father is Satan, the liar and murderer from the beginning. Christ is holiness itself, being the perfect image of the Father. The Antichrist is the human personification of wickedness, being as it were, Satan incarnate. Satan is the Anti-God of the Old and New Testaments. But since he acts here on earth through intermediate human agents, he fashioned evil men in the Old Testament into mini-anti-gods and anti-messiahs. When Christ, the Son of God, became man, then Satan fashioned many of his anti-gods into mini-antichrists and he is preparing even now one Antichrist par excellence to destroy the Church in the last days.

Christ is the ever-faithful Son of God. The Antichrist is the great apostate.

Even after this composite portrait of the Antichrist put together from the Scriptures, the doctrine of the Antichrist remains a great mystery. We will indicate some of the obscurities therein in the following chapters. Scriptures do not give us a perfectly focused portrait of the Antichrist. For, as Cardinal Newman notes often, in treating of this problem of prophecy, Revelation does not intend to provide us with complete answers in all details, but purposely leaves truths revealed with some aura of mystery, the better to purify our faith in the fires of trial and to keep us alert, fighting, and faithful in the uncertainty of expectation.[61] For the Antichrist can only be understood in the context of the total war being waged in human history over men in which God, his Christ, and the saints are being attacked by Satan, his devils, and their earthly accomplices. Through the double-pronged attack of temporal persecution and spiritual seduction the forces of Satan and the Antichrist attempt to scuttle God's plan for the salvation of men. Whoever cooperates in the Antichrist's work of spiritual destruction becomes an agent culpably involved in some grave measure in the working out of the mystery of iniquity, the mystery of Satan and of the Antichrist. Now this satanic enterprise has been going on without respite since the fall of angels and men from the day of creation. All men, whether they like it or not, must find themselves at the heart of this struggle where no human resources can ever assure man of victory. But

[61] John Henry Cardinal Newman, *Tracts for the Times*, Vol. 5, 1838–40, Advent Sermons on Antichrist, (London: J. Rivington, 1840), pp. 1–54 .

where men would of themselves be vanquished, the Lamb of God will conquer and His faithful witnesses will conquer with him. Moreover, they will rejoice for all eternity in their common victory.

Chapter 4

The Antichrist and the Greek Fathers

The influence of the Greek Fathers on Christianity has been over the ages a profound and enduring blessing. Hence we would like to know what they teach about the Antichrist. But at once we must specify what is meant by the title "Fathers." Chronologically the title "Fathers" is clearly defined as far as the Greek Church is concerned. Historians of literature, philosophy, and theology date the Greek patristic age as comprising the first seven centuries following the age of the apostles. Of course there were many writers of theology in those seven centuries, many orthodox and many, many heretical authors. Important as each author was for his own age and place, the totality of Greek patristic geniuses may be summed up in a few outstanding authors—creative men, original thinkers themselves, representative in their own works of the profoundest theological thinking of such universal influence and authority in their own and future times as to direct the channel of patristic achievements in the East and to bridge thereby the gulf between East and West. Such authors have made the whole world a participant in the glory that was Greece and the grandeur that was Rome in the context of a supernatural vision and way of life. Most of the Greek Fathers were dead by the end of the fifth century, but their works lived on in the compilations of their numerous disciples and imitators.

It would be unwise to attempt a canon of the Fathers—a list acceptable to all who follow this subject with professional interest. But tradition in the Church has established the acceptable marks of a "Father of the Church." No writer or teacher is accepted as a "Father of the Church" who, beyond his witness and work in dogma, did not live in orthodox communion with the Church, and whose life was not eminent for sanctity. Thus the popular term for "Father of the Church," sanctioned by the usage of centuries, is applied to ecclesiastical writers who were preeminent for sanctity of life and heavenly wisdom in their teachings and writings, and who persevered in the communion of the Faith until death. This is not to say, however, that formal heretics did not exert an enormous influence on the development of the Faith, both by their positive contributions and, unfortunately, by their negative exaggerations on faith and morals. Their stubborn attempts to sustain these exaggerations as part of the truth led to their excommunication from the body of the Church. Though many of the latter were great scholars, they cannot be called "Fathers" in a sense that is approved by all the faithful.[62]

But why do we consult the Greek Fathers on the matter of Christian dogma, morals, and prophecies? Because of the proximity of these Fathers to the apostles themselves. This proximity to the college of the apostles gives the Greek Fathers great authority in the early Church. They are in the direct line of descent of the living Christian tradition, and great weight must be given to their teachings and writings. Irenaeus, one of the Greek Fathers whom we will consult on the Antichrist, explains the importance of

[62] James Marshall Campbell, *The Greek Fathers* (New York: Longmans, Green, 1929), pp. 5–10.

direct contact with the apostles for the preservation of the deposit of the Faith and the living traditions of the Catholic Church.

> The blessed apostles, then, having founded and built up the church, committed into the hands of Linus the office of the episcopate. Of this Linus, Paul makes mention in the Epistles to Timothy. To him succeeded Anacletus; and after him, in the third place from the apostles, Clement was allotted the bishopric. This man, as he had seen the blessed apostles, and had been conversant with them, might be said to have the preaching of the apostles still echoing in his ears and their traditions before his eyes. Nor was he alone in this, for there were many still remaining who had received instructions from the apostles.[63]

And then referring to his own close connection with St. John, the beloved disciple of Jesus, Irenaeus wrote:

> But Polycarp also was not only instructed by apostles, and conversed with many who had seen Christ, but was also, by apostles in Asia, appointed bishop of the church in Smyrna, whom I also saw in my early youth, for he tarried on earth a very long time, and, when a very old man, gloriously and most nobly suffering martyrdom, departed this life, having always taught the things which he learned from the apostles, and which the church had handed down, and which alone are true. To these things all the Asiatic churches testify, as do also those men who have succeeded Polycarp down to the present time,—a man who was of much greater weight,

[63] The Writings of Irenaeus, *Against Heresies*, trans. Rev. Alexander Roberts and Rev. W. H. Rambaut, Vol. 1 (Edinburgh: T & T Clark, 1884), pp. 261–262.

and a more steadfast witness than Valentinus and Marcion and the rest of the heretics.[64]

St. Irenaeus

Before the Christian Era there came out of the non-Greek East a curious philosophy concerning the problem of evil called Gnosticism. Though pre-Christian in origins, it set itself to reinterpret paganism and Judaism, changing them radically by its novel interpretations. There is no defining Gnosticism, so many were its sects, so contradictory its tenets, so flagrant its borrowings of ideas and phraseology from the philosophies and religions it met in its wanderings. But all through the confusion of its metastasizing systems ran the fundamental theme of pessimism — the doctrine that matter is a deterioration of spirit, that the universe is the principle of evil, uncreated by and in opposition to the Deity. Salvation for the Gnostic consisted in knowledge, the vision of God, communication with the divine here on earth. Gnosticism made ecstasy the means of the most perfect knowledge and the ultimate aim of religious life. It was a simple matter of time before the philosophy of the Gnostics contaminated the religion of the Church. With its rich and obfuscating amalgam of rites, belief, and magical practices, Gnosticism attempted to explain the origin of evil, human destiny, the relations between matter and spirit, between God and His creation, between God and Jesus Christ. This strange syncretism entered the Church and won from traditional Catholicism some of the Church's first theologians, scholars, and many of its bishops. Of course, Gnosticism also provoked strong

[64] Ibid., pp. 262–263.

traditional reaction, including one of the masterpieces of Catholic writing, the *Adversus Haereses* of St. Irenaeus.

Who was St. Irenaeus? He was one of the most sympathetic figures in whom all the tendencies of his time seemed to meet. He was born apparently between AD 135 and 140 in Asia Minor, and in his youth was a disciple of the famous bishop of Smyrna, St. Polycarp, who was, in turn, the disciple of St. John. In the year 177, Irenaeus appears in Rome as the envoy of the Church of Lyons, recounting to the Roman Church the details of the famous persecution then raging. He had himself suffered in that persecution that gave many martyrs to the Lyonnese Church: among them its aged bishop, Pothinus. Irenaeus was elected to succeed him and ruled for twenty to thirty years. He is the last recorded student of the personal pupils of the apostles. He became the first great systematic expositor of the Faith handed down by the apostles. Tradition tells us that he died a martyr.

As the busy missionary bishop of Lyons, a frontier diocese, Irenaeus found time to become the adversary par excellence of Gnosticism, delivering it a mortal blow in his classic work, *Against Heresies*, from which it never recovered. No innovator, Irenaeus presented no revolutionary theories, no new explanations of the Faith. On the one hand, he exposed and refuted those multiform Gnostic heresies that prevailed in the latter half of the second century; and, on the other hand, he presented a clear exposition and defense of the Catholic Faith. But he so restated the old traditional Faith in relation to the danger of Gnosticism that his very restatement took on a universal value for all times. This method of defense has stood up not only as an adequate refutation of Gnosticism but, by anticipation, of all and every heresy the Church has had to face since her infancy. Simply summarizing the legacy of all who had preceded him, setting forth once again the traditional belief and practice of the Church as he knew it, he ends by sketching a theological theory of the Church and its teaching office that all subsequent discussions have merely developed. Thanks largely to his work, the Church did not become Gnostic, although many Catholics became Gnostics. In this precious book Irenaeus established for all time the criterion of truth in every confrontation between the Catholic Church and her adversaries. The issue is always the simple one of the living tradition handed down from the apostles against the new speculations. Heresies base their veracity on the virtuosity and depth of human learning; Irenaeus based the truth on the teaching authority of the Church. Gnostics ridiculed the deposit of the Faith as being "teaching fitted for simpletons." Irenaeus accepted this gibe of the Church's modernizing children and established the truth of Catholicism and the errors of the heretics on no other basis than the general belief in the traditional nature of Catholic teaching and the general acceptance of the claim of the rulers of the Church to decide what was tradition. It was ever thus, and will ever be thus, that the Church has passed, and will always pass, unscathed through myriad doctrinal, moral, and religious crises that attack her throughout the ages. Irenaeus repeats the tradition in order to refute those thinkers whose special error was that they claimed to arrive at the fullness of Christianity solely through the avenue of "Knowledge," the Greek word for knowledge being *Gnosis*.[65]

[65] Philip Hughes, *A History of the Church*, Vol. 1 (New York: Sheed and Ward, 1934), pp. 84–92.

Irenaeus on the Antichrist

In refuting Gnosticism, Irenaeus traces their doctrines back to Simon Magus, the magician mentioned in the Acts of the Apostles, who attempted to buy from St. Peter the power of miracles and of calling down the Holy Spirit on whomever he would. Irenaeus hints that we have in Simon a foreshadowing of the Antichrist. He quotes Luke's Acts of the Apostles:

> But there was a certain man, Simon by name who before time used magical arts in that city, and led the people of Samaria astray, declaring that he himself was some great one, to whom they all gave heed, from the least to the greatest, saying, This is the power of God which is called great. And to him they had regard, because that of a long time he had driven them mad by his sorceries.[66]

Irenaeus goes on to relate St. Peter's reaction to Simon's monetary offer.

> Your money go to destruction with you because you have thought that the gift of God could be purchased with money. You have no part or lot in this matter because your heart is not right before God. Repent, therefore, of this wickedness of yours and pray to God that perhaps this thought of your heart may be forgiven you. For I see you are in the gall of bitterness and in the bond of iniquity.[67]

Irenaeus further relates that Simon refused to repent and set himself up against the apostles whom he considered merely as more advanced magicians than himself. In order to gain their

[66] Acts 8:9–11.
[67] Ibid., 8:20–23.

secret of producing wonders Simon applied himself with still greater zeal to the study of the whole art of magic. Such was the marvelous advancement and proficiency he attained that he bewildered and overpowered the multitudes with the number and variety of the wonders he wrought. Irenaeus relates that the emperor Claudius Caesar honored Simon with a statue on account of his magical prowess. Then Simon himself claimed to be a god and sought divine honors from his followers. He fathered Gnosticism and a host of other heresies to prove his claim to divinity. For he taught his followers that he himself appeared among the Jews as the Son, but descended in Samaria as the Father, while he came to other nations in the character of the Holy Spirit. The mystic priests created by Simon's diverse heretical sects practiced profligate lives and magical arts. They used exorcisms and incantations, love potions as well as charms and any other curious arts they could press into service, such as the arts of interpreting dreams and of sending dreams.[68] In the times of the Antichrist there will be many such heretical sects and messengers of Satan practicing similar abominations, corrupting truth and morals and bringing disaster upon the world and the Church, so unbridled will men be in their madness against God, so arrogant, impious, and irreligious in spirit against Christ and His Church.

When he speaks directly about the Antichrist, Irenaeus refers to him as a definite particular human person. The Antichrist is to be the Archrebel among men even as Satan is the Archrebel among the angels. In the Antichrist will be summarized and brought to plenitude all the iniquities and impostures that have taken place from the moment of the fall of the angels, through the fall of man, comprising the evils perpetrated by the

[68] The Writings of Irenaeus, *Against Heresies*, op. cit., pp. 88–89.

generations before Noah and the flood, the evils perpetrated by
the perverse generation that crucified Christ, those against his
Church right up to and including the flood of crime that will
be ushered in by the arrival of the "man of sin." In other words
the Antichrist will be the culmination and recapitulation of all
evils chosen in angelic and human history.[69] For the present,
the Antichrist is like a crouching lion as his many weaker pre-
decessors sow the seeds of evil and prepare the field of the
cosmic and social universe for his coming. When the hour of
the fullness of iniquity has struck, the Antichrist will come.
Aided mightily by Satan who will be loosed temporarily from
the bottomless pit, he will unleash his final, all-out assault on
man and God in a spirit of heinousness and hatred never before experienced or even imagined. The whole power of apostasy will find its plenitude in this beast who will rise from the
turbulence of the sea of nations and will seek to be honored as
if he were God.

Irenaeus also sees in the person of King Nebuchadnezzar
another forerunner of the coming Antichrist. For the king had
a golden statue struck sixty cubits high and six cubits wide. He
ordered all his subjects, under penalty of being thrown into a
fiery furnace, to fall down and adore the statue at the sound of
the trumpet. But the Jews Ananias, Misael, and Azarias—known
by their Babylonian names as Sidrach, Misach, and Abed-
nago—refused to perform this act of idolatry and were thrown
into the cauldron of fire, foreshadowing thereby the type of
trial the just would suffer in the last days who refused to adore
the statue struck in honor of the Antichrist. The young men

[69] W. Wigan Harvey, *Sancti Irenaei, Libros quinque adversus Haereses*,
Vol. 2 (Ridgewood, NJ: Gregg Press, 1965), pp. 391, 405, 406.

witnessing to the true God in the fiery furnace are types of the witnesses who will testify for Christ and die for his Church before the idolatrous king known as the Antichrist. Irenaeus not only finds in the statue of Nebuchadnezzar a prefiguration of the future statue in honor of the Antichrist, but he also finds in its measurements of sixty cubits of height and six cubits of width a symbolic prefiguration of the number whereby the Antichrist will be identified—666. He reasons thus: the six hundred years of Noah's life, after which the apostasy of men from God that occasioned the flood was culminated, and the numbers of the cubits of the statue of Nebuchadnezzar, on account of which the just were cast into the fire, signify the numbers of the name of that man in whom at the last times every apostasy, injustice, iniquity, false prophecy, and imposture of man's six thousand years of history will be recapitulated. Because of the plentitude of evil personified in that man, the Antichrist, the heavens and the earth will come to an end in a deluge of fire.[70]

Irenaeus reminds his readers that the Antichrist will come suddenly. He quotes St. Paul: "When men will be hailing peace and security, at that moment ruin will fall upon them."[71] He refers to the prophet Jeremiah to emphasize not only the sudden coming of the Antichrist but also to identify the Jewish tribe from which the Antichrist will arise. "The snorting of horses was heard from Dan; all the land was moved at the sound of the neighing of his warriors. And they came and devoured the land and all that was in the city and its inhabitants."[72]

---

[70] Adelin Rousseau, *Contre les Heresies*, Book V (Paris : Éditions du Cerf, 1969), pp. 369-371.

[71] 1 Thess. 5:3.

[72] Jer. 8:16.

It is because the Antichrist will arise from the tribe of Dan, whose members will follow him into apostasy, that the tribe of Dan is not counted in the Apocalypse among the Jewish tribes seen before the throne of the Lamb in the glory of heaven. So theorizes Irenaeus and many other ecclesiastical writers who follow the earliest traditions.

Since he will be evil, as it were, personified and, according to Irenaeus' expression, the maximum of malice, *recapitulatio universae iniquitatis*,[73] the Antichrist will supersede idols by himself, opposing and exalting himself above all that is God, or that is worshipped. He will sit in the Temple of God at Jerusalem, seducing those who will adore him as if he were the Christ. Our Lord Himself hinted at the willingness of the Jewish leaders to be seduced by the Antichrist when He upbraided the Scribes and Pharisees for rejecting Him, His message, and His miraculous works. "I have come in the name of My Father, and you do not receive Me. Another will come in his own name and him you will receive."[74] This other, Irenaeus tells us, is the Antichrist, the Archenemy of Christ, wicked judge who fears not God nor reveres men. He will come in his own name and establish his world dominion with the cooperation of evil angels and men.

Concerning the Antichrist's rebuilding and possession of the Temple of God at Jerusalem, and his sacrilegious cult there, Irenaeus finds its prediction in the book of Daniel: "And the holy place shall be made desolate. And strength is given to him against the continual sacrifice. And he shall cast down truth as well as justice. And he shall do and prosper."[75]

[73] Harvey, *Sancti Irenaei, Libros quinque adversus Haereses*, op. cit., p. 402.
[74] John 5:43.
[75] Dan. 8:11–12.

The angel Gabriel explains to Daniel the things that shall come to pass at the end of this malediction.

> And after their reign, when iniquities shall be grown up, there shall arise a king of a shameless face, and understanding dark sentences; and his power shall be strengthened, but not by his own force (but by the devil's). He shall lay all things waste, and prosper and accomplish more than can be believed. He shall destroy the mighty and the saints. Craftiness shall be his in great measure leading to his great success. His heart shall be puffed up; in his abundance of all things he shall kill many and lead many into perdition. And he shall confirm the covenant with many in one week, and in the half of a week the victim and the sacrifice shall fail, and there shall be in the Temple the abomination of desolation even to the consummation and to the end. And the half of the week signifies three years and six months, the time of his reign and power ... which will be destroyed by the coming of the Lord of lords and the King of kings.[76]

Concerning the exact name of the Antichrist, Irenaeus says that it is a secret kept by God until the man of sin arrives. He warns his readers not to try to guess the name from the number of the beast, 666. He tells us that those who saw and spoke with St. John in person were also warned by the beloved disciple not to play the guessing-game or the numbers-game with the name of the Antichrist. Irenaeus adds that those who fix on a certain name for the Antichrist from their own speculations will be easily deceived by him when he arrives under his own name. They will not be aware that he has yet come and hence the Antichrist

---

[76] Dan., 8:23–27.

will easily seduce them for they will not be on their guard against him.[77] Moreover, the Holy Spirit will not give us the name of the Antichrist ahead of time, but only when we must know it. The Antichrist is not worthy to be heralded ahead of time by a special name announced by messengers from heaven. Such divine revelations of special names for the coming of servants of God into history are made in the cases of certain holy prophets and of the Son of God, all of whom were destined to bring salvation to men and glory to God. Since the Antichrist is to come suddenly and disappear suddenly, as if he had never existed, God has not revealed his name ahead of time. One does not herald the name of a person who will never exist in the divine life, who will be vanquished forever by both the first and second death. Irenaeus cautions patience in awaiting the accomplishment of the prophecy that will reveal the Antichrist and his personal characteristics. To begin the game of name guessing—or the numbers game—in order to discover the exact name of the Antichrist is to open up an endless futile activity that will waste valuable time and energy and never solve the problem.[78]

St. Cyril of Jerusalem

St. Cyril was born in Jerusalem in AD 315, a few years before the outbreak of the Arian heresy. He lived to see its suppression by the Edict of Theodosius, 380, and to take part in its condemnation by the Council of Constantinople in the following year. He became bishop of Jerusalem and one of the most outstanding exponents of sacramental theology. But in his battles against Arianism, he was three times deposed and driven from Jerusalem,

[77] Rousseau, *Contre les Heresies*, Book V, op. cit., p. 387.
[78] Ibid., p. 385.

his See. During his third and longest forced exile—367-379—Jerusalem was given over to heresy and schism, to the violent strife of rival factions, and to extreme licentiousness in morals. St. Gregory of Nyssa, who was commissioned by a council held at Antioch in 378 to visit the Churches in Arabia and Palestine, "because matters with them were in confusion, and needed an arbiter," has given an account of the prevailing corruption. "If divine grace were more abundant about Jerusalem than elsewhere, sin would not be so much the fashion among those who live there; but, as it is, there is no form of uncleanness that is not perpetrated among them; rascality, adultery, theft, idolatry, poisoning, quarreling, murder are rife."[79]

The major work of St. Cyril is his *Catecheses*, instructions for neophytes during Lent and Paschal-tide. It constitutes a major source for the "Liturgy of St. James," the Syriac Liturgy. Cyril was deeply aware of Catholic unity, directing his hearers that on coming to a strange city or town they ought not to ask merely for the church, but for the "Catholic Church." In the summer of 382 a synod of Eastern bishops met at Constantinople. From the synodal letter addressed from this body to the bishops assembled at Rome we read as follows: "Of the Church in Jerusalem, the Mother of all the Churches, we make known that Cyril, the most reverend and most beloved of God, is Bishop, and that he was canonically ordained long ago by the Bishops of the province, and that he has very often fought a good fight in various places against the Arians."[80] This justification by the synod is the last recorded incident in Cyril's life. He died in 386. Here we will

---

[79] *Nicene and Post-Nicene Fathers*, Vol. 7, *Cyril of Jerusalem and Gregory Nazianzen, Introduction to Cyril* (Edinburgh: T & T Clark, 1994), p. x.
[80] Ibid., p. xi.

give his teaching on the Antichrist as it appears throughout his *Catechetical Lectures.*

Cyril of Jerusalem on the Antichrist

The Antichrist will be Christ's counterfeit; he will be raised up by Satan to discredit the truth; a sorcerer's sorcerer, he will perform many amazing deeds, all wondrous lies, by the art of sorcery. This great Deceiver is awaited eagerly by that race which rejected Christ as its king and Messiah. St. Cyril uses the same argument put forth by Irenaeus to prove this: "But if another shall come in his own name, him you will accept." This other is the Antichrist, coming on his own authority and posing as the true Messiah.[81]

In discussing the preparations for the coming of the Antichrist, Cyril emphasizes the deep moral decay of his own times. Hatred of the brethren is making room for the Antichrist; for the devil prepares beforehand the divisions among the people, and especially among Christians on what is true or false doctrine, good and evil morals. This very day there is a great falling away; thousands have abandoned the truth. The Church is filled with heretics in disguise who are the forerunners of the Antichrist. The true Christ comes from above, first in silence, weakness, and solitude, as a suffering Savior. But in His Second Coming He will come again from above, but this time with the blast of a trumpet as Judge in the glory of His Father, accompanied with legions of bright angels. On the other hand, the Antichrist comes from below, from the earth, a magician, expert in diabolical arts. He shall seize the power of the Roman Empire and

---

[81] Ibid., *The Catechetical Lectures* of St. Cyril, Archbishop of Jerusalem. The whole Lecture XV is on the Antichrist and the last things, pp. 104–114.

falsely style himself the true Christ, deceiving the Jews, who are looking for an anointed one with a political kingdom, and seducing the Gentiles by his magical illusions.[82] At first the Antichrist will put on a show of mildness, as though he were a learned and discreet person. He will act the part of a man of soberness and benevolence. But once he has established himself as totalitarian master of both Jews and Gentiles, he will drop the mask of benign graciousness. Then will begin his career of open crime, characterized by all kinds of heinous deeds and lawlessness. He will outstrip in maliciousness all the unrighteous, ungodly persons who have gone before him, displaying against all men, but especially against Christians, a murderous spirit driven on by a lust for cruelty. He will be a tyrant run amuck in the blood of the saints for three and one-half years.[83]

In relating the Antichrist's rise to world power, Cyril follows the traditional explanation of Daniel's vision on this event. The reign of the Antichrist will begin when he gains control of the kingdoms that once made up the Roman Empire. Ten kings will be reigning in different areas of the empire. Then an eleventh king, the Antichrist, will arise and seize total power. Three of the kings he will conquer outright and the remaining seven he will win over to subjection to himself. The angel Gabriel explains the vision of the ten kings to Daniel thus: "The fourth beast shall be a fourth kingdom upon the earth, which shall surpass all kingdoms. And the ten horns of this beast are ten kings that shall arise; and another king shall rise up after them, who shall surpass in wickedness all who were before him ... and he shall speak words against the Most High. A blasphemer

---

[82] Ibid., pp. 104–114.
[83] Ibid.

the man is and lawless, not having the kingdom from his fathers, but having usurped the power by means of sorcery."[84]

The Antichrist and Rebuilding the Temple

An important event in the life of St. Cyril is his prediction of the failure of the Emperor Julian the Apostate to rebuild the Temple of Jerusalem. Julian, a contemporary of Cyril, had apostatized from the Faith as a student in Athens.[85] Now as emperor he was attempting to restore ancient heathenism and galvanize it into some sort of glorious new life. In order to discredit the Christian belief that a sentence of everlasting destruction had been pronounced by Christ against the Temple, Julian aspired to restore its ancient glory. But the Christians put their faith in the words of Christ and were convinced Julian would fail in his attempt. The historian Rufinus records the fact that "lime and cement had been

---

[84] Ibid.

[85] Gregory Nazianzen was a student at Athens with the young Prince Julian, afterward the emperor who apostatized. Gregory claims even at this early period to have foreseen and dreaded Julian's accession. "I had long foreseen," he wrote, "how matters would be from the time that I was with him at Athens. He had come there shortly after the violent measures against his brother, having asked permission of the Emperor to do so. He had two reasons for this sojourn—the one more honest, namely, to visit Greece and its schools; the other more secret, known only to a few persons, namely, to consult with the heathen priests and charlatans about his plans; because his wickedness was not as yet declared. Even then I made no bad guess about the man, although I am not one of those skilled in such matters; but I was made a prophet by the unevenness of his disposition and the very unsettled condition of his mind. I used these very words about him: 'What an evil the Roman State is nourishing,' though I prefaced them with a wish that I might prove a false prophet." Quoted in *Nicene and Post-Nicene Fathers*, pp. 190-191 from Oration V of St. Gregory Nazianzen.

brought and all was ready for destroying the old foundations and laying the new." After studying the prophecies in Daniel concerning the "times," the predictions of our Lord in the Gospels, and the visions of St. John in the Apocalypse, Cyril remained certain that Julian, though a forerunner of the man of sin, was not the Antichrist. Hence, without any special private revelation, Cyril predicted that Julian would fail in his attempt to rebuild the Temple of Jerusalem, a feat that only the Antichrist was destined to accomplish. In that same year 363 Julian was killed in his Persian campaign and the whole project was abandoned by the new Emperor Jovian who, as a believer in the Nicene Creed, gave the Church a period of comparative peace.[86]

Cyril emphasized the fact that the Antichrist alone, and no other potentate, would rebuild the temple of Jerusalem. For the Antichrist would abhor all other idols, wanting himself to be the only idol adored. Thus he must seat himself in his own rebuilt Temple as God. Coming to the Jews as their Christ, he would demand worship of them. That is why he would have to make a great account of the Temple, so as to completely beguile the Jews as a new Solomon rebuilding the House of God and calling it his own house. Cyril held that the Antichrist would come at a time when "there shall not be left one stone upon another in the Temple of the Jews."[87] As far as Cyril was concerned, that doom upon the Temple was not yet accomplished in his day, nor did he expect it be completed until the coming of the Jewish Antichrist who would restore the Temple shortly before the end of the world. For Cyril could see that the old Temple, destroyed by the Romans under Titus, still had stones upon stones. Hence Cyril

[86] Ibid., pp. ix, x.
[87] Matt. 24:2.

expected events of nature and history—earthquakes, storms, floods, new building projects, the decay of time, etc.—to destroy slowly all the stones of the old Temple. Once this happened, another sign heralding the advent of the Antichrist would have been accomplished. However, it was Cyril's conviction that the final destruction of the Temple of Jerusalem, that rebuilt by the Antichrist, would take place only at the Second Coming of Christ, at the end of the world. Only then would the prophecy of our Lord, as stated in Matthew, "not a stone will be left upon a stone," actually be fulfilled.

Martyrs under the Antichrist

When he meditated on the persecution that would be perpetrated by the Antichrist against the Church, Cyril was able to compare the persecutions of his own day to what would happen in the times of the Antichrist. He predicted that the persecutions directed by the Antichrist would be the worst the world had ever known, or would ever know. And the martyrs suffering under these persecutions would be the most blessed of all martyrs.[88] Here is how he describes the scene:

There will be a time of affliction, such as never happened since there was a nation upon the earth till that time. The fearful monster, the great serpent, the unconquerable enemy of mankind ready to devour.... The Lord, knowing the greatness of the enemy, in mercy to the godly, says, "Let those who are in Judea flee to the mountains." However, if any person feels within himself a strong heart to wrestle with Satan, let him remain (for I do not despair

[88] *Catechetical Lectures* in *Nicene and Post-Nicene Fathers*, Lecture XV, pp. 104–114.

of the Church's strength of nerve), let him remain and let him say, "Who shall separate us from the love of Christ?" ... But thanks be to God who has confined the greatness of that tribulation to a few days; for He says, "But for the elect's sake those days shall be shortened"; and the Antichrist shall reign only three and a half years—a time, times and a dividing of times.... Blessed surely he who shall then be a martyr for Christ! I consider that the martyrs of that season will be greater than all martyrs; for the former martyrs wrestled with man only, but these, in the time of the Antichrist, will battle with Satan himself in person. Persecuting emperors slaughtered the former martyrs; but they did not pretend to raise the dead, nor make show of signs and wonders; but here there will be the persuasion both of force and fraud, so as to deceive, if possible, even the elect. Let no one at that day say in his heart, "What could Christ do more than this or that? By what power does this man work these things? Unless God willed it, he would not have permitted it." No, the Apostle warns you saying beforehand, "God shall send them a strong delusion," —not that they may be excused but condemned, namely those who believe not in the truth, that is, in the true Christ, but take pleasure in unrighteousness, that is, in the Antichrist.... Prepare yourself, therefore, O Man, you have the signs of the Antichrist; and remember them not only for yourself, but communicate them also freely to all around you. If you have a child according to the flesh, delay not to instruct him of these things now. If you are a teacher, prepare also your spiritual children, lest they take the false for the true. "For the mystery of iniquity is already at work." I fear the wars of the nations; I fear the divisions among

Christians; I fear the hatred among brethren. Enough! But
God forbid that it should be fulfilled in our days. However,
let us be prepared.[89]

On the essentials concerning the prophetic history of the Antichrist and his deeds, as represented in this chapter from the writings of Sts. Irenaeus and Cyril of Jerusalem, the other Greek Fathers, such as Clement of Alexandria, Athanasius, Basil the Great,
Gregory of Nyssa, Gregory of Nazianzus, Chrysostom, etc., all
agreed. They accepted the traditional teaching on this matter that
was handed down from the apostles, even though in some minor
details concerning the Antichrist prophecies, details not the subject of this study, they held diverse opinions. For all the Fathers
and theologians unanimously concur in this belief as to the Antichrist's individuality. Consequently, his personal existence and
future event must be considered as an object of divine faith.[90]

---

[89] Ibid.
[90] P. Huchede, *History of Antichrist* (Rockford, IL: Tan Books and
Publishers, 1969), pp. 11–12.

Chapter 5

The Antichrist and the Latin Fathers

In the preceding chapter two essential marks that identify a "Father of the Church" were recorded. First, the writer or teacher of Catholic Faith and morals had to persevere unto death in a life of orthodox communion with the Church. Second, that life had to be eminent for sanctity. Let us briefly recall how the Church historically arrived at her basic requirements for declaring certain ecclesiastical teachers and writers "Fathers of the Church."

The New Testament used the word *Father* to indicate a teacher of spiritual truths by whose means the soul of man could be born again and grow up into the likeness of the holiness of Christ. Paul had written: "For though you have ten thousand pedagogues in Christ, yet you have not many fathers. For in Christ Jesus through the Gospel did I beget you. Therefore, I beg you, be imitators of me as I am of Christ."[91]

The first teachers of Christianity seemed to be collectively called or spoken of as "the Fathers." Thus bishops and priests engaged in the apostolate of writing and teaching about the Faith enjoyed this title. It is not surprising, therefore, that appeals were often made to the writings and teachings of these

---

[91] 1 Cor. 4:15, 16.

clergymen in order to settle doubts that arose about the Faith. This procedure was valid enough as long as bishops and priests kept teaching the deposit of the Faith in its full purity. In the second century bishops were orthodox; but in the third century they were often found wanting; in the fourth century they were the leaders of schisms and heresies. It became apparent that bishops as well as priests—and some brilliant ecclesiastical lay scholars—were fallible and often enough became heretics, misrepresenting the Faith to be what were, in fact, their own false philosophies. Inevitably a new criterion and appeal was sought, one of more enduring value, in deciding who was a true "Father of the Church." To the two characteristics already listed—perseverance in orthodox communion with the Church and eminent holiness of life—the Church now added the following marks of a Father of the Church: 1) the teacher must enjoy a certain antiquity (looked at from the present day); 2) he could enjoy citation by a General Council; 3) he could enjoy citation in public Acts of popes addressed to the Church; 4) he could enjoy an encomium in the Roman Martyrology as *sanctitate et doctrina insignis*, i.e., "outstanding for sanctity and doctrine"; 5) he could enjoy the public reading of his work in Churches; and 6) he could enjoy citation with praise as being an authority on the faith by one of the more celebrated Fathers. In all this, it was clearly understood that the consensus of the Fathers was not expected in minor matters touching aspects of doctrine, morals, religious history, or customs.[92]

[92] John Chapman, "The Fathers of the Church," in *The Catholic Encyclopedia*, Vol. VI, ed. Charles George Herbermann (New York: Gilmary Society, 1913), article on "The Fathers of the Church" by John Chapman, pp. 1–18.

It is interesting to note that through most of the fourth century while the Arian heresy was raging, the controversy turned upon scriptural arguments pro and con. Appeals to past authority were few indeed. Thus, appeal to the Fathers was never the most imposing *locus theologicus*, for they could not easily be assembled so as to form an absolutely conclusive test. On the other hand, up to the end of the fourth century there were practically no infallible definitions, except condemnations of heresies chiefly by popes. It was, therefore, to the living authority that appeals were made. The famous statement of Pope St. Celestine became the rule for orthodox teaching and Christian conduct. *Desinat incessere novitas vetustatem.* "Let novelty cease to attack antiquity."

In 434, St. Vincent of Lerins produced his famous document, the *Commonitorium*. In it he wholeheartedly adhered to the rule of Pope St. Celestine. He quoted it as an authoritative and irresistible witness to his own doctrine that where *quod ubique,* or *universitas est incertum,* i.e., where universal agreement on a point of doctrine is uncertain, the faithful must then inquire into the *quod semper* or *antiquitas,* i.e., into the constancy and antiquity of the Church's teaching on the matter. Now the Ecumenical Council of Ephesus had been held in the same year (431) in which Pope St. Celestine had written his famous letter containing the rule: "Let novelty cease attacking antiquity!" The Acts of this Council were before St. Vincent as he wrote his *Commonitorium* and it is clear from his document that he looked upon both pope and council as decisive authorities. St. Vincent had to establish this truth before composing and enunciating his famous canon, *quod ubique, quod semper, quod ab omnibus*—that is, *universitas, antiquitas, consensio.* It was not really a new criterion for orthodoxy, else it would have committed suicide by the mere novelty of its very expression. But never had the doctrine been so admirably phrased, so limpidly explained, so adequately exemplified. Even the law of the evolution of dogma is defined by St. Vincent in language that can hardly be surpassed for exactness and vigor. St. Vincent's triple test is wholly misunderstood if it is taken to be the ordinary rule of faith. Like all Catholics of his time, St. Vincent himself took the ordinary rule to be the living Magisterium of the Church and he assumes that the formal decision in cases of doubt lies with the Apostolic See. But cases of doubt arise when no such decision is forthcoming. Then it is that the three tests are to be applied, not simultaneously, but, if necessary, in succession.[93]

St. Augustine

Perhaps the most illustrious of all the Fathers—Greek or Latin—is St. Augustine (354–430), Bishop of Hippo in Africa. He has the unique fame of having routed in his lifetime three heresies—Manichaeism, Donatism, and Pelagianism. He was perhaps the greatest controversialist the world has ever known. His tremendous success as an apologist for the Faith was due as much to his zeal in persuading men to accept the truth as to his skill in refuting their errors. Besides this he was not merely the greatest philosopher among the Fathers; he was really the only philosopher. As a philosophical theologian he has no superior, except perhaps his own son and disciple, St. Thomas Aquinas, who quotes him as much, if not more, than he quotes Aristotle. Augustine was himself a Platonist. As a commentator and original thinker, he cared little for the letter, everything for the spirit. Yet his harmony of the Gospels shows that he could attend to

[93] Ibid.

history and details. No one perceived the theological-philosophical overtones of history as profoundly as did Augustine. Pope Leo XIII in his encyclical on historical studies, *Saepenumero*, bade historians to take St. Augustine as their guide. "All history in a way shouts out that it is God whose providence governs the varied and continual changes of mortal affairs, and adapts them, even in spite of human opposition, to the growth of his Church."[94] No one understood or exemplified this truth with greater brilliance and profundity than did St. Augustine in his masterful work *De Civitate Dei*. Pope Pius XII returned to the theme of the two cities, expounded by St. Augustine in his great work, in an allocution to historians in 1956: "As the great St. Augustine said with classical precision: what God proposes that comes about, that happens, even though it happens slowly, it happens ceaselessly. God is truly the Lord of history."[95]

St. Augustine was also a renowned professor of rhetoric before his wonderful conversion. Yet, like St. Cyprian, and even more than St. Cyprian, he put aside as a Christian all the artifices of oratory that he had mastered so well. He retained correctness of grammar and perfect good taste, together with the power of speaking and writing with colloquial plainness. Large-minded and far-seeing, he was also very learned. His *De Civitate Dei* reveals the vast amount of reading he did. What is even more inspiring is that it puts him in the first place among apologists for the Faith. Before his death he was the object of extraordinary veneration. It has been remarked that there is about this many-sided bishop a certain symmetry that makes him an

---

[94] C. M. Eberhardt and C. Newman, *A Summary of Catholic History*, Vol. 1 (St. Louis: B. Herder Book Company, 1961), p. 5.

[95] Ibid.

almost faultless model of a holy, wise, and courageous shepherd of souls. Because he grasped so quickly and thoroughly the large and long view of God's economy of salvation, because he was a profound philosophical theologian, it was St. Augustine in the West who completely systematized the complicated doctrine of the Holy Trinity, which had led so many of the Eastern theologians into particular heresies. It is well to remember, as we follow St. Augustine's thought on the Antichrist, that this holy bishop in all his writings and preachings remained essentially a penitent inflamed with a grateful love of God.

Background: St. Cyprian

We present here a sketch of St. Cyprian's problems with the surrounding pagan people and their authorities in order to give a minimal historical background against which the thought of St. Augustine, some two hundred years later, on the destiny of the Church in her war with the city of Satan and its antichrists can be appreciated. St. Cyprian became bishop of Carthage in the year 250, only months before the Emperor Decius' edict stating that all Roman citizens must perform a public act of sacrifice to the gods of the empire or else go to their death. Cyprian, who was an avid reader of Tertullian, displayed in his own writings a clear eschatological orientation. In an address to Demetrian, Cyprian answers charges that the recent calamities of famine, drought, war, plague, and social chaos are attributable to the Christians. This work, short and restricted in its scope, reflects some of the vivid Tertullian apocalyptic polemic against the Roman State, against the world as led captive by the demons. "Caesars are necessary for the world," claims Tertullian, that very world which in his view is soon to meet its end. Tertullian paints a picture, wondrous in its grim details, of that everlasting spectacle that Christians will enjoy from their vantage point in the new Jerusalem—of kings and governors, actors, wrestlers and charioteers, all tortuously tossing in the fiery billows of hell. He is not against the world of God's creation, but against the world that has become the Babylon, the mother and whore of idolatry and obscenities. "For the world is God's, but the goings-on of this world are the devil's."[96]

In this work, as often elsewhere, Cyprian writes as a man utterly convinced that the day of the Lord is at hand. But his conviction is of such serenity that he considers an extended study of older apologetic themes pointless.[97] Cyprian tells Demetrian that he is merely asserting the facts about the imminent end of the world and he appeals to Demetrian to repent and believe while there is yet time. The failure of the crops, the absence of winter rains and of summer sun, the murderous plague, the raging of repeated wars, all offer ample testimony that the world is running down and will soon come to its final demise. Christians have long known that "in the last times evils would be multiplied and misfortunes varied." These occurrences are just as natural as the arrival of old-age decrepitudes in a man, yet no one thinks of blaming Christians for the latter misfortunes. Moreover, physical disasters are simply the concomitants of widespread moral rottenness: corruption in the courts and the buying off of judges, avarice in the market place, violence in public life, the wholesale and shameless seizure of the property of the dying. Added to all this is the debasement of the people in the public, degrading worship of crocodiles, snakes, apes, and stones. Finally there is

---

[96] Quoted by Robert F. Evans in his *One and Holy* (London: SPCK, 1972), pp. 8–11.

[97] Ibid., p. 38.

the general persecution of the innocent Christians. Physical decay, moral evil, idolatrous religion, the oppression of God's people are simply four indicators pointing in the same direction: the great and terrible day of the Lord when an avenging God will take to Himself those who have been signed with the blood of Christ and will condemn the pagans to hell, a hell whose fire is never extinguished. Thus Cyprian wrote to the proconsul Demetrian.[98]

Augustine also lived in times of mounting religious and social chaos. The Church of his day had to suffer many anxieties and adversities. The sack of Rome provoked vigorous pagan reaction against the Church. Italy and Africa were in panic over the ravages of the Goths. Gothic-Arian mercenaries debilitated the faith of the troops. There was a widespread revival of paganism, of idolatry. Augustine saw that the new situation in which the Church found herself called for new duties in the hierarchy and the faithful. In the midst of this crisis, Augustine put before the Latin world a theological structure of breathtaking brilliance that possessed strong lines of continuity with previous Christian thought yet was thoroughly attuned to the new conditions of the Church in a falling and hostile empire. Never was Augustine disposed to argue that *traditio* was a small matter.[99]

Augustine had three purposes in writing *The City of God*. First, he wished to demonstrate that neither a pagan nor the Christian religion could insure a State against the military and other temporal vicissitudes common to human society as such. Second, he sought to prove that, as regards religion, the Roman Empire could do nothing better than become a Catholic empire, thereby

[98] Ibid., pp. 38, 39.
[99] Ibid., pp. 65, 70–71.

furthering among men the worship of the true God and the enjoyment of that true tranquility of order which is the peace that comes from Christ. Third, he undertook to reveal that the ultimate destiny of the Catholic Church is not in the slightest degree tied to the fortunes of the Roman Empire.[100]

The Two Cities

For Augustine the war between the heavenly city and the earthly had its origin and background in the war between the fallen angels and the holy angels before the creation of man and his universe. Before human history the City of God was already established in heaven among the glorified angels, while the City of Satan already existed in hell among the damned angels. The two cities began not here on earth, but beyond the material universe, God being king of the heavenly, Satan tyrant of the diabolical city.[101] Now it was God's plan that no intelligent being, created in His own image and likeness, would be exempt from the honor and opportunity of choosing his Creator with a love of preference. When God created man in grace, He invited him to choose between remaining in holiness, to become a glorified citizen of heaven, and becoming morally evil and thus a damned citizen of hell. When Lucifer seduced our first parents, he projected into human history his own City of Satan among men. But when Adam repented and God promised him that He would send a Savior, the seed of a woman, to redeem mankind, He established the foundation for that City of God among men which was to conquer the City of Satan at the end of time. The two cities have

---

[100] Ibid., p. 112.
[101] *The City of God*, trans. Marcus Dods, (New York: Modern Library, 1950), Bk. XI, c. 13.

two contradictory loves. The City of God is founded and moved by love of God that fundamentally unites its citizens to God and to each other in a communion of saints. For a people is an assemblage of rational beings united in fellowship by their agreement as to the truths they profess and the faith they live. But more than this, since the last word in salvation is not with the head but with the heart, a people is an assemblage of spiritual beings united in fellowship by their agreement as to the divine, angelic, and human persons they adhere to in love. Self-love, pride, and the lust for domination govern the earthly city. Humility, truth, patience, and love of God are the driving forces of the heavenly city. The earthly city is moved by the love of self even unto the contempt of God. The heavenly city is moved by the love of God even unto the contempt of itself. The former glories in itself; the latter in the Lord. The former seeks glory from men; the latter's full glory is found in God. The city of the world glories in its own wisdom; the city of God in the incorruptible wisdom of God.[102]

The brothers, Cain and Abel, are the types of the two cities. Cain, the fratricide, is the founder of the earthly city. A man of the world overcome by envy, he slew his brother. Like his spiritual father, Satan, Cain became a liar and murderer from the beginning, for he hated his brother Abel for no other reason than that Abel was good and pleasing to God while he himself was evil and rejected by God. Cain built cities to last in this world; Abel built no city; he was a pilgrim in this world, traveling through toward the heavenly city. The struggle that fell out between Cain and Abel illustrates the incompatible ideals of the two cities. Cain is the figure in time of Satan who rebelled

[102] Ibid., Bk. XIX, cc. 21, 24.

against God, of the Jews who slew Christ and of the Antichrist who attempts to destroy the Church by war and persecution. Abel prefigures in himself the holy angels in his fidelity, Christ crucified in his innocent death, and the persecuted Church in his sufferings for his fidelity to God. For all the good are hated, like Christ, without cause. Abel used the world and its creatures that he might glorify God and enter into the joy of his Lord. In this, too, he prefigures Christ and His Church; both come to glorify God in His creation and in his saints. But Cain is a type of Satan, of the Jews, of the Antichrist in that he used the world for his own enjoyment and aggrandizement; he attempted to abuse God in order to increase his enjoyment, power, and rule over the world. In this Cain is the figure of Satan, the Jews, and the Antichrist especially because all these strive to dethrone God and become Lords of the world in their own names.[103]

Here on earth the City of God is the pilgrim Church striving in history to enter fully into the blessedness of the Holy Angels and the vision of God. But, unlike the City of God in heaven, the Catholic Church is not sealed against sinful members, against traitorous citizens. In this world there is no eschatological perfection in the Church. Her citizens must continually be drawn toward their final perfection, must still be gradually released from varying degrees of ignorance and infirmity. Her citizens must continue to pray daily that their sins be forgiven. For the Church, which is truly and finally holy and without blemish, having neither spot nor wrinkle, is the Church that in the lives of its fighting, suffering members is still being prepared—the heavenly Church or perfect City of God. Augustine says that the wrath of God will break equally upon the pagan world and upon

[103] Ibid., Bks. XV–XVIII.

many, perhaps most, in the Church on earth. The Antichrist will be the final test, the final divine scourge against a world steeped in apostasy and idolatry. For the city of the Antichrist will be like the City of Babylon, a word that means confusion. This city will be powerful and wonderful in construction, and it will gain supremacy over the whole world. It plans to make itself so high and mighty that it will challenge the heavens, blaspheme God, and indeed make of men "hunters against God."

The Church, the City of God in time, is composed of sinners and saints, of tares and wheat. Here and now God alone can infallibly distinguish those who are to end up tares rather than wheat. For men to attempt to uproot the tares from the Church would be to be lacking in the virtue of patience, to refuse to allow to God what only He can do.[104] For God accomplishes, in the mysterious way He grants the grace of perseverance, the awesome demonstration that no spiritual security, no saving regeneration is possible except as His unqualified gift. But the exercise of patience does not exclude the use of ecclesiastical discipline for heretics and public sinners. It merely means that the exercise of discipline requires great sensitivity, circumspection as well as courage. Now bishops possess magisterial and jurisdictional authority in the Church. They are obliged to maximize the conditions that will assist the faithful in their journeys toward the beatific vision. Hence, bishops may also be obliged to excommunicate, if all other remedies have failed. Weak brethren must be protected by good shepherds from heretical wolves who would devour the Faith and the faithful. Moreover, both faithful and heretics must be taught that the wages of sin are serious and offending Christians will be brought to amendment by the prompt use of external persuasions. Then, too,

---

[104] Ibid., Bk. XX, cc. 5, 9.

bishops will apply disciplinary measures promptly and courageously, if they realize that heretics are not so much brothers who
need a bit of talking to as they are rather a solid structural encampment of the earthly city within the heavenly city to subvert the
latter. From the camp of heretics within the Church, one must
expect not only the ideological warfare of impostors, claiming to
be faithful citizens of the true City of God, but one must expect
from these impostors violence as well. The Antichrist will find
many allies in his fight against the Church from the encampment
of heretics within the Church.

Augustine on the Antichrist

In harmony with all the other Fathers and theologians of antiquity, Augustine held that the Antichrist will be an individual
person. For him the word *Antichrist* is not a generic term signifying all heretics, schismatics, apostates, infidels, or impious, antichristian movements and empires. He writes: "Truly Jesus
Christ will extinguish by His presence the last persecution
which is to be made by the Antichrist. It is written that Christ
will slay him by the breath of His mouth, and empty him with
the brightness of His presence."[105] Augustine also has recourse
to Daniel's prophecies about the end of the world. Daniel recounts the last judgment in such a way as to indicate that the
Antichrist must come first. Daniel sees four beasts, signifying
four kingdoms and the fourth is conquered by a certain king
who is recognized as the Antichrist. And after the Antichrist's
conquests, Daniel sees the eternal kingdom of the Son of Man,
that is to say, of Christ. "My spirit was terrified, I Daniel, in the
midst of my body, and the visions of my head troubled me."

[105] Ibid., Bk. XVIII, c. 53.

Augustine maintains that whoever reads this passage, "even half-asleep," cannot fail to see that the kingdom of the Antichrist shall fiercely assail the Church before the last judgment of God shall introduce the eternal reign of the saints. It is patent, too, from the context that the *time, times and half a time*, means a year, two years and half a year, that is to say, three and one-half years, the length of the Antichrist's reign. Augustine concludes: "As for the ten kings, whom, as it seems, the Antichrist is to find in the person of ten individuals when he comes, I own, I am afraid, we may be deceived in this, and that he may come unexpectedly while there are not ten kings living in the Roman world."[106]

Then in working out the schedule of apocalyptic events, Augustine writes:

> In connection with the (Last) Judgment the following events shall come to pass, as we have learned: Elias the Tishbite shall come; the Jews shall believe; the Antichrist shall persecute; Christ shall judge; the dead shall rise; the good and the wicked shall be separated; the world shall be burned and renewed. All these things we believe shall come to pass; but how, or in what order, human understanding cannot perfectly teach us, but only the experience of the events themselves. My opinion, however, is that they will happen in the order in which I have related them.[107]

Augustine on Paul concerning the Antichrist

Augustine gives an interesting commentary on what the apostle Paul wrote about the coming of the Antichrist, the Second

[106] Ibid., Bk. XX, c. 23.
[107] Ibid., Bk. XX, c. 30.

Coming of Christ, and final judgment on the day of the Lord. The passage he interprets is:

> We beseech you, brethren, by the coming of Our Lord Jesus Christ and our being gathered together unto him not to be hastily shaken from your right mind, nor terrified, whether by spirit or by utterance, or by letter attributed to us, as though the day of the Lord were near at hand. Let no one deceive you in any way, for the day of the Lord will not come, unless the apostasy comes first, and the man of sin is revealed, the son of perdition, who opposes and is exalted above all that is called God, or that is worshipped, so that he sits in the temple of God and gives himself out as if he were God. Do you not remember that when I was still with you, I used to tell you these things? And now you know what restrains him, that he may be revealed in his proper time. For the mystery of iniquity is already at work; provided only that he who is at present restraining it, does still restrain, until he is gotten out of the way. And then the wicked one will be revealed, whom the Lord Jesus Christ will slay with the breath of his mouth and will destroy with the brightness of his coming. And his coming is according to the working of Satan with all power and signs and lying wonders, and with all wicked deception to those who are perishing. For they have not received the love of truth that they might be saved. Therefore, God sends them a misleading influence that they may believe falsehood.[108]

Clearly Paul is writing of the Antichrist and of the day of final judgment. But the final judgment cannot come unless he comes

[108] 2 Thess. 2:1–11.

first who is the apostate. All the ungodly are apostates, but the Antichrist is the apostate par excellence. It is not certain what temple the Antichrist will use to accept divine worship, whether the ruined and restored temple of Solomon or a Church. Yet the apostle, it would seem, would not call a temple of an idol or demon the temple of God. Some think, therefore, that the Antichrist in this passage refers not specifically to the prince of evil himself, but to his whole body, the mass of people who adhere to him as their prince. Others think that the Antichrist will act as if he were the temple of God himself, as if he were the Church itself. As regards the hindrance or cause of delay preventing the coming of the Antichrist, Augustine records various interpretations put forth in his day. Some think Paul is referring to the Roman Empire, but indicates it in a subtle manner, lest being more explicit, he should incur the calumnious charge of wishing ill to the empire that it was hoped would be eternal. And in using the words "the mystery of iniquity is already at work," he alluded to Nero whose deeds seemed to be the works of the Antichrist. Hence, though dead, some supposed Nero would rise again. Others denied Nero was dead, but asserted that he had gone into hiding to give the impression he was dead, and that he was living at a vigorous age, waiting the proper time to come forward and regain his kingdom as the Lord of the world, the Antichrist. Augustine's dry comment on these theories is: "I wonder that men can be so audacious in their conjectures."[109]

Yet Augustine holds it a reasonable theory that the Roman Empire must be taken out of the way, that is, fall, before the Antichrist is revealed. Others think the words, "You know what is withholding" and "the mystery of iniquity is already at work,"

---

[109] *The City of God*, Bk. XX, c. 19.

refer to the wicked and the hypocrites who remain within the Church. When these traitors have reached a number so great as to shake the foundations of the Church, they will furnish the Antichrist with many allies, that is, a large group of subversives working within the Church to destroy her, and this is the mystery of iniquity because it is hidden. That is why Paul exhorts the faithful to hold tenaciously to the faith. "Only he who holds, let him hold until he be taken out of the way," that is, until the mystery of iniquity that is now hidden, until the subversives within the Church are revealed, identified, taken out of the way, and spewed out of the bosom of the Church. Indeed this is the same mystery recorded in the epistle of John the Evangelist. "Little children, it is the last time: and you have heard that the Antichrist shall come; even now there are many antichrists; whereby we know that it is the last time. They went out from us, but they were not of us; for if they had been of us, they would no doubt have continued with us." Hence the Church must rid herself of these many heretics whom John calls antichrists. On their departure they will then join the Antichrist who will be revealed to the whole world.[110]

Augustine on the Millennium

John the Evangelist speaks of two resurrections in the Apocalypse. Some Christians have misconstrued the passage into "ridiculous fancies." When he speaks of the first resurrection, John is indicating the rise of the soul from the death of sin to the life of grace for the sinners who hear the voice of the Son of Man and accept Him as their Savior. This is the resurrection from the first death, the death of the soul in ungodliness and wickedness

[110] Ibid., Bk. XX, c. 19.

in time. Those who persevere in the life of the first resurrection will also be preserved from the second death—from damnation in hell after the final judgment. Thus they will also enjoy the second and final resurrection, that of the glorified body and soul united in heaven at the end of time. "And I saw an angel come down from heaven.... Blessed and holy is he that has part in the first resurrection; on such the second death has no power; but they shall be priests of God and Christ and shall reign with him a thousand years."

On the strength of this passage, many have erroneously held that the first resurrection is future and bodily. They have been especially influenced by the number of a thousand years, as if it were fitting, in the economy of salvation, that the saints should enjoy a sort of Sabbath or sabbatical of a thousand years' rest, a holy leisure from labor after the six thousand years of tumultuous struggle from the moment of man's fall into sin. Misinterpreting the Psalmist's statement, "One day with the Lord is a thousand years, and a thousand years is as one day," they concluded that it was fitting that, on the completion of the six thousand years of toil and trouble, there should follow a kind of seventh day Sabbath in the succeeding thousand years. And in order to celebrate this Sabbath rest the saints will rise from the dead in the first resurrection. Now this opinion would not be too objectionable if it were believed that the joy of the saints during that thousand years of Sabbath would be a spiritual joy, flowing from happiness in the presence of the glorified Christ and of God. Augustine states: "For I myself too once held this opinion." But those who still hold this opinion about the first bodily resurrection and the thousand years of Sabbath have corrupted the whole theory. They claim that during this period the saints will leisurely enjoy immoderate carnal banquets, overflowing with large supplies of meat and drink as not only to shock temperate souls but to surpass even the credulity of gluttons. Only the carnal-minded can conceive and adhere to such a myth of the millennium. We call such believers chiliasts, a term we may literally reproduce by the name of millenarians. It would be tedious to refute their opinions point by point. Rather let us see how Scripture should be understood on this matter.

It was for the binding of the devil who held the human race captive in a sea of sins that the evangelist John saw in the Apocalypse "an angel coming down from heaven, having the key of the abyss and a chain in his hand. And he laid hold on the dragon, that old serpent which is called the devil and Satan, and bound him a thousand years," that is restrained his power so that he could not seduce or capture those who were to be saved. These thousand years may be understood in two ways.

First, we can consider that man is living in the last millennium, that thousand years of the six thousand of the world's history to date. We are living as it were in the sixth day of the world's history. This age is to be followed by a Sabbath that will have no evening and during which the saints are to enjoy endless rest. Thus speaking of a part under the name of the whole, the evangelist calls the last part of human history, the part, that is, which is yet to expire before the end of the world—a thousand years. Second, there is the explanation that John used the thousand years as an equivalent for the whole duration of the world, since one thousand is considered the perfection of numbers and fittingly marks the fullness of time. Augustine prefers the first interpretation. Thus during the sixth day of the world's history, during this sixth millennium, the devil is bound and prohibited from seducing the nations that belong to Christ, those predestined to enjoy eternal life. For the present, then, unable to seduce the nations from which the Church is gathered and which he formerly seduced before the Church existed, the devil awaits the termination of this sixth day, of this last millennium, before he is to be turned loose for his final assault on God and His Church. All are agreed, of course, that Satan seduces even now and draws to damnation those souls and nations not predestined to eternal life.[111]

At the termination of the thousand years, the devil will wage a violent war for three and one-half years, in league with all his wicked angels and godless human forces, on the camp of the saints. Now this is allowed, even willed, by divine design. For in what more striking way could God allow the malicious power of Satan to be made evident to the whole of creation? Or in what more challenging way could God give His saints the opportunity of demonstrating their steadfast fortitude and fidelity to Himself and His kingdom? Moreover, the final struggle will reveal to all creation the good use God makes of the wickedness of His enemies. For the City of God will conquer these mighty adversaries only by the power of God and will thus bring greater glory to Christ, the redeemer, helper, and deliverer of all captive souls and nations willing to follow Him.

Now the devil was bound not only when the Church began to be more widely extended among all nations beyond Judea, but he is bound even now and shall be bound until the end of the millennium. And when he is loosed, what will become of the little ones? Will Satan's power prevent the children of Christians from being baptized? Christian parents will have to use clandestine methods to bring their babes to the laver of regeneration.

---

[111] Ibid., Bk. XX, c. 7.

The real meaning of the thousand years is that the saints are reigning at the present time with Christ in His kingdom the Church. For the Church is now, today, His kingdom. True, the saints are reigning in another, far different way than the peaceful reign they will enjoy in heaven. Christ has said: "Lo, I am with you always even to the end of time, unto the consummation of the world." Surely it is during this present time that the scribe brings forth from the treasury of the Church new things and old. At the same time sainted souls are reigning with God in heaven while awaiting the resurrection of their bodies even during these last thousand years at whose completion Satan will be turned loose against all mankind.

When the thousand years are completed, Satan will be loosed and through the agency of the Antichrist, he shall seduce nations from the four corners of the earth, nations known as Gog and Magog, whose number of soldiers is as the sands of the sea. These organized powers will make war and bring upon the camp of the saints the final, cruelest persecution ever mounted against the Church. The entire City of God will be assaulted by the enemy forces of the City of the Antichrist. For the nations called Gog and Magog are not to be understood as some barbarous nations, but those nations everywhere in which the devil dwells and holds sway over the leaders and their peoples. Thus the camp of the saints, wherever it is found throughout the earth, will be encompassed by the savage persecution of her enemies. But the forces of the Antichrist will be impotent to lure the saints to their ranks and the last divine punishment will be the fire that flashes from heaven to consume that impious army. Augustine understands the first beast, the one arising from the sea, to be the Wicked City of Satan, while the second beast, the one arising from the earth, is his false prophet, the Antichrist. When all these enemies are conquered

and thrown into the pool of eternal, inextinguishable fire, then
the figure of this world will pass away in a universal conflagration,
even as once before the world was covered and nearly all men destroyed in the deluge known as the universal flood.[112]

St. Gregory the Great (540–604)

Gregory the Great, Pope and Doctor of the Church, is one of the
most notable figures in ecclesiastical history. His influence on
the doctrine, organization, and discipline of the Catholic
Church is enormous. We must look to him for the explanation
of the religious situation of the Middle Ages. He is the father of
the evolution of the form of medieval Christianity. Indeed, almost all of the leading principles of later Catholicism are found,
at least in germ, in the work and writings of Gregory the Great.[113]

Gregory's work and thought developed within a historical
cauldron of severe wars and dislocations in Italy and the Christian world at large. In the mid-sixth century the Italian peninsula
was devastated by Justinian's wars to regain Italy from the Ostrogoths. Then Byzantine Italy was governed by an imperial func-
tionary, the exarch, from his residence in Ravenna. But scarcely
a decade after the victory over the Ostrogoths, the Lombards
began conquering northern Italy. By 593, the third year of
Gregory's pontificate, the Lombard king, Agilulf, was besieging
Rome, a trial bringing apocalyptic miseries to Christendom and
graphically portrayed in Gregory's homilies on the prophet Ezekiel. Moreover, the early 590s brought drought, famine, plague
on a gigantic scale. Religious affairs were snarled not only by the

[112] Ibid., Bk. XX, cc. 7, 8.
[113] G. Roger Hudleston, "St. Gregory the Great," in *The Catholic Encyclopedia*, Vol. VI, pp. 780–787.

traditional Arianism of the Gothic tribes, but also by the schism in Gaul and northern Italy in reaction from the Council of Constantinople's condemnation in 553 of the "Three Chapters," i.e., writings of Theodore of Mopsuestia, Theodoret, and Ibas. The Western schismatics were convinced that in approving this action the papacy had been party to a renunciation of the Christology of Chalcedon and had in fact, if not in words, accommodated itself to Monophysitism. Even Queen Theodelinda, a powerful ally of Gregory, caused him great pain by going over to the cause of the schismatics. Then there was the continuing claim of the patriarch of Constantinople that he should be called "universal bishop," a claim that was not new in Gregory's time, but that he resisted with ardent animus. Thus Gregory's pontificate was tried and purified in times of severe struggles on more than one front. The multiple strains he experienced he related directly with a high pitch to an eschatological expectancy. His conviction that the Antichrist was near and that the end of all things was at hand is apparent everywhere in his writings.[114]

We get a panoramic perspective of Gregory's thought concerning the Church, her struggles, and destiny, when we read his immense commentary running to thirty-five books, which he wrote on the book of Job. It is known as his famous *Magna Moralia* or simply as *Moralia*. It offers Pope Gregory's existential account and reflections on the mission and sufferings of the Catholic Church in the hostile world of the sixth century.

Gregory and the Church

The Church is the suffering Church. Job is the type of both Christ and the Church. In this dual role Job signifies Gregory's

---

[114] Evans, *One and Holy*, op. cit., p. 140.

sense of the Church in crisis and trial. Job typifies in his own sufferings both the sufferings of Christ and the Church throughout history, and the union of Christ and His Church in their rejection by the world.[115] Job's innocence in the face of his accusing friends offers Gregory the opportunity to analyze anew the question of the relation between sin and the Church as eschatological community. He calls Job's friends heretics even as the Church must label many of her unfaithful members.[116] Of course, Gregory had to worry in his day over Arians, neo-Nestorians, Monophysites, and Donatists all claiming to be orthodox teachers of the faith. There are then Job's wife and Elihu to complete the *dramatis personae*. The former typifies the carnally minded within the Church, the latter the proud in the Church. In all these relationships there exists the struggle of the elect versus the reprobate within the Church. Gregory treats of three major themes within the Church: the intrusion of power and pride, the tug of war between the contemplative and active life, and the question of the elect.[117]

Gregory on the Antichrist

In both his letters and the *Moralia* Gregory is constantly preoccupied with the problem of power within the Church. Unfortunately, clerics and lay people, princes and paupers within the Church are found to be attached to the things of this world and attached to the love of power over men. The love of God had grown cold and the exaltation of self over others had become one of the chief signs of Satan's freely prowling presence within

[115] *Moralia* of Gregory the Great, trans. John Henry Parker (London: J.G.F. & J. Rivington, 1844), Praef. 14, 15; Bk. VII, c. 29.
[116] Ibid., Praef. 15.
[117] Ibid., Praef. 14, 19.

the Church. The massive intrusion into the Church of the lust for power is itself a sign of the imminent coming of the man who is the Antichrist for the final struggle between light and darkness before the end of all things. Gregory repeatedly depicts the antithesis between Christ with His body the Elect Church and Satan with his body the damned community. In time the Church is destined to suffer at the hands of those lusting chiefly for worldly power and glory. Such wicked Christians manipulate the Body of Christ to serve their own satanic ends. The tension between Christ and the Antichrist is heightened by the fact that the Antichrist, on his arrival, will unite within himself both the power of this world and "apparent holiness." Gregory is convinced that he is living at a time when the smoke of hell is pouring from the nostrils of the Antichrist before this false Messiah stands fully revealed before the world. When writing to the patriarch of Constantinople to protest that worthy's claim to the title of "universal bishop," Gregory condemns the connivance at the court of the secular persons who have prompted the bishop to his satanic effrontery. Then when writing to the court he denounces the pride of his brother bishop as a sign that the times of the Antichrist are near. He laments elsewhere, too, these dire defects in bishops: 1) they too easily assume airs of inflated authority inappropriate to their spiritual office; 2) they too often do not devote themselves to their proper office of preaching the Gospel.[118]

In his sermon to the citizens of Rome during the siege of the city by the Lombards, Gregory's theme was that the end of the world was at hand. The times were disturbed; the nations at war

[118] Ibid., Bks. XIV, c. 27; XV, cc. 32ff; c. 69; XVI, c. 15; XXXII, cc. 25-28; XXX, c. 63; XXXIV, c. 8; XIX, c. 23; Epistles 1-36.

with one another; earthquakes, pestilence, and famine were over-whelming countless cities. Italy was being smitten by the sword and crushed under the heel of the Gentile foe; the blood of the human race was spilt and streaming forth unto thousands of deaths. All that was needed were the signs in the sun, moon, stars and they seemed not far off as one could fear from the violent changes in the atmosphere. During the battles between the Christians and the Lombards, fiery ranks in the heavens were reported. All that was now needed was the confounding of the waves of the seas.[119]

In his *Moralia*, as he is commenting on the book of Job, Gregory compares the destruction of Jerusalem to the end of the world. When Judea rejected Christ and the apostles, the Jewish nation was ruthlessly destroyed and scattered to the four winds under the Roman Emperor Titus. There was no one to save that rebellious nation from the wrath of God. Now at the end of time, when Satan is on the point of destroying the Catholic Church through the agency of a seemingly unconquerable Antichrist, two illustrious preachers, two olive trees, two candlesticks will stand before the Lord of the universe. Elias and Enoch, their deaths delayed, will come after the fullness of the Gentiles has come into the Church. They will restore all things in Christ and defeat the Antichrist.[120]

In commenting on the following words of Job, Gregory again sees the Antichrist. "For he has stretched out his hand against God and has strengthened himself against the Almighty. He has run against Him with neck raised up, and is armed with a fat neck." These words apply to the head of all the unjust, the

[119] Ibid., pp. 3, 4.
[120] Ibid., Bk. IX.

Antichrist. For the Antichrist finds his strength in fighting God; he exalts himself in the world, glorifies himself there with evil deeds, and wins the acclaim of the world thereby. Now in time is his hour of triumph, brief but brilliant. He is lionized by hordes of wicked followers anxious to imitate him in satisfying their criminal lusts. Such becomes the intensity of the Antichrist's ill will against God that he challenges God, raises his fists against Him, blasphemes Him, thus inflating his neck and whole being with his own pride. God permits him to succeed for a time in a career of crime. But this very ephemeral success inflates his ego all the more, swells his neck with pride, and prepares him as a brand for eternal burning.

The contrast between Christ and the Antichrist could not be more pronounced than in their respective relations to revealed truth. The Incarnate Truth has chosen the poor, uncultured, and simple to preach the inestimable truths of the Gospel. The Antichrist, the condemned man, whose form the apostate angel, Satan, possesses at the end of the world, chooses the wise of this world, the double-minded, the arrogant intellectuals to preach lies about revealed truth.[121] That is why Job quickly prays for the utter destruction of the head of the unjust: "Let the memory of him perish from the earth and let not his name be renowned in the streets." Again, Gregory tells us Job is speaking of the Antichrist. The memory of Satan and his evil kingdom is everywhere celebrated where the Antichrist is victorious. For the Antichrist undertakes to diffuse the glory of Satan throughout the earth and universe; he wants to gain for the kingdom of Satan terrestrial and celestial glory. But he will not prevail. The Lord Jesus will destroy him. Job indeed predicts: "He shall drive him out of

[121] Ibid., Bks. XII, XIII.

light into darkness and shall remove him out of the world. His seed shall not subsist, nor his offspring among his people, nor any remnants in his country. They that shall come after him shall be astonished at his day, and horror shall fall upon them that went before."[122]

In all this commentary of his *Moralia* Gregory tells us that the holy man, Job, saw in a vision that the destruction of the Antichrist would come at the end of the world.[123] That is what he predicts when he says: "Let him curse it that has cursed the day, even him who shall take the great whale." For the Antichrist is the evil spirit who is in league with night itself, the son of darkness. At the end of the world he will pass himself off as light, as the day, pretending to be God himself, while deceitfully claiming for himself as the "great whale" the brightness of the Deity, exalting himself above all that is called God or that is worshipped.[124]

The Antichrist will run wild against the just with such cruelty and hatred that even the elect will be struck with extraordinary fear; the saints will be driven out into the wilderness; many of them will be martyred. Then Elias and Enoch will be recalled from their special places back to Jerusalem to enter the arena against the Antichrist and, after exposing the falsity and wickedness of this son of perdition, these prophets of God will, in imitation of their Lord Jesus Christ, suffer in their flesh the fury of the Antichrist, dying at his hands the death of martyrdom. But in the end these tabernacles of wickedness, this kingdom or synagogue of Satan, will be cast into the pool of eternal fire.[125]

---

[122] Ibid., Bk. XIV.
[123] Ibid., Bk. IV.
[124] Ibid., Bk. IV.
[125] Ibid., Bk. XIV.

Gregory continues his commentary thus: it is said that the basilisk is the king of serpents. Now the head of the reprobate is the Antichrist. The myth relates that the basilisk is hatched from a serpent brooding over a cock's egg. But the evils of the satanic asp are put into the egg so as to nourish the emerging basilisk and to form it into a member of the prince of iniquity whose mystical body of evil in time is headed by that chief basilisk the Antichrist.[126] In speaking of the Antichrist's seductive power, Gregory comments on Job's statement that "he will drag every man after himself and drive innumerable men before himself." The word *man* here signifies the worldly wise, skilled in human affairs. But how does the Antichrist drag, even before his coming, an innumerable crowd of men and, after his coming, all men? It is because the ancient enemy, once he enters into a reprobate man, kidnaps even the last man under the yoke of his damnation. He captures all men whom he discovers living a carnal existence. Before he has manifested himself, he drags innumerable carnal men; yet he does not succeed in dragging them all because each day, thanks to penance and prayer, some return to a life of justice. Nevertheless, if he still captures innumerable persons, while he is not yet present in the world as a person, it is because there go before him evil agents who sow and scatter the paralyzing seeds of his wicked kingdom. When the Antichrist accomplishes the astonishing prodigies before the eyes of all men during his day in the sun, it will not be innumerable men he will capture, it will be all men, all carnal men who seek their delights in the goods, interests, pleasures of this world. Such evil persons will submit themselves to his power without a struggle—indeed with pleasure.[127]

[126] Ibid., Bk. XV.
[127] Ibid., Bk. XV.

In his zeal to advance the well-being of the whole Church, Gregory the Great was haunted by the imminent presence of the mighty, mysterious Antichrist. He saw the Antichrist assuming both the oppressive power of this world and the aura of holiness. He saw the Antichrist binding all the particular embodiments of power hostile to the Church into a unity marching against the Church. These hostile forces were: heretical professors of Christian faith; Christian emperors at Constantinople who turned their backs on the defense of Catholic Italy, who prevented imperial servants from becoming monks, who unlawfully deposed bishops who supported the pretensions of a bishop in their capital who claimed for himself a universal episcopate over the Church. Then there were the Arian invaders of Italy, the neo-Nestorian schismatics recently rejuvenated by the profession in their faith of the Lombard queen. There were also bishops and even papal agents who would not resist the temptation to exploit the powerless and to affect the posture and manners of power. Gregory thought that the Antichrist bound all these movements into a hostile unity. Here was the presence of the "world" as reprobate within the Catholic Church, the commingling of the two cities with their two loves. And this evil presence brought upon the Church the agony of the final eschatological woes while it was also bringing the city of man to the edge of the last abyss.[128]

Despite his agonizing eschatological expectations about the imminent presence of the Antichrist, the end of the world, the arrival of the final judgment, Gregory the Great was a man of profound faith and zealous action. Though the end of the world was near, the future of the Church and its saving mission to all

---

[128] Evans, *One and Holy*, op. cit., p. 152.

men and nations must nonetheless be planned, administered, and advanced. For that purpose Gregory dispatched a group of monks under the leadership of one, Augustine, for the purpose of converting the Angles of England into children of God. Apocalyptic fears could never paralyze the Church's efforts to convert and sanctify the world.[129]

---

[129] Ibid., p. 153.

Chapter 6

The Antichrist in Medieval Thought

A profusion of medieval art and literature demonstrates how popular were such religious themes as the advent and reign of the Antichrist, the mission of Enoch and Elias, the fifteen signs of doom
and the Day of Doom itself among the preachers and faithful of
that period. Such subjects appealed powerfully to the imagination
of consummate artists, writers, preachers, and to their audiences.
Many masterpieces have survived to bear witness to the vivid life
these truths had in the souls of great painters, poets, preachers,
and commentators on Holy Scripture. The art and literature of
eschatology has collected some of the greatest masterpieces of all
time. One need only stand transfixed before Michelangelo's final
judgment in the Sistine Chapel or travel in a trance with Dante
in his *Divine Comedy*.

Medieval sermon collections and homiletic literature reveal
the hypnotic attraction such topics as the Antichrist and the Day
of Doom had for preacher and people. Of course, one principal
aim was to reprove vice by awakening salutary awe and fear in the
face of the terrors to come from the Antichrist and at Doomsday.
Another explanation for the high interest in these terrifying
themes was the periodical announcement of the approaching
end of the world. The end of time, sometimes to the exact date,

was predicted then even as it is today. But the twelfth century had far more prophets of Doomsday than has the twentieth. Of course, the fact that the Middle Ages were an era of faith and unity in faith can explain the greater credence given such predictions. In today's age of divided Christianity and widespread skepticism and atheism, although interest in these religious themes is still high, curiosity over the sensational rather than credence in the revelational aspects of these matters drives the masses to read the books and see the movies that treat of these subjects. But when medieval preachers, artists, and savants reverted time and again to serious treatment of the subject of the Antichrist, they made a deep spiritual impression on the minds and hearts of the populace.

As early as the beginning of the eighth century, we find several discussions of the Antichrist and the last judgment in the writings of the Venerable Bede. Many scholars hold that Bede copied such subjects literally from Latin sources and introduced them to the English. Certainly Bede, after St. Jerome, is regarded as the originator of one of the lists of fifteen signs of doom that will precede the end of the world. Moreover, even a cursory look at the literature of eschatology of the Middle Ages reveals that these works on the Antichrist and Doomsday are based on the treatises of the early Fathers of the Church.[130]

In the reign of St. Louis IX (1235–1270), Agobard in his *De Judaicis superstitionibus* (*Concerning Jewish Superstitions*) expressed the wish that all treatises on the Antichrist might be gathered

[130] Brother Linus Urban Lucken, "Antichrist and the Prophets of Antichrist in the Chester Cycle," Ph.D. diss., Catholic University of America, 1940. The whole book has been most helpful on the literature written on the Antichrist during the Middle Ages. Its research and bibliography have been most helpful to my work.

112

together, apparently with the hope that the confusion resulting from so many conflicting versions might in this way be settled. Scarcely a century went by without some fervent resurgence of interest in the person and history of the Antichrist. Mathias von Janow testified that the Antichrist had become such a thoroughly discussed figure that, if he were to appear then, in the fourteenth century, even the smallest child would be able to recognize him. And Bousset concludes his article in the *Encyclopedia Britannica* with the statement: "To write the history of the idea of the Antichrist in the later Middle Ages would be almost to write that of the Middle Ages."[131]

The perennial interest in the Antichrist and the repeated warnings of his near approach were often connected with party struggles, religious and political. Each party regularly accused its rivals of being forerunners of the Antichrist. The practice was especially common in the religious controversies of the Reformation period, but it is found much earlier within the Catholic Church from a political viewpoint in the conflict between the Guelphs and the Ghibellines, and in the quarrel centered about the Spiritual Franciscans. This particular phase of the Antichrist prediction and its political application is a cause of much confusion, but it will not concern us here. For the purposes of convenience the interpretations of the Antichrist may be classified in three groups: the political adaptations, the Jewish conception of the Antichrist as a monster, and the purely religious Christian account. We are not concerned with the first two in this work. We are concerned here simply with the religious portrayal of the subject. It may be said,

---

[131] Wilhelm Bousset in his article on the Antichrist in the *Encyclopedia Britannica*, 14th ed., Vol. 2,. p. 60ff.

however, that the interpretations concerning the person and career of the Antichrist from the beginnings, through the Middle Ages to the Reformation and to modern times, are all so many witnesses to the popularity of this mystery of salvation history.[132] The frequent recurrence of the theme of the Antichrist and its repeated use for polemical purposes testify also to its utility and fertility.

From time to time, men of high learning and sanctity, convinced of the imminence of the Day of Doom, allowed themselves to be deceived into believing that the Antichrist had already come. As early as 380, St. Martin of Tours asserted his belief that the Antichrist was then living, but as yet still a boy. In the eleventh century, Bishop Ramieri of Florence was definitely certain of the Antichrist's existence. St. Norbert, the founder of the Order of the Premonstratensians, assured St. Bernard that the Antichrist was then living as his contemporary. In the thirteenth century, the so-called Joachimites, whose whole life and activity were largely dominated by the conviction that the end of time was at hand, pointed out the Antichrist in living persons and set definite dates for the end of the world. Naturally, the dates had frequently to be postponed, but new ones were readily fixed, as conditions seemed to justify. Berthold of Regensburg, the famous German preacher, was at one time influenced by Joachimite ideas, as was also Arnold of Villanova. The celebrated preacher of the fifteenth century, St. Vincent Ferrer, asserted definitely that the great enemy of Christianity had been born in the year 1403. To these examples many references from vernacular literature to a contemporary living Antichrist could be added.[133]

[132] Lucken, op. cit., p. 10.
[133] Ibid., p. 9.

A Profile of the Antichrist

So many characteristics have been attributed to the Antichrist in the many treatises devoted to him that an exhaustive anatomy is impossible in the incomplete mosaic on his figure and his features presented here. In the words of the Catholic exegete Atzberger, the subject of the Antichrist is one of the most comprehensive chapters in the history of eschatology, as it is also one of the most difficult, elusive, and indefinite. "From the day when the word (Antichrist) was first coined, it has assumed every variety of shape, has fitted with equal precision the most contrarious things and persons." From the few concise scriptural references to him ecclesiastical and secular writers have developed a lengthy and elaborate "Antichristology."[134]

As we mentioned earlier, we restrict ourselves in this primer on the Antichrist to a consideration of the character of the Antichrist from a religious standpoint. The medieval literary portraits of the Antichrist from this standpoint are many and varied, but there is one work in particular that serves admirably our purpose of giving a representative summary of the common medieval consciousness of the character of the Antichrist. That work is the *Epistola Adsonis ad Gerbergam Reginam de Ortu et Tempore Antichristi—Letter of Adso to Queen Gerberga on the Origin and Time of the Antichrist.*[135] This letter was written by Adso, a monk and later abbot of Moutieren-Der, sometime about the middle of the tenth century. The work is an important document on the Antichrist, offering as it does a convenient summary of earlier patristic

[134] Ibid., p. 10.
[135] Ibid., p. 11. The text is printed in Migne, P.L., 101. Col. 1291ff. Also in Karl Young, *Drama of the Medieval Church*, II (Oxford: Clarendon Press, 1933), pp. 496–500.

teachings, while exercising a considerable influence on subsequent developments of the doctrine of the Antichrist.

Adso addresses himself at once to the meaning of the name *Antichrist*. The name signifies that the Antichrist will be opposed to Christ in every respect: *Quia Christo in cunctis contrarius erit, id est Christo contraria faciet.* "Because he will be contrary to Christ, he will perform deeds opposed to Christ." Adso then appears to contradict himself, for he goes on to point out many characteristics of the Antichrist and incidents in his career that parallel the figure and history of Christ. Of course, the opposition will be primarily and substantially interior, a metaphysical, moral opposition on the spiritual and supernatural level of being and living. As far as exterior appearances and actions are concerned, there will be parallels to offset the contraries. The explanation is simple. The Antichrist will not only oppose Christ, but he will also openly ape Christ in order to deceive the masses.[136]

Thus, let us present a summary of the various meanings that have been suggested for the name of the Antichrist. Malvenda gives a brief explanation of the different interpretations of the name, demonstrating that the Greek prefix anti (αντι) may signify not only opposition (*contrarietatem*), but also equivalence (*aequipollentiam*), or substitution (*subrogationem*), or even equal power (*aequalem potentiam*).[137] Douglas Hyde makes an interesting observation in his article on a medieval Irish account of the Antichrist:

As for Antichrist himself, the general opinion seems to be that his name is derived from *anti* (αντι) "against," meaning an opposer of Christ, but it may also be taken to mean "one

[136] Ibid., pp. 11, 12.
[137] Thomas Malvenda, *De Antichristo Libri Undecim*. Roma, 1604, quoted by Lucken, op. cit., p. 12.

resembling Christ in appearance and power," as *antitheos* (αντίθεος) means "one who resembles God" in Homer, and later *antistrategos* (αντιστρατηγος) "a propraetor," *antebasileus* (αντιβασιλεύς) "one who is king during an interregnum." And this meaning seems to be in the mind of the author of this story when he says that Antichrist will raise people from the dead "in imitation of Christ."[138]

In a reference to the spelling in the title of the Chester plays *The Prophets of Antichrist* and *The Coming of Antichrist*, W.W. Greg has still another suggestion to make as to the probable meaning of the word: "I believe all manuscripts (of the Chester cycle) are consistent in the spelling *Antechrist*. No doubt the scribes did not distinguish very clearly between *anti* and *ante*, but there may also have been some confusion, between Antichrist as the opponent of Christ and the same as precursor of the second coming of Christ."[139]

The interpretation given by Adso was common enough. Yet many characterizations of the Antichrist seem based on "one resembling Christ in appearance and power." In harmony with his interpretation Adso lists a few traits of the Antichrist that are contrary to the character of Christ. Christ is humble; the Antichrist will be proud. Christ came to raise the lowly and redeem sinners; the Antichrist will reject the humble and glorify sinners and teach the vices that are contrary to Christian virtues. He will contemn evangelical law, seek his own glory, and will call himself the omnipotent God.

[138] Douglas Hyde, "Medieval Account of Antichrist," in Gertrude Schoepperle Loomis, *Medieval Studies in Memory of Gertrude S. Loomis* (New York: Columbia University Press, 1927), p. 393.

[139] W.W. Greg, *The Play of Antichrist* (Oxford: Clarendon Press, 1935), p. xxiii, note 2.

Then Adso gives details that demonstrate parallelism rather than antithesis. The Antichrist will be born of Jewish parents, of the tribe of Dan, but his mother will not be a virgin, as many believe. As the Holy Ghost came into the heart of Mary, so will the devil enter into the mother of the Antichrist, and his diabolical power will always support the Antichrist. Babylon will be his birthplace, but he will be reared and instructed in Bethsaida and Corozaim. After his education under malignant spirits, he will go to Jerusalem and set up his seat of power in the Temple that he will have restored. He will submit to the rite of circumcision, proclaiming he is the son of the omnipotent God. His first converts will be kings and princes. His influence will be extended from sea to sea, largely through force and persuasive eloquence. He will perform many acts of power and great miracles, even raising the dead to life. There will be three principal means that he will employ to seduce men: miracles, gifts, terror. Those who believe and follow him will be marked on the forehead with a sign. For three and one-half years he will reign and, at the end of that period, he will destroy Enoch and Elias, who will have previously opposed and unmasked him by preaching the true faith. These, in brief outline, are the contents of Adso's letter on the Antichrist.

Something more needs to be said about the element of "parallelism." Throughout the historical development of the prophecy on the Antichrist, even before Adso, the innovations that appear from time to time are based to a greater or lesser extent on the scriptural passages referred to earlier in this work. But many phrases in the development of the portrait of the Antichrist can be explained by "parallelism," whereby events and traits in the life and character of Christ suggest similar events and traits in the life and character of the Antichrist. Many of the new features developed can be satisfactorily accounted for in this way.

Following the common medieval idea of the Antichrist as expressed in Adso's letter, we can come to these conclusions. The Antichrist will be a false Messiah whose success in deceiving his victims will depend largely on his possession of traits and powers that ape and recall those of Christ. We frequently find in the writings of the Fathers this expression: *sicut in Christo ... ita in Antichristo.* "As in Christ ... so also in the Antichrist."[140] Even as early as Hippolytus, in the third century, we find an emphasis placed on the parallelism between the character of Christ and the hypothetical character of the Antichrist. This early writer of the Greek Church stresses, as the chief trait of the Antichrist, the hypocrisy by which he affects humility and meekness in order the better to deceive the unwary. In his treatise *On Christ and the Antichrist*, Hippolytus sets forth the following parallels:

> For the deceiver sets to liken himself in all things to the Son of God. Christ is a lion, so Antichrist is also a lion; Christ is a king, so Antichrist is also a king.... The Saviour came into the world in the circumcision, and he will come in the same manner. The Lord sent apostles among all the nations, and he in like manner will send false apostles. The Saviour gathered the sheep that were scattered abroad, and he in like manner will bring together a people that is scattered abroad. The Lord gave a seal to those who believed in him, and he will give one in like manner. The Saviour appeared in the form of man, and he too will come in the form of man. The Saviour raised up and showed his holy flesh like a temple, and he will raise a temple of stone in Jerusalem.[141]

[140] Lucken, op. cit., p. 15.
[141] St. Hippolytus in *Ante-Nicene Fathers*, Vol. 5, eds. A. Roberts and J. Donaldson (New York: Scribner's Sons, 1903), p. 206; cf. also p. 247.

The same point was made by Origen, the famous contemporary of Hippolytus:

> I hold that there exists not only the word Christ, but also the word, the Antichrist; there exists Christ the truth and the Antichrist the counterfeit truth; there is the wisdom that is Christ and the false wisdom that is the Antichrist.... We discover all the virtues personified in Christ and all the counterfeit virtues incarnated in the Antichrist.[142]

Parallelism, then, seems to have been a popular method for determining the characteristics of the Antichrist during the Middle Ages. Eventually, the Antichrist was pictured in almost every respect as the *simia Christi*. One explanation for the tendency of portraying the Antichrist under this aspect was the common teaching in the Church that Christ would appear at His Second Coming in the same human form in which He ascended into heaven. And in order that he might deceive even the elect, it would be only too natural for the Antichrist, so the medieval writers thought, to assume as nearly as possible the traits that would induce the Jews to recognize in him the Son of God come to judgment. Of course, there are other reasons for the popular representation of the Antichrist as the "simia," or ape, of Christ.

One common medieval concept of the devil pictured him as "aping," or imitating, God in his many activities, and the representation of the Antichrist as the ape of Christ was, no doubt, merely the transfer of this idea. For the Antichrist was often conceived of

---

[142] Lucken, op. cit., p. 16. He gives the Latin, which is as follows: *Puto, quia non solum est sermo Christus, est et sermo Antichristus; veritas Christus, et simulata veritas Antichristus; sapientia Christus, et simulata sapientia Antichrustus. . . . Invenimus omnes virtutes esse Christum, et omnes simulatas virtutes Antichristum.*

as the incarnation of the devil himself. Even if this satanic identity were denied, as it was by some alert medieval writers who pointed out the metaphysical impossibility of a mere creature possessing two different natures simultaneously, nevertheless all agreed that the mission of the Antichrist was diabolical. Thus, he is almost everywhere represented as being attended and inspired by an evil spirit. It was easy, therefore, for the popular mind to conceive the Antichrist as the *simia Christi*, just as his master Satan was seen as the *simia Dei*.[143] Here we see how fruitful the study of parallelism in the notion of the Antichrist has been.

The Antichrist in Medieval Drama

Though a popular subject in the theological and homiletic writings of the Middle Ages, the subject of the Antichrist was even more popular in medieval plays. The earliest, by far, of the dramatic representations of the Antichrist prophecy is the Latin play *Antichristus* from the monastery of Tegernsee in Upper Bavaria. It is dated about 1160 and is one of the earliest dramas to be written in Germany.

The play opens with the Roman emperor decreeing that all kings of the earth must again pay tribute to the Roman Empire. He dispatches messengers to demand and supervise compliance. The king of the Franks yields only when defeated in battle. The kings of Greece and Jerusalem yield at once. Now the enraged king of Babylon mounts a campaign to destroy Christianity. He attacks Jerusalem, but the city is saved by the timely arrival of the emperor and his troops. The emperor enters the empty Temple of Jerusalem after his victory and places his crown and imperial insignia before the altar, declaring that Christ alone is the true

---

[143] Ibid., p. 17.

imperial king and ruler. Then the emperor returns home, leaving Ecclesia, who had accompanied him to Jerusalem, to remain in the temple in the company of the pope.

At this moment the Antichrist makes his entrance. While Ecclesia, Gentilitas, and Synagoga are praying their doctrinal creeds, hypocrites enter sanctimoniously and win over the laymen and king of Jerusalem. Then the Antichrist, master of the hypocrites, himself appears accompanied by Hypocrisy and Heresy whom he charges with the responsibility of corrupting laity and clergy. The Antichrist then conquers the king of Jerusalem, crowns himself and ascends the throne of the temple. Meanwhile the king of Jerusalem flees to the king of the Teutons, and Ecclesia, after enduring much harassment and suffering, is driven from the temple. She returns with the pope to the seat she shared with him and the emperor at home.

The Antichrist then moves to subjugate all kings of the earth, sending messengers to demand submission. The kings of Greece and France are easily conquered by threats and bribes. He receives their homage and puts his mark on their foreheads. But the sturdy king of the Teutons offers resistance; he rejects bribes, gifts, threats. Indeed, he wins battles over the armies of the Antichrist. Finally, in desperation, the Antichrist is driven to perform miracles in order to gain the Teuton king. In the presence of the king the Antichrist heals a lame man and a leper. But the Teuton king remains uncertain about the Antichrist's honesty and authority. Finally, the Antichrist raises a dead soldier to life and the king of the Teutons bends his knee and receives the brand of the Antichrist on his forehead. The Teuton king now leads the Antichrist's armies against Gentilitas and the king of Babylon; he conquers them. Then, through the craft of the hypocrites, Synagoga submits to the Antichrist who now comes forward as the absolute ruler of the whole world.

But, at this point in history, the prophets Enoch and Elias return to the stage of the earth. They preach the truths of Christianity, convert Synagoga, denounce and unmask the usurper. The enraged Antichrist promptly kills the prophets and Synagoga. Then while he is in the act of declaring his divine omnipotence, thunder crashes down over his head; he collapses and all his followers flee in panic. The play closes with Ecclesia, arms wide open summoning the fleeing to repentance and a return to the Christian Faith, while a chorus is singing the praises of God.[144]

In Italy in the fourteenth century Alessandro D'Ancona, in his *Organi del Teatro Italiano*, published a drama on the Antichrist and the Last Judgment: *Lauda Drammatica Dell'Antichristo O Del Giudzio Finale*, "Dramatic Canticle of the Antichrist and of the Last Judgment." The same principal events generally recorded in the life of the Antichrist are represented with a few slight changes. Instead of Michael, the Archangel Gabriel kills the Antichrist. This Italian play concludes with the stage directions for carting away the corpse of the Antichrist: *Satana cum aliis demonis conducit eum in infernum.* "Satan with other devils drags him into hell."[145] A French dramatic poem, *Le Regne de l'Antechrist*, "The Reign of the Antichrist," which dates from 1240, also contains the usual story. Moreover, in the literature of the Middle Ages there are references to many Antichrist plays that have not survived in manuscript to our day.[146] In the fifth chapter of his book *De Investigatione Antichristi*, "Concerning the Study of the Antichrist," Gerhoh bemoans the practice

[144] Ibid., pp. 28–30.
[145] Ibid., p. 31.
[146] Ibid., p. 32.

of presenting theatrical spectacles in the churches. His greatest
wrath is directed against the many plays portraying the wicked
life and deeds of the Antichrist.[147] In the chronicle of Giuliano
da Cividale are found references to two elaborate plays on the
role of the Antichrist, one performed in 1298, the other in
1304, both in the town of Cividale.[148] In Zurich, about 1353, a
play on the Antichrist enjoyed long popularity.[149] *The Pricke of
Conscience* is a fifteenth-century account of the Antichrist, usually ascribed to Richard Rolle of Hampole. This account of the
Antichrist is preceded by a list of ten signs of the coming final
judgment and followed by the more generally known fifteen
signs attributed to St. Jerome. Some details of the usual story
are changed. The Antichrist is begotten of a sinful man and a
woman in whom the devil has entered; the good angel assigned
to him at his birth flees as witches, necromancers, and other
disreputable characters take charge of his education. He succeeds through false preaching, miracles, gifts, terror, and the
aid of an evil spirit who descends from the air upon his followers. He feigns resurrection from the dead, causes rain to fall,
stone images to speak, and fire to come down from heaven.
The Jews welcome and follow him. He is opposed by the preaching of Enoch and Elias, but destroys them after 1260 days. They
rise again and ascend to heaven after three and one-half days.
But the Antichrist then reigns for three and one-half years. His
first fifteen days of absolute power are a reign of terror. At age
thirty-two and one-half the Antichrist is slain on Mt. Olivet by
the sword of the Archangel Michael. The jubilation of his

147 Ibid., p. 20.
148 Ibid., p. 21.
149 Ibid., p. 22.

followers is cut short suddenly and a general slaughter ensues. Forty-five days are allowed by God for repentance before the end of the world and the final judgment.[150]

Finally, there is the famous drama called *The Coming of Antichrist*. It is dated about 1328 as the next to the last play of the Chester Cycle, which consists of some 23 or 25 religious dramas.[151] In his *The Chester Plays*, Wright observes that "the play very fully represents the common medieval legend on the subject" (of the Antichrist).[152] But there are several variations on details that do not really change substantial or Catholic doctrines, as they are represented in the Adso letter. The principal ones are: 1) the Antichrist's attribution to himself of definite prophecies; 2) his denial of Christ's divinity; 3) the fact that all women will love him; 4) the role of the four kings, converted by Enoch and Elias, whom the Antichrist slays together with the prophets; 5) the miracle of turning trees upside down and having their fruit grow from their roots; 6) the Antichrist's sending of the Holy Spirit; 7) his distribution of several countries as gifts; 8) his extended debate with Enoch and Elias; 9) the role of the Antichrist's doctor who advises the Antichrist to curse the prophets; 10) Elias blessing bread and discounting the Antichrist's miracles; 11) the role of the demons carrying off the corpse of the Antichrist, condemned to hang by his heels in hell for all eternity; 12) the resurrection of Enoch and Elias; 13) the Archangel Michael leading the prophets into heaven.[153]

[150] Ibid., pp. 36, 37.
[151] Ibid., pp. 47ff.
[152] Thomas Wright, *The Chester Plays*, I (London: Printed for the Shakespeare Society, 1843), p. 224.
[153] Lucken, op. cit., p. 68.

The Antichrist

The Fifteen Signs of Doom

Several passages of the New Testament enumerate in a general way the signs of the approaching Doomsday. In the Gospel of St. Matthew, chapter 24, Christ warns his disciples against false prophets and enumerates certain signs such as pestilence, famines, and earthquakes, as well as "wars and rumors of wars." In the Gospel of St. Mark, chapter 13, several definite signs are indicated, particularly in the passage, "But in those days, after that tribulation, the sun shall be darkened, the moon shall not give her light. And the stars of the heaven shall be falling down, and the powers that are in heaven shall be moved." The Apocalypse, chapter 16, speaks of the plagues ensuing from the seven vials. The Epistles of St. Paul to the Thessalonians announce the "man of sin."[154]

Taking these scriptural passages as points of departure, theologians usually enumerate the following more generally accepted events as signs of the Day of the Lord:

1. The preaching of the Gospel throughout the world
2. The conversion of the Jews
3. The return of Enoch and Elias
4. A general falling away from Christian faith
5. The reign of the Antichrist
6. Persecution of the just and the disturbances of nature
7. The sign of the Son of Man appearing in the heavens
8. Universal conflagration
9. The advent of Christ with great power and majesty[155]

Once we compare these general signs numerically listed as such nowhere in the Bible with the more explicit and fully

[154] Ibid., p. 111.
[155] Ibid., p. 112.

developed medieval versions of the fifteen signs of Doomsday, it is easy to see how the human imagination, taking off from the New Testament passages, has created many legendary lists that gripped and pleased the people of the Middle Ages. It is popularly thought that the apocryphal fourth book of Esdras was the stimulant for the detailed accounts of the approach of Doomsday. The book was widely known in the first centuries of the Christian era, and was frequently quoted by the Fathers of the Church. Its date could be set anywhere from 30 BC. to AD 218. It helped frame the popular belief in the Middle Ages concerning the last things. The first account that fixes the number of the signs of doom at fifteen and assigns them to fifteen successive days appears in the writings of the Venerable Bede. Here is the first version of the fifteen signs as made known in England by Bede, a version that influenced all Europe — indeed all Christendom:

1. The sea will rise forty cubits and will be as a wall.
2. It will recede again, so as scarcely to be seen.
3. It will be normal as at the beginning.
4. Marine animals will cry out.
5. Waters will burn.
6. All plants will be covered with a bloody dew.
7. All buildings will be destroyed.
8. Stones will strike each other and divide into three parts.
9. Earthquake.
10. Hills and valleys will be leveled.
11. Men will come forth from caverns and run about as if mad.
12. Stars will fall.
13. The dead will rise.

14. All living will die so that they may arise with the dead.
15. The earth will burn.[156]

These signs are much the same as those that appear in two other important versions, one ascribed to Peter Comestor, the other to St. Thomas Aquinas. All three refer to St. Jerome as their source, but there is no treatment of the signs of doom anywhere in the extant works of St. Jerome. Perhaps a lost work of his contains this list.

St. Thomas touches the theme of the Antichrist only lightly and indirectly, when he is explaining that the prophets Enoch and Elias were not taken up into the heaven of the glorified before they died, but were taken to some hidden terrestrial paradise to await their final mission on earth—their confrontation with the Antichrist. St. Thomas writes: "Elias was taken up into the atmospheric heaven, but not into the empyrean heaven, which is the abode of the saints: and likewise Enoch was translated into the earthly paradise, where he is believed to live with Elias until the coming of the Antichrist."[157]

But St. Thomas addressed himself very directly to the signs of Doomsday. He wrote in his *Summa Theologica* as follows:

Further Jerome mentions fifteen signs preceding the judgment. He says that on the *first* day all the seas will rise fifteen cubits above the mountains; in the *second* day all the waters will be plunged into the depths, so that scarcely will they be visible; on the *third* day they will be restored

[156] Ibid., p. 119.
[157] St. Thomas Aquinas, *Summa Theologica* III, q. 49, art. V, Reply obj. 2, English translation by the Fathers of the English Dominican Province, Vol. 16, 2nd ed. (London: Burns Oates and Washbourne, 1926), p. 333.

to their previous condition; on the *fourth* day all the great
fishes and other things that move in the waters will gather
together and, raising their heads above the sea, roar at
one another contentiously; on the *fifth* day, all the birds
of the air will gather together in the fields, wailing to one
another, with neither bite nor sup; on the *sixth* day rivers
of fire will arise towards the firmament rushing together
from the west to the east; on the *seventh* day all the stars,
both planets and fixed stars, will throw out fiery tails like
comets; on the *eighth* day there will be a great earthquake,
and all animals will be laid low; on the *ninth* day all the
plants will be bedewed as it were with blood; on the *tenth*
day all stones, little and great, will be divided into four parts
dashing against one another; on the *eleventh* day all hills
and mountains and buildings will be reduced to dust; on
the *twelfth* day all animals will come from the forest and
mountains to the fields, roaring and tasting of nothing;
on the *thirteenth* day all graves from east to west will open
to allow the bodies to rise again; on the *fourteenth* day all
men will leave their abode, neither understanding nor
speaking, but rushing hither and thither like madmen; on
the *fifteenth* day all will die and will rise again with those
who died long before.[158]

After listing the fifteen signs of doom attributed to St. Jerome,
St. Thomas gives his own assessment, in which he tends to mini-
mize them:

When Christ shall come to judge he will appear in the form
of glory, on account of the authority becoming a judge. Now

[158] Ibid., Vol. 20, pp. 88-89.

it pertains to the dignity of judicial power to have certain signs that induce people to reverence and subjection; and consequently many signs will precede the advent of Christ when he shall come to judgment, in order that the hearts of men be brought to subjection to the coming judge, and be prepared for judgment, being forewarned by these signs. But it is not easy to know what these signs may be: for the signs which we read in the Gospels, as Augustine says, writing to Hesychius about the end of the world, refer not only to Christ's coming to judgment, but also to the time of the sack of Jerusalem, and to the coming of Christ in ceaselessly visiting his Church. So that, perhaps, if we consider them carefully, we shall find that none of them refers to the coming advent, as he remarks: because these signs that are mentioned in the Gospels, such as wars, fears, and so forth, have been from the beginning of the human race: unless perhaps we say that at that time they will be more prevalent: although it is uncertain in what degree this increase will foretell the imminence of the advent. The signs mentioned by Jerome are not asserted by him; he merely says that he found them written in the annals of the Hebrews: and, indeed, they contain very little likelihood.[159]

Medieval and Modern Millenarianism

In the very early days of the Church, indeed at the time of St. John the Evangelist, the heresy of millenarianism was taught by Cerinthus. He organized a sect that taught that after Christ's Second Coming an earthly paradise would be established and endure for a thousand years. This misconception was derived

[159] Ibid., Vol. 20, pp. 88–89.

from a too literal interpretation of the Apocalypse where John wrote: "And he laid hold on the dragon, the ancient serpent, who is the devil and Satan, and bound him for a thousand years. And he cast him into the Abyss and closed and sealed it over him, that he should deceive the nations no more, until the thousand years should be finished. And after that he must be let loose for a little while." Cerinthus added other alien elements to his millenarianism. He taught that Christ was the son of Mary and Joseph, and that the Holy Ghost descended upon him only at His baptism. It is said that St. John was enjoying the public baths in the company of his faithful friends one day, when Cerinthus entered with his fellow heretics. Immediately the beloved disciple and his friends started to leave, exhorting all present to do the same, lest the public structure collapse while harboring such a heretic and enemy of truth.[160]

We have already seen how St. Augustine dismissed the millenarian legend with contempt. In his time the paradise of one thousand years after the Second Coming of Christ was interpreted in a grossly sensual fashion. Old heresies die hard and even have a life of resurrection. In 1210, the disciples of the Abbot Joachim of Fiore claimed to be the Church of the Holy Spirit, destined to succeed the outworn, corrupt, overly rich old dispensation. The notion that the Church had failed, and the divine revelation had now been entrusted to a faithful, spiritual remnant was fostered by millenarian speculations. Joachim's comments and preachings on the Apocalypse stirred up a hornet's nest. He had a reputation for holiness and learning, and he infected his age with an eschatological frenzy. Even Pope Gregory

---

[160] C.M. Eberhardt and C. Newman, *A Summary of Catholic History* (St. Louis: B. Herder Book Company, 1961), p. 69.

IX began one of his bulls with these words, "Since the evening of the world is now declining." Clearly Joachim left the world in suspense; the abbot died in 1201, after announcing the coming of the Antichrist for the year 1260.[161]

Joachim's followers held that the Incarnation and Passion of Christ were not the high point of the divine mercy to man. The reign of Christ was but a preparation for a more perfect dispensation, the reign of the Holy Ghost. This was now about to begin. There would no longer be a Church; the pope would joyfully resign his power to a new order of contemplatives; the active life would cease and all Christendom would become a vast monastery of contemplatives, vowed to absolute poverty. Moreover, the law of spiritual effort would cease and, the Holy Spirit being poured out in a new and perfect effusion of gifts and graces, the law of spiritual joy would reign unhindered. Pope, cardinals, hierarchy, systematic theology, canon law—these not only would disappear but their very presence and survival were hindrances that delayed the coming of the new age. The first duty of the faithful soul, then, was to abandon them, to abandon the reign of Christ, to leave the bark of Peter for the bark of John, and to prepare the way for the reign of the Holy Spirit. With these false doctrines went a medley of speculation, preached and rhymed about everywhere. The end of the world was imminent; the Antichrist waited in the wings of the stage of history. The type of man he would be and where he would be found were the subject of endless sermons and treatises.[162]

---

[161] Ronald Knox, *Enthusiasm* (New York: Oxford University Press, 1950), p. 110.
[162] Philip Hughes, *A History of the Church*, Vol. 3 (New York: Sheed and Ward, 1947), pp. 35, 36.

Ronald Knox interprets the revolt against the Church by the Franciscan "Spirituals" in a very profound manner. He writes:

> The protest, in any case, was really a protest against the whole notion of an institutional, that is "visible Church." That there could be tares in the wheat, that worthless fish as well as eatable ones could be found in the net, was a doctrine incomprehensible to Wycliffe and Huss, for all their insistence on the Gospel. For the enthusiasts there is only one Church, a Church "invisible." Its members consist of the names which are written in the book of life, whatever their sectarian affiliations. "The true Church," in Wycliffe's opinion, was the whole community of those persons, whether clergymen or laymen, who were ultimately to be saved, and these persons were predestined. The pope himself, if not predestined, was not a member of the Church.... Their real belief, like that of all enthusiasts, was that it did not matter who founded your particular religious group, or when. What mattered was that you should follow Christ; if you did that, you were *ipso facto* inside the only Church that counted.[163]

In the fifteenth century, Cardinal Nicholas of Cusa, the first complete example of the Renaissance man, an original, brilliant thinker, sometimes called the last great "original" of the Middle Ages, gave his generation and his readers some three centuries' grace, predicting that the world would not outlast 1734.[164] The Anabaptists of Holland also revived the legend of chiliasm. They held that the existing world order was about to end and an earthly millennium was to succeed during which the saints

---

[163] Knox, op. cit., pp. 112, 113.
[164] Ibid., p. 137.

would reign. Their great missionary Melchior Hoffmann announced the Second Coming for the year 1553, and suspended baptisms for two years in order to prepare for it. Hoffman died in prison before his fixed date arrived. But the apocalyptic spirit survived him; the Munsterite Anabaptists predicted a terrible vengeance on the godless before the Easter of 1534 and that the tenth man should not remain alive in Munster itself, which, they said, was the city of the Lord, the new Jerusalem.[165] All chiliastic movements outlive the nonfulfillment of their prophecies. The prophets of the millennium, when proven wrong, always discover errors in their calculations and arrange new schedules for coming apocalyptic events.

In 1652 James Milner, a Quaker, predicted that the world would come to an end the following December.[166] The whole Camisard revolt in France is set against a strong apocalyptic background. Jurieu dated the downfall of the Catholic Church for 1690 in France; the two witnesses, according to him, were already awaiting their resurrection at the end of three and one-half years.[167] In 1730, as a reaction to the papal bull *Unigenitus*, the Abbe Etimare, a Jansenist, announced that the Church had unchurched herself, that salvation was to be found among the faithful remnant of Catholics who were appealing against the bull. This led him to take steps that betrayed his enthusiasm into fantasy. He began commenting on the Apocalypse. He concluded that the Gentiles had apostasized, that the conversion of the Jews was at hand, that Elias would appear at any moment. The war of the Beast had begun in 1730 and would end in 1733.[168] In 1761 the Methodist

---

[165] Ibid., p. 137.
[166] Ibid., p. 150.
[167] Ibid., p. 358.
[168] Ibid., pp. 378, 379.

enthusiast George Bell confidently announced to his parishioners the end of the world for 1763. John Wesley may have been remotely to blame for Bell's eccentric religious conduct.[169] For all enthusiastic movements, in their efforts to detach the people from worldliness, fall into the language and mentality of chiliasm. In his own early days as an evangelist John Wesley had spoken in the manner of the Fraticelli and the French prophets as if the coming of Christ was at hand. In England in 1830, Edward Irving claimed the last days were upon humanity. He called the newly founded University of London the Synagogue of Satan. Glossolalia broke out in Irving's congregation and before long, to the scandal of many but to his own delight, his sermons were interrupted by prophets predicting all sorts of fantastic, final events.[170] In 1758 in North America, Shaker Ann Lee announced that she was a new female Messiah. In 1786 another Shaker, Jemima Wilkinson, claimed to be the new, female Messiah. Neither woman knew the other though both resided in New York. They differed in their blueprints for the future. Jemima believed, up till 1820, and some of her followers believed even after her death in that year, that she was immortal. But Ann Lee taught that the millennium had begun in 1770, and her promise was that there would be a great increase and permanent establishment of the Church on American soil.[171] Then there were the pietistic groups, the "perfectionists" as they are sometimes called. They were convinced that they were living the perfect life here and now. Ebel, for instance, believed he was preparing his converts for the life of the resurrection, in that they neither married nor were given in marriage, for they were

[169] Ibid., pp. 545, 546.
[170] Ibid., p. 552.
[171] Ibid., p. 559.

already like the angels in heaven. Prince went further; he believed that he and his little group had already entered the resurrected life; redeemed in the flesh as well as in the spirit, they were enjoying the millennium here and now.[172]

Has the millennium legend ceased to attract members of the Catholic Church? Unfortunately, by no means. In 1977 two Catholic priests, Fathers John W. Tombler and Hubert J. Funk, wrote a book called *The Raptured*. The subtitle is "A Catholic View of the Latter Days and the Second Coming." The blurb on the front cover reads: "A first in the field of Catholic publishing. This future view of a one-world religion with headquarters in Rome and headed by an Antipope written by two Catholic priests will cause some rumblings in the Vatican."

Chapter 8, entitled "The Millennial Kingdom," puts complete trust in the legend that Christ and the saints will reign on the earth, after the death of the Antichrist, for one thousand years. Jerusalem is to become the world capital; the Jews will accept Christ. All those in the state of grace at Christ's Second Coming, when he will slay the Antichrist, will be rapt up into heaven alive. Then begins the millennium during which Christian principles will prevail everywhere; wars will cease; few children will be born during these years (the authors remind Zero Population Growth organizations that they will be delighted with this arrangement). But at the end of the thousand years all mayhem breaks loose again, for Satan is loosed and with Gog and Magog—but this time not with the Antichrist, who has already been conquered and is in hell hanging by his heels—wages a major war against the Catholic Church. Christ conquers for a second time and the Antipope and the Antichrist in hell now return to the pool of fire for all eternity. The abyss is sealed forever.[173]

This entire explanation is naive theology-fiction; it runs counter to all Catholic teaching and living tradition. Unfortunately, it is sensational; it is written in journalese as those in search not of truth, but of best-seller sales and perhaps a big bonus for movie rights for an apocalyptic extravaganza. The lack of reverential reasoning is appalling; the misuse of Scripture is scandalous. Contradictions abound everywhere. In an age of confusion of faith, such a detailed schedule of coming apocalyptic events could only be produced by a secularized spirit. The authors started out to produce, in their own words, "a block-buster." Instead they begot a monstrous hallucination. The incompetence of the whole myth is apparent when it calls for two world cataclysms, one against the Antichrist at the Second Coming of Christ, and one against Satan at the end of the thousand-year utopia. Still worse, there is then to be a third coming of Christ in final victory. Nowhere in Scripture is a third coming of Christ called for. We must conclude, then, that enthusiasm for novelty and the sensational with regard to apocalyptic mysteries inevitably leads many into the cauldron of chaotic fantasy.

[173] John W. Tombler and Hubert J. Funk, *The Raptured* (East Orange, NJ: Trumpet Press, 1977), pp. 147–154.

Chapter 7

Newman and the Antichrist

John Henry Newman is beyond doubt one of the greatest minds and noblest persons of the nineteenth century. In him we have a rare, yet winsome, combination of learning, originality, sound judgment, profundity, and holiness. A divine philosopher, man of letters, and pastor of souls, Newman was the leader of the Oxford Tractarian Movement and the most illustrious of English converts to the Catholic Church. His long, yet meteoric, career spanned the years 1801 to 1890.

Having loved and immersed himself in the works of the early Fathers of the Church, Newman became in his own right such a master of Catholic philosophy, theology, morals, and Scripture that he can truly be called a nineteenth-century Father of the Church. Even in his own day he accomplished lasting work. He resuscitated the Fathers, brought into relief the sacramental system, paved the way for an astonishing revival of the long-forgotten ritual, and gave the clergy a new hold upon thousands at the moment when, in England, Erastian principles—theories of secular supremacy in religious affairs—were on the eve of triumph. Throughout his life the motto of Oxford remained his continual inspiration: *Dominus illuminatio mea,* "The Lord is my light." And two of the most important rules that guided his conduct toward God and his fellowmen were: "Holiness rather than peace" and "Growth the only evidence of life." His greatness consisted in the harmony of his genius of the first rank with a deep spiritual temper, in a personality no less winning than sensitive. Indeed, among the literary stars of his time, Newman was distinguished by the pure Christian radiance shining in his life and writings. He is the one Englishman of that era who upheld the ancient Creed with a knowledge and fervor that only the early Fathers possessed. In the exposition of that Creed he developed and used a Shakespearean force of style and a zeal worthy of the saints. It is this unique combination that raised him above the lay preacher *de vanitate mundi* like Thackeray and that gave him a place apart from Tennyson and Browning. Newman is the great Christian and Catholic apologist, the Augustinian type of controversialist in an epoch of agnosticism amid the forces of evolution.[174]

On a voyage to North Africa, Italy, western Greece, and Sicily (December 1832–July 1833), Newman the Anglican stopped in Rome and for the rest of his life the city laid a spell of religion upon him that was never to be diminished. At Leonforte in Sicily he took seriously ill with a fever and was nursed back from the jaws of death by a peasant. Yet during his illness Newman was convinced that he would not die, that God was calling him to some religious high mission. He cried out: "I shall not die; I have not sinned against the light." On his way home, while his ship was becalmed in the straits of Bonifacio, Newman sought God's guidance toward the truth

[174] William Barry, "John Henry Newman," in *The Catholic Encyclopedia*, Vol. X, ed. Charles George Herbermann (New York: Gilmary Society, 1913), pp. 794–800.

and his Church in his famous poem-prayer, "Lead, Kindly Light," deservedly treasured today by all nations, especially English-speaking peoples.[175]

Back in England, Newman began "The Tracts for the Times," as he tells us with a smile, "out of my own head." He was trying to justify his own religious apostolate in the Anglican Church which he held to be one branch, along with the corrupted Catholic Church and the Greek Church of the true Church. He held that these three were accidental ritual variations of the one true Christian society. In 1841 his "Tract 90" tried to reconcile the Anglican Thirty-Nine Articles with the Council of Trent, an impossible undertaking even for the genius of Newman. During the previous eight years of writing the tracts, Newman took his motto from the *Iliad*: "They (the enemies) shall know the difference now." During these years he won victory after victory only to be defeated finally by his own weapon when "Tract 90" antagonized the Anglican hierarchy. Censored severely, he retired to his tent in Littlemore, a broken champion, in 1841. But in 1845, after four years of silence, study, prayer, and penance, Newman was received into the Catholic Church on October 8, 1845 by Father Domenico Barbieri—today Blessed Barbieri—a Passionist mystic who had long sacrificed himself as a missionary for the conversion of England.[176]

Even in his Anglican days Newman was a great preacher. But he preached without eloquence or gesture of popular gifts. His genius was a thrilling earnestness and a knowledge of human nature seldom equaled. When published it was said his sermons "beat all other sermons on the market as Scott's tales

[175] Ibid.
[176] Ibid.

141

beat all other stories." Their chastened style, fertility of illustra-
tion, and sharp energy have lost nothing by age. In tone they
are severe and often melancholy, as if the utterances of an isolated prophet crying in the wilderness. His eight volumes of
Parochial and Plain Sermons are admirable in their profound interpretation of Scripture and, though written in his non-Catholic period, have very little in them to which Catholics can
object. His Catholic *Sermons to Mixed Congregations* exceed in
vigor and irony all other sermons ever published by him. For
once he became a Catholic, his genius bloomed out with a
force and freedom it never displayed in the Anglican communion. Listen to the words of R. H. Hutton on Newman the
Catholic convert: "In irony, in humor, in eloquence, in imaginative force, the writings of the later and, as we may call it, the
emancipated portion of his career, far surpass the writings of
his theological apprenticeship."[177]

Because of Newman's Tracts, patristic studies became the
order of the day. His first volume, *The Arians of the Fourth Century*,
dealt with creeds and sects of that heresy. His *Apologia Pro Vita
Sua* gives us the key to his mental development and his judgment
on the great religious revival known as the Oxford Movement. It
also devastated Charles Kingsley's accusation against the Catholic Church. "Truth," wrote Kingsley, "for its own sake has never
been a virtue with the Roman clergy. Father Newman informs us
that it need not, and on the whole ought not, to be; that cunning
is the weapon which heaven has given to the saints wherewith to
withstand the brute male force of the wicked world which mar-
ries and is given in marriage." In his brilliant annihilation of this
calumny, Newman won great admiration for himself and the

[177] Ibid.

Catholic Faith.[178] We can only mention here some of Newman's other important works. *An Essay on the Development of Christian Doctrine* aimed at harmonizing the apparent variations in dogma with the Catholic Church's claim to be the same Church that goes back to the apostles in an unbroken living tradition. Newman's theory of the organic development of dogma in the crucible of historical trials is a magnificent contribution to the understanding of the economy of salvation as God reveals its secrets in unrolling history. His *Idea of a University* exhibits a range of thought, an urbanity of style, a pregnant wit, and an understanding of the nature of Catholic education that is brilliant and unrivaled. It is still the best exposition and defense of Catholic educational theories in any language. But Newman is also a poet and playwright. His *Dream of Gerontius* far excels the meditative verse of modern bards by its felicitous shadowing forth in symbols and dramatic scenes of the world beyond this vale of tears.

Besides being a master of thought and style, Newman was a mystic and prophet who enjoyed the deepest insight into the future of the Church. It is under this aspect of his genius that we will consider his treatment of the Antichrist. For Newman always looked beyond the immediate future in his love and concern for the Church. In a lecture given at Dublin on "A Form of Infidelity of the Day," he seems to have anticipated the great apostasy from the Church via the heretical road of Modernism and neo-Modernism. He called this heresy "the religion of reason," and condemned it as the ruin of all revealed truth, of all supernatural faith. He foresaw the total loss of the Church's temporal power; he predicted the positive role of the faithful in the infallible teaching of the Magisterium. To his own

---

[178] Ibid.

generation he became a Jeremiah, decrying the abandonment of the Faith by many in the Church and the disease of religious liberalism within its bosom.

Despondency was his prevailing mood and, though he was long under a cloud of suspicion for heresy both in and outside the Church, Newman never despaired. He clearly, courageously expounded, defended, and advanced the Catholic Faith to all who would listen. Though gracious and even tenderhearted, Newman's peculiar temper included deep reserve. He had not in his composition, as he says, "a grain of conviviality." He was always the Oxford Scholar, no democrat, suspicious of popular movements, but keenly interested in political studies and affairs as bearing on the fortunes of the Church. Yet his motto as a cardinal, "*Cor ad cor loquitur*," "Heart speaks to heart," reveals that this great Catholic genius was one in mind and heart with the most illustrious of all the Fathers, St. Augustine, who had written: "The final word is not with thought, nor with reason, nor with the head, but with love, with the will, with the heart." Newman expressed his thought on the Antichrist in four famous Advent sermons on that subject: The Times of Antichrist; The Religion of Antichrist; The City of Antichrist; The Persecution of Antichrist.

1. The Times of the Antichrist

Newman consults Holy Scripture, the Fathers of the Church, and great historical figures in order to describe events that will usher in the times of the Antichrist. The day of the Antichrist will not come until there is a great falling away from God, Christ, and the Church. This frightful apostasy and the advent of the man of sin shall precede Christ's final coming. Yet the coming of the Antichrist shall be prepared by "false prophets," "false Christs," "the showing of signs and wonders," "iniquity abounding," and "love waxing cold" in the whole world. These signs will tell us that the day of the Lord is near, even at the doors, for the Antichrist comes immediately before the Second Coming of Christ. Two other great signs will herald the imminent coming of the Antichrist. There will be worldwide confusion and trouble, "great tribulation, such as was not from the beginning of the world until this time," and "this Gospel shall be preached in all the world for a witness unto all nations; and then shall come the end."[179]

But what is the meaning of the words "the mystery of iniquity is already at work"? According to Newman, they mean that in all times, even in St. Paul's day, there are shadows, forebodings, earnests, and evil elements preparing for the day in which wickedness will arrive in all its fullness. Just as there have always been types of Christ preceding and preparing the way for the coming of Christ, so the shadows of the Antichrist will precede him. Even the days of the apostles typified the last days; there were false Christs, national then, and international upheavals. Then the true Christ came in judgment to destroy the unfaithful among the Jews. "In truth," Newman writes, "every event in the world is a type of those that follow, history proceeding forward as a circle ever enlarging.... For every age presents its own picture of those future events which alone are the real fulfillment of the prophecy which stands at the head of them all."[180]

---

[179] John Henry Newman, Advent Sermons on Antichrist, in *Tracts for the Times*, Vol. V (London: J.G.F. & J. Rivington, 1840), pp. 1–54. Note Well: here we give only the references to the sermons; the references to the scriptural quotes are found in the sermons and need not be repeated here.

[180] Ibid., pp. 4–5.

We have seen that St. Paul told the Thessalonians that the Antichrist could not come in their era because something or someone was restraining his coming. What was this restraining power that delayed the manifestation of the enemy of truth? "Now you know what restrains him that he may be revealed in his proper time." Who or what is this restraining power? According to Newman, it is generally admitted to be the Roman Empire. Just as Rome succeeded Greece in Daniel's vision, so the Antichrist succeeds Rome and Christ the Savior succeeds the Antichrist.[181] Newman argues that the Antichrist has not yet come because the entire Roman Empire has not yet been thoroughly vanquished, has not yet disappeared from the face of the earth. Newman thought that important vestiges of the Roman Empire survived into the nineteenth century. For the ten horns or kingdoms, of which Daniel speaks, and into which the Roman Empire will be divided, still exist. Until they are thoroughly removed the Antichrist will not come. Out of the little horn will eventually arise the Antichrist, "with the eyes of a man and a mouth speaking great things."

The Antichrist will embody the spirit of infidelity par excellence. Newman claimed that this malignant spirit, this fierce and lawless principle, was at work even in his own day.[182] This spirit of ambition, the mother of all heresy, schism, sedition, revolution, and war was being held back by the framework of society and government that Newman's time inherited, a representative of Roman power, a still functioning legacy of the Roman Empire to the modern world.

Newman asks whether the Antichrist will be one man, an individual, or a power or a kingdom? The Holy Scripture, the

---

[181] Ibid., p. 5.
[182] Ibid., p. 6.

Newman and the Antichrist

living tradition of the Church and the consensus of the Fathers led him to conclude that the Antichrist will be one man, a person. For he is called in Scripture "the man of sin," "the son of perdition," "the adversary and rival of all that is called God or worshipped," "the one who sits as God in the temple of God, proclaiming himself to be God." He is the wicked one "whom the Lord shall consume with the spirit of His mouth and shall destroy with the brightness of His coming.... Whose coming is after the working of Satan with all power and signs and lying wonders." Then, too, Daniel speaks of the Antichrist "subduing three kings, speaking words against the Most High, thinking to change times and laws, ruling for a time and times and the dividing of time." Again: "The judgment shall sit and they shall take away his dominion, to consume and destroy it unto the end." Daniel also relates the duplicity whereby he comes to power.

> In his estate shall stand up a vile person, to whom they shall
> not give the honor of the kingdom; but he shall come in
> peaceably, and obtain the kingdom by flatteries.... And
> such as do wickedly against the covenant shall be corrupt
> by flatteries; but the people that do know their God shall be
> strong and do exploits.... And the king shall do according
> to his will; and he shall exalt himself, and magnify himself
> above every god, and shall speak marvelous things against
> the God of gods, and shall prosper till the indignation be
> accomplished.... Neither shall he regard the God of his
> fathers, nor the desire of women, nor regard any god; for
> he shall magnify himself above all. But in his estate shall
> he honor the God of forces, and a God whom his fathers
> knew not shall he honor with gold and silver, and with
> precious stones and pleasant things.

St. John says of this wicked person:

> There was given him a mouth speaking great things and
> blasphemies; and power was given unto him to continue
> forty and two months. And he opened his mouth in
> blasphemy against God, to blaspheme His name and His
> tabernacle and them that dwell in heaven. And it was given
> him to make war with the saints, and to overcome them;
> and power was given him over all kindreds and tongues and
> nations. And all that dwell upon the earth shall worship
> him whose names are not written in the book of life of the
> lamb slain from the foundation of the world.[183]

Newman also presents an argument from probability to persuade his reader that the Antichrist will be an individual person.
He chooses three remarkable shadows, among many that could
be selected, that answer closely to the descriptions of what the
Antichrist will be and do when he comes. For if the types and
forerunners of the Antichrist are famous historical persons, then
the Antichrist will have to be even more so a world-famous person. From the shadows of the Antichrist we can learn much
about the substantial Antichrist.

Prior to the advent of Christ, perhaps the most remarkable
shadow of the coming fulfillment of evil in the Antichrist was
the heathen, King Antiochus, of whom we read in the book of
the Maccabees. Daniel also has much to say about this shadow,
his terms and descriptions clearly pointing to King Antiochus
and simultaneously to the Antichrist. These terms imply that
Antiochus *was* a type of that monster who will ravage the Church
at the end of time.

[183] Ibid., p. 8.

Antiochus was a savage persecutor of the Jews. Some Jewish apostates, seeking the power and pleasures of this world, made a covenant with him. They made themselves uncircumcised, forsook the holy covenant with God, joined the heathen, and sold themselves to perform all manner of mischief. When Antiochus had conquered Egypt, he advanced against Israel and Jerusalem. He sacked the city, profaned the temple, removed the golden altar, the candlestick of light, all the sacred vessels, the vials, the censers of gold, the veils, the crowns, the golden ornaments; he pulled down every sacred symbol. Claiming to be God, he massacred the people, set fire to Jerusalem, and "pulled down the houses and walls thereof on every side." Then he rebuilt the city of David; he settled the sinful nation in the city, wicked men and women, and fortified it. Then King Antiochus assimilated the Jews under his heathen laws, demanding that they abandon the law of God under penalty of death. The Jews accepted the religion of a pagan idolatry, sacrificed to false gods, and profaned the Sabbath. The king forced other impieties upon the Jews. Those who remained faithful to their covenant and Sabbaths he put to death. But the majority polluted the sanctuary, visited the altars and groves of idols, and sacrificed swine's flesh and unclean beasts. Finally, Antiochus set up a great idol or, in the words of history, "the Abomination of Desolation" upon the altar, and built idol altars throughout the cities of Judah. When he had torn the books of the law into shreds, he consigned them to the fire. "Here," says Newman, "we have presented to us some of the lineaments of the Antichrist who will be such and worse than such, as Antiochus."[184]

Another such shadow was the Emperor Julian the Apostate. He lived between AD 331 and 363. His example also indicates

---

[184] Ibid., pp. 8–10.

that the Antichrist will be one person, not a kingdom or power.
Julian fell away from the Catholic Faith, mounted a persecution
of Christians and attempted to reestablish pagan idolatry as the
religion of the empire. He proudly undertook to rebuild the
temple of Jerusalem, having gathered all the men and materials
to do so. But trouble in the eastern part of his empire called him
to the front to quell an uprising. In the ensuing battle Julian was
killed and his plans to crush the Church were totally frustrated.[185] Newman presents the false prophet Mohammed as a third
historical shadow of the Antichrist. This shadow began his imposture about six hundred years after Christ and his armies tore
at the soul and body of Christ in the fierce religious wars they
waged against the Church.[186] Finally Newman refers indirectly
to the godless leaders of the French Revolution who attacked
the Church fiercely, laicized France, and spread revolt against
God and His Church throughout Europe and the world. In
every case of a forerunner of the Antichrist, Newman demonstrates how the apostasy of the people from the true God prepared the coming of these heralds and types of the Antichrist
and led to the wholesale slaughter of a religious society.[187] First
the people of God in large numbers discarded their sacred religion *and then* the enemy was allowed to come in. The great
apostasy is always the harbinger of the shadows and substance
of the Antichrist. The Jews first abandoned God, then came
Antiochus; Christians first fell away into Arianism, then arose
Julian the Apostate and the persecution; the heresies of Nestori-
anism and Eutychianism destroyed the faith of millions, then

---

[185] Ibid., pp. 8, 11.
[186] Ibid., p. 10.
[187] Ibid., p. 10.

came Mohammed. The agnosticism and atheism of the Enlightenment paved the way for the Reign of Terror under Robespierre and the Jacobins.[188]

Newman then reflects on his own times to see if there are growing signs of the coming of the Antichrist. "Is the enemy of Christ and his Church to arise in our times from a certain special falling away from God?" Without answering yes or no, Newman describes the conditions of his time as favorable to an early arrival of the Antichrist. There are evidences to convince us that we are entering the Age of Apostasy. For apostasy is being formed, gathering forces, gaining ground on the Church every day. Everywhere in the world, but quite visibly and formidably in the most peaceful, civilized nations, we are witnessing a supreme effort to govern men and dominate the world without religion. It is a widely accepted and spreading dogma that nations should have nothing to do with religion, that religion is merely a private matter, an affair of one's own conscience. In effect it is widely accepted that Truth is neither a personal nor a social need and, therefore, society ought to allow Truth to fade from the face of the earth. It is considered futile social action to continue to advance a system of Truth and absurd to attempt to hand it on further developed organically to our posterity. In almost every country there is a united, powerful movement to crush the Church, to strip her of power and place. Everywhere we discover a feverish, litigious endeavor to get rid of religion in public activities—in schools, in mass media, in social transactions, in political affairs. Societies are said to be built on the principle of Utility, not on the principle of Truth. Experience, not Truth or Justice, is accepted as the end or rule of state activities, enactments of law included. Numbers not Truth is the final ground for maintaining this or that creed, morality,

[188] Ibid., pp. 11, 12.

151

or law, it being generally believed that the many are always in the right, the few in the wrong. Even the Bible is given so many meanings over and against its obvious one that it is reduced to having no meaning at all, to being at best a pleasant myth, at worst a dead letter. In the end religion is denied any objective, historical reality such as is displayed in written dogmas, ordinances, and sacraments. Religion is rather confined to each person's inner feelings, experiences, and psychological reactions. Thus cast into the dark world of variable, evanescent, volatile feelings, religion is discredited in the minds of many when it is not already destroyed.[189]

"Surely," continues Newman, "there is at this day a confederacy of evil, marshalling its hosts from all parts of the world, organizing itself, taking its measures, enclosing the Church of Christ as in a net, and preparing the way for a general apostasy from it.... This Apostasy and all its tokens and instruments are of the evil one and saviour of death." How does the Evil One bring about the apostasy? "He offers baits to tempt men: he promises liberty, equality, trade and wealth, remission of taxes, reforms. He tempts men to rail against their rulers and superiors in imitation of his own revolution. He promises illumination, knowledge, science, philosophy, enlargement of mind. He scoffs at times gone by, at sacred traditions, at every institution which reveres them. He bids man mount aloft, to become a god. He laughs and jokes with men, gets intimate with them, takes their hands, gets his fingers between theirs, grasps them and then they are his." Newman was convinced that the shadows of the Antichrist in his day, some one hundred years or so ago, were thickening and lengthening as the age of darkness approached.[190]

[189] Ibid., p. 12.
[190] Ibid., pp. 13, 14.

2. The Religion of the Antichrist

Newman takes directly from St. John the Evangelist the characteristic that will reveal the Antichrist when he comes. He will openly deny our Lord Jesus Christ to be the Son of God come in the flesh from heaven. In fact, the denial of Christ can be called the spirit of the Antichrist; those who deny Christ can be said to have the spirit of the Antichrist; to be like the Antichrist, to be themselves antichrists, albeit on a smaller scale. "Who is a liar," asks St. John, "but he who denies that Jesus is the Christ?"

St. Paul and St. John speak of the same enemy of the Church. This is discovered from the similarity of their descriptions. Both claim that the spirit of the Antichrist was already at work in their day. "That spirit of the Antichrist," says St. John, "is *now already* in the world." "The mystery of iniquity is *already* at work," says St. Paul. Both describe the enemy as being scarred with the same special sin—open infidelity. St. John writes: "He is the Antichrist who denies the Father and the Son." St. Paul identifies him in like manner as "the adversary and rival of all that is called God, setting forth himself as if he were God." In every case we find the same blasphemous denial of God and religion. And St. Paul scores the final blasphemy: "He will oppose all existing religion, true or false, all that is called God or worshipped."

The prophet Daniel decries the same reckless impiety in the Antichrist:

> The king shall do according to his will; and he shall exalt himself and magnify himself above every god, and shall speak marvelous things against the God of Gods, and shall prosper until the indignation be accomplished.... Neither shall he regard the God of his fathers, nor the desire of women (that is, as it would appear, the Messiah,

to be his mother being the especial privilege and object of hope among the Jewish women), nor regard any god—for he shall magnify himself above all.

Christ's words to the high priests plotting His death also give a deeply prophetic allusion to the blasphemous designs of the Antichrist. "I am come in My Father's name, and you do not receive Me; if another shall come in his own name, him you will receive." This, according to the Fathers, is a prophetic allusion to the Antichrist whom the Jews will mistake for the Christ. He comes in his own name, not from God, as even the Son of God came, who, if any, might have come with the power of his essential divinity.[191]

Then there are the Scripture passages that speak generally of the impieties of the last age of the world, impieties that will usher in and be completed in the culmination of evil in the Antichrist.

Many shall be purified and made white and tried. But the wicked shall do wickedly; and none of the wicked shall understand ... in the last days perilous times shall come, for men shall be lovers of their own selves, covetous, boasters, proud, blasphemers, disobedient to parents, unthankful, unholy, without natural affection, truce-breakers, false accusers, incontinent, fierce, despisers of those that are good, traitors, heady, high-minded, lovers of pleasures more than lovers of God, having a form of godliness but denying the power thereof; scoffers walking after their own lusts, and saying, Where is the promise of His coming?; despising government, presumptuous ... self-willed, not afraid to speak evil of dignities ... promising men liberty, while themselves the servants of corruption.

[191] Ibid., p. 17.

Newman then expounds on why the Antichrist is to be connected with the Jewish race. The Antichrist will come saying: "I am Christ." But the Jews, having rejected the true Christ, will now have to undergo the judicial punishment imposed upon themselves by their stubborn blindness to the light of Christ. They will be taken in by the false Christ. For the Antichrist will be the consummate, the complete deceiver, "whose coming," says St. Paul,

> is ... with all wicked deception to those who are perishing because they have not received the love of truth, that they might be saved. Therefore, God sends them a misleading influence that they may believe falsehood, that all may be judged who have not believed in the truth, but took pleasure in wickedness.

Since the Antichrist will pose as the Messiah, it has been universally accepted by the Christian tradition that he would be of the Jewish race and observe the Jewish rites.[192] Moreover, according to St. Paul, the Antichrist will "sit in the Temple of God,"—the Jewish Temple—according to the Fathers. Our Lord's own words support this prediction when he speaks of "the abomination of desolation" (an expression denoting the Antichrist in his full wickedness), "standing in the holy place." Then, too, St. John describes the Antichrist's persecution of the two witnesses of Christ, Elias and Enoch, as taking place in Jerusalem. "Their dead bodies shall lie in the street of the great city, which is spiritually called Sodom and Egypt, where also Our Lord was crucified."

Newman then asks a most important question. Will the Antichrist profess any sort of religion? Scripture tells us that he will

[192] Ibid., p. 18.

worship neither true nor false God. For the Antichrist is "to exalt himself over all that is called God or worshipped." He will set himself forcefully against idols and idolatry. Yet Daniel writes: "In his estate shall he honor the God of force, and a God whom his fathers knew not shall he honor with gold and silver, and with precious stones and pleasant things. Thus shall he do in the most strong holds with a strange god, whom he shall acknowledge and increase with glory." The meaning of the words "God of force" and "a strange God" is, according to Newman, "quite hidden from us and probably will be so till the event." Yet some sort of false worship is certainly predicted as the mark of the Antichrist, despite the fact that Daniel asserts that "he shall set himself against all idols," as well as against the true God. This apparent contradiction should not surprise the faithful. For it is generally known to the saints that infidelity leads to superstition and blasphemers are really cowards. Take the example of Catholic France, which during the French Revolution became a laicized, atheistic state. Atheism was absolutely professed as the state religion. In spite of this, a certain strange worship was set up. The state leaders forced a Catholic archbishop to come forward and declare publicly that there was no God. They closed the churches, and seized and desecrated the gold and silver vessels from the sanctuaries. They formed mock processions of men clad in priestly garments and singing profane hymns. They annulled the divine ordinance of marriage, reducing it to a mere civil contract. They exalted the very negation of religion, their living blasphemy into a kind of god, calling it Liberty. And they literally worshipped it as a divinity. Rejecting Christ as an impostor, they decreed in the public assembly of the nation the adoration of Liberty and Equality as divinities. And they appointed festivals in honor of Reason, the Country, the Constitution, and the Virtues. They determined that tutelary gods, even dead men, were to be canonized, and consecrated and worshipped; and they enrolled in the lists of these some of the most notorious infidels and profligates. This infatuated, godless people tried to reinstate the old Roman democratic worship, as if to prove that Rome, the fourth monster of the prophet's vision, was not dead. They even raised a statue to Ceres, a Roman divinity, and appointed a festival in her honor. This new pagan religion of atheistic France demonstrated that the evil spirit of old Rome was still active in the world, though its name was almost extinct. In the end these apostates bowed down to the goddess of Reason in the person of a nude prostitute whom they placed on the high altar of Notre Dame cathedral in Paris.[193]

In summarizing the religion of the Antichrist, Newman stresses these conclusions of the Fathers of the Church. (1) The Antichrist will come out of the Roman Empire, upon its division into ten kingdoms. (2) The Antichrist will come up suddenly out of it upon these ten, subdue three of them, and finally all of them. (3) The Antichrist will then blaspheme, puffed up with power and glory, and use great words against the Most High. (4) After remaining torpid for centuries, the Roman monster will awake at the end of the world and be restored in all its laws and forms. (5) The system of Augustus, founder of the Roman Empire, will be adopted and established by the Antichrist to his own aggrandizement and glory. (6) This is the fourth monster, whose head was wounded and healed—the empire was destroyed and divided into ten. (7) This time the Antichrist, a man of power and wonderful resources, will heal and restore this monster so that it will vigorously fight once again against the camp of the

[193] Ibid., pp. 20–22.

saints. (8) The name of the Antichrist is the very number 666, which will reveal him as "the Abomination of Desolation." But the true meaning of his name will remain a mystery until the historical event of the Antichrist's arrival takes place.[194]

In short, the Antichrist will be an open blasphemer, opposed to all worship true or false. He will be a persecutor of the Church, but a patron to all the Jews, a restorer of their worship. He will be the author of a novel kind of worship. He will appear suddenly from the end of the Roman Empire, which was once and now sleeps. He will knit that Roman Empire again into one, engraft his Judaism and new paganism onto the old discipline of Caesar Augustus, thereby earning for himself the title of Roman king, and the divine honors of an emperor. He will rule for three and one-half years and then pass away as suddenly as he appeared.[195]

3. The City of the Antichrist

The intimate connection of the city of Rome with the exploits and reign of the Antichrist leads Newman to speculate that Rome may turn out to be the city of the Antichrist in the last times. Even the Fathers of the Church leaned heavily toward this interpretation. The influence of the Roman Empire permeates the Gospels, the Acts of the Apostles, the Epistles, especially of Paul and the Apocalypse. Christ was born, lived, suffered, and died under the Romans. St. Paul, a Roman citizen, was at times protected, at times persecuted, and finally executed by Roman power. The same is true, though to a lesser degree, with the other apostles. The great city that ruled over

[194] Ibid., pp. 23–26.
[195] Ibid., p. 26.

the kings of the earth first severely persecuted and finally promulgated Christianity.[196]

In chapter 17 of the Apocalypse, St. John describes the great city of Rome under the image of a woman: she is cruel, profligate, impious. She is arrayed in worldly splendor and costliness, in purple and scarlet, in gold and precious stones and pearls. She sheds and drinks the blood of the saints, becomes drunk on it. She is called "Babylon the Great," to signify her power, wealth, profanity, pride, sensuality, and persecuting spirit. When St. John was writing his Apocalypse, the city of Rome was the historical embodiment of the above description. Newman tells us: "There never was a more ambitious, haughty, hardhearted and worldly people than the Romans; never any, for none else had ever the opportunity, which so persecuted the Church. Christians suffered ten persecutions at their hands and very horrible ones, extending over 250 years."[197]

St. John represented this city of sin as an abandoned woman, seated on a "scarlet-colored monster, full of names of blasphemy, having seven heads and ten horns." This image drives us back to Daniel's prophetic description in which the four great empires of the world are shadowed under the figure of four beasts—a lion, a bear, a leopard, and a nameless monster, this last different from the rest, "dreadful and terrible and strong exceedingly." This is surely the same beast that St. John saw; the ten horns identify it. Now this fourth beast in Daniel's vision is the Roman Empire: "the beast," therefore on which the woman sits is also the Roman Empire. History bears out this interpretation, for Rome, the mistress of the world, might

[196] Ibid., p. 28.
[197] Ibid., p. 29.

well be said to have sat upon, and been carried about triumphantly on, that world which she had subdued and made her creature. Daniel explains the ten horns of the Beast to be "ten Kings that shall arise" out of this empire. St. John agrees, saying: "The ten horns which you saw are the ten kings, which have received no kingdom as yet, but receive power as kings one hour with the beast." Then, too, in an earlier vision Daniel speaks of the empire as destined to be "divided," as "partly strong and partly broken." Moreover, this empire, the beast of burden of the woman, was at length to rise against her and devour her; it would do this in the time of its divided existence. "The ten horns which you saw upon the beast, these shall hate her, and shall make her desolate and naked, and shall eat her flesh and burn her with fire." Such was to be the end of the great city of iniquity. Lastly, three of the kings, maybe all of them, are said to be subdued or won over by the Antichrist, who is to come up suddenly while they are in power. Thus does Daniel prophesy the event: "Another shall rise after them, and he shall be diverse from the first, and he shall subdue three kings, and shall speak great words against the Most High, and shall wear out the saints of the Most High, and think to change times and laws; and they shall be given into his hands until a time, times and a dividing of time." This power that rises up against the kings is the Antichrist. And here we should observe how Rome and the Antichrist are further related to each other in the prophecy.

Rome is to fall before the Antichrist rises. For the ten kings are to destroy Rome; then the Antichrist appears to supersede the ten kings. St. John makes this rather clear: "The ten horns shall hate and devour the woman." And Daniel says: "I considered the horns, and behold, there came up among them another little horn with eyes like the eyes of a man and a mouth speaking great things." That is the Antichrist.[198]

Newman tries to determine how far these prophecies have been fulfilled, and what remains to be accomplished. The Roman Empire did break up; it divided into a number of separate kingdoms—France, Germany, England, Italy, etc. Yet it is difficult to number the ten kingdoms accurately and exactly. Then, though Rome has been sacked often most fearfully, yet it has never suffered from ten parts of its own empire. Rather it has been brought down by barbarians who came from outside the empire. Moreover, Rome still exists today as a city, whereas it was to be "desolated, devoured and burned with fire." Finally, Rome has not as yet fulfilled another description of the city of Satan. She has not taken "the golden cup in her hand full of abominations," nor made "the inhabitants of the earth drunk with the wine of her fornication," expressions implying a successful worldwide seduction. This she has not done to date.[199]

The Roman Empire has not yet been divided into ten kingdoms, so the time for the Antichrist has not yet come. And all the Fathers say that the ten kingdoms are to come at the end of the world and last but a short time. Then the Antichrist will come upon them suddenly. Can one say today whether the Roman Empire is gone or still with us, however attenuated? In one sense it is gone, for it is divided into kingdoms. In another sense it is not, for the date cannot be assigned on which it came to an end, and much could be said for its continued existence, though this be a mutilated and decayed existence. The Roman

[198] Ibid., p. 30.
[199] Ibid., p. 31.

Empire must someday revive for ten vigorous kingdoms must arise from her and be conquered by the Antichrist before the end comes.

The prophet describes the resurrection of Rome thus: "'The beast,' that is, the Roman Empire, 'the monster that you saw, *was and is not*, and *shall* ascend out of the abyss *that was and is not and yet is*.' Moreover, the ten kings and the empire will rise together, the kings appearing at the time of the monster's resurrection, not when it is languid and torpid. 'The ten kings ... have received no kingdom as yet, but receive power as kings one hour with the beast.' If the Roman Empire is still prostrate, the ten kings have not yet come; and if the ten kings have not yet come, the destined destroyer of the woman, and the full judgments upon Rome, have not yet been realized."[200]

However much she may have suffered throughout history, the full measure of God's judgment has not yet fallen upon Rome. It did fall upon Jerusalem, the holy city. That city and its people rejected God and Christ. God sent the Roman legions under the emperor, Titus, to destroy completely apostate Jerusalem and Israel. The divine vengeance fell upon the holy city, then turned against the Roman Empire, which was disorganized, broken in pieces by insurrections, plagues, famines, and earthquakes, while countless hosts of barbarians attacked it from all sides and even burned and pillaged Rome itself. Yet the Roman Empire and the city of Rome remained in existence. The Goth, the Hun, the Vandal plundered Rome, but did not annihilate her. Why has Rome been granted so far such special treatment in God's providence?

It was the consensus of serious thinkers in the early Church that the barbarian invasions were merely a preliminary

[200] Ibid., p. 32.

punishment sent by God upon a wicked Roman Empire and city of Rome. In the end they predicted, God would completely destroy the city by the fury of the elements. Gregory the Great wrote in his Dialogues: "Rome shall not be destroyed by the nations, but shall consume away internally, worn out by storms of lightning, whirlwinds and earthquakes."[201] Yet Rome has not yet been wholly and irrevocably destroyed because God has always had a faithful people in that city. Babylon, Sodom, and Gomorrah were wholly rotten, hence wholly destroyed. But Rome received the Church as a guest. Christians dwelt there, suffered there, prayed there. They were the life and salt of the very city that persecuted them. St. Augustine used this same argument against his pagan brethren who blamed all the catastrophes that befell the empire and the city of Rome on the Christians. Augustine pointed to the cities that had sinned and had been visited with divine chastisements; he showed that they had perished altogether, whereas Rome was still preserved. Here, he said, was the fulfillment of God's promise to Abraham; for the sake of the faithful Christians in it, Rome was chastised, but not utterly destroyed. Historical facts bear out the truth of this interpretation. Alaric, the fierce conqueror, arrived at the gates of defenseless Rome. Yet he exhorted his troops "to respect the churches of the Apostles St. Peter and St. Paul, as holy and inviolable sanctuaries." Fifty years later Attila the Hun advanced against the city. Pope St. Leo was successful in arresting his plan to destroy the city. Then a few years later, came Genseric, the most savage of barbarian conquerors. Pope Leo again mitigated the fury of the barbarians. Though they pillaged the city, they kept their promise to the pope to spare

[201] Ibid., p. 35.

the unresisting multitude, and to protect the buildings from fire and the captives from torture. Here is displayed the wonderful rule of God's loving providence. The Church suffers daily with the world and in so doing sanctifies the world. Total divine vengeance is still suspended over the city of Rome because the Christian Church still lives, suffers, witnesses, and dies a martyr's death there, interceding for the city, sanctifying and saving it.[202]

Newman concludes that Rome may be spared until the end of time. Then, too, just as Babylon is a type of Rome and of the world of sin and vanity, so Rome in turn may be a type also, whether of some other city, or of the proud and entire deceiving world. The woman is said to be Babylon as well as Rome; so again she may be something more than Rome, a city of sin that is yet to come or is building toward being the capital of the Antichrist's empire. Perhaps the total ruin depicted by the prophets for the city of the Antichrist applies to the general wickedness of the whole world at the time of the Antichrist. Certainly tragic judgments came upon Rome when her empire was taken from her. Her persecutions of the Church have been in a large measure punished by God. Scripture's predictions about her have been fulfilled. Whether she is to be judged finally and destroyed utterly depends first on whether righteous men in the city will save her, and second, whether the prophecy of final, complete destruction relates in its fullness to Rome or to some other city of which Rome is a type. But if Rome is to be judged, this must be before the Antichrist destroys the ten kings. The ten kings are to destroy Rome and the Antichrist will last a short time in power. The prophecy, it seems, has not yet been fulfilled, whatever one decides about Rome. For the Roman Empire has not yet been divided into

[202] Ibid., pp. 36–37.

ten kingdoms; it has not yet risen to devour the woman, whoever she stands for, nor has final judgment come crashing down upon the woman. At any rate and by any interpretation the city of the Antichrist will be a city plagued with sin; it will be a sacrilegious city, an idolatrous city, the mystical society of Satan upon the earth.[203]

4. The Persecution of the Antichrist

Persecutions are a characteristic mark of Christ's Church. They are not a *necessary* lot of the Church, but one of the appropriate badges, a sign by which one recognizes that she belongs to her crucified founder. Christ makes it clear that His Church is to have the same lot as He had. His life and hers in time begin and end in persecution. He ascended from her and left her in persecution; He will come back and find her in the worst persecution of all time. The prophets all speak of this most dreadful prosecution yet to come upon the Church. Christ Himself predicted it:[204] "Then shall be great tribulation, such as was not since the beginning of the world to this time, no, nor ever shall be; and unless these days had been shortened, no flesh would be saved; but for the sake of the elect, these days shall be shortened."

Some of the principal texts from Scripture that Newman uses to indicate the final worst persecution, that of the Antichrist, against the Church are as follows:

Another shall rise after them, and ... he shall speak great words against the Most High, and shall wear out the saints of the Most High, and think to change times and laws; and they shall be given into his hand until a time, times and a dividing of time: that is three and one-half years.

[203] Ibid., pp. 38–39.
[204] Ibid., pp. 41–42.

They shall pollute the Sanctuary of strength, and shall
take away the Daily Sacrifice, and they shall place the
Abomination that makes desolate, and such as do wickedly
against the Covenant shall be corrupted by flatteries; but
the people that do know their God shall be strong and do
exploits. And they that understand among the people shall
instruct many; yet they shall fall by the sword and by flame,
by captivity, by spoil many days.

Many shall be purified and made white and tried; but
the wicked shall do wickedly .. . and from the time that the
Daily Sacrifice shall be taken away, and the Abomination
that makes desolate set up, there shall be a thousand two
hundred and ninety days.

Then shall be great tribulation, such as was not since
the beginning of the world.

The beast that ascends out of the bottomless pit shall
make war against them and shall overcome and kill them....
And they that dwell upon the earth shall rejoice over them
and make merry and shall send gifts one to another because
these two prophets tormented them that dwell on the earth.

And the woman fled into the wilderness where she has
a place prepared of God, that they should feed her there a
thousand two hundred and threescore days.

And there was given unto him a mouth speaking
great things and blasphemies; and power was given unto
him to continue forty and two months. And he opened
his mouth in blasphemy against God, to blaspheme His
name and His tabernacle and them that dwell in heaven.
And it was given unto him to make war with the saints
and to overcome them . . . and all that dwell upon the
earth shall worship him, whose names are not written in

the book of life of the Lamb slain from the foundation of the world.

I saw an Angel come down from heaven, having the key of the bottomless pit and a great chain in his hand; and he laid hold on the dragon, that old serpent, which is the devil and Satan, and bound him a thousand years ... and after that he must be loosed a little season ... and shall go out to deceive the nations which are in the four quarters of the earth, Gog and Magog, to gather them together to battle: the number of whom is as the sand of the sea. And they went up on the breadth of the earth and compassed the camp of the saints about and the beloved city.[205]

The early Christians interpreted these passages as terrifying persecution that the Antichrist would inflict on the Church in the last days. All previous persecutions were considered pallid preludes to the final tribulations. For in all previous persecutions the Church had also been somewhat sheltered in various places. In the final, universal persecution she will have no place to hide. Moreover, never before was a persecution attended with the cessation of all religious worship. But in the final trials, "they shall take away the Daily Sacrifice," words which the early Fathers interpreted to mean that the Antichrist will suppress for three and a half years all public religious worship. Instead the Antichrist will have himself set up, in the symbol of the statue struck in his image and likeness and miraculously made to move and speak by the power of Satan, in the restored Temple of Jerusalem, there to receive the adoration and other honors from his idolatrous followers. But the last and worst persecution will be advanced with

[205] Ibid., pp. 42–44.

a marvelous eruption of "lying wonders," miracles more stupendous than those the magicians of Egypt effected with Satan's power against Moses. Whether these miracles are real or pretended, or the result of the Antichrist's virtuosity in manipulating the forces of science, makes little difference. For they will produce in the masses the same effect as if they were genuine miracles. They will overpower the imaginations and wills of millions who will decide to abandon the true God and follow the Antichrist. "There will be signs and wonders," says our Lord, "inasmuch that, if it were possible, they shall deceive the very elect." And St. Paul speaks of the Antichrist as one "whose coming is after the working of Satan, with all power and signs and lying wonders, and with all deception of unrighteousness in them that perish, because they received not the love of truth, that they might be saved. And for this cause God shall send them strong delusion that they should believe a lie."

And St. John: "He does great wonders so that he makes fire come down from heaven on the earth in the sight of men and deceives them that dwell on the earth by the means of those miracles which he had power to do in the sight of the beast."[206]

Newman thus lists four aspects of the final persecution mounted by the Antichrist. It will be fiercer, more horrible, more awful than all earlier persecutions taken singularly or collectively. It will effect the cessation of the ordinances of grace, especially of the Daily Sacrifice. It will set up the open, legal establishment of infidelity coupled with a blasphemous, habitual way of life even within the holiest recesses of the Church. It will be supported and advanced with a marvelous power of working miracles. Then Newman goes on to comment on the

[206] Ibid., pp. 44–45.

first aspect alone, that is, the sharpness, cruelty, and universality of the trials.

A brief survey of the history of the Church will convince any reader that cruelties more shocking than those suffered by the early Christians are almost unimaginable before the event. Even St. Paul's recording of the persecutions before his time do but weakly describe the trials the Church suffered in his day and afterward. Jewish saints were tortured, mocked, scourged, imprisoned, stoned, sawn asunder, tempted, slain with the sword, driven out to wander in sheepskins and goatskins, left destitute, afflicted, abandoned. These were the persecutions visited on the faithful prophets under the Law. As they anticipated the Gospel in doctrine, so did they anticipate the Gospel in sufferings. But the persecutions against the Gospel were much sharper, even as the Gospel doctrine was much clearer.[207]

Newman then relates the bloodcurdling martyrdom of Sts. Sanctus, Maturus, Attalus, and Blandina. They were tortured by turns in every possible way from morning till evening, their bodies being burned, mangled, and pierced in every part. But their constancy in the Faith exhausted their persecutors. Then red-hot plates were fastened to the tenderest parts of the body. But they still survived their sufferings and grew more radiant in the Faith. Some days later they were taken to the games and went through every torture again, as if they had suffered nothing before. Scourged, forced into red-hot iron chairs, dragged around by the beasts, they finally came to their victorious end. Blandina, however, was hung on a cross, placed so as to be devoured by the beasts turned loose on her. Then scourged, she was placed in a basket, thrown to a bull and died under the tossings of the furious animal.

[207] Ibid., p. 46.

Then Newman briefly relates the unspeakable tortures the Arian Vandals inflicted on four hundred bishops of Africa, and ten years later, two hundred and twenty more; and later still on some four thousand Christians faithful to the orthodox creed. Hard labor in unhealthy places, exile, long marches across burning sands, torture, laceration with scourges, burnings with hot irons, the cutting off of limbs, these were but some of the tortures that preceded their violent deaths. Yet even these supreme tortures did not prevent the early Fathers from predicting far worse cruelties for the Church in the days of the Antichrist.[208]

It is certain that the final persecution has not yet come and that we must therefore prepare for its arrival. All ages in the Church have been convinced that Scripture has foretold this coming catastrophe. Every generation of Christians has been on the watch, looking out more anxiously as time advances. Signs do occur in history from time to time, not to fix the day, but to remind us that the Antichrist and the final struggle between the Church and her enemies is daily approaching. Other signs tell us that the universe and the planets are growing old; our earth keeps crumbling away under the forces of nature and the abuse of man. The night is far spent; the day is at hand. Shadows begin to move; the old forms of the Roman Empire, with us from the time of Christ, heave, tremble, and nod toward a fall. When they go, the Antichrist will be released, announced, and acclaimed. But he will disappear in a short, fearful season. And then Christ will come in power and glory.[209]

One might use the analogy of a man slowly dying on his bed for the present condition of the Roman Empire. It exists and yet

[208] Ibid., pp. 47–48.
[209] Ibid., pp. 49–50.

does not exist. It has relapses, recoveries, days of coma and days of consciousness. It is not dead yet on its deathbed; it lingers, rallies, fails. It is a matter of time; the illness is terminal, but the exact day of demise is uncertain. It will die, no doubt, with some violence and convulsions. The Antichrist is the head of this empire, but the empire must finally die to make way for his ascendency to full power. Thus death is hastening forward, surely, irrevocably, whether it takes a few years more or less. It may come after our time or that of our children, for we are all creatures of a day and a generation is like the striking of a clock. But the empire, the world, human society are tending to dissolution; their days are fast running out, ever decreasing in numbers.[210]

Another anxious sign that Newman took as an indication of the approaching power of the Antichrist was that in his day the power of Islam was visibly declining. Lastly, he mentions another remarkable token of the approaching end. Referring to the Apocalypse, he recalls that it is predicted that in the last persecution Satan will be loosed from his prison, will deceive the nations, Gog and Magog, and unite them all in a war against the Church. Newman observes, moreover, that the northern nations will be stirred up against the Church. This has happened twice already. First the Goths and Vandals attacked the Church and became Arian heretics. Second, the Turks attacked the Church after they were deceived into the false religion of Islam. Were these nations the shadows of the Gog and Magog to come in the future? Newman thought that perhaps they were. At any rate, he saw in his day the nations of the North gathering strength as never before; and these nations were bitter enemies of the Church. This he took as a sign of the advance of the Antichrist;

[210] Ibid., p. 50.

it was perhaps only a preparation, a warning, a call to sober thought on things to come; perhaps it was only a cloud in the sky warning about the advancing storm.[211]

Newman concludes his comments on the last persecution, the persecution of the Antichrist thus: it may not be a persecution of blood and death, but of craft and subtility—not of miracles but of natural wonders and marvels of human skill, human acquirements in the hands of the devil. Satan may adopt the more alarming weapons of deceit—he may seduce us in little things, move the Church, not all at once, but little by little from her true position. He has had much success in this tactic in the last centuries. He has moved every part of the Church away from the truth of Christ, from the old faith upon which it was built. It is Satan's policy to split us and divide us, to dislodge us gradually from the rock of strength. When he has divided the whole of Christendom, the final persecution may come. When we are full of schism and heresy, what better time for the appearance of the Antichrist? When Christians have flung themselves into the arms of the world, Christ's enemy, when they depend for their protection on the world and have surrendered their independence, honor, and strength to its approval, then will the Antichrist burst upon them in fury, then will the idolatrous nations open the flood gates of wickedness and overrun the Church and the world with the hatred and cruelty that is let loose from the abyss of hell. Then will Satan and the Antichrist have their hour, their last hour of darkness upon the earth. For they and their wicked followers will suddenly disappear into the never-ending darkness of eternal perdition.[212]

---

[211] Ibid., p. 51.
[212] Ibid., pp. 51–52.

Chapter 8

Modern Shadows of the Antichrist

In 1632 Tommaso Campanella (1568–1639), a Dominican friar, wrote a book entitled *De Antichristo, Concerning the Antichrist*. Philosopher, poet, theologian, and somewhat of a scientist, Campanella was strongly influenced by Plato, Plotinus, Joachim of Fiore, and by the natural philosophy of Bernardino Telesio, whom Francis Bacon proclaimed *novorum hominum primus*, "the first modern man." An original and bold thinker, as well as political activist, Campanella fell afoul of the Church and political authorities and of the Inquisition composed of his fellow Dominicans. He was in and out of government and Church prisons frequently, as he failed or succeeded in proving his orthodoxy and sanity. All told he spent thirty years in prison and became famous for his suffering and learning. It was while he was in a Neapolitan jail that he wrote *De Antichristo*. At heart he always wished to be thoroughly Catholic, but his audacity of thought and political action (publicly and in writing he defended Galileo twice) made him a controversial figure. Consequently, authorities feared and restrained him. In his political philosophy he envisioned for mankind a Christian utopia that he described in his classic work, *The City of the Sun*. In this theocracy the Church would be the bond of unity among men and nations; the papacy would be the ethical institution for peaceful universality. Christ would be the supreme ruler worthy of divine honors; the apostles would receive the highest esteem and reverence. The political rulers of this City of the Sun would be Christian philosophers and men of wisdom in all fields of human endeavor. Campanella was convinced that his mission in life was to write and fight against tyranny, sophistry, and hypocrisy, from which all evils flowed, and to promote God, truth, and decency.[213]

Campanella states that all godless tyrants and all sophistical heretics are antichrists, for they are types of and participators in the evil that the greatest Antichrist will one day bring to culmination. Never had there been so many precursor antichrists at one time in history as there were in his day. Mohammed, Calvin, Wycliffe, and Luther had already prepared the proper milieu in the world for the appearance of the Antichrist. In fact, Campanella reports the opinion of a famous preacher, Serafino Frimano, that Luther is without a doubt the last precursor of the greatest and cruelest Antichrist. Even the famous Robert Bellarmine subscribed to this thesis. For Luther has all the characteristics that are directly opposed to the virtues of St. John the Baptist, the saintly precursor of Christ. Luther is full of deceit, tyrannical, cruel, fraudulent, and envious. He is a thousand times a liar; he is a reed shaken by the wind; he is dressed in soft clothing, frequenting the palaces of Danish kings, of the Grand Duke of Saxony, of Count Palatino, of the Marquess of Brandenburg. John the Baptist gave up secular clothing, dressed in a hermit's garb, and went into the desert, living a life dedicated to God through penance and the practice of virginity. Luther became the enemy of chastity and virginity when he threw off his

---

[213] Francesco Grillo, *Tommaso Campanella in America* (New York: S.F. Vanni, 1954), pp. 11–17.

religious garb and eloped with a nun. He ridicules the sacraments beginning with Baptism, the rite begun by John the Baptist. Luther seems to have been predicted as the precursor of the Antichrist. The famous preacher of the Dominican Order, Vincent Ferrer, predicted shortly before the birth of Luther that the precursor of the Antichrist was near, and he described him with the marks that we have delineated here. Many took Vincent's words to mean that the Antichrist was already born and would reveal himself shortly, probably in about thirty years.[214] As if to bring St. John the Evangelist up to date, Campanella quotes him: "Dear children, it is the last hour, and you have heard that Antichrist is coming, so now many antichrists have arisen.... Every spirit that does not confess that Jesus Christ has come in the flesh, is not of God, but is of Antichrist, of whom you have heard that he is coming and now is already in the world."[215]

As he studied the activities of the enemies of the Church in his day, Campanella went on to identify them as forerunners of the Antichrist. Among the armed precursors of the Antichrist he indicated the king and queen of England, the kings of Scotland, Denmark, Norway, the princes of Saxony, the Palatinate, Brandenburg, the Conde and his Huguenots, the Orange family, the Stuarts, King Cristierno and the other heads of the French, Swiss, the Bohemians, the Swabians with other heretics of the times. Then there was the false prophet Mohammed who multiplied and scattered his militant sect everywhere like a plague. This pestilence invaded Asia, Africa, Greece, Hungary, in all almost three hundred kingdoms. Certainly Mohammed has to be

---

[214] Tommaso Campanella, *De Antichristo* (Roma: Centro Internazionale Di Studi Umanistici, 1965), Latin on left page, Italian on right page, pp. 11, 13.

[215] 1 John 2:18; 4:3.

counted as a precursor of the Antichrist for he denies the Father and the Son, and empties out Jesus by denying His divinity. All of these heretics are like the heretic Cerinthus, whom St. John avoided like the plague; all these heretics divide Christ, deny His divinity and hope to create a paradise for wicked, unclean, unrepentant sinners. In truth, only Italy and Spain have thus far been saved from the heretics and the Mohammedans, though in the past these nations suffered much at the hands of the latter. Yet even today these nations are experiencing very bitter trials because of the heretics. For as St. Bernard said: "They [these Christian nations] were embittered because of the trials they suffered at the hands of tyrants; they were even more embittered because of the trials they suffered at the hands of heretics and they are now most embittered because they are suffering betrayal from their own Pharisaical children and sophists, from whom there can never proceed true Christian peace." Campanella concludes that he has demonstrated from the prophets of old and from those of his own day that the Church is once again the slave of the Babylonia of infidels, Mohammedans, heretics, schismatics, sophists, and hypocrites. And she will remain such a slave until the time of the nations is accomplished and a new Cyrus shall arise as her liberator. Campanella adds that Sts. Bridget, Catherine of Sienna, and Dionisio the Carthusian, together with other holy persons, are awaiting the Savior's coming, which they had foreseen in private visions. Thus, the Antichrist's seat of authority is presently being established and many of his horns of power have already appeared. In fact, Aristotle, Averroes, and Machiavelli, who are popular subjects of study in the schools, are creating many antichrists—young men who graduate from the schools imbued with their falsities and who become chalices brimming over with the wrath of God, which they pour out on the sun, the hierarchy of the Church, the secular princes, and the doctrine of Christ, obliterating the light of revelation with their clouds of endless heresies. Some of these heresies have swept down from the North where Calvin, Wycliffe, Luther, and legions of Protestants are ravaging the flock of Christ. At the same time and in a similar manner, but coming from the East and South, the Mohammedan heresies have created black clouds of novel opinions in the primitive Christian world. Then, too, the terrible schism that has divided the Muscovite and Greek Christians has torn the beautiful tunic of Christ. Therefore, we must conclude with St. Gregory the Great and with St. Bernard that the stage is set for the arrival of the Antichrist. This historical hour has been prepared, concludes Campanella, by bad religious, heresiarchs, pseudo-prophets, new Pharisees and Sadducees. All the Fathers of the Church agree that a host of precursor antichrists must prepare the way for *l'Antichristo Massimo*, for the Super-Antichrist, even if they disagree on the individual person who will be the Antichrist. Even the Protestants agree with us on the point concerning the cloud of precursor antichrists that will be the advance guard of *The Antichrist*.[216]

Campanella presents another serious insight concerning the role of the Antichrist. He states that not only are godless tyrants, false prophets, and heresiarchs types of the Antichrist, but the kingdoms they capture and corrupt, the movements they organize and direct, the evil philosophies of life they spread and the sects they spawn are also symbolically to be called antichrists and precursors of the Antichrist. There are examples of this type of interpretation in Holy Scripture. In Daniel and in the Apocalypse the Antichrist is described under

---

[216] Campanella, op. cit., pp. 13, 15.

the name of the great multiple beast. By the beast, Daniel means not only a single man who is the head, as when he indicates Alexander the Great as the one-horned goat, and Darius, King of Persia, as the two-horned ram, but Daniel is also indicating their kingdoms. Then, too, when the sacred writer speaks of Ammon, Moab, Esau, and Israel, he is pointing out not only the individuals who bore this name in life, but also their clan, tribe, kingdom. So too when the Antichrist is mentioned his kingdom is also considered as the Antichrist. Thus in Daniel again, the lion means the king and the kingdom of the Assyrians; the bear the king and kingdom of the Persians; the leopard the king and kingdom of the Greeks; and the fourth beast with ten horns points to the king and kingdom of the Romans. But perhaps the best example to use in demonstrating this analogy is that found in the New Testament. The name *Christ* is applied not only to the incarnate Son of God, but to the Church herself, the kingdom of God, the Mystical Body of which He is the head.[217]

Campanella here touches a truth developed more explicitly and brilliantly by later theologians and philosophers. The Church is described today as the prolongation of Christ in time and the history of mankind. It was always known by prophets and holy men that evil is not merely personal but social and seeks a society of subjects for its permanent establishment as the City of Satan opposed to the City of God. Thus evil movements are merely apes of social movements toward God and goodness. For God is goodness itself. As such He tends to diffuse and share His goodness with others. But God is an all-holy Family, the Blessed Trinity, and He wants to share His holiness

[217] Ibid., pp. 15, 17.

with men through the prism of the family. He wants to establish a society of sanctified subjects. Man is lost or saved in families, societies, churches, movements. He loses himself eternally if he remains in evil societies founded by precursor antichrists; he is saved eternally if he perseveres in the society of the saints founded by Christ Himself in His Church. The Family of Holiness, the Blessed Trinity, has decreed from all eternity that the members of the family of man should be sanctified by their acceptance in adoration, love, and service of the divine family. Christ is the only way to incorporation into the glorified communion of saints. The Antichrist and his shadows, personal and societal, are the way to the dismal alternative, the community of the wicked in the City of Satan.

Perhaps the most tragic example in all history of antichrists leading a nation astray is to be found in what happened in Jerusalem when Christ was brought to trial before Annas, Caiphas, and Pilate. The high priest Caiphas, the former high priest and his father-in-law, Annas, the Sanhedrin, the chief priests and the Pharisees—all united in a conspiracy, not only rejected Christ and had him unjustly executed, but they also prevented the nation at large of the Chosen People from accepting the Redeemer God had sent them. St. Paul, recalling with sorrow this crime of his nation, would gladly have exchanged his own salvation, were such a deed morally permissible, for the return of his countrymen from the ranks of the Antichrist to the ranks of the followers of Christ. Another insight into the relationship between the precursor of the Antichrist and the kingdom, movement, or sect he guides and corrupts is revealed here. The personal figure of the Antichrist fades and dies after a few years, but his movement usually survives for centuries after, causing unmeasured spiritual ruination to millions upon millions, to nation upon nation throughout the whole world. To this day, the Chosen People have not recovered from the betrayal of their leaders some well nigh two thousand years ago; to this day they have not accepted Christ. And to this day there are millions of Protestants, Mohammedans, and other heretics who, through no fault of their own, are afflicted with blindness toward the truth because of the sickness they inherited from their antichrist ancestors.

We have considered in the previous chapter Newman's treatment of several anticipations of the Antichrist that have already occurred in history. In that treatment Newman's most recent example of a precursor of the Antichrist was the revolt of France against the Church and the persecution the eldest Daughter of the Church inflicted on the faithful under the Jacobin leaders, which reached its bloody climax during the Reign of Terror. That was about two centuries ago. Since that time many more shadows of the Antichrist have appeared in history. We want to study a few of them now. For they are infinitely more cunning, far crueler, better organized, and amazingly more competent in burning down the world. The Church is bleeding at their hands; Christ is dying in countless millions. Bishops, priests, religious in the tens of thousands have been imprisoned, exiled, separated from families, from the faithful, and even murdered. Thousands of Christian churches and schools have been closed; thousands of schools dedicated to the teaching of militant atheism have been opened. The preaching of the Gospel, the performance of corporal and spiritual works of mercy have been forbidden to bishops, priests, faithful. And not infrequently the faithful are placed under so-called Catholic bishops, priests, and superiors who turn out to be men of the godless government instead of men of God, hirelings instead of shepherds. And under pressure from such Judases the poor faithful are often compelled to hawk atheistic propaganda in the cause of the coming Antichrist and his master Satan. Millions of believers stray like sheep without a shepherd; they are also under twenty-four-hour surveillance by secret police. Tens of millions of children of Christian parents are forcibly incorporated in the red pioneers, march behind blood-red banners and are brought up in savage hatred of God, Church, and country.

But perhaps in order to better understand the all-pervading crises of our times—religious, moral, social, political—and the better to prepare for the coming catastrophes, it would first be well to get a panoramic view of the dark disorders inflicted on the Church in the past by countless shadows of Antichrist. In his *Short History of the Church*, Monsignor Philip Hughes summed up the situation of the Church at the end of the second century thus:

> Already we are seeing the appearance of types that will never cease to reappear throughout two thousand years; Catholics who propose to explain Catholicism by synthesis with the intellectual life of the time; Catholics who look back from the difficulties of the moment to a far-off golden age of primitive faith; Catholics who turn from an official teaching that does not encourage their personal likings to an alleged private inspiration that sets them apart from ordinary teaching. In one sense Church History is a web where threads such as these do but cross and recross.[218]

In one sense the history of the Catholic Church is a long procession in which precursors of the Antichrist appear, age after

---

[218] Philip Hughes, *Short History of the Church* (London: Burns & Oates, 1967).

age, to attempt the destruction of the Catholic Church. Our Lord promised that the gates of hell would not prevail against His Church. And the Church overcomes each successive assault of antichrists through the fidelity of that remnant of her citizens who refuse to succumb to despair and are willing to die for the Faith. It is said by many that the Church is presently suffering the greatest crisis of her long history. Yet this reality should not be an excuse for abandoning her. Catholics do not become members of Holy Church because of their merely human spiritual leaders, whatever their rank or moral stature. Catholics do not do Christ nor His Church a favor by adhering in faith and baptism to them. Rather Christ and His Church bestow on mankind the pearl of greatest price by receiving its members into His Mystical Body, the one Ark of Salvation, however battered or storm-tossed she may be. Christ grants human persons the greatest privilege imaginable on earth by choosing them to be members of His kingdom on earth.

There are truly dark disorders in the Catholic Church today and in the darkness many souls become disoriented and tend to lose their way. They become confused, unable to put events into their proper perspective; they become irritated when there is no sign of light and are tempted to panic; they become angered when led astray by false shepherds and are tempted to bolt from the flock of Christ, to go off on their own.

Jean Ousset, who ranks among the world's most distinguished writers, restores a sense of perspective to embattled Catholics. He reminds us that a time of dark disorder is a time for standing fast and fighting. In the darkness on Calvary, Mary and John remained standing beside the cross. Many of Christ's disciples—including the first pope—fled. Dark disorder, then, is a challenge to fidelity, to take our stand beside Mary and John beneath the cross of the dying Christ. The devil and his anti-christs never give up, nor will ever give up, as long as the time of man's trial and pilgrimage on earth lasts. Soldiers of Christ must match this determination for evil with their own determination for sanctity. Then Jean Ousset presents a long list of "dark disorders" with which many antichrists have scourged the Mystical Body of Christ throughout the ages. Heresies, schisms, revolts, persecutions, despicable betrayals, all hurled at the Bride of Christ to destroy her.

2nd Century: Gnosticism, Docetism (condemned by St. John the Evangelist), Marionism, Montanism

3rd Century: Manicheans

4th Century: Eutychians, Donatists, Macedonians, Helvidians, Arians

5th Century: Monophysites, Nestorians, Pelagians

6th Century: Semi-Pelagians

7th Century: Menethelites

8th Century: Iconoclasts

9th Century: Iconoclasts

10th Century: Simony and other abuses

11th Century: Berengarians

12th Century: Albigenses, Waldenses

13th Century: Albigenses

14th Century: Wycliffe

15th Century: The "Great Schism," two antipopes at one time, and other grave disorders

16th Century: Calvin, Luther, Zwingli, Henry VIII

17th Century: Jansenists, Rationalists

18th Century: Jansenists, Quietists

19th Century: Modernists, Old Catholics

20th Century: Neo-Modernism, Teilhardism[219]

Newman reminds us that during the time of the Arian heresy, it was the bishops, priests, theologians that fell for the false doctrine; the laity remained faithful and supplied the Church with many martyrs. But even among the bishops and theologians the opposing parties at times were not clearly defined. Not too many enjoyed the clarity, serenity, and sureness of an Athanasius or a Hilary. One could not always point unmistakably to heretics and schismatics on one side and with certainty to the orthodox on the other. To complicate matters even more, emperors entered the fray on both sides and called councils on their own authority. The poor popes had to be diplomatically agile and yet doctrinally firm. For crises of heresies from the very beginning even to our own day leave Catholics experiencing "dark times," not often knowing which side to take or who is on what side. There are sharp disagreements among bishops, priests, theologians; each side claims to be defending a doctrine handed down in the deposit of the Faith; each claims to have the true sense of the Church's living tradition and that it is really the faithful witness

---

[219] Jean Ousset, "Dark Disorder within the Church," *Christian Order*, January 1974, pp. 19-33.

to its generation on the matter in dispute. When such dark and chaotic disorder reigns on matters of faith and morals, many other pernicious fruits are produced by this tree of heretical controversy. Such are suspicions, betrayals, cowardice, polemics, insults, riots, tortures, murders, apostasies. Think of the "dark disorder" created by the heretic Dioscoros at the Council of Chalcedon in 451, the infamous council where Flavian, the orthodox bishop, and the papal legates were violently, so violently, attacked that Flavian died three days later from shock and the injuries received, while the papal delegates escaped. Pope Leo the Great rejected this council entirely calling it *non iudicium sed latrocinium*, "not a council at all, but a get together of bandits." Consider the "dark disorder" of the Great Schism with two and even three popes hurling abuse at one another to the scandal of the whole Christian world. Reflect on the black disorder of the Council of Basel that declared the pope suspect. Then, too, look back on the dark disorder of the trial of Joan of Arc at the hands of a bishop, a vice inquisitor, several abbots, and the cream of the doctors of Paris university who were later to become the *periti*, "experts" at the infamous Council of Basel, which opened shortly after St. Joan was executed by being burned at the stake.[220]

Modern Intellectual Shadows of the Antichrist

The examples just cited give us some ancient shadows of the Antichrist. Now we will consider more modern successors to those shades. There are three main sources of what I consider the most dangerous revolution the Church has ever had to face, a revolution that is still scourging her severely. This revolution is a process of "self-demolition," as Pope Paul VI once called it, and

---

[220] Ibid., pp. 27, 28.

it aims at driving the Church to the end of "the road to perdition." Modernism is that heresy called by St. Pius X, who temporarily halted its spread in 1908, "the synthesis of all heresies."[221] The trinity of parents responsible for the perversion known as Modernism are: (1) its religious ancestor is the Protestant Reformation; (2) its philosophical parent is the Enlightenment; (3) its political pedigree comes from the French Revolution. Father A. Vermeesch, S.J. has written: "The essential error of Modernism is nothing less than the perversion of dogma, the critique of supernatural knowledge according to the false principles of contemporary philosophy."[222] The fallen away, excommunicated priest-intellectual the Abbe Loisy, called the Father of Modernism, agrees with the Vermeesch statement. He writes: "In reality all Catholic theology, even its fundamental principles, the general philosophy of religion, divine law, and the laws that govern the knowledge of God, come up for judgment before this new court of assize."[223] And Professor M. Perrin, in his classic work on this heresy, *Modernisme dans L'Eglise*, corroborates the statement of Abbe Loisy: "Modernism is that humanitarian movement whose ambition is to eliminate God from all social life."

Thus, the Abbe Loisy is certainly an intellectual precursor of the Antichrist. He adhered to, wrote in favor of, taught a heresy against the authority of the Church that aims at destroying the Catholic Faith and Church. Other modern intellectual shadows of the Antichrist that have subordinated the Catholic

[221] St. Pius X, Pascendi Dominici Gregis: *On the Doctrine of the Modernists* (Boston: St. Paul Editions, 1907), pp. 48–51.
[222] A. Vermeesch, "Modernism," in *The Catholic Encyclopedia*, Vol. X., ed. Charles George Herbermann (New York: Gilmary Society, 1913), pp. 415–421.
[223] Ibid., p. 415.

Faith to contemporary philosophy are prominent atheists whose great influence is very much with us today. It was the philosopher Feuerbach who formulated in precise terms the modern humanistic atheism that is so widespread today. In his *Essence of Religion*, he wrote: "I aim to change the friends of God into the friends of man; believers into thinkers, worshippers into workers, candidates for the other world into students of this world; Christians, who, on their own confession are half-animal and half-angel, into men, whole men."[224] Earlier he had pointed out his plan for secularizing man when he wrote that he would transform "theologians into anthropologians ... religious and political footmen of a celestial and terrestrial monarchy and aristocracy into free, self-reliant citizens of earth."[225] Nietzsche, in his crusade to develop an elite of supermen, turned out to be another giant and intellectual forerunner of the Antichrist. He proclaimed "the death of God," not merely the God of the metaphysicians but of the theologians as well. Andre Gide shrewdly analyzed the sickness of Nietzsche's spirit to be an insane jealousy of Jesus Christ. Nietzsche's wrote his *The Antichrist* to oppose Christ and in his last work, *Ecce Homo*, sets himself up as the victorious rival of Him whose teaching he proposed to supplant. Nietzsche suffered from a God-complex he hoped to share with the superatheists he planned to create. We read in his *The Antichrist*:

> The Christian conception of God—God as god of the sick, God as spider, God as a spirit—is one of the most corrupt conceptions of the divine ever attained on earth.

[224] Ludwig Feuerbach, *The Essence of Religion*, trans. George Eliot (New York: Harper Torchbooks, 1957), p. 170.
[225] Ibid., p. 14.

It may even represent the low-water mark in the descending development of divine types. God degenerated into the *contradiction* of life, instead of being its transfiguration and eternal Yes! God as the declaration of war against life, against nature, against the will to live! God—the formula for every slander against "this world," for every lie about the "beyond!" God—the deification of nothingness, the will to nothingness pronounced holy![226]

Following in the footsteps of the individualistic revolution of 1789 that, under the influence of Rousseau and the Encyclopedists, made an idol of abstract Liberty, Proudhon, a nineteenth-century socialist, attempted to set revolution in opposition to revelation. He invited the Catholic Church to preach a revolutionary morality to the sovereign people. He asked her to abolish whatever is theological and ecclesiastical in her institution. He advised her to relinquish all her possessions to the commune, to release all monks, nuns, and priests from perpetual vows, in short, to "desacralize" herself, and to do away with clergy, with hierarchy. Let her preach revolution and her salvation will be assured in this world. This was the same temptation offered the Church by Modernism, which asked the Church to lead a movement to humanitarian progress in this world. In imitation of her Master, the Church refused to accept this worldly mission.[227] One need only reflect on these demands for a short time to realize how all-pervasively the Proudhonian perfume has penetrated religious events in the Church since the close of the Second Vatican Council.

---

[226] Friedrich Nietzsche, *The Antichrist*, in *The Portable Nietzsche*, trans. Walter Kaufmann (New York: Viking Press, 1954), pp. 585–586.

[227] Joseph Proudhon, *La Justice dans la Revolution et dans L'Eglise*, Vol. 3 (Paris: Garnier, 1858), pp. 602–603.

Karl Marx rejected Proudhon's dreams as being reactionary and utopian Socialism. Marx also intended to liberate man, as did the other godless thinkers mentioned above. But he was determined to direct man toward a different goal. Rousseau placed all his hope for liberating man in the "general will"; Proudhon in "justice" attained through the organ of collective reason functioning in discussion groups discovering ideas and pursuing rights. But Marx placed his hope in the "proletariat" whose period of dictatorship would fade into the classless society, after it had crushed classes through class warfare. For Marx, religion and God had to be abolished as drugs that kept man enslaved in a destitute existence.[228] Here again we have testimony of effective intellectual shadows of the Antichrist who prepared individuals and societies, indeed whole nations, as godless subjects ready to be dominated by the coming Antichrist.

Step by step the liberation, which in the eighteenth century granted man a godless individualistic freedom and democracy, and in the nineteenth century granted him godless socialistic egalitarianism, expanded from the field of thought and burst, in an everonrushing flood, into the field of man's multifaceted activities or conduct. Freud gave this liberation a new face; he taught man to liberate himself from sexual repressions that lie at the root of his fears and failures. Marx wanted to destroy religious alienation through the abolition of capitalistic property. Freud saw religion as a collective neurosis that psychoanalysis had the mission to dissolve.[229] Taking these positions as a point of departure, Wilhelm Reich advanced further. He proclaimed the necessity for a sexual revolution capable of

---

[228] Marcel Clement, *Christ and Revolution* (New Rochelle, NY: Arlington House Publishers, 1974), p. 40.
[229] Ibid., p. 41.

establishing "a revolutionary morality" of sexual drives. Thus man would be freed from capitalistic morality, from Church morality, the repressive morality of the dominating class.[230]

Coherent with the sexual revolution, which is pivotal to a cultural revolution, are the demands made by an agitated, titillated public today. In the name of total liberation the public demands the widespread use of contraception, the right to free and state-financed abortion, the right to trial marriage, the right to choose homosexuality, to enter lesbian and homosexual marriages. These are not marginal demands but are essentially linked to the movement of the total liberation of man from God, from morality, from restrictive positive laws, from the canons of reason. Progressively these demands deny the very nature of man; they are now moving to the denial or cancellation of the marriage institution as such. Before women were free not to marry; now the rule is being changed to "women must not marry."[231]

Such is the scope, in its full impetus, of the unlimited liberation of man, of this godless utopia. Rousseau dreamed of a political, Marx of an economic, and Freud of a sexual liberation. But all of these intellectual forerunners of the Antichrist are agreed on this fundamental dogma. The complete liberation of man must be, can only be, founded on his total liberation from the God of revelation and the religion and Church He established. Today we are witnessing the final fruits of these pernicious doctrines. Though opposed to each other in accidentals for a short time, these various godless philosophies of life are now commingling into a system of thought, a code of

[230] Ibid., p. 41.
[231] Ibid., p. 42.

acting, not necessarily in the minds of the intellectual shadows of the Antichrist, the idea-men, the ideologues, the theoreticians, but in the collective mentality of the masses who, in their mad rush for the utopia of unrestricted liberty, are not even aware of the fine differences of opinion expressed among their intellectual manipulators. The system of thought among these intellectual antichrists may be multiform, but it is unified in its basic inspiration—hatred of God and of religion. This hatred is expressed by a rejection of human nature defined as a creature dependent on a Creator and his established cosmic, moral, spiritual, and supernatural order. Rousseau put it well: "He who dares to attempt to found a people must feel himself capable, so to speak, of changing human nature."[232] For Marx the collective man "creates" himself throughout history. "For the Socialist Man, so-called world history is nothing other than the creation of man through human work."[233]

Thus, liberated man, resenting his essential creaturehood and God the author of it, rejects God himself and promotes himself from creaturehood to Godhood. It is the same rebellion of the old serpent Satan: "I will not serve! I will rise above the throne of God! I will be God!" It must be stressed that this mania for man to recreate himself is the source of inspiration for Freud, Reich, Marcuse, and all the intellectual shades of the Antichrist. Marcuse blames man's incapacity to attain beatitude "in time." Thus, the "idea of integral human liberation must necessarily contain the vision of the struggle against time.... But the fatal enemy of lasting gratification is TIME, the inner

[232] J. J. Rousseau, *Complete Works*, Vol. VI (Paris: Éditions Dalibon, 1824), p. 4.
[233] J. Y. Calvez, *La Pensée de Karl Marx* (Paris: Éditions du Seuil, 1956), pp. 301, s. 99.

finiteness."[234] For man who would be God, there must also be the exhilarating experience of living in the divine milieu of limitless perfection. Man must be eternal, above time, immutable, beyond containment, absolutely perfect. Our intellectual shadows of the Antichrist, imitating Satan deceiving our first parents, have promised rebellious man these divine honors and conditions, but they cannot fulfill their promises. Like Satan they are liars and murderers from the beginning. For when man strives to become God on Satan's or his own terms and not on God's terms, he becomes his own end, attempting in arrogant pride an impossible self-delusion—to change his human nature into the nature of God, to recreate himself through rebellion, through work, to conquer time and all human finitude. This way lies madness and suicide for totally liberated man who then turns on his fellowmen and inflicts on them the "abomination of desolation."

Modern Activist Forerunners of the Antichrist

Thus far we have briefly analyzed some of the major, modern intellectual forerunners of the Antichrist, the brilliant theoreticians who are preparing mankind for the coming of the kingdom of the Antichrist. We have indicated how their various false philosophies are gradually commingling, becoming incarnated and unified in the consciousness and conduct of the secularized masses. For ideas have consequences and violent ideas—such as violate nature and nature's God—will produce violent leaders inspired by such ideas who will strive to implement false philosophies of life by violently imposing them on society. Now we know

[234] Herbert Marcuse, *Eros and Civilization* (Boston: Beacon Press, 1955), p. 191.

that the Antichrist will be a political genius, a conqueror of and ruling dictator over all the kingdoms of this world, as well as an intellectual genius. Hence not only will he make use of brilliant heretics to lay the intellectual foundations of his kingdom, but he will also make use of charismatic activists, politically talented, proficient leaders, master tacticians who will ruthlessly establish his dictatorship of power.

Let us identify some of the sinister political forerunners of the Antichrist whom the intellectual shadows of the Antichrist begot for our age of violence. Hitler, a power maniac with a cunning, crooked wisdom, proclaimed Nietzsche the official philosopher of Nazism. Slight adjustments were made in Nietzsche's godless philosophy of superman so as to render it efficient in the spread of Nazism. The Superrace replaced the Superman; the blond, German, pure race became the idol of the Germans and the master of all other races. Naturally, Nietzsche's violent virtues of the will over reason were kept and developed to a pitch of frenzy. They were then put to serve in a militarism that sought to dominate all Europe. Hitler, the activist genius and forerunner of the activist Antichrist dictator-to-come, after persecuting all religions and making a religion of race, plunged Europe and the whole world into a war that slaughtered millions upon millions of soldiers and innocent noncombatants and destroyed whole cities and nations. Nazism made of Catholic Europe a material and spiritual wasteland in which the victorious seeds of godless Communism have taken root and flourished. Mussolini was another politically active forerunner of the Antichrist; he divinized the omnicompetent Socialist State. He joined Hitler in a war from which he hoped to come forth as the emperor of the newly refounded, post-Christian Roman Empire. And he fought the Church of Christ over the souls of youth whom he would degrade to being slaves of the religion of Fascism. Stalin, child of Marx's ideology, was one of the bloodiest political forerunners of the Antichrist. He adapted Marx's Communism to the benefit of his own lust for total power. For over seventy-four years now, militant organized atheism has been crushing the Christian soul of Holy Mother Russia. Since the Second World War it has tortured the Christian nations behind the Iron Curtain. In the Far East, under the bloody direction of Mao Tse-tung, Communist atheism has put eight hundred million Chinese into a vast concentration camp behind the China Wall and the Bamboo Curtain. While in the Western Hemisphere, the bloody dictator Fidel Castro has reduced to material and spiritual destitution some 7 million Catholic Cubans. Thus the godless plight and plague of Communism has exacted from the human race a chilling, exorbitant price in blood, lives, and terror. It is estimated that in all his purges, collectivization plans, and persecutions of religions, Stalin murdered some 60 to 90 million people. In China Mao was even more ferocious, having a much larger population to torture; he is said to have massacred from 94 to some 130 million. Then, too, the costs in sheer terror are incalculable; hundreds of concentration camps hold tens of millions of slave workers; a vast internal machinery for spying and repression strikes terror into the hearts of all. Never before, not even in a world that included German Nazism and Italian Fascism, has a regime spawned such gigantic, competent organs of surveillance, denunciation, punishment, censorship, and intimidation. No governments in all history have invented so many "crimes against the state" or applied the death penalty so extensively as have Communist regimes. Nor have any governments used judicial trials as such exquisite means of torture and confession. In former revolutions, terror and torture ended with victory. In Russia, in China, in Cuba persecution and brutality have grown in scope and ferocity after the security and power of the new tyrants was assured. It is a fair guess that over the years no fewer than 50 million Soviet citizens experienced the hell of the slave-labor system for periods of one to twenty-five years. And the millions and millions of Chinese prisoners working in slave communes will probably never be accurately calculated. Then there are the cruel psychological costs to the human race of godless Communism in its absolute control of the flow of news and ideas of truth. Andre Gide, after his journey through the USSR that cured him of his illusions about Communism, said: "I doubt that in any country in the world, even Hitler's Germany, is thought less free, more bowed down, more terrorized."[235] Moreover, the godless zealots of Communism have established centers of spying and subversion in every country in the world. Their call to revolution and violent rebellion is beamed everywhere; it is broadcast twenty-four hours a day, for these centers work as effectively, ceaselessly, and secretly as the law of gravity, pulling down to destruction every civil and religious community striving for social justice and spiritual peace. Eugene Lyons in his book *Workers' Paradise Lost* emphasizes the cost to the world of triumphant, godless Communism:

> The communist blight, I repeat, is everywhere. The havoc it works has not been limited to governments and institutions. Its poisonous effects have been wider and deeper on the minds of men the world over. Sincere progressives in all countries have been disoriented and corrupted by support of, or flirtation with communist doctrines and practices. Men and women of intellectual and moral stature—among

[235] Eugene Lyons, *Workers' Paradise Lost* (New York: Paperback Library, 1967), p. 365.

them educators, and religious leaders who influence young minds—not to mention the millionfold Lumpen-intelligentsia in the noncommunist world, found themselves defending slave labor, glorying in the Big Lie, shouting "Hoorah for murder!" when the killers were communists.[236]

The territorial and ideological ambitions of God-hating Nazism and Communism were insatiable. One remembers the cynical Stalin-Hitler Pact that unleashed World War II. It allowed Nazi Germany and Communist Russia to invade and divide between themselves Catholic Poland. Here is another frightful example of how the political forerunners of the Antichrist, and their totalitarianisms of brown or red coloration, so easily and quickly commingled to cooperate in the rape of a Catholic nation. This need not have astonished anyone, for both dictatorships had plenty in common; both eroded traditional intellectual and ethical standards; both provided a rationale for inhumane activities under "revolutionary" or "liberating" slogans. Self-deception and self-justification, springing from colossal pride, enabled these inhumane regimes to enact programs of deplorable cruelties with what they considered to be clear consciences. After all, godless tyrants regard terror and torture merely as superficial blemishes on society, necessary cauterizations for the liberation of man from addiction to the hallucinations of God and religion. Hence, today there is no crisis anywhere in the world—from Asia to the Caribbean, from Africa to the Middle East—in which the blood-drenched hands of militant Communism are not deeply involved. Since 1917 the Communist, godless shadows of the Antichrist have kept the

[236] Ibid., p. 374.

earth in continuous bloody turmoil, ferocious civil wars, competing subversionary tactics, contradictory propaganda campaigns all fomented and encouraged for the purpose of creating a mankind without God, a mankind hating God, a humanity united, under the shadows of the Antichrist, in its fight against Christ and His Mystical Body.

In the Far East, in another great power, Satan held sway during those same years over the Japanese people. They were spiritually enslaved to the idolatry of emperor-worship. Their politically activist leaders were also militarists bent on undertaking expansionist wars at the cost of their neighbors. Hence these activist precursors of the Antichrist joined with Nazi Germany, Communist Russia, and Fascist Italy in World War II. One good result of Japan's defeat is that the nation has abandoned the religion of emperor-worship. But, on the other hand, it has been so eaten out by the secularism and materialism of the West, that it has become the greatest anti-life clinic in the world, ploughing under every year millions of its most precious resources—its babies whom it murders in the womb. This avalanche of murders against innocent, defenseless persons is already a great victory for the forces that are the precursors of the Antichrist in Japan.

But if the atheistic dictators turned out to be monsters, if the emperor of Japan demanded worship from his subjects and victories from his soldiers, the leaders of the free world were hardly models of reason. In a way they turned out to be just as immoral and perhaps even crueler because for a while they posed as champions of human dignity and freedom. England went into World War II to preserve the freedom of Poland; the U.S. entered the same to preserve Europe from the dictatorships of Nazism and Fascism. By accident, because of Hitler's blunders, the Allies found themselves fighting at the side of the godless

Russian regime. But bearing arms together with that immoral monster, the headiness of their victory and the temptation to play God together in rearranging the world to suit their whims, led our leaders to betray the cause of the human race—peace with justice. Churchill and Roosevelt entered the power game against Stalin and lost to that consummate power maniac. At Yalta they betrayed Poland and all the Eastern European countries, agreeing to Stalin's complete control of them as satellites of the Soviet hegemony. The rest of the world would be divided into spheres of influence under the domination of the U.S., Great Britain, and China.[237] Hence, the peace finally worked out was little more than an agreement among power-hungry thieves. Leaders such as Roosevelt and Churchill who betrayed the basic rights of their own allies and sold them into slavery can only be considered precursors, shadows of the Antichrist. For, though they had the opportunity as victors powerful enough to establish an order of justice and peace, they established instead worldwide injustice and disorder. For they flirted with Communist power, initiated its lustful immorality and allowed Communism's armed and organized way of life to become the most universal, effective agent for evil in the world. If the hegemony of the Antichrist is predicted to be the most universal, treacherous, cruel, and murderous confederation of nations ever organized in an evil cause, then Churchill and Roosevelt who, knowingly and willingly, cooperated in the creation of the worldwide Communist hegemony can justly be called precursors of the coming Antichrist. Consider the historical evidence.

[237] Robert I. Gannon, *The Cardinal Spellman Story* (New York: Doubleday Company, 1962), p. 222.

On September 2, 1943, Cardinal Spellman, "the personal representative" of President Roosevelt to the Holy See, had an hour-and-a-half conversation alone with the president. During the course of that conversation the cardinal learned from the president of the United States, the most powerful man in the world, at that moment considered to be "on top of the world," the following dismal news: 1) At the end of the war Communist Russia would be allowed to take under her sphere of influence Finland, the Baltic States, and the eastern half of Poland, Bessarabia. 2) The European people would have to endure Russian domination, in the hope that in ten or twenty years they would be able to live well with the Russians. 3) The United States and Britain could not oppose the Russians. 4) Austria, Hungary, and Croatia would be allowed to fall under the Russian protectorate. 5) The future League of Nations must be made up of only the big four—U.S., Great Britain, Russia, and China. 6) Small states would form a consultative assembly without right to decide or vote. For example, at the armistice with Italy, the Greeks, Yugoslavs, and French asked to be co-signers. "We simply turned them down," said Roosevelt. For they have no right to sit in where the big ones are. Only the Russians were admitted because they are big, strong, and simply impose themselves. Thus, the coming treaty of peace and the League of Nations was to be founded on the principle of "might makes right," not on the principle of Justice and Liberty.[238] To put it mildly, Cardinal Spellman was shocked at the callous indifference of his "dear friend" to the rights and liberties of millions of people in many peace-loving nations who, when they could, fought as America's allies. In an earlier first meeting, the president and

[238] Ibid., pp. 222, 223.

the cardinal had agreed against their critics about America entering the war, that this was a special war, not a war to save any particular country like Great Britain; it was a war to save human liberty without which man could not achieve his ideals in life. And now the president of the United States was airily consigning millions of human beings to political slavery, labor camps, and execution cellars. French president Charles De Gaulle was also shocked by Roosevelt's nonchalant revelation to him of this heartless plan. He recounts this high level tête-à-tête with Roosevelt in his *Memoires of the War*. De Gaulle never had any use for Roosevelt from that time on.[239] It was clear to both the cardinal and De Gaulle that the president of the United States, taking Churchill along with him, had capitulated to Communist secularism, atheism, and totalitarianism after the Allies had successfully fought these same spiritual plagues in Nazism, Fascism, and Japanese militarism. This inability and unwillingness to see the struggle between atheistic and confessional forces in its metaphysical, transcendent dimensions was the cause of the colossal blunders of Churchill and Roosevelt, blunders that have brought our modern world to the verge of another, this time nuclear, world war. Both Roosevelt and Churchill barred De Gaulle, who saw the struggle in its proper perspective, from the Yalta Conference where the details of the betrayals were finalized in documentary form. But as far back as 1933 President Roosevelt's blindness on the nature of godless Communism and his superficial assessment of its threat to the freedom of all nations was already revealed in an interview he gave Father

---

[239] Charles De Gaulle, *Memoires of the War*, Vol. 3, 1944–46, trans. Richard Howard (New York: Simon & Schuster, 1960), pp. 90–102.

Edmund Walsh, S.J., founder of the School of Foreign Service at Georgetown University. Father Walsh related the incident in his book *Total Power*. Roosevelt asked Father Walsh's advice on whether the United States should recognize Soviet Russia. Father Walsh pointed out that if he did, he would be opening the United States to a flood of Soviet spies entering through diplomatic channels. He stressed that Communism was messianic, dead serious, in its drive to conquer all nations. The president laughed heartily, commenting that he could handle old Joe Stalin who was friendly and civil and only wanted peaceful relationships with the West. Needless to say, the president recognized Soviet Russia.[240] Such naivete in the president of the strongest nation in the world proved a serious blunder. The successors of Stalin, following his shrewd tactics, are gradually isolating America and her allies, while sapping their will to defend liberty. Already Russia and her allies have successfully gained control of vast regions of Asia, Africa, India, Cuba, and are moving ahead politically and militarily in Mexico, and in South and Central America. Everywhere they are advancing and the free world is shrinking and retreating. The allies of the Antichrist are growing in number, expanding ever further over the face of the globe and dominating more and more millions, even billions, of men.

We mention here two mind-boggling crimes which demonstrate that at base there is precious little difference between the inhumanity of godless Communism and that of the materialistic West. In September 1939, as a result of its invasion of Poland, the Red regime of Russia sent to concentration camps 200,000 Polish prisoners of war. Most of the Polish officers and several thousand soldiers were sent to camps at Starobelsk, Kozielsk, and Ostachkov.

[240] Edmund Walsh, *Total Power* (New York: Doubleday, 1948).

In April 1940 there were about 15,000 of them there, including 8,700 officers. Only 48 were ever seen again. In April 1943 the Germans announced the discovery of mass graves containing executed Poles in the Katyn forests near Smolensk. The bodies found at Katyn, 4,143 in number, represented only those who had been in the Kozielsk camp. What happened to the Poles in the other two camps remains unknown. The Nuremberg judges examined the Katyn Affair from July 1 to 3, 1946. There was no doubt left that these prisoners of war were killed in cold blood by the Russians and it is just about a foregone conclusion that the same tragic fate was met by the other 10,400 men.[241] There are solid stories that a number of Polish prisoners were packed into old barges and scuttled in the White Sea. There are other persistent stories of a mass execution and burial of thousands of Poles resembling Katyn in the neighborhood of Kharkov. Here is an example of mass execution carried out without trial against prisoners of war whose only crime was that of defending their country against godless, unjust aggressors. And the mass execution was carried out in complete secrecy as a routine administrative measure. It is hard to imagine that the Antichrist, when he comes to power, will be crueler or more efficient in persecuting the just than these competent forebears of his.

At the end of World War II, six million Soviet men, women, and children were stranded beyond their native borders. They had been imported as slave laborers and were liberated from the power of the Nazis by the victorious Allied armies. Several million of them refused to return to the hell of Communist Russia, for only hardships, humiliations, concentration camps, and

[241] Robert Conquest, *The Great Terror* (New York: Macmillan, 1969), pp. 482–483.

execution awaited them there. But to placate the Soviet dictator, the U.S. and its allies, under the direction of President Roosevelt, used force to repatriate these runaway subjects who were pleading for political asylum in the more humane countries of the West. One of the American prosecutors at Nuremberg, Thomas J. Dodd, later U.S. senator from Connecticut, reported on the matter:

> During my participation in the Nuremberg war crimes trials, in the postwar period, I learned something of the desperation and hatred and terror of the hundreds of thousands of Russian war prisoners and slave laborers held by the Nazis, whom we, through incredible ignorance, returned against their will to the Soviet authorities. My soul is still tormented by the nightmarish accounts of mass suicides, in which men slashed their wrists with tin cans and women jumped with their children from upper story windows rather than face return to Soviet Russia.[242]

While Allied forces were driving the desperate prisoners like cattle into trucks and trains, a Soviet Repatriation Commission was engaged in an all-sweeping manhunt to catch in its net every one of its terrified, hiding-out countrymen. In the end all but a half a million were herded back to Russia where they were treated like deserters and subjected to purges. Even the loyal ones were purged for, having been infected by the freedom of the West, they could no longer be reliable or useful for the Communist cause. The vast majority of these men never saw their families again, but were dispersed to alien areas in various labor camps and, like the executed Polish soldiers, lost forever to history

[242] Lyons, op. cit., pp. 133–134.

And here we would indicate one of the darkest deeds ever perpetrated by a big ally against a little ally that was under attack, engaged in a struggle for its very existence and actually winning that war against the Communists when it was struck down by its so-called defender of liberty. I speak of the John F. Kennedy Administration's cold, calculated, heavily financed destruction of the legitimate Ngo Dinh Diem government in South Vietnam. Falling for the Communist trap set by their burning of Buddhists, the leftist American press, led by the *New York Times*, accused the so-called Catholic regime of Diem of mounting a religious persecution by approving those burnings. As Diem so justly asked of an American reporter: "Why does the Western press keep calling this government Diem's Roman Catholic government? Kennedy is a Catholic but nobody calls his government the Roman Catholic Kennedy regime."[243]

What Diem probably did not know was that the anti-Catholic Liberal Party in New York City had given Kennedy about 210,000 votes, the actual margin with which he squeaked to victory over Nixon. Hence President Kennedy held in his possession an IOU, a reminder that at some time he would be called upon to repay the Liberal Party for services rendered in his victory. While Diem, the faithful Catholic, was defeating the Communists in his country, the Communists started the political ploy of burning Buddhists and the leftist press in America started the false propaganda that

---

[243] Marguerite Higgins, *Our Vietnam Nightmare* (New York: Harper and Row, 1965), p. 162. The author recalls her phone call to Roger Hilsman on hearing of the assassination of Diem thus: "'Congratulations, Roger,' I said. 'How does it feel to have blood on your hands?' 'Oh, come on now, Maggie,' said Roger. 'Revolutions are rough. People get hurt.'" Thus did Hilsman, Pilate-like, wash his conscience of the murder of an ally in which he was a chief mover.

Diem was behind it all. It was at this point that the Liberals made their demand to President Kennedy that Diem must go. The smear campaign accusing Diem of ordering the burnings was made despite the fact that Diem had some seventeen Buddhists in his government and a UN investigating committee found no evidence of governmental persecution of Buddhists. But the leftists were not to be inconvenienced by the truth. The gold-plated liberals and Communist sympathizers in the Kennedy camp hollered all the more for Diem's head. One was reminded of the Jewish crowd yelling for the crucifixion of Christ against the evidence of his innocence. The favorite liberal tactic was to undermine Diem's image by a flood of vicious rumors inundating press, radio, and TV. In fact, in the company of other priest friends and family relatives, I saw and heard President Kennedy on a Labor Day TV show, a year before the *coup d'etat* that destroyed Diem, call upon the people of Vietnam to change the head of their government if they hoped to continue getting American aid. While the Communists pushed mobocracy and murder in Vietnam, the leftist journalists in America scattered lies about Diem on the journalistic winds blowing in the whole world. New Frontiersmen were in hot pursuit of their designated victim. Their first ploy was to get the ambassador to Vietnam changed. So Ambassador Nolting was recalled. Then Kennedy shrewdly sent a Republican, whose faded image needed repolishing if he were to win the nomination in the upcoming convention, to do the dirty work of a Democratic administration. After all, if disaster followed the coup, it could be blamed on Ambassador Henry Cabot Lodge, the Republican with ardent aspirations for the White House. On his arrival in Vietnam, even before presenting his credentials to President Diem, Lodge first visited the Communist-infested Buddhists centers, insulting the president thereby by an act that violated every rule of diplomatic protocol. He also encouraged the generals and the radicals who were planning a *coup d'etat* by seeming to put the United States on their side.[244]

Meanwhile at the State Department in the United States the leaders of the Diem-must-go school, the high-ranking liberal leftists Averell Harriman, Assistant Secretary for Political Affairs, and Roger Hilsman, Assistant Secretary for Far Eastern Affairs, had George Ball, Undersecretary of State—whom they sought out on the Chevy Chase Golf Course—summarize by phone to President Kennedy—vacationing in Hyannis Port—the gist of a cablegram they were sending to South Vietnam. The "cleared" cablegram gave the green light to the Vietnam generals opposed to Diem to depose him by a *coup d'etat*.[245] The rest is ugly history; Diem was assassinated by his generals, the president of Vietnam whose personal incorruptibility was legendary. Vietnam and the U.S., after the assassination of President Kennedy in a similar manner three weeks later in Dallas, were then plunged into the maelstrom of a war they were destined to lose with frightful carnage to men and the destruction of mountains of material treasure. Today the Khmer Rouge monsters of the Communist regime are practicing genocide against Vietnam, Cambodia, and the surrounding captive tribes. Following the shameful American retreat from South Vietnam, hypocritically acclaimed as a "blessed peace," hundreds of thousands of the "boat people" drowned in the ocean or perished in huge refugee centers that were prevented from receiving essential foods and medicines.

The cast of participants that engineered this betrayal must be seen as types of the Antichrist. Religion, the Catholic religion,

[244] Ibid., p. 185.
[245] Ibid., p. 188.

was a key issue in this sordid affair, and like the Antichrist these atheistic liberals hated a ruler who was a practicing follower of Christ. Moreover, just as the Antichrist, while posing as the true Christ, will perform murderous and lying crimes, so too these participants in one of America's blackest betrayals, posing as champions of civil and religious liberties, knowingly lied about the true situation and performed deeds worthy of Satan—liar and murderer from the beginning. Moreover, when the Antichrist finishes his work, there will remain behind a bleak wasteland of intellectual darkness and bloody oceans of human sufferings. The tragic fact is that today in Vietnam, because of the American betrayal, atheistic Communism rules supreme in another nation; the name and light of Christ are anathema and the Catholic Church with its millions of faithful have sunk into the silence and slavery of a vast concentration camp.

An objection might be advanced that the political figures participating in these tragic historical events ought not to be projected as types of the Antichrist. For often these atheistic figures do not know about, do not reflect on, or if they know of him, reject outright the very idea of an Antichrist. The objection implies that the person can be considered a type of the Antichrist only if he knows about and consciously imitates the Antichrist. This is an erroneous conclusion. It springs from the fact that one implies that man can divide all history into sacred and secular compartments with no relationship existing between them. The fact is that man and history never existed, nor ever will exist, in a merely secular, natural dimension of being. God created man and called him to his destiny solely in a supernatural dimension of history. God's providence and economy of salvation functions only in a supernatural key. There never existed a wholly naturally good human race; there existed in the beginning only a supernaturally good human race, for the persons of our first parents were created in the holiness of grace as children of God destined for the face-to-face vision of God in heaven. Therefore, whatever actions man performs in history have supernatural effects for good or evil, whether the performer of these actions is a believer, a theist, or an atheist. There exists only salvational, supernatural history, however much man may, for his convenience, divide history in his mind into secular and sacred. The prophets of God, the men of faith, believers see and evaluate all human conduct *sub specie aeternitatis*, under the light of eternity. Thus Daniel, the prophet of God, saw in King Nebuchadnezzar of Babylon, who persecuted the Chosen People of God, the precursor of the final Antichrist. Whether King Nebuchadnezzar realized his role made no difference concerning this truth. The Maccabees saw in the wicked emperor Antiochus who destroyed the temple of Jerusalem, a true type of the Antichrist. Whether Antiochus believed in an Antichrist made little difference; he was doing the work of Satan, the work the final Antichrist would do with consummate skill. The popes saw in Attila the "scourge of God;" the Fathers saw in Nero a type of the Antichrist; St. John saw in the emperor Domitian a type of the Antichrist. Finally the example of Christ's vision will help us see this truth. Christ rebuked the head of the apostles St. Peter, immediately after proclaiming him the Rock and first pope, in these frightening words: "Get behind me Satan, for you are a scandal to me; for you do not mind the things of God, but those of men." Peter had attempted to dissuade Christ from accepting the Passion and death awaiting Him. Certainly subjectively, Peter thought he was advising Christ in kindness, sympathy, and love, hoping to save Him from that terrible fate. Peter never saw himself doing Satan's work. But the fact of the economy of salvation is that the Passion and death of our Lord was decreed by the Loving Father and ratified by the two other Holy Persons of the Holy Trinity; it was the Holy Will of God. Thus, even though unaware of the satanic nature of his advice, Peter was acting the role of Satan who would certainly have willed to prevent the Passion and crucifixion. Hence Peter was a type of Satan, even a type of the Antichrist, as all men are when they oppose the Holy Will of God. It took our Lord's strong enlightening words to bring Peter to abandon that satanic stance. So today and all through history, politics and political actions cannot be separated from their spiritual and supernatural matrixes or effects. In this very real and true sense, the persons represented in the historical examples presented in this chapter are types, precursors, shadows, earnests of the Antichrist. Only a person of faith will see and accept this divine vision of reality.

Shadow of the Antichrist in the Holy Land

No consideration of the signs of the Antichrist would be complete if we did not reflect on the awesome events that have taken place in the Middle East and the Holy Land. According to Scripture and the Fathers of the Church, one of the events that must prepare the world for the coming of the Antichrist is the return of the Jews as a nation to their homeland in Jerusalem. They as a nation will be given another chance, an additional special grace, to accept Christ as their Messiah. The prophet Hosea predicted as much:

> For the children of Israel shall sit many days without a king, and without prince, and without sacrifice, and without altar, and without ephod, and without teraphim; and after this the children of Israel will return and shall seek the Lord their God and David their king; and they shall fear the Lord and His goodness in the last days.[246]

[246] Hosea 3:4, 5.

Moses makes the same prediction: "After all the things afore-said shall find you, in the latter days you shall return to the Lord, your God and shall hear His voice."[247] St. Paul makes the same prediction in his own way. "Has God cast away His people?" Then he adds: "That blindness in part has happened to Israel until the fullness of the Gentiles should come in, and so all Israel should be saved, as it is written."[248] Augustine, Gregory, and the Fathers hold that the conversion of the Jews in the last days is a truth of divine faith.

Today, through the crucible of three wars, the Jews have established their nation in Jerusalem. Moreover, the Zionist government in power considers all Jews anywhere in the world as citizens of the Israeli state and demands their first loyalty.[249] It invites Jews to emigrate from foreign countries and settle in Israel. Thus the process of the "ingathering" of the Jews from the diaspora is everywhere in full swing. Here, however, we run into a difficult task of reconciling two prophecies that are apparently contradictory.[250] (1) The Antichrist will seduce the Jews and thus be received as their Messiah in Jerusalem. (2) Elias will convert the Jews. Fortunately Sacred Scripture provides us with a distinction that clarifies the difficulty. "And at that time your people shall be saved, everyone shall be found written in the book" of life.[251] "And all that dwelt upon the earth adored him, whose names are not written in the Book of Life of the Lamb."[252]

[247] Deut. 4:30.
[248] St. Paul, Rom. 11:25, 26.
[249] Alfred M. Lilienthal, *What Price Israel* (Chicago: Henry Regnery, 1953), pp. 229–234.
[250] P. Huchede, *History of Antichrist* (Rockford, IL: Tan Books and Publishers, 1969), p. 33.
[251] Dan. 12:1.
[252] John, Apoc. 13:8.

According to these texts, a portion of the Jews, choosing to remain in a worldly, earthly life adhering to the Antichrist, will remain obstinate and prevent themselves from being listed in the book of life. But the greater part will hear the voice of Elias (and of Enoch) unmasking the deceitfulness of the Antichrist, and will be converted to Christ. The final conversion of the Jews is predicted in many places in the Bible.

But what can be said of the developments within the Israeli state? Is the state attempting to return to the religious Judaism of old? Or has it become a nationalistic state just like the secular states of Europe? Actually, political Zionism is really Jewish secular nationalism. Much as Zionist propaganda would like to equate Zionism with Judaism, political Zionism cannot be an intrinsic core of Judaism. For Zionism is essentially ethnic and territorial. It is the Jewish political philosophy for the secular nation-state. It has elevated the Jewish desire for political power above the Jewish religious vocation. Unfortunately, the Jewish secular state, guided by the principles of Zionism, has become the ultimate glory of the Jews today; Jewish secular nationalism is today supreme in Israel; it is the apotheosis of the naturalistic, humanitarian, humanist Jew. And in order to advance this humanistic utopia dramatically, the Knesset, ruling body of the State of Israel, together with the prime minister, Menachem Begin, recently legally established the Holy City of Jerusalem—both the Jewish and the occupied Arab sections—as the capital of the State of Israel. In moving its capital from Tel Aviv to Jerusalem, Israel further antagonized the major religions, the United Nations, and, indeed, the whole world. Moslems, Protestants, Roman and Greek Catholics see in this move another arrogant step toward the secularization of the Holy City and the desacralization of the holy places. Will the rebuilding of the Temple be the next step, followed closely by the erection of the statue of the Antichrist before which all men will be commanded to fall in adoration? Whatever may be the future, it is a fact that the whole world is presently alarmed that a religious world war may break out at any moment in the Holy Land. Certainly the establishment of the nationalistic State of Israel with a secularized Jerusalem as its capital has fulfilled another sign predicted by Christ for the coming of the Antichrist: "In those days you shall hear of wars and rumors of wars. . . . For nation will rise against nation, and kingdom against kingdom." This is the reality in the Middle East today.

Traditional religious Judaism taught the principles of ethics, justice, mercy, and fidelity to the one True God who had chosen the Jewish race to prepare itself and mankind for the coming of God's Son who would redeem all men. Zionism is not interested in God's covenants with the Chosen People for their own and for all men's salvation. Zionism has chosen to create a secular state seeking wealth, power, prestige, and more land. The founding Fathers of Zionism did not share the traditional religious beliefs of devout Jews. Hence they did not return to Zion physically in order to return to God spiritually. They returned to create a secular utopia. They returned to seek a readjustment in the modern world's conditions for Jewish welfare, i.e., to destroy the indignities of anti-Semitism and the government pogroms of Eastern Europe and Russia. These ends are good in themselves, but they have cancelled out the transcendent spiritual goals given Israel by God. A homeland for Jews was for the founders of Zionism primarily a secular quest patterned on the nationalism of nineteenth-century Europe, especially the nationalism of Germany.[253] Exemplifying the opposition of religious Jews to a Zionistic secular state is the statement of Rabbi Joseph Hayyim Sonnenfeld:

> With regard to the Zionists what shall I say and what am I
> to speak? There is great dismay in the Holy Land that these
> evil men who deny the Unique One of the world and of His
> Holy Torah have proclaimed their power to hasten redemp-
> tion for the people of Israel and gather the dispersed from
> all ends of the earth. They have also asserted the view that
> the whole difference and distinction between Israel and the
> nations lies in the nationalism, blood and race, and that
> the faith and the religion are superfluous.... For us in the
> Holy Land it is a sure sign that Dr. Herzl comes not from
> the Lord but from the "side of pollution."[254]

Yet, though philosophically and religiously atheistic, Zionism would exploit religious trappings to further its credibility. That is why the religious symbols of Judaism have been grafted onto the political paraphernalia of the Zionist state, thus desacralizing them. Moreover, as a result of continual tension concerning Israel's survival, a permanent state of war with her Arab neighbors, victories, defeats, invasions, occupation of Arab lands, and the daily threat of perpetual terrorism, Jews all over the world have sympathetically rallied to the cause of Zionism. Yet a perceptive Jewish philosopher like Martin Buber points out the danger of this unreflective enthusiasm. "Zionism," he writes, "has degenerated into *sacro egoismo* (sacred egoism)," and has made "an idol of

---

[253] Gary V. Smith, introductory note to *Zionism: The Dream and the Reality* (London: David & Charles, 1974), pp. 11–18.
[254] Ibid., pp. 13, 14.

the people," of the race.[255] Another philosopher of international renown, Gabriel Marcel, in a postscript written to his play *The Sign of the Cross*, which treats the theory that exaggerated Semitism leads to exaggerated anti-Semitism, warns of the errors and illusions to which so many well-intentioned Israelites have succumbed since the end of World War II:

> No one can question the fact that the problem of Israel has regained dramatic intensity. Today, as I am informed, conversions are growing among the Jews, but, on the other hand, a laicized and enraged Judaism is threatening to degenerate into a new form of nazism as indefensible as the former breed. Between these two extremes, there are many Jews of genuine faith and good will. This play is written for their reflection.[256]

Then, too, contrary to Zionist ideology, the greatest periods of Jewish creative accomplishments have been associated with pluralistic civilizations in their time of expansion and tolerance: in the Hellenistic period, in the Arab civilization of North Africa and Spain, and in Western Europe and America.[257] God gave the Chosen People a set of universal, transcendent values—monotheism, the natural law preached by the prophets, the prophecies of salvation, the tablets of the ten commandments, covenants of love with Himself; these values arose from the universal, supernatural vision and vocation given this people, a vocation that was to prepare them to receive His Son within themselves and to go

---

[255] Ibid., p. 17.

[256] Gabriel Marcel, *Le Signe de la Croix*, in *Vers un Autre Royaume*, (Paris: Plon, 1949), p. 161.

[257] I. F. Stone, "For a New Approach to the Israeli-Arab Conflict," in Smith, op. cit., pp. 197–217.

out to the rest of the world as ambassadors of Christ the Redeemer. Zionism, however, is a myopic view of Jewish aspirations; it seeks merely narrow values: an exclusive homeland, survival, security with no transcendent vocation for itself and other nations. The magnificence of the prophets lay in their overcoming narrow ethnocentricity and projecting the Chosen People toward the splendor of their divine calling, i.e., being God's agents of truth and holiness to all nations. But Zionism has clamped down on the State of Israel a Lilliputian nationalism that has so divided the Jews from all other nations that international Semitism is again on the rise, wars are habitual between Israel and her Arab neighbors and international distrust, resentment, and fear of the Israeli state is growing. Here lies the profound difference between Jew and Israeli; the former maintains his relationship to God and a sense of spiritual mission to all mankind; the latter is obsessed with his own tribe's earthly welfare.[258]

According to Hannah Arendt, prominent author, "today reality has become a nightmare" for all nations, but especially for the Zionist State of Israel, which considers itself cut off altogether from the human community, a nation where Jews want to live among Jews alone, no matter what happens in history. But down that road lies social suicide according to Arendt:

> Some of the Zionist leaders pretend to believe that the Jews can maintain themselves in Palestine against the whole world and that they themselves can persevere in claiming everything or nothing against everybody and everything. However, behind this spurious optimism lurks a despair of everything and a genuine readiness for suicide that becomes extremely dangerous

[258] Ibid., p. 211.

should they grow to be the mood of Palestinian politics. There is nothing in Herzlian Zionism that could act as a check on this; on the contrary, the utopian and ideological elements with which he injected the new Jewish will to political action are only too likely to lead the Jew out of reality once more.[259]

Therefore, because it is founded on atheistic philosophical and political Zionism, the Israeli state has had to equip itself for survival and expansion in this world. It has become a powerful military state with a superb army, air force, and navy, all being now equipped with nuclear weapons. It has perhaps the most efficient police and secret service corps in the world. Such a secular, earthbound state could easily become the political and military power base for the Antichrist when he comes. For the Antichrist will be in perfect accord with the ideals of such a Zionist state. For the Zionist State of Israel represents the apostasy of the Chosen People from fidelity to their one True God. And as we know, the Antichrist will come when there is a general apostasy, an apostasy of the Jews from the God of Abraham, Isaac, and Jacob; an apostasy of Christians from belief in Christ as the God-Man who came to redeem all mankind. Both those apostasies in virulent form are with us today. Moreover, the State of Israel has demonstrated that it has the will and ability to go to war and win the secular goals to which its heart is attached. Thus when the Antichrist comes to power as head of such an efficient, superbly equipped, scientific state, founded on "nationalism, race and blood," he will be able to conquer the rest of the world. He will be the first, the only Jew to reign with political, economic, military power over the whole world from his capital city, Jerusalem,

[259] Hannah Arendt, "The Jewish State: Fifty Years After—Where Have Herzl's Politics Led?," in Smith, op. cit., pp. 67–80.

the city in which our Lord was crucified. Thus through the crucible of wars, cosmic upheavals, the witnessing of Elias and
Enoch, their martyrdoms and resurrections, the victories and
miracles of the Antichrist, the Jews and the whole world will be
given the final grace to accept or reject Christ, to accept or reject
Satan in his emissary the Antichrist.

Once again the Jews will have to choose between a Caesar,
this time, the Supreme Caesar, the Antichrist, or the Christ,
the Son of God as their king and ruler. The Jews, though dispersed for two thousand years throughout all regions and nations, have, nevertheless, maintained their identity. No other
people has been able to do this. The Chosen People, no matter
how distantly they fled from God or separated from their
homeland, could never erase from their consciousness the fact
that God, Who chose them and made a solemn covenant with
them, was still their true king and ruler, the fact that God still
expected them to fulfill the special vocation He entrusted to
them. Hence even today in the Zionist State of Israel there is
an agonizing hunger among many Jews to get back to the God
of Abraham, of Isaac, and of Joseph. There is a growing, vocifer-
ous dissatisfaction with the atheistic Zionist state. Many young
Jews in Palestine are discovering the life of Christ for the first
time and are coming to Christianity. They are coming to realize
that Judaism was meant to be a light to the nations and a covenant of the peoples. They are seeking a spiritual Zion, not a
materialistic Zionism. Rabbi Kaufmann Kohler expressed this
ideal thus:

> The fundamental principle ... to be accentuated more
> than any other is that Judaism is no more a national reli-
> gion than its God is a tribal God ... Judaism is a universal

system of truths and ethics, destined to become the religion of humanity.

... the Jew's place is in the world among nations. His task and scope are international and not confined to a little territory he may call his own.

... This ideal Zion of humanity not built by human hands, a spiritual Zion for all mankind is the goal, the aim.[260]

Now the Antichrist, when he comes, will attempt to satisfy this intense spiritual hunger of God's people. But he will do so by posing as the true Christ, rebuilding the Temple, performing lying wonders and thus sweeping the people with enthusiasm and blind frenzy into the practice of idolatry—the adoration of himself and Satan. Therefore, the developments in the Holy Land, the historical unfolding of the national life of the State of Israel bear close watching and study by all men, but especially by Christians, to whom our Lord said: "And when you see the abomination of desolation (the Antichrist) standing where it ought not (in the rebuilt temple of God demanding and accepting adoration from his slaves) ... and when these things begin to come to pass, look up, and lift up your heads, because your (final) redemption is at hand.... Watch then, praying at all times, that you may be accounted worthy to escape all these things that are to be and stand (in heaven, not fall into hell) before the Son of Man."

---

[260] Ibid., p. 15.

Chapter 9

The Antichrists Within

When he was rector of the Catholic University of Ireland, which he helped to create, Cardinal Newman found some spiritual relief in the fact that he lived in an age when unbelief made its attacks against the Catholic Church "from a position over against us in citadels of its own, confronting us in broad daylight and with a direct assault." This was preferable by far, he contended, than living in a time, as in the Middle Ages, when "Catholicism was the sole religion in Christendom, and unbelief necessarily made its advances under the language and guise of faith." In a lecture to the student body of 1853 entitled "A Form of Infidelity of the Day," Newman said:

> Though it cannot be denied that at the present day, in consequence of the close juxtaposition and intercourse of men of all religions, there is a considerable danger of the subtle, silent, unconscious perversion and corruption of Catholic intellectuals, who as yet profess, and sincerely profess, their submission to the authority of revelation, still the danger is far inferior to what it was in one portion of the Middle Ages. . . . And I have no hesitation in saying . . . that I prefer to live in an age when the fight is

in the day, not in the twilight; and I think it a gain to be speared by a foe, rather than to be stabbed by a friend.[261]

What Newman was spared has become the challenge of contemporary Catholics. We are living in an age when the fight for the Faith is in the twilight, when the enemy without has found allies against us among the members of our own household. We are witnessing today worldwide secularization of Catholic doctrines, values, and institutions. A generation that is contesting God and His revelation in Christ is simultaneously presenting man with a new, apocalyptic adventure in a rivalry calculated to rob God forever of the allegiance of men's minds and hearts. The whole Sacred Magisterium in union with the Holy Father is striving tirelessly to provide the light and courage needed to call back the nations to their divine destiny. They are concentrating on the mission of leading the embattled Church and the world through the chaos, dissent, infidelity, and treason of our times. Quite naturally, the Magisterium and the faithful have looked to Catholic intellectuals for supporting leadership and guidance in this crisis. Indeed, they have entrusted into their hands the all-important scientific and spiritual formation of their children in the hope of restoring, through the future leadership of these witnessing youths, all things in Christ. Yet in this revolutionary age when, thanks to the marvelous means of communication, the control of the many by the few is a practical, effective technique, it becomes quite easy to conquer a people through the conquest of their own intellectuals, through an undermining and subverting of their religious, political, and educational institutions.

[261] John Henry Newman, *The Idea of a University* (New York: Image Books, 1959), p. 352.

Antichrists in the Academy

Events happening in Catholic universities today are making the Catholic community, and the larger Judaeo-Christian community as well, anxious about the intellectual, religious, social, and political activities of these institutions. If we recall briefly the essence and purpose of a university in general and of the Catholic university in particular, we will understand how and why universities have degenerated from their noble natures and abandoned their loftiest ideals, why they have become, as it were, schools that lead men not to Christ but to the Antichrist.

Newman tells us that "the university is a place of *teaching* universal *knowledge*.... Such is a university in *essence*, and independently of its relation to the Church."[262] Now it has always been a reasonable lay and Catholic understanding that the university administrator, professor, or student, like every other student, is bound to patriotic duty and, in harmony with that, to a dedication to the common objectives of the intellectual-moral search for truth and integrity—united by common agreement on the methodology, demonstrations, and experiments suitable to the enlargement and perfection of each discipline of learning. Moreover, scholars, scientists, philosophers, and theologians have always agreed that this community of minds, created by the vision and needs of larger religious and civic communities, is meant to be at the service of these larger communities that continue to inspire and sustain them.[263]

Even when he speaks of the secular university, Newman emphasizes its constant need of the Church's assistance and of its theological fulfillment if it is to truly teach *universal* knowledge:

---

[262] Ibid., p. 7.

[263] Rev. Joseph F. Costanzo, S.J., "Academic Freedom and the Intellectual," Cork University publication, 1960.

But, practically speaking, it (the university) cannot fulfill its object duly ... without the Church's assistance; or, to use the theological term, the Church is necessary for its *integrity*. Not that its main characters are changed by this incorporation: it still has the office of intellectual education; but the Church steadies it in the performance of that office.[264]

A university, I should lay down, by its very nature professes to teach universal knowledge. Theology is surely a branch of knowledge: how then is it possible for it to profess all branches of knowledge and yet exclude from the subjects of its teaching one which, to say the least, is as important and as large as any of them?[265]

The Catholic university is a community of minds associated together to teach and research the natural sciences, the social sciences, history, literature, philosophy, theology, and so on. But what distinguishes the Catholic university, and what distinguishes any school of particular confession, is that it provides explicitly for a faculty of theology that teaches its own religious creed as a science, that is, as a body of organized, researched dogmas and precepts, known as its religious philosophy of life. The Catholic university has a theology faculty that scientifically teaches and researches the articles of the Creed of the Catholic Faith. "The Catholic college or university seeks to give the authentic Christian message an institutional presence in the academic world. Several things follow from this. Christian commitment will characterize this academic community. While fully maintaining the autonomy concomitant to its being a college or university, the institution will manifest fidelity to the teachings

[264] Newman, op. cit., p. 7.
[265] Ibid., p. 61.

of Jesus Christ as transmitted by his Church. The advancement of Christian thought will be the object of institutional commitment. The human sciences will be examined in the light of Christian faith. The best of the Christian intellectual and spiritual tradition will be blended with the special dynamism of contemporary higher education in a way that enriches both."[266]

The Catholic school and especially university is a community of minds that also provides a chapel on the grounds, a place for worship and the administration of the sacraments and the religious aid of spiritual counselors. In such schools there is no compromise between natural goals of academic excellence and the higher goals of sanctity, namely the goals of the Catholic Church to transform all natural truth in the new light of its relationship to the truth of Revelation. Nor is there any compromise between the natural goal of moral excellence and the higher goal of the Catholic Church in the field of human conduct, namely the elevation of natural goodness to the transcendent level of holiness through man's acceptance of the grace of salvation in Christ. Once again Cardinal Newman is our teacher on the mind of the Catholic Church in founding her schools and universities. Relating why Pope Pius IX wanted a Catholic university in Ireland, Newman said:

> Surely what he (the Pope) does, he does for the sake of religion. And if he encourages and patronizes art and science, it is for the sake of religion. He rejoices in the widest and most philosophical systems of intellectual education, from an intimate conviction that the truth is his real ally, as it

[266] U.S. National Conference of Bishops, Letter on Education, "To Teach as Jesus Did," in *L'Osservatore Romano*, English edition, November 4, 1972, p. 7.

is his profession; and that knowledge and reason are sure ministers to faith.... Nothing short of this can be his aim, if, as it becomes the successors of the Apostles, he is able to say with St. Paul, "I do not judge myself to know anything among you, except Jesus Christ and Him crucified." ... When the Church founds a university, she is not cherishing talent, genius or knowledge for their own sake, but for the sake of her children, with a view to their spiritual welfare and their religious influence and usefulness, with the project of training them to fill their respective posts in life better, and of making them more intelligent, active members of society.[267]

Moreover, the Catholic Church is historically the mother of the universities. At a time when Western Christianity was united by the bond of the Catholic Faith, the Middle Ages produced its most unique and original achievement—the universities. Antiquity created the schools of Athens and Alexandria. The Academy and the Lyceum of the Peripetetics and the Porch of the Stoics were the intellectual fruits of its genius. But what is the distinctly Catholic and medieval stroke of genius in the creation of the universities, of which our own are the modern heirs, is the institutional embodiment of the educational ideal, the organization of the various faculties of arts and sciences, and the interdependent hierarchy of all the sciences under the light of the science of Revelation. This unity in diversity brought them all to the full complement of learning and wisdom. Before the revolt of Luther, eighty-one universities were dispersed throughout Christendom and the majority of these were founded by papal charters. Once again the excellent doctor for our times in these matters is Cardinal Newman:

[267] Newman, op. cit., pp. 8, 9.

The Middle Ages is the age of the universities; it is the classical period of the Schoolmen; it is the splendid and palmary instance of the wide policy and large liberality of the Church as regards philosophical inquiry. If there ever was a time when the intellect went wild and had a licentious revel, it was at the date I speak of. Was there ever a more curious, more meddling, bolder, keener, more penetrating, more rationalistic exercise of the reason than at that time? ... Did the Church take a high hand with philosophy then? No!... It was a time when she had temporal power and could have exterminated the spirit of inquiry with fire and sword; but she determined to put it down by *argument*; She said: "Two can play at that and my argument is the better." She sent her controversalists into the philosophical arena. It was the Dominican and Franciscan doctors, the greatest of them being St. Thomas, who in those medieval universities fought the battle of revelation with the weapons of heathenism. It was no matter whose the weapon was; truth was truth all the world over. With the jawbone of an ass, with the skeleton philosophy of pagan Greece did the Samson of the schools put to flight his thousand Philistines.[268]

Unfortunately, today the Catholic university has become restless in its natural home, the Catholic Church. Everywhere it is loosening its filial bonds with the Teaching Church and, often enough, deliberately cancelling out its Catholic connection. Already, like Henry VIII of England who certainly was and is a shadow of the Antichrist, some former Catholic universities have confiscated Church property and treasures and turned them over

[268] Ibid., pp. 423, 424.

to use in purely secular projects. They have appropriated schools, colleges, universities, properties, and monies that have generously flowed into astronomical figures from the hearts of Catholic parents and faithful who gave not only their children to Catholic schools, but their savings in the belief that the religious education given in those schools would prepare men for profitable lives in time while leading them in holiness to the beatific vision in eternity. These former Catholic universities, like Judas, traitor and forerunner of the Antichrist, have turned over to the enemy for a price, the Christ who is the supreme Teacher and Master of the truly Christian school. When asked why they strive to erase their religious and Catholic character, the religious leaders of these universities display an incoherent inability to define themselves, their policies, their goals or even their continued existence. Money is the root of their rejection of their Catholic commitment; they have been choked by the cares and riches of this world. We have been forewarned that the Antichrist would win many over from Christ by bribes and gifts of wealth. The strategy of these unfaithful universities or of their leaders is to don secular clothing, intellectually and physically, and to slip into the secularizing surroundings of the governmental and foundational financial worlds—there to gain eligibility for the vast educational monies made available by these worldly powers to self-proclaimed aconfessional schools. But to the man of spiritual vision money is seen as merely the superficial explanation for the Catholic college cop-out from the Church. The unhealthy fever for money is merely a symptom of a deeper spiritual malady. The mysterious explanation is that the Catholic school or university, in the persons of its leadership and often of its religious teachers, prior to its sellout to secularism, had already so devaluated the

Faith that Catholicism had finally become negotiable for material gains. Today there is such a general apostasy of once Catholic schools from the Faith that the Antichrist would find himself right at home in the heretical, revolutionary, immoral atmosphere that pervades those campuses and classrooms. Gradually, over the years the essential purpose of the Catholic university has been radically changed. Lusting after secular academic excellence, huge student bodies, expensive science complexes, notoriety, publicity, political clout, and financial power, the leaders of Catholic universities somehow lost sight of the unearthly purpose and spirit of the Catholic university. Thus, in today's Catholic university, intellectualism is preferred to Catholicism; scientism to faith, relativism to truth, immanentism to transcendence, subjectivism to reality, situationism to moral integrity, and anarchism to authority. The essential purpose of the Catholic university has *de facto* been changed, despite the lip service that is still paid to the original Catholic ideal. Conduct flows from convictions and when the conduct is consistently depraved it is because the convictions have been corrupted. For example, Judas, forerunner of the Antichrist, had radically changed his deepest convictions about the person and mission of Christ before he sold his Lord for thirty pieces of silver. No virtuosity at contorted rationalization can mask the massive turning away from the Catholic ideal that has taken place in the Catholic universities of the United States. The light and love of the world have made tragic advances against the light and love of Christ. Once again in Cardinal Newman, prophet for our age of apostasy, we find a profound explanation of how Catholic universities have abandoned the Faith and even become hostile to revealed truth and to the Magisterium that guards and guarantees its veracity:

It is no sufficient security for the Catholicity of a university, even that the whole of Catholic theology should be professed in it, unless the Church breathes her own pure and unearthly spirit in it, and fashions and moulds its organization, and watches over its teaching, and knits together its pupils, and superintends its actions.... It cannot but be that if left to themselves, they will, in spite of their profession of Catholic truth, work out results more or less prejudicial to its interests. Nor is this all: such institutions may become hostile to the revealed truth in consequence of the circumstances of their teaching as well as of their end. They are employed in the pursuit of liberal knowledge, and liberal knowledge has a special tendency, not necessary or rightful, but a tendency in fact, when cultivated by beings such as we are, to impress us with a mere philosophical theory of life and conduct, in the place of Revelation.... It is not that you will at once reject Catholicism, but you will measure and proportion it by an earthly standard. You will throw its highest and most momentous disclosures into the background; you will deny its principles, explain away its doctrines, rearrange its precepts, and make light of its practices, even while you profess it.... This intellectualism first and chiefly comes into collision with precept, then with doctrine, then with the very principle of dogmatism.... In a country which does not profess the faith, it at once runs, if allowed, into skepticism or infidelity; but even within the pale of the Church and with the most unqualified profession of her Creed, it acts, if left to itself, as an element of corruption and debility. Catholicism, as it has come down to us from the first, seems to be mean and illiberal; it is a mere popular religion; it is the religion of illiterate ages or servile populations or barbarian warriors; it must be treated with discrimination and delicacy, corrected, softened, improved, if it is to satisfy an enlightened generation. It must be stereotyped as the patron of the arts, or the pupil of speculation, or the protege of science; it must play the literary academician, or the political partisan; it must keep up with the age; some or other expedient it must devise, in order to explain away, or to hide, tenets under which the intellect labours and of which it is ashamed — its doctrine, for instance, of grace, its mystery of the Godhead, its preaching of the Cross, its devotion to the Queen of the Saints, or its loyalty to the Apostolic See.

Let this spirit be freely evolved out of that philosophical condition of mind ... and it is impossible but, first indifference, then laxity of belief, and then even heresy will be the successive results. Here then are two injuries which Revelation is likely to sustain at the hands of the master of reason unless the Church, as in duty bound, protects the sacred treasure which is in jeopardy. The first is a simple ignoring of theological truth altogether, under the pretense of not recognizing differences of religious opinion; ... The second, which is of a more subtle character, is a recognition indeed of Catholicism, but (as if in pretended mercy to it) an adulteration of its spirit.[269]

We have already seen that Newman contended that the university was an incomplete and stunted world if it tried to function in isolation from the truths of religion and particularly

[269] Ibid., pp. 223–225.

from the assistance of the Catholic Church. Speaking specifically of the Catholic university Newman stressed that "it is ancillary certainly to the Catholic Church, first because truth of any kind can but minister to truth; and next, still more, because nature will ever pay homage to grace, and reason cannot but illustrate and defend Revelation; and thirdly, because the Church has a sovereign authority, and when she speaks *ex cathedra*, must be obeyed."[270] Pope Pius XII, stressing that the Catholic university (and school) exists to serve the Church as well as the intellect, said: "The Christian school (at every level) will justify its existence in so far as its teachers—clerics or lay persons—religious or secular, succeed in forming staunch Christians."[271] Despite this clear, Catholic, papal teaching, the Catholic university today refuses to submit to the Magisterium. In 1967 the Land O'Lakes statement on "The Nature of the Contemporary University," endorsed by prominent officials of leading Catholic universities, contains this declaration of independence from the authority of the Magisterium: "To perform its teaching and research functions effectively the Catholic university must have a true autonomy and academic freedom in the face of authority of whatever kind, lay or cleric, external to the academic community itself.... There must be no theological or philosophical imperialism; all scientific and disciplinary methods and methodologies must be given due honor and respect. This means that the intellectual campus of a Catholic university has no boundaries and no barriers.... The whole world of knowledge and ideas

---

[270] Ibid., pp. 414–415.
[271] Charles E. Rice, *Authority and Rebellion* (New York: Doubleday, 1971), p. 174.

must be open to the student; there must be no outlawed books or subjects."[272]

In the Spring of 1969, the representatives of leading Catholic universities throughout the world and members of the Vatican Congregation for Catholic Education met in Rome. Again the universities attending this meeting adopted a statement that called for complete independence from the Church. It said that the Catholic university "is limited by no other factor than the truth it pursues. Every limitation imposed on the university which would clash with this unconditioned attitude for pursuing truth would be intolerable and contrary to the very nature of the university."[273] But in October 1969 the Vatican's Congregation for Catholic Education met in plenary session and strongly reaffirmed the authority of the Magisterium, which extends in the Catholic university "not only to truths of the faith, but also to those matters connected with the truths of the faith":

> To fulfill (its) mission, a Catholic university must be seen as existing not only in the world, but also in the Catholic community and therefore, it is related to those who preside over the Catholic community, the Catholic hierarchy. Obviously, the specific purpose of the Catholic university cannot be realized if those whose proper function is to be the authentic guardians of the deposit of faith are relegated to a marginal place in its life and activity.[274]

Once again at the Second International Congress of Delegates of Catholic universities, held in the Vatican under the auspices of

[272] Ibid., p. 174.
[273] Ibid., pp. 176, 177.
[274] Ibid., p. 178.

the Congregation of Catholic Education from November 20 to 30, 1972, the position of the Church was strongly contested and rejected. After much frank discussion, the plenary session of the delegates from all parts of the world, led by a large, militant North American faction, rejected the following amendment that was proposed to harmonize the liberty of the Catholic university with the universal mission of the Catholic Church to spread the teaching of Jesus and to bring all men to salvation:

> The truth which the Catholic university has to research and transmit has a double source: science and revelation. Therefore, the Catholic university, in its statutes and regulations has to provide adequate means to guarantee, in an autonomous and efficacious manner, fidelity in research and in teaching not only to science but also to Catholic doctrine, in conformity with its essential note of "fidelity to the Christian message as it comes to us through the Church."[275]

In effect, then, the religious leaders of certain Catholic universities voted to reject any institutional, statutory, academic allegiance to the teachings of Jesus Christ as transmitted by His Church through the Magisterium. Can one imagine a more antichristian activity than institutional apostasy from Christ and His Church through the calculated revolt and disobedience of religious leaders who receive all their authority, their existence as religious, the institutions they run from the authority of the Church herself? In rejecting this amendment, these leaders rejected their "necessary ancillary and ministrative" vocation in the Church. Imitating the role

---

[275] From the documents of this Congress at which I was an observer. These documents are in my file.

that the Antichrist will play, they placed themselves on a par with the Vicar of Christ and His Church, a position they ought never to have usurped. They became antichrists, dividing the Church, dividing Christ by introducing rebellion and revolution within Catholic institutions of learning and within religious orders and congregations. At the same time they demonstrated a crude insensitivity to the grave responsibility of the Hierarchy for the salvation of the souls committed to their care, many of whom are having their faith and morals undermined precisely on the campuses of modern Catholic universities where contradictions of the Church's teachings are being academically featured and officially tolerated, if not fostered. Moreover, the fierceness with which this amendment was opposed evinced a coldly uncharitable indifference to the needs of the students who, in the words of Pope Pius XI, "have a strict right to instruction in harmony with the teaching of the Church, the pillar and ground of truth."[276] As if foreseeing the rebellion of our day in the academic world against the Church, Newman wrote, à propos of the Catholic Church's presence in Catholic universities:

> Hence a direct and active jurisdiction of the Church over it and in it is necessary lest it should become the rival of the Church with the Community at large in those theological matters which to the Church are exclusively committed—acting as a representative of the intellect, as the Church is the representative of the religious principle. The Church has no call to watch over and protect science; but towards theology she has a distinct duty; it is one of the special trusts committed to her keeping. Where theology is, there she must be; and if a university cannot fulfill its name

---

[276] Rice, op. cit., p. 177.

The
The Antichrist

and office without recognition of revealed truth, she must be there to see that it is a *bona fide* recognition, sincerely made and consistently acted upon.[277]

Now leaders and communities of Catholic universities, who set themselves up as rivals of the Church with the Community at large, are definitely playing the role of the Antichrist. For the essence of the Antichrist is that he exists to supplant Christ, His truth, His way, His life. In fleeing from the bosom of the Catholic Magisterium into the arms of the Secular Magisterium, they often justify their apostasy by arguing that there is an inner incompatibility between the demands of the Church for orthodox teaching with Christian morals and the academic freedom inherent in the adventure of university education. In a word, they picture the Church, even as her enemies do, in the role of always and necessarily impeding free research, free expression, and free publication. They would have it that the Church shackles the intellect and the will, suffocating the former, binding the latter. Newman rejects this false accusation. "First, then, as to the fundamental principle of religion and morals, and again as to the fundamental principles of Christianity, or what are called the *dogmas* of the faith—as to this double creed, natural and revealed—we, none of us, should say that it is any shackle at all upon the intellect to maintain these inviolate. Indeed, a Catholic cannot put off his thought of them; and they as little impede the movements of his intellect as the laws of physics impede his bodily movements."[278]

The trouble with this understanding of academic freedom is that it takes for granted as a truth what is a falsity, indeed a complete illusion, namely, that academic freedom is absolutely

[277] Newman, op. cit., pp. 222, 223.
[278] Ibid., p. 425.

234

immune from any reasonable bounds, limitations, or restrictions. No human freedom is absolutely immune to restriction. Freedom is no longer freedom when it is reduced to being the unhindered pursuit of one's whims and desires. This is especially true of freedom exercised in the field of philosophy where conflict with the authentic and infallible teachings of the Church is foreseeable. A true understanding of academic freedom, therefore, is in order so as to distinguish it clearly from academic license.

Academic freedom derives from the rational nature of man. It is rooted in the intellectual activity of man whereby he is called to a dominion and stewardship of the universe through a conquest of truth. *Positively*, then, academic freedom is a generous guarantee to the unimpeded access to the evidence of truth in any given science. Thus, academic freedom is always bounded by the canons and axiomatic truths of each discipline of learning. Thus, again positively, academic freedom is both purposive and responsible. It has its own built-in rules; its requirements are conditioned by predefined directions toward the truth of its particular science. The moral right to academic freedom arises from the inviolability of the proper action necessary to its scientific achievements of truth, founded on man's connatural inner dynamism of the human intelligence's hunger for truth. *Negatively*, academic freedom means at the very least the immunity from unreasonable restrictions, both from within and from outside the academic community, of the right to communicate the results of one's researches through lectures and publications, and the right to be immune from unreasonable restriction in the pursuit of the teaching profession.[279]

[279] Rev. Joseph F. Costanzo, S.J., *This Nation under God* (New York: Herder & Herder, 1963), pp. 407–425.

We are now in the position to ask, "How is academic freedom violated?" Scholars, scientists, and philosophers hold that whenever one of their members ventures consciously and freely to teach as truths doctrines that contradict the clearly established dogmas or unconditional truths of their disciplines, then such a member of the university is abusing his academic freedom, putting it in the service of stupidities or known falsehoods instead of using it to advance the horizons of truth. Now every science has its dogmas, theology, philosophy, and all the natural sciences. Dogmas are not only the ultimate answers to some fundamental questions; they also prompt further questioning and research, leading thus to enlarged, more profound truth. Now Newman was well aware of the scourge of false prophets and teachers of novelties in the universities. And he comes down hard against them:

> There is a demand for reckless originality of thought, and a sparkling plausibility of argument ... a demand for crude theory and unsound philosophy, rather than none at all. It is a sort of repetition of the "Quid novi?" of the Aeropagus, and it must have an answer. Men must be found who can treat, where it is necessary, like the Athenian sophist, *de omni scibili* (of whatever is knowable). The teaching of such men is so offhand, so ambitious, so changeable. It increases the seriousness of the mischief ... that they can give no better guarantee for the philosophical truth of their principles than their popularity of the moment, and their happy conformity in ethical character to the age which admires them. I am far indeed from allowing in any matter which even borders on religion, what an eminent Protestant divine has advocated on the

most sacred subjects—I mean the "liberty of prophesying."
I have no wish to degrade the professors of science, who
ought to be prophets of the truth, into mere advertisers
of crude fancies or notorious absurdities. I am not pleading that they should at random shower down upon their
hearers ingenuities and novelties; or that they should
teach even what has a basis of truth in it, in a brilliant,
offhand way, to a collection of youth who may not perhaps hear them for six consecutive lectures and who will
carry away with them into the country a misty idea of
the half created theories of some ambitious intellect.[280]

A Catholic university that allows professors and lecturers to
attack the authentic teachings of the Church, whether they are
infallibly defined or not, is not faithful to the best canons of
scholarship, nor to the Church or its own students who have a
right in justice to receive the divinely revealed truths in their
pristine purity. We know that Satan and the Antichrist snare
millions of souls through their fascination for novel doctrines
and their enthusiasm for revolutionary morals. This is the snare
that promises man-come-of-age updated, original theology and
free-from-scruples, easy morality. Catholic universities that have
thus conformed to the world's desires are not exercising their academic freedom responsibly. Thus when eighty-seven Catholic
theologians, acting as forerunners of the Antichrist, from diverse
Catholic universities issued a violent attack against *Humanae
Vitae* within thirty hours of its release to the world, the whole
world witnessed a scandalous performance that, for its record
speed and intemperate tone, could scarcely be praised as mature

[280] Newman, op. cit., 426–427.

research, much less taken as a model of a responsible exercise of academic freedom. Commenting on the scholarly incompetence and spiritual irresponsibility of the signers of the *Statement*, whose rebellious minds and angered hearts made them foreshadows of the Antichrist, Father Joseph F. Costanzo, S.J. writes:

> Time has the numbing effect of dimming the memory of the asperities of this contestation of a solemn and definitive papal teaching, but the spiritual wounds inflicted upon the faithful may be long in mending. The raw aching fact is that scandal was given. These dissidents did interpose their pastoral counsel between the Supreme Pastor of the Universal Church and the faithful in a grave matter of morality touching intimately the conscience of spouses.... Summarily, my own appraisal of the *Statement* is that it is a supercilious pastiche of highly questionable postulates, such as the crude charge that the Roman Pontiff does not correctly understand Catholic ecclesiology, the referrals to past reversals of authoritative papal announcements on matters about which even onetime Protestant scholarship has long since become too embarrassed to regurgitate, the position that *Humanae Vitae* is at variance with the affirmations of Vatican II and demonstrates no advance upon *Casti Connubii*, etc.... The *Statement* constitutes a bold and novel ecclesiology which ... none of the Pontiffs, Councils, and Fathers of the Church have ever known, and surely one that might have drawn unusual interest had it been proposed to the Fathers of Vatican II as the Dogmatic Constitution of the Church.[281]

[281] Rev. Joseph F. Costanzo, S.J., "Academic Dissent: An Original Ecclesiology," in *The Thomist*, XXXIV, October 4, 1970, pp. 636–637.

When rebellious theologians, of international fame, are officially invited by many Catholic universities to address large student bodies and to attack, to the glee of these unformed youth, the nature of the Church, its infallibility, its priesthood, its papacy, its moral code, then this can scarcely be called a performance of profound scholarship or reasonable freedom. Rather it is a prostitution of the teaching profession, a sham performance by disaffected members of the Church who are exploiting for personal publicity and publication purposes the itching ears of youthful audiences as yet unable or unwilling to endure sound doctrine because they have been so often titillated by novelties and fascinated by foolish fables. Newman knew and exposed the infidelity of such forerunners of the Antichrist:

> Every now and then you will find a person of vigorous or fertile mind who relies upon his own resources, despises all former authors, and gives the world, with the utmost fearlessness, his own views upon religion, or history or any other popular subject. All his works may sell for awhile; he may get a name in his day; but this will be all. His readers are sure to find on the long run that his doctrines are mere theories, and not the expression of facts, that they are chaff instead of bread, and then his popularity drops as suddenly as it rose.[282]

When a woman lecturer, with no particular qualifications as a theologian, is invited to address large student bodies at many Catholic universities and during her lecture ridicules Christ, the holy Mother of God, and attacks the Church's teaching on contraception and abortion, then hosting Catholic universities

[282] Newman, op. cit., p. 152.

cease to be centers for Christian wisdom and become schools for scandal; then they are preparing not soldiers of Christ, but soldiers of the Antichrist. When the president of the oldest Catholic university in the United States, Georgetown University, publicly refuses to "take an official position" in favor of the solemnly taught, conscience-binding truth and morality of *Humanae Vitae* on the flimsy excuse that "the encyclical has divided theologians and bishops," even though as a Jesuit he has vowed fidelity to the pope and papal teaching, then one can see in the very Company of Jesus the disease of spiritual infidelity, the apostasy in high places from the Teaching Church that prepares the coming of the Antichrist. This spirit of apostasy is incarnated in a spiritual position utterly despised by St. Ignatius of Loyola—the temporizing, calculating, uncommitted stance of the man of half measures, the man addicted to worldly wisdom and approval, the man who refuses to cast in his lot with Christ and his vicar, the pope. Now this presidential cop-out, imitated by many religious teachers and Catholics in the university world, has caused incalculable scandal to students, alumni, and the whole Catholic, not to say non-Catholic, world. When Catholic universities, against the expressed commands of the Vatican, hire as teachers in their theology departments laicized priests and known heretics, then disobedience degenerates into the open rebellion characteristic of antichrist-types and a form of academic revolution introduces religious chaos on the Catholic campus, which then becomes the breeding ground for militant enemies of Christ and His Church. But the whole Catholic community, on and off campus, suffers from this arrogant rebellion, for confusion, resentment, suspicion, and hatred are diffused everywhere in the whole of society. Then, too, when the very scientific teaching of and in favor of Catholic theology is substituted for by a program in religious studies or religious sociology in which all theologies are laid out smorgasbord style and the students are invited to choose what they like, since no one theology is better or truer than another, then the faith of Revelation is effectively denied and the spiritual sickness of indifference infects the faculty, students, parents, and the whole of society; then society is made ready for the coming of the Antichrist, since it is bereft of all faith. Concerning the suppression of revealed theology of the Catholic Faith in a university, Newman long ago revealed what would happen once this was done. "If you drop any science out of the circle of knowledge, you cannot keep its place vacant for it; that science is forgotten; the other sciences close up, or, in other words, they exceed their proper bounds and intrude where they have no right.... The same is the case with the subject matter of theology; it would be the prey of a dozen various sciences if theology were put out of possession; and not only so, but these sciences would be plainly exceeding their rights and capacities in seizing upon it. They would be sure to teach wrongly where they had no mission to teach at all."[283] Thus, in default of well-trained theologians, Catholic universities that have banished or down-graded the science of theology by allowing heresy to be taught, are turning out religious sociologists, porno-theologians, savants of comparative religious studies who have the audacity to tell the Teaching Church that she has been wrong these past two thousand years in her understanding and preaching of the dogmas of the Resurrection, the Virgin Birth, Original Sin, salvation, angels, devils, hell, purgatory, heaven—indeed there is no limit to their babblings nor to the depth of their theological incompetency.

[283] Ibid., p. 105.

But as if scandals in the field of doctrine were not enough, we are now witnessing scandals in the field of spiritual and moral advice stemming from priests and university and even seminary publications. Once again the oldest Catholic university in the United States is the scene of this new shock to the Christian and popular mind. Financed by student fees, directed by a priest faculty member, and distributed by the undergraduate student government, a booklet entitled "Human Sexual Response-Ability" endorses homosexuality: "Careful reflection might very well indicate that this type of lifestyle is the most honest and healthy for him and her." The booklet also endorses contraception: "Emotional and sexual relationships can happen to all of us. So, to those romantically involved, to the recreation minded, and to the would be William (and Wilhelmina) the conquerors, we must emphasize the responsibility to learn about and to use any of the proven contraceptives available."[284]

Patrick Cardinal O'Boyle, Ordinary of the Diocese of Washington, D.C. at that time, where the booklet was printed and distributed, stigmatized the pamphlet as "potentially dangerous to spiritual welfare," warning his flock that the denial of Catholic dogma "is there for any reasonable, alert person to grasp." Moreover, he called upon the Georgetown University officials to have the booklet withdrawn as a source of scandal and incompatible with the Catholic character of the university. The president of the university refused to cooperate with the archbishop and disclaimed, Pilate-like, all responsibility for the publication of this evil book, despite the university connections mentioned

---

[284] *The Human Sexual Response-Ability* written by students of the Department of Obstetrics and Gynecology, Georgetown University, directed by Rev. R. C. Baumiller, S.J., Washington, D.C., 1972, pp. 4ff.

above without whose aid the pamphlet would not have been born and diffused on campus. Once again, Pilate-wise, a Superior and son of St. Ignatius washed his hands publicly of an evil he was bound to remove, this time his duty of preventing the pamphlet's wicked influence on souls. His excuse was once again woefully weak. He claimed the pamphlet was a student project and hence not an "official" work of the university. In effect, the president rejected all responsibility for this Catholic university's concern for the spiritual and intellectual welfare of its students and, of course, he served notice to the Hierarchy and the Church that on Catholic university campuses, the Church should neither be seen nor heard. Could the Antichrist himself be more dictatorial than this? Academic license not freedom, academic free-thinking not scientific truth and revelation have now become the new secular gods of too many Catholic universities. Once again Newman vividly relates the disaster these shadows of the Antichrist create within the Church:

> It is a miserable time when a man's Catholic profession is no voucher for his orthodoxy, and when a teacher of religion may be within the Church's pale, yet external to her truth. Such has been for a season the trial of her children at various eras of her history. It was the state of things during the dreadful Arian ascendency, when the flock had to keep aloof from the shepherd, and the unsuspicious Fathers of the Western Councils trusted and followed some consecrated sophist from Greece or Syria. It was the case in those passages of medieval history when simony resisted the Supreme Pontiff or when heresy lurked in the universities. It was a longer and more tedious trial while the controversies lasted with the Mono-physites of old and with Jansenists of modern times.

A great scandal it is and a perplexity to the little ones of Christ to have to choose between rival claimants upon their allegiance, or to find a condemnation at length pronounced upon one whom in their simplicity they have admired. We, too, in this age have our scandals, for scandals must be. It is a great gain when error and false teachers are exposed, for then they cease to deceive the simple.[285]

We have briefly examined what immeasurable damage certain shadows of the Antichrist within the Church have inflicted on educational institutions of the Church. Many religious leaders of Catholic universities, colleges, schools—institutions that are treated as moral persons under the statutes of both canon and civil law because they have been incorporated under both these systems of law—have effectively transferred complete control, authority, management, and ultimate administrative responsibility of these institutions to lay boards of trustees or mixed boards of trustees in such a way that the parent religious order, congregation, institute, have lost effective control over such moral persons. This legal act is in fact an unjust alienation and transfer of ecclesiastical property to another legal entity. This unjust alienation and transfer of Church property violates the property rights of the Church and of the religious order to whom the institution belongs. Neither the Church nor the order gave permission nor entered into the confiscation of this property from the religious domain, nor approved of its consignment to purely secular owners for purely secularized purposes.[286]

[285] Newman, op. cit., pp. 360–361.
[286] Rev. Adam J. Maida, *Ownership, Control and Sponsorship of Catholic Institutions* (Harrisburg, PA: Pennsylvania Catholic Conference, 1975). The book treats of the unjust legal transferral of Church property to the secular domain.

However, evil as these legal apostasies are, there are other, more serious, dreadful consequences that ex-Catholic universities must answer for. In taking their religious communities out of the Catholic Magisterium on their own initiative, such religious leaders or administrators have violently changed the vocation of their own members. They have done this without any authorization from the Holy See nor from the Major Superiors of these orders who alone have the right to even consider such changes, subject to the approval of the Holy See. Moreover, without ever having even consulted these religious, they have callously imposed on them the role of teaching in secularized universities. This has divided and embittered the majority of religious communities whose morale is low and whose teaching members are shrinking through desertion, dislodgement, and death. How often have I heard disillusioned religious express in their own lamentations the noble sentiments found in this thought of Newman!

> If indeed this university ... were set up for the promotion of any merely secular subject . . . then indeed I should be out of place ... in being here at all. For what reason could I in that case have had for having now given some of the most valuable years of my life to this university, for having placed it foremost in my thoughts and anxieties—I had well nigh said to the prejudice of prior, dearer and more sacred ties—except that I felt that the highest and most special religious interests were bound up in its establishment and in its success?[287]

Then, too, the teaching religious communities are dying from lack of replacement by new and younger religious. Secularization has turned off the tap of vocations, but even more ominously, it

[287] Newman, op. cit., p. 453.

has driven off young religious who might have been won to the lecture halls, had the academic venture remained a Catholic apostolate. For there is no attraction, neither from the natural nor supernatural viewpoint, to teaching in a secular university while living in a religious community. The very incompatibility of ideals keeps both communities, the academic and the religious, in constant turmoil. The result is that the religious community's hold on its university, financial and spiritual, becomes very tenuous and finally breaks. This radical change brings religious communities face to face with radical, hostile, secularized, and even paganized students, with inimical faculty members and a world that despises the religious for their flight from their original high commitment. However civil or polite the world may appear in its public demeanor, it can never forget that these religious are to be likened to those who put their hand to the plow and turned back. Neither heaven, hell, nor the world loves a quitter. It may not be too harsh to say that these communities are on the road to academic and religious extinction and this by the hand of their own leaders who have performed another function of the Antichrist, namely, to bring the Church down into ill repute. This prophecy of extinction might be considered to be too lugubrious, were it not for an interview I read between a reporter of Fordham Magazine and the new president of that legally secularized university:

> Q. Let's turn for a moment to the position of the Jesuits. Historically, Father, Jesuits have been the backbone of the university. Their contributions to what Fordham has become are immense. Yet their numbers ... have declined, especially in the past ten years or so. What role or roles do you see the Jesuits playing in Fordham's future?

A. Jesuit tradition has been to develop works or institutions and then pass them to others all across the world. You will find many traces of institutions started by Jesuits which, for one reason or another, passed from Jesuit control and were even deprived of Jesuit presence. Personally, I am deeply committed to higher education and I would like to see Jesuits continue in this work, but their activity in higher education and even in an institution such as Fordham will be based on individual efforts much more than on group presence. A university such as Fordham simply could not be operated by the Jesuits as a group and I don't think it should. The university has a role that goes beyond that of an individual religious community. We Jesuits should do our best to serve the University, but we should not be surprised if our role declines.[288]

One reads in this answer a complete coming to terms with the secularization of a once great Jesuit university. One reads a willingness to see Jesuits work as isolated individuals, no longer as the Company of Jesus seeking the greater glory of God in the scientific training and sanctification of youth. One reads with amazement that the goal of achieving better secular higher education goes beyond the goal for which St. Ignatius founded religious communities and their schools, colleges, and universities. One reads of an incredibly new dedication for Jesuits, to serve as best they can a new god—the Secular University in the Secular City. And finally there is that complete stoical resignation to decline and disappearance from the apostolate of higher education on the university plane. And these spiritual cop-outs are presented by a Jesuit

[288] *Fordham Magazine*, Fall 1972, pp. 7, 8.

president of a secularized university to his confreres, living in a religious community of which this president is not the religious superior, as new ideals for their lives as Jesuits and companions of Jesus. Could the Antichrist himself tempt religious men with such a mean worldly vision? And this is represented as a victory of the Society of Jesus, to have its well-trained men work as intellectual loners, competitors with lay professors, for the betterment of secularized higher education! Could any role be more dismal for men who have dedicated themselves to the greater glory of God and the sanctification of souls in the service of Holy Church? Can one find a more tragic fulfillment today of the parable of the Vine and the fallen branches? Even this tragedy was foreseen and explained by Newman:

> The grace stored in Jerusalem and the gifts which radiate from Athens are made over and concentrated in Rome. This is true as a matter of history. Rome has inherited both sacred and profane learning; she has perpetuated and dispensed the traditions of Moses and David in the supernatural order and of Homer and Aristotle in the natural. To separate these distinct teachings, human and divine, which meet in Rome, is to retrograde; it is to rebuild the Jewish Temple and to plant anew the groves of Academus.[289]

The Antichrists and the New Christianity

From what we have considered above it is clear that intellectuals have awakened the world to the spirit of rebellion.[290] Some

[289] Newman, op. cit., p. 206.
[290] Julien Benda, *The Treason of the Intellectuals* (New York: William Morrow, 1928), pp. 4, 7, 10.

Catholic intellectuals, playing the role of forerunners of the Anti-christ, have helped create a spiritual wasteland, a condition of crisis and confusion within the whole Christian world, but especially within the Catholic Church. They are questioning and protesting almost everything—dogma, morals, sacraments, liturgy, govern-ment. Their spirit of defiance is animated by the fires of social ha-tred, a hatred that rejects the sacred. Political passions have achieved an ascendancy over Christian virtues within the Christian world. As apostles of the modern mind in a technocratic world dedicated to humanistic atheism, many Catholic intellectuals keep clamoring for their rights, using politics, litigation, demonstrations, and even violence to get them. Intellectuals have organized political hatreds today, have made these passions universal, coherent, homogenous, permanent, preponderant. Anyone can hear, read, and recognize them in crude daily newspapers, radio broadcasts, and TV docu-mentaries.[291] The Christian world is dying because of its apostasy from Christ, His Church, and their transcendent God. The erosion in Christian faith is founded on the evanescence of the Christian mind. And this loss of the Christian mind is due largely to the treason of Catholic intellectuals who have gone lusting after the wisdom of the world. We are witnessing today the eclipse of true theology, that is, the study of God and of God's creatures in rela-tion to Him as known by reason and revelation through the teach-ings of Christ and His Church as she contemplates, follows, and grows up in Him. What is taught as theology today is not the sci-ence of God, but the science of men's thoughts about God. This amounts to a historical and genetic study of the leading ideas of all religions, a discipline that does not assume or even investigate the truth of these ideas, but is solely interested in discovering the steps

[291] Ibid., p. 45.

of evolutionary process whereby they have come to be what they are.[292] There is no true theology today because there no longer exists a Christian mind, a consciousness aflame with love for the teachings of Jesus Christ. Mr. Harry Blamires, an intelligent, sensitive Christian layman realized this tragic condition of man as far back as 1963. At that time he wrote a book entitled *The Christian Mind*, from which we quote the opening paragraphs:

> There is no longer a Christian mind.
>
> It is a commonplace that the mind of modern man has been secularized. For instance, it has been deprived of any orientation towards the supernatural. Tragic as this fact is, it would not be so desperately tragic had the Christian mind held out against the secular drift. But unfortunately the Christian mind has succumbed to the secular drift with a degree of weakness and nervelessness unmatched in Christian history. It is difficult to do justice in words to the complete loss of intellectual morale in the twentieth-century Church. One cannot characterize it without having recourse to language which will sound hysterical and melodramatic.
>
> There is no longer a Christian mind. There is still, of course, a Christian ethic, a Christian practice, a Christian spirituality. As a moral being, the modern Christian subscribes to a code other than that of the non-Christian. As a member of the Church, he undertakes obligations and observations ignored by the non-Christian. As a spiritual being, in prayer and meditation, he strives to cultivate a dimension of life unexplored by the non-Christian. But as

[292] E. L. Mascall, *Theology and the Gospel of Christ* (London: SPCK, 1977), p. 18.

a *thinking* being, the modern Christian has succumbed to secularization. He accepts religion—its morality, its worship, its spiritual culture; but he rejects the religious view of life, the view which sets all earthly values within the context of the eternal, the view which relates all human problems—social, political, cultural—to the doctrinal foundations of the Christian Faith, the view which sees all things here below in terms of God's supremacy and earth's transitoriness, in terms of Heaven and Hell.[293]

It should not surprise us, then, that the modern secularized Christian, as a *thinking* being, has created a new Christianity. We have already observed that St. Pius X stigmatized "Modernism as the synthesis of all heresies." Now the secularized mind, led by agnostic philosophers and theological skeptics, because it has abandoned the supernatural view of reality, looks at God and Revelation in an *immanentist* rather than *transcendentist* manner. Hence, such a mind concocts evolutionary, immanentist explanations of God, religion, dogma, the sacraments, Scripture, the Church, and its Magisterium. All faith, religion, and revelation is subjected to criticism by science and personal experience. Divine revelation is imperfect and, therefore, subject to continual, indefinite progress corresponding to the progress of reason. Prophecies and miracles of Scripture are the poetical imaginings of men, to be sure great men. Dogma is merely man's approval of his refined formulas on religious experience. As experience changes and evolves so must dogma take on new, even contradictory meanings. All religions arise from experience and lead to salvation; the advantage of one over the other rests merely in the liveliness or vividness of its formulas. Christianity, of course, has

[293] Harry Blamires, *The Christian Mind* (London: SPCK, 1963), p. 3ff.

pounded out the most brilliant formulas. But indifferentism follows, if one religion is as good as another, and the result arises that it is considered divisive for the Church to work at making converts to the Catholic Faith.

Now the first aim of Catholic Modernists, as forerunners of the Antichrist, is to convert the Church of Rome to Modernism and then the universal Church. They insist that "the Roman Pontiff can and ought to conform with contemporary progress, liberalism and civilization." Really, like the Antichrist when he comes, they seek to create a Church in their own image and likeness—a small, Gnostic, elite Church of worldly-wise intellectuals who will dominate the religious thinking and practice of the whole human race. Scandalized that Christ founded His Church for all men, especially for outcasts, it is small wonder that these shadows of the Antichrist exhibit an indifference to official Catholic teaching and express an irreconcilable animosity to the custodian of this truth, the Magisterium.

Today neo-Modernism has regrouped its forces under such titles as "Catholic Opposition," or "Catholic Dissent," or "Christian Critics." Of course this opposition, dissent, and criticism is leveled against "the institutional Church," not against the enemies of the Church. As we will notice from their doctrines, policies, and spirit, the mind of these Catholics is not merely secularized; it is rather desacralized and has succumbed to a sacrilegious demagoguery that would substitute for Catholicism a Christian Socialism that is really a utopian seducer of the human spirit.

On November 17–18, 1973, the Christian Critics held an international assembly in Lyons, France. At the end they proclaimed the "New Christianity," and sent their document for approval to the Permanent Council of the French Episcopate. The document was rejected by the French bishops as being "a veritable alteration in the fundamentals of the Catholic Faith." Here are the five main characteristics of this "New Christianity":[294]

1) *Anthropocentrism:* Man not God is the center of religion, God is found solely in the face, functions, fortunes, and future of man. The primacy of man is identified with the primacy of God. 2) *Immanence in the World:* The kingdom of God is here not hereafter. Salvation means liberation from social sin, i.e., from ignorance, hunger, underdevelopment, political oppression, economic exploitation. Personal sin is no longer relevant in today's historical context. The new Catholics, enlisting under Socialism's banner, must achieve the kingdom of God by destroying capitalism. 3) *The New Evangelism:* The true meaning of the Gospels is economic not spiritual, arising from service to the poor; only the poor and their socialistic champions can understand the Gospels. The Magisterium has misinterpreted the meaning of the Gospels these two thousand years, using them to exploit the poor and remain in power with the mighty of this world. 4) *The New Ecclesiology:* The Church is part of the world; she does not exist for herself, but to serve the world. Hence, she must dissolve all her own institutions. In her liturgical life, any members may function as priests. In her jurisdictional life, local churches must be autonomous, for all authority comes from the faithful who share co-responsibility. 5) *The New Passion for Christ:* But this love is not for Christ the God-Man. Rather it is for Christ who is only a great man—the Man-for-others, the friend, the defender, the liberator of the poor, indeed, the revolutionary and Grand Subverter, aiding the poor to overthrow all corrupt institutions, the traditional Church included. Here we have mini-antichrists within the Church sowing the seeds of heresy, dissension,

---

[294] "The New Christianity," *Homiletic and Pastoral Review*, November 1976, pp. 54–61.

suspicion, and violence. Their resentful apostasy from the teaching of the Church must be answered and they must be unmasked as shadows of the Antichrist within the Church.[295]

In brief reply to these errors, therefore, it must be noted: 1) A religion of man must deny God and produce a decapitated love for man who is lovable only because God loves him and died for him. 2) The straitjacket of immanence prevents salvation from entering man's history from above; it denies the eschatological kingdom and reduces religion to being a mere political ideology, an exercise in utopian futility. 3) The Gospels belong exclusively to the Catholic Church who authentically gathered them together. Moreover, she alone possesses the Holy Spirit as the soul of her being, that Spirit who is the author, inspirer, and source of Holy Scripture. 4) The Church, as the unique creation of Christ and the Holy Spirit, is in but not of this world. Her mission to sanctify men in time as a people of God will be completed in glory for all eternity. 5) The Christ of the neo-Modernists is a nonhistorical fiction, tailored to push Socialist and Marxist ideology through the means of propaganda.

Already this propaganda has increased communist, atheistic influence within the Church.[296] The *National Jesuit News* produced a document entitled "National Planning and the Need for a Revolutionary Social Strategy: A Christian-Maoist Perspective." Therein we read that "the Society of Jesus must purge itself of its bourgeois social consciousness and identify with the proletariat," i.e., develop a social communist consciousness. Moreover, according to Father Dennis Willigan, S.J. of the University of North Carolina, this "document has been circulated among Jesuits in a

---

[295] Ibid., pp. 54–61.
[296] This and the following examples of "Liberation Theologists" actions are taken from *The Mindszenty Report*, June 1977, a monthly report put out by the Cardinal Mindszenty Foundation, St. Louis, MO.

number of provinces and has received a generally favorable reaction in as much as it represents a step toward the construction of a revolutionary social strategy for the Society (of Jesus) which is explicitly neo-Marxist and Maoist."

Then, too, Jesuit Father Juan Alfaro, who teaches at the Pontifical Gregorian University in Rome, told the October 1976 meeting of the International Theological Commission that "Christ was a kind of Palestinian Che Guevara." In the *National Catholic Reporter*, journalist Desmond O'Grady admits that though the Vatican remains staunchly anti-Marxist, nevertheless, "from the Philippines to Portugal there are Catholics who claim Marxist analysis is most pertinent to their situation." Che and Mao Tse-tung; Ho Chi Minh and Karl Marx are their "saints." Today "Catholic-Communist dialogue," begun in the early 1960s, has culminated in the open alliance of Catholics with atheistic Marxism. Prime Minister Fidel Castro has stressed the importance of "Marxists and honest Christians working together," Radio Havana reported September 2, 1977. According to the broadcast the dictator of Cuba said that a "strategic alliance" must be formed between Marxists and Christians "so that the Latin American revolution can move forward." "Progressive priests, most of them foreigners," says the *New York Times* on May 5, 1978, are playing leading roles in the guerrilla movements throughout Central America: for example, in Nicaragua, the North American Capuchins, and "in Honduras, Jesuit priests actually created the most radical of three peasant organizations" battling the government. Alan Reding of the *New York Times* notes how this clever tactic is working. "Because of the angry reaction of the South and Central American governments under attack by the guerrillas," he says, "the Catholic hierarchies are being forced to take the side of their progressive clergy," dismissing the possible consequences of a Communist take-over.[297]

Then, too, many priests and religious as guerillas have joined the movement called the theology of liberation. Their prime religious spokesmen today are Gustavo Gutierrez of Peru; Juan Luis Segundo of Uruguay; Hugo Assman of Brazil (now in exile); and Miguel Bonino of Argentina. In North America spokesmen for the "Liberation Theology Movement" include Father Charles Curren of Catholic University; Father Antonio M. Stevens-Arroyo, C.P., executive secretary of the Hispanic Consultation of Theology in the Americas; Gregory Baum of Canada, former Augustinian priest; and Father David Tracy of the University of Chicago, who was elected president of the Catholic Theological Society in 1976.[298]

The Theological Society is currently causing controversy and confusion with its recently released "Human Sexuality: New Directions in American Thought," which rejects traditional Catholic teaching on sex and sin. "Liberation theologists" are waging what Monsignor George A. Kelly, Director of Advanced Studies in Catholic Doctrine at St. John's University, describes as ideological "guerrilla warfare" against the Church on the campuses of Catholic universities, colleges, and seminaries. And in many instances they are being aided by advisors to our bishops who should be warned of the dangers in supporting their schemes. For example, in 1975, Father Sergio Torres, an exile from Chile where he headed the "Christians for Socialism" under Marxist president Allende, organized a week-long "Theology in the Americas" conference in Detroit described by the liberal *National Catholic Reporter* as a gathering of "North American Christian leftists and Latin American

[297] Ibid.
[298] Ibid.

Liberation Theologians." Part of the bill for this meeting—about $15,000—was picked up by the U.S. Conference of Catholic Bishops. More assistance in promoting "liberation theology" comes from the world headquarters of the Maryknoll Fathers where Father Torres operates from an elegant estate on the Hudson River. His associates include Father Miguel D'Escoto, director of communications for Maryknoll who claims that capitalism "is intrinsically wrong at its base," even though his order's missionary work is supported primarily by capitalist dollars donated to the Maryknolls.[299]

Liberation theologists claim that they combine "radical social activism with theological reflection" to produce a "blend of Marxism and Christianity." Communism—they prefer the word Marxism—offers the best solution to the world's woes. They dismiss the experiences of millions upon millions who have been murdered or still languish in Communist caves and concentration camps as unimportant. Father Juan Segundo rationalizes thus: "The history of Marxism, even though oppressive, offers right now more hope than the history of existing capitalism." The question of priests and religious resorting to armed conflict and terrorism is described by the theologians of liberation as "counter-violence methods." In other words, guerrilla priests are only reacting to the violence perpetrated by "oppressive governments" with "counter" measures that may happen to be Cuban-made rifles or terrorist bombs. Liberation theology "makes liberation the central Christian symbol" replacing nineteenth- and twentieth-century emphasis on reconciliation, says Father David Tracy. "Liberation theology has never bothered to hide its contempt for a presumptuously 'Roman' theology,"

[299] Ibid.

responds ex-Jesuit Peter Hebblethwaite, former editor of the English Jesuit magazine *The Month*. Both Fathers Tracy and Hebblethwaite are part of a "symposium in print" offered by the Paulist's *New Catholic World* magazine in its current May/June issue devoted to "Christian/Marxist Dialogue."[300]

Others writing for this special edition include liberation theologist Father Antonio Arroyo on "Marxism and Hispanic Movements in the U.S." and Margaret Schuler who is active in "American Christians Toward Socialism" and claims to having been "nurtured by the Gospel and informed by Marxist insights." The Paulist Spring book catalogue coos contentedly over the Christian/Marxist dialogue thus: "More than a decade ago, Teilhard de Chardin said that Christians and Marxists were 'traveling on the same road' and would eventually 'finish up by finding each other on the same mountain peak.' Today, Christians in France and Italy are boldly advocating a 'strategic alliance' with Communism. In many other parts of the world, Christian thinkers are advocating a 'theology of liberation.' In this book theologian Peter Hebblethwaite tells us how the encounter reached its present status and where it might lead in the future."[301]

The future is already present. In 1965 a Communist document, printed in Red China in Spanish for Latin American use, outlined plans to take over the Catholic Church not by making war on the Church, but by capturing it through subversion, infiltration and propaganda. The document claimed that it would be necessary "to progressively replace the religious element" in Church teaching "by the Marxist element; we shall gradually

---

[300] Ibid.
[301] Ibid.

transform the false conscience of the Catholics to the true conscience, so that they will eventually come around to destroying,
by themselves and for themselves, the divine images which they
had themselves created. This is our line of struggle for victory
against the counter-revolutionary Catholic Church." How well
this tactic has succeeded is demonstrated in another new book
published by the Paulist Press entitled *The New China: A Catholic
Response.* Here is a news story distributed by Religious News Service on April 6, 1978, concerning this book:

> Four Jesuit theologians—two of them Americans—have
> indicated in a new book that the Communism of Mao Tse-
> tung is more akin to Christianity than the religions of the
> East and that the Holy Spirit may be using Communism to
> lead the Chinese people to Christ. According to the book,
> some Christian virtues are being practiced by followers of
> Mao and Mao's version of Communism may well prepare
> China to accept Christianity. The moral teachings of Mao
> Tse-tung have produced a generation of Chinese who really
> put the good of the people above their own advantage (ac-
> cording to one of the Jesuit authors). I would not hesitate to
> say that the Holy Spirit may be using the Little Red Book of
> Mao's thoughts as an instrument in leading many Chinese
> to a love of their neighbor. Communism is preparing the
> way for the Gospel.... Mao's ideology can speak to the
> Christian need for personal development, for the evolution
> of the total Christian community, and for more productive
> Christian action and thought." Is it possible that these Je-
> suit forerunners of the Antichrist, using Satan's tactics of
> the big lie in writing this book, this atrocious apology for
> Mao, the mass murderer of millions in China, never read

in the *Guinness Book of World Records* that Mao is the world's all-time mass executioner? At least 94 million, and more probably up to 130 million, Chinese have been ruthlessly slaughtered since 1949 by Mao's Communist regime, and God alone knows how many he slaughtered before coming to total power.[302]

Here then is updated, Red Modernism eating out and fragmenting the Church. It is the new-styled cradle of religious revolution—militant, socialistic, terroristic, Marxist. It advocates a theology of violence, a morality of total, especially sexual, permissiveness. Father Louis Bouyer describes it in a recent book of his, *The Decomposition of Catholicism*. A British poet, playwright, and novelist wrote in his epic work, *The Deserted Village*, these famous words: "Ill fares the land to hastening ills a prey where wealth accumulates and men decay." Today this line can easily be adapted to the far greater tragedy of "the deserted Church." "Ill fares the Church to escalating ills a prey where doubt accumulates and men betray." Here is a brief summary of some of the statistics on the decomposition of Catholicism due to inroads made by the treason of intellectual shadows of the Antichrist directing the movement of updated neo-Modernism as a battering ram against the Church from within and from without.

Statistics of Decomposition

Mass Attendance: England & Wales: There has been a decline of about 16 percent from 2,092,667 in 1962 to 1,752,730 in 1974. This decline must be considered in relation to the fact that

[302] Ibid.

there had been an annual increase before, and for the first years after, the Council of Vatican II. These Mass attendance figures are provided by the Catholic Educational Council. *France:* According to the figures published by *La Croix*, the official daily of the French Church, on June 30, 1975, there has been a decline of 66 percent in Mass attendance; 41 percent were attending in 1964, only 14 percent were attending in 1975. *Holland:* Official figures issued by the *Catholic Social Institute* (K.A.S.K.I.) and published in *Dagblad* on March 26, 1971, reveal that 64.4 percent attended Mass weekly in 1966. This has declined to 47.2 by 1970. According to the *Catholic Herald* of May 18, 1975, the figure had declined to 30 percent by 1975, a total decline of 54 percent. *Italy:* *The Catholic Herald* of October 18, 1974, cites a figure of 53 percent in 1956 according to the Italian journal *Epoca*. In the *Universe* of September 14, 1973, Father S. Burgalassi, sociology professor at the Lateran University, gave a figure of 27 percent for regular Mass attenders. This represents a decline of 50 percent. The *Tablet* of September 4, 1976, quotes a figure of only 10 percent of Mass attenders among Rome's working class, which, according to the *Tablet* "seems to indicate that religious practice has notably declined in Italy during the past 5 years." *U.S.A.:* In a survey based on statistics published in the official Catholic Directory, *Time* magazine, in its May 24, 1976, edition, revealed a decline from 71 percent in 1963 to 50 percent in 1974, a decline of 30 percent in Mass attendance among Catholics.

Vocations to the Priesthood: England & Wales: According to figures cited in the *Times* of July 15, 1974, there has been a 25 percent decline in seminary enrollment since 1964. Nothing is said of the quality of the training given in the seminary. *France:* Seminary enrollment has declined by 83 percent from 1963 to 1973 as reported in the *Irish Catholic News*, March 20, 1975, which cites the official French National Centre for Vocations. In 1973, 151 new seminarians were enrolled and 422 left. In 1974, 191 entered and 205 left. This represents a figure of 45 percent more leaving than entering over the two years, in addition to the 83 percent decline in enrollment. Figures published in the *Tablet* for June 1, 1974, reveal that as a result of deaths, defections, and decline in ordinations, it was expected that the overall figure of 40,994 priests in France in 1967 would have declined to 21,820 by the end of 1975, a decline of 47 percent. *Holland:* Figures taken from the same source as those cited for Mass attendance reveal a 97 percent decline in ordinations and a 97 percent decline in the enrollment of students for the priesthood. Every seminary in Holland had been closed by 1970, and the 108 students studying theology in that year were in university faculties and the possibility of more than a very small proportion ever being ordained is minimal. Ordinations now number about a dozen in a really good year, with deaths and defections up to about 250 each. *Italy:* There has been a 35 percent decline in ordinations and a 45 percent decline in the number of seminarians between 1967 and 1973 (*Irish Catholic*, August 7, 1975). *U.S.A.:* There had been a decline of 64 percent in seminary enrollment between 1967 and 1974 and 25 percent of American seminaries had closed, according to the figures published in the *Homiletic and Pastoral Review* in October 1975. Over 10,000 have abandoned the priesthood since the Council (*Time*, May 24, 1976). *Female Religious:* The world total of nuns has declined by 24.6 percent in the four years 1970–1974. During this period the decline in the U.S.A. was 38.5 percent (*Catholic Herald*, May 9, 1975). Since the Council 35,000 nuns have abandoned their convents in the U.S.A. (*Time*, May 24, 1976). The total number of nuns declined by 50,000 from 1966 to 1976 (figures from the official U.S. Catholic Directory, published May 27, 1976).

Conversions: England & Wales: The Catholic Directory gives figures of 15,794 for 1959 and 5,253 for 1974, a 67 percent decline. Moreover, in 1963, there were 136,350 baptisms and in 1974 only 80,587, a decline of 59 percent (Catholic Directory). *U.S.A.: The National Catholic Register,* September 12, 1976 reports a "downward skid" or a 49 percent drop in baptisms from preconciliar figures.

The figures show a pattern of stagnation in the Catholicism of the West. Figures from such countries as Belgium and Germany, not cited here, conform to the prevailing trend downward. No attempt is made to assess the trends in Africa and Asia. However, it is noted that countries behind the Iron Curtain show a much healthier pattern. Croatia, Poland, Slovenia show the Church flourishing with plentiful vocations. In these countries pressure and persecution from Communism have really strengthened both the Catholicism and nationalism of the people. Equally detailed figures have been cited concerning the decline of the Catholic educational system, for example, in the U.S.A. where Catholic schools and colleges are closing at the rate of one a day. Or we could have cited the decline of the established Catholic press throughout the West. Moreover, precise figures are not available for the catastrophic flight of youth from Catholicism. In England the optimistic figure is 65 percent of the youth have left Christianity. It must also be born in mind that a very high proportion of those still claiming to be Catholics have become *de facto* Protestants by making themselves the sole arbiters of those aspects of Christian Faith and morals they feel inclined to accept. In the U.S.A., for example, 83 percent of Catholics have rejected the teaching of *Humanae Vitae* on the immorality of artificial birth control (*Time,* May 24, 1976).

Such is the spiritual wasteland that the neo-Modernist forerunners of the Antichrist have produced. They are preparing a
godless, morally corrupt society as the proper milieu for the coming of the Antichrist. Man's infidelity and immorality are the
cause of the coming of the Antichrist, but God makes use of him
as a scourge to separate the evil from the good, the wheat from
the chaff. Professor George Santayana, famous agnostic of our
era, in his book *Winds of Doctrine*, made a trenchant critique of
the Modernism of his day and it applies even more justly to updated Modernism. He wrote: "Modernism ... is the love of all
Christianity in those who perceive that it is all a fable. It is the
historic attachment to his Church of a Catholic who had discovered that he is a pagan.... Modernists are men of the Renaissance, pagan, pantheistic in their profounder sentiment, to
whom the hard and narrow realism of official Christianity is offensive just because it presupposes that Christianity is true.... As
for Modernism, it is suicide. It is the last of those concessions to
the spirit of the world which half-believers and double-minded
prophets have always been found making; but it is a mortal concession; for it concedes that everything in Christianity, as Christians hold it, is an illusion." And remarking wryly on the Modernists' opposition to Rome, Santayana writes: "The modernist
feels himself full of love for everybody ... except the Pope."[303]

There is a sure way of escaping the disease of Modernism and
its carriers, the shadows of the Antichrist, and that is total dedication to the teaching of the Apostolic See of Rome. "He speaks
in vain," writes St. Maximus in the sixth century, "who tries to
persuade me of the orthodoxy of those who refuse obedience to

[303] George Santayana, *Winds of Doctrine* (Gloucester, MA: Peter Smith,
1971), pp. 25–27.

his Holiness, the Pope of the Most Holy Church of Rome." And Cardinal Newman, prophet and doctor of our times, warns us not to follow ourselves in matters of faith and morals, but to follow Christ and His Church. He writes:

> Be our mind as heavenly as it may be, most loving, most holy, most zealous, most energetic, most peaceful, yet if we look off from Him (Christ and His Church) for a moment, and look towards ourselves, at once these excellent tempers fall into some extreme or mistake. Charity becomes over-easiness; holiness is tainted with pride; zeal degenerates into fierceness; activity eats up the spirit of prayer; hope is heightened into presumption. We cannot guide ourselves. God's revealed word is our Sovereign rule of conduct; and therefore, among other reasons, is FAITH so principal a grace, for it is the directing power which receives the commands of Christ and applies them to the heart.[304]

Now the neo-Modernist precursor of the Antichrist is a person who trusts in himself alone; he has lost his faith in Christ, but cannot steel himself to admit it. Yet, jealous of the faithful, he would rob them of the faith and holiness to make them companions of his own misery. Therefore, the Modernist mini-antichrist must make use of the big lie, like his master Satan. He has to fill the traditional dogmas with new content, new Christianity. He uses the right words—God, Christ, grace, eternal life, kingdom of God, sin, salvation, heaven, hell, death, resurrection. But he empties them of all Catholic meaning. For him the more a thing changes, the more it remains the same. Today the neo-Modernists

---

[304] John Henry Newman, *Parochial and Plain Sermons*, Vol. II (Westminster, MD: Christian Classics, 1966), pp. 278-279.

in the Church are the heralds of the Antichrist. Am I becoming an unreasonable alarmist or succumbing to melodramatic hysteria in saying this? It will help to ponder the words that St. Pope Pius X wrote more than thirty years ago in reference to the antichristian movement of Freemasonry, which was attacking the Church from outside, and to the movement of Modernism, which was simultaneously subverting the Church from within. And remember as you read the pope's sober words that the apostasy from the Church today is immeasurably greater now than it was then: "There is room to fear that we are experiencing the foretaste and beginnings of the evils which are to come at the end of time, and that the Son of Perdition, of whom the Apostle speaks, has already arrived upon earth."[305]

---

[305] Pope St. Pius X, Encyclical *Suprema Apostolatus*, 1903.

Chapter 10

Detente All Round:
Catalyst to the Antichrist?

La detente, in its original meaning, signified the trigger of a gun. Lâcher la detente means "to pull the trigger." Through wider application la detente came to mean a catch that starts or stops a movement, a gadget for releasing the striking of a clock, a control piece. Thus the pulled trigger fired the cocked gun; the released catch set off the wound-up alarm.

In the spiritual world, therefore, it would be the aim of the tactic of detente to dissipate dangerous tensions, to soften eyeball to eyeball confrontations, to set off alarms for protective actions. But there are two ways of resolving confrontations on the basic issues of human justice, freedom, and dignity. First, by surrendering to the enemy, either outrightly or by making counterfeit compromises disguised as wisdom under face-saving slogans. Second, by meeting the enemy courageously and forcing him to retreat from his evil aggressions. Unfortunately, in today's confrontation between what's left of the Christian West and the atheistic East, the West has taken the first road—that of verbally disguising its full retreat before the forces of atheistic evil. For today the policy of detente merely indicates a slow maneuvering for sly surrender to tyrants. It is a policy instrument that degrades the art of thinking, conversation, and, above all, the art of home and foreign politics by dragging all social communication into the dust and dreariness of fatalistic defeatism. Vainly hoping to relax international tensions and avoid nuclear war, the free West regularly succumbs to the demands of the monolithic East. This policy of detente is one of tragic self-delusion; it dissipates no dangerous tensions. Hence it is bound to be a failure on the political, economic, and military level because it was, and is, a continuing betrayal on the moral and religious level of human relations. It is a superficial, simplistic policy, lacking vision and depth. For this tactic of detente is doing nothing to reinforce the foundations below that are crumbling away and threatening a sudden collapse of the Western world. Attempting with detente to treat merely the symptoms of the sick society, the leaders of the West do not yet realize that detente itself is the essential virus in its own malignant sickness. Let me explain.

Religious Detente: Apostasy from God

The root evil of the tactic of political detente is to be found in man's metaphysical, moral, religious flight from and rejection of God. For man's social attitudes on the fundamental relations of community life, his just claims and moral obligations are determined by his care or carelessness about his relationship to God. Even godless socialist Proudhon had to marvel at how political problems were assumed into theology. In his *Confessions of a Revolutionary*, we read: "It is a cause of wonderment to see how in all political problems we invariably stumble up against theology." But Donoso Cortes in his "Essay on Catholicism, Liberalism, Socialism," commenting on Proudhon's wonderment at God's presence everywhere in politics, writes: "There is nothing here that should cause surprise except the surprise of Proudhon. For theology, by the very fact that is the science of God, is the Ocean that contains and embraces all the sciences, just as God is the Ocean that contains and embraces all things."[306] And it was the great St. Augustine who said that in its roots every serious political problem has a causal nexus with faith or lack of faith in God. The Psalmist long ago had written: "Unless the Lord builds the house, they labor in vain who build it."[307] This is a truth that applies to nations as well as to families and the Church.

Thus the fundamental evil of detente is that man has abandoned faith in and love for God. Man has sued first for separation then divorce from God and followed this rupture with a new engagement and remarriage to his new love and idol, technological humanism. Mankind is living in an age in which the West denies God through an addiction to technological scientism while the East escalates a messianic war against God through its addiction to dialectical materialism. The West has divinized Security and Technocracy; the East, Science and Revolution. But in both camps atheistic humanism has become the state religion. And both of these systems of secular humanism eclipse the person, eliminate his freedom, deny his human-divine value, and subject him to the tyranny of technological impersonalism. The alarming signs of the times testify to a fierce spirit of evil advancing everywhere. It is the spirit of detachment, detente, flight from, even rebellion against God and man. Hitherto the powers of government in each country, as yet relying on God and reason, were firm and vigorous enough to restrain this rebellion. But today many agnostic countries can barely contain

---

[306] Donoso Cortes, *Ensayo Sobre el Catolicismo, el Liberalismo y el Socialismo* (Buenos Aires: Editorial Americalee, 1943), p. 23.
[307] Psalm 126.

that lawless spirit, while many others have actually legalized the principle of lawlessness itself, the principle of license masquerading as liberty.

We are reminded of St. Paul's warning to the Thessalonians. In the last days there will be an awful, unparalleled outbreak of evil everywhere. This will be called the great apostasy. We ask ourselves: Does universal detente in the face of evil merely put the mask on what is today the great apostasy? At any rate, St. Paul reminds us that in the midst of this general falling away a certain Man of Sin, having the image of Satan and breathing hatred toward God and man, will suddenly appear. He will exercise frightening preternatural powers of destruction against the just. This Child of Perdition will be so special and singular an enemy of Christ that he will be called the Antichrist.[308] For just as types of Christ went before Jesus, heralding His coming, so shadows of the Antichrist have already preceded him, indeed are even now preceding him, to prepare the way for his coming. We recall the warning of St. John the Evangelist to the Christians of his day: "Little Children, it is the last time ... even now there are many antichrists whereby we know it is the last time."[309] But compared to the Archantichrist, all forerunners of him were so many mini-antichrists. This Super-Antichrist will orchestrate revolutions so expertly that the very framework of society will shatter into pieces under his wicked wand. In a stunningly evil way, he will knit together his totalitarian rule of heresy, sedition, revolution, schism, war—indeed of every evil movement—and hurl them effectively against the Church. Preceded by apostasy, conceived in apostasy, gestated in apostasy, born in apostasy, and raised up

[308] 2 Thess. 2:1-11.
[309] 1 John 2:18.

to manhood in apostasy, the Man of Sin will come to total power through a general, universal apostasy. In other words, the Antichrist could never have existed except for the decision of the majority of persons in the East and West to apostatize from God and join the forces of atheism.

Am I foolishly playing the prophet of gloom and doom in saying that we are entering the Age of Apostasy? Are there no evidences to convince us that some such apostasy is being formed, gathering forces, gaining ground on us every day? It must be admitted that in the West the conflict between the children of the New Humanism and the faithful is escalating in ferociousness. The spirit ruling in the great cities is avaricious, luxurious, self-dependent, irreligious, ungodly, falsely liberal, and sacrilegious. In fact a specific madness of modern society is its assault on the sacred. Suddenly the Secular City of Harvey Cox has degenerated into the Sacrilegious City of Jesus Christ Superstar in which the Son of God made man is reduced to being a moronic "hippie." And as if that blasphemy were not enough, word comes from Denmark that the makers of the idols of the Sacrilegious City have some devilishly creative ideas they mean to immortalize in a new film. We read in *The Christian Science Monitor* for August 10, 1973: "Meanwhile, in Denmark protest is mounting over another film about Jesus (still in the making). Thousands of people from Europe, the U.S., Japan and Africa are expected to demonstrate in Copenhagen ... against the film which, its director says, will portray Jesus as a bank robber and a lover. The state-controlled film institute has granted Danish director Jens Joergen Thorsen about $100,000 for the film."[310] On Sunday August 26, 1973, Pope Paul VI, addressing a large gathering of

---

[310] *The Christian Science Monitor*, Friday August 10, 1973, p. 8.

the faithful, condemned the film with holy zeal and anger: "We cannot remain silent and hide our personal sorrow about such an ignoble and blasphemous outrage which intends to deform the inviolable figure of Our Saviour, the supreme act of our faith and love.... Christ is being made a laughingstock, the victim of sacrilege and filthy lies: this is the reality! Where is our common moral and civil conscience? Can we allow our social existence to be degraded to such a point?"[311] The offspring of the New Humanism are agnostics, atheists, apostates, lovers of this world with tastes, opinions, habits immersed in materialism, with hearts riveted to the vagaries of time, minds moulded by vanities of passing pleasure, with thoughts rising no higher than personal comforts and gains, with a haughty contempt for the Church, her ministers, her sacraments, her devotions, her lowly faithful; with a lust for rank and station, an ambition for the splendor and fashions of the world, an affectation for refinement, a dependence upon their own powers of reason, a habitual self-esteem and finally with an utter insensibility to the heinous sins they are committing against God and man.

At first the Catholic Church seemed impregnable to the assaults of the forces of hell. To outsiders she looked impressive, coherent, immense; they admired her clarity of doctrine, her sure guidance in morals, her firm authority, her unified counterattack against spreading religious skepticism, savage totalitarianism, and perverse hedonism. She was seen as the last and strongest bastion against the advance of organized, militant, atheistic barbarism. Moreover, a steady in-gathering of converts buttressed her fight against the forces of desacralization. Then the tower of truth and holiness began to topple from an earthquake within. Apparently there had been a hidden

[311] L'Osservatore Romano, English edition, September 6, 1973, p. 2.

fault, a serious weakness down deep in the members of the Catholic Church. This weakness was found, it seemed, in the Church's leaders and especially among its prestigious intellectuals. It took the Council called Vatican II, the Council that, in the words of Pope John XXIII, was summoned to Rome "to bring the modern world into contact with the vivifying and perennial energies of the Gospel!"; it took this Council to discover that too many of its own members had been nurturing for a long time a secret desire to join the world and that now, abusing the Council itself as an authoritative pretext, such lovers of this world were opening the gates of the Church so as to bring the faithful into contact with the stultifying and deadly energies of neo-Modernism. The result has been that the humanistic pretensions of the secular world have been vastly exaggerated for Catholics and the development of a serious inferiority complex has reduced many of them to confessing cravenly and obsessively nothing but Catholic depravities, as if the Church, instead of being the Mystical Body of Christ, had been in fact all along the sacrilegious Body of the Antichrist. These "New Church" Catholics had become scandalized over the Catholic Church's allegedly intransigent, dogmatic, authoritarian, rigid, anti-Semitic, legalistic, Constantinian, triumphant, Roman postures and policies. We have all heard these snide slogans flung against the Church as rocks for her stoning. Indeed, a fascination for the secular with a tendency toward the sacrilegious had already eroded the sense of the sacred in these "New Church" Catholics. And under the influence of this fatal sickness, their hypercritical, even delirious, dialogue had reduced the number of conversions to the Faith significantly while increasing enormously the desertions of Catholic priests, religious, and laity to the world of unbelief.

The tragic results of secularism's eclipse of the sense of the sacred among the "New Church" Catholics are everywhere in evidence.

There are the serious divisions among Catholics on essential matters of faith and morals, errors concerning God, the historicity of the Gospels, the Real Presence, the Divinity of Christ, infallibility, the Resurrection, the nature of the Church and its salvational ministry, and many, many others too numerous to mention—all these have divided and mutilated the flock of Christ. To the scandal and sadness of men of good will everywhere, even priests have cheapened the sacred convictions and holy places of the multitudes. They have violently occupied cathedrals, rudely interrupted holy liturgies, raucously challenged legitimate civil and sacred authority.

But the problem, of course, is not principally sacrilegious words and deeds. We must not mistake the symptom for the disease. The radical disease is a general loss of faith, a religious exhaustion that twists the souls of men from God and attaches them with enthusiasm to every clever and caustic criticism that corrodes the realm of the sacred and glorifies the city of this world. Religious sociologist Harvey Cox did not foresee that his brilliant Secular City would become that sacrilegious cesspool in which a decadently permissive society would exalt, in its novels, dramas, movies, paintings, liturgies, popular arts, and frenzied music, savagery and sexuality. But you need not take my word for this social slide into spiritual sliminess.

In his book entitled *Trousered Apes*, Professor Duncan Williams wholeheartedly agrees with Leslie Fiedler that "there is a weariness in the West which undercuts the struggle between Socialism and Capitalism, democracy and autocracy, a weariness with the striving to be men."[312] Admitting that the news of God's death "has permeated, secularized and radically changed every aspect of Western

---

[312] Duncan Williams, *Trousered Apes* (New Rochelle, NY: Arlington House Publishers, 1971), p. 43.

thought and society," Professor Williams proceeds to document abundantly that, as a result of the banishment of God from society, "the Western world and its culture is saturated with violence and animalism.... We are teaching savagery and are naively appalled at the success of our instruction."[313] He demonstrates effectively how the literature of the times both reflects and provokes the escalating barbarism and defeatism that is creating the satanic society, ready to enthusiastically acclaim the Antichrist when he comes. Commenting on the Theatre of the Absurd that degenerates into the Theatre of Revolution and then into the Theatre of Cruelty, Professor Williams writes:

> What shocks an audience today will be acceptable tomorrow and thus the contemporary dramatist is constantly impelled to seek further excesses to gratify a warped taste which he has himself implanted in the public mind.... The whole modern cult of violence and animalism is in essence an admission of defeat. Since we cannot be men to any idealistic extent, let us lapse into barbaric animalism but, still clinging to vestiges of a past which we hate but cannot escape, let us clothe our defeat in high-sounding terms: "alienation," "cult of unpleasure," "realism," and similar jargon. Yet all this fashionable phraseology cannot conceal the fact that the Emperor has no clothes. The literature of today lacks certain essential qualities. It no longer satisfies man's need for beauty, order and elevation, and to this extent it is incomplete and stunted. It contains, as Trilling has observed, an anti-civilizing trend, and to this is closely linked a cult of ugliness, a morbid

[313] Ibid., p. 29.

concentration on the baser elements of life, a clinical obsession with the bizarre and with the grossly sensual and degrading aspects of human nature.... The contemporary playwright or producer might well take as his motto, *Apres moi, la secheresse* (After me, the drought), and congratulate himself that he is writing before a morbid public appetite demands scenes of such repellent realism that actors and actresses will have to be killed on stage in order to satisfy it.[314]

Doctrinal Detente: Flight from Revelation

All the enemies of God, but especially the "New Church" Catholics, as heretics and rebels against God and His Church, bear the characteristic mark of the Antichrist. That brand is their denial that our Lord Jesus Christ is the Son of God who has come to redeem men. St. John the Evangelist states that the denial of Christ is aptly called the spirit of the Antichrist. Thus these modern enemies of Christ within the Church radiate the spirit of the Antichrist, are disciples and forerunners of the Antichrist, and can be called antichrists or mini-antichrists.

It is hardly surprising that the City of Satan, in its attack on the Catholic Church, would concentrate its big guns on two major doctrines that constitute the heart of the Catholic Faith: 1) the Eucharist as the real substantial presence of the true eternal sacrifice of Jesus Christ in the consecrated host; 2) the Virgin Mary as the Mother of God. Both these mysteries are reduced to being Christian developments of old pagan myths, fables that attempted to explain the origin of the universe through monistic

---

[314] Ibid., pp. 40, 72.

and cosmological forces. Daily within the Church one is sad-
dened at the waning reverence for the Eucharist and shocked at
the growing blasphemies against the Eucharist and the Mass. The
Mystery of Iniquity has opened an offensive against the Mystery
of Faith. In the opinion of the ex-canon M. Roca, found in his
book, *Glorieux Centennaire,* the mystery of the Incarnation was
not an assumption of a human nature by Jesus Christ, the Second Person of the Blessed Trinity. It was merely "an innoculation
of the divine into the human." It is thus that the masses, all unknown to themselves, receive the divine influence in their moral
ways and secret acts. It is also thus that in the rites of the Church,
this divine innoculation is admirably symbolized in the ceremonies of Baptism, the Eucharist, and the other sacraments. Thus
the Eucharist considered as a rite is merely a symbol, but considered as the cosmological reality that it expresses, it is the presence
of the Cosmic-Christ, of the Christo-humanity in everything.
Therefore, in reality transubstantiation is only the presence of
Christ in the human. Civilization, whether advancing or regress-
ing the flow of history and human communications, will become
"communion" for everyone through an osmosis of cosmic dimensions. This is a species of Christo-genesis rooted in evolution.[315]

This mythical "Eucharistization" concocted from the theories
of Teilhard de Chardin is supposed to be the phenomenon
through which Christ assimilates to Himself humanity and,
through humanity, the universe itself. Thus transubstantiation,
by divinizing the universe, enlarges and prolongs Christ's incarnation. The Word inserts itself through this innoculation into

[315] M. Roca, *Glorieux Centennaire,* p. 537. Quoted by *Si, Si, No, No,* a
monthly periodical published in Rome, Italy, Marzo 1976, Anno
II, Numero 3.

the cosmic elements. It is true that Teilhard attributes a secondary character to these phenomena that for him flow out of the
consecration of the Mass. But it must be noted that if this procedure of "Eucharistization" is dialectically turned, as an antithesis,
to the innoculation posited by Roca, the result is such a convergence that what the Council of Trent defined as "the immediate
and individual presence of Christ in the consecrated host"
through the admirable and singular conversion of transubstantiation can no longer be clearly distinguished as being distinct from
the original, creative, universal presence of God in all things.
From such an explanation one gets the impression that "cosmic
holy communion" is a real possibility and that sacramental transubstantiation is merely its symbol. Thus the sacrament of the
Holy Eucharist is counterbalanced, and the idea of the communion of all men among themselves is considered the real holy
communion in the "Christo-Social-Spirit." We read Roca again:
"This holy communion for all men takes the place of sacramental
communion and it can happen that transubstantiation operates
in all men more rapidly than in so-called Christians who accept
the empty formula and dead letter of the Sacrament of the Eucharist.... Here is what I call transcendental and rational theology. The theologians of the future will accept this explanation
and type of theology."[316]

Such variations on Gnosticism, symbolism, and Modernism
attack the authentic teaching of the Magisterium on the Holy
Eucharist. They are to be rejected with zealous contempt, for
they are the work of the shadows of the Antichrist. We now
emphasize three errors concerning the Blessed Virgin. Just as
Christ is not the Son of God, but an innoculation of the divine

[316] Ibid., p. 537.

into the human, so Mary is not the Mother of God. Rather she is the key to all cosmogonies, i.e., the fulfillment of all goddesses created by the pagans to explain the origin of the universe, the fulfillment of Gaia, Demetra, and Iside. Mary thus represents the living, Feminine Principle or Immaculate Wisdom and is united with the Masculine Principle, the Celestial Divine Spirit, from whose spousal union a new divine race of men comes forth. Mary thus received a priesthood, which however has remained hidden up to our times. Today, as knowledge of women has developed, women, in consequence of Mary's priesthood, may become priestesses themselves and even papal consorts in the Church of the Future. Roca concludes as follows: "Thus under two parallel tiaras and in a cloud of incense men will behold the Pope and his Consort pontificating together as spouses, symbols of the sacred, divine Duality—the Power of Masculinity and Feminity, the Spirit and the Anima, the two universal principles of the celestial Diade and of the androgynous (hermaphroditic) priesthood."[317] These fables are nothing but a marvelous mixture of the theories of updated Gnosticism, Catharism, and Cabalism, all occult religious philosophies condemned as heresies by the Church.

Detente as Liturgical Demolition

Once again we find that Cardinal Newman foresaw another serious attack upon the Christian Faith. This time he warned Christians against innovators who would relax Christian forms and usher into the Church liturgical frenzy. Such devotees of change question every Christian form of prayer, every posture of devotion, every devotion itself, and the very personal or traditional

---

[317] Ibid., pp. 497, 506, 507.

symbols of the Faith. Their lust for innovation is used as a battering ram against the stability of long-established, time-tested sacred rites, which have been witnesses and types of precious Gospel truths for Christian communities. Hurriedly, even violently, they replace divine forms with new diluted Masses, new prayers, new sacraments, new churches, new terminologies—all of which confuse the faithful. Newman writes: "No one can really respect religion and insult its forms. Granted that forms are not immediately from God, still long use has made them divine *to us*; for the spirit of religion has so penetrated and quickened them, that to destroy them is, in respect to the multitude of men, to unsettle and dislodge the religious principle itself. In most minds usage has so identified them with the notion of religion, that one cannot be extirpated without the other. Their faith will not bear transplanting.... Precious doctrines are strung like jewels upon slender threads."[318]

Liturgical detente has led to the loss of the sense of the sacred. To realize this tragic event we must reflect on what the sense of the sacred really comprises. The sacred is a mystery. It heralds the presence here and now of the world above, the world of the divine, and it fills man with incomparable reverence. The sacred reveals that the religious sphere is set apart, wonderfully superior and distinct from the rest of man's existence. But this apartness, far from precluding contact between the religious and natural spheres of man's existence, is actually a precondition for their fruitful intercommunion. Sacredness is one of those ultimate data perceived in and by itself, unexplainable, indivisible, mysterious. Sacredness is a reality that does not exist solely outside

[318] John Henry Newman, *Parochial and Plain Sermons*, Vol. II (Westminster, MD: Christian Classics, 1966), pp. 75, 76.

man as a knower, but it invades and involves the whole man as a free person. The sacred seizes each man in his ontological, intellectual, psychological, and historical developments.[319]

Thus the sacred must be approached, not with curiosity the way we approach an objective problem, but with awe and trembling, the way we approach mysteries. For the sacred represents the divine call from above, forcing the man of good will, like Moses before the burning bush, like the three apostles before the transfiguration of Christ, to his knees in a prostration of adoration. The challenge emanating from the sacred is so powerful that man cannot remain indifferent to it. In the presence of God, the Source of Sacredness, man either adores with the prayer, "Thy Will be done," or rebels with the cry, "I will not serve!" Thus God is the ineffable Someone at the summit of every experience of the sacred. This Summit of the Sacred claims the first place in every intelligent being's life, angels and men. Religion is man's response to the sacred, to God, the Supreme Ruler, Prior, Independent yet ever-present Other. The sense of the sacred presents man with these paradoxical experiences. God is presented as totally Other, transcending man, yet He is simultaneously experienced as being intimately present, nearer to man than man is to himself, filling man with awe and yet desiring to give Himself to man in intimate communication and communion. St. Paul reminds us that "in Him we live and have our being."

The sacred also brings man the experience of God's brilliance and luminosity. Thus man's response to God is his response to the numen or the numinous, that is, to the wholly illuminating,

---

[319] Alice von Hildebrand, Chap. IV in *Introduction to a Philosophy of Religion* (Chicago: Franciscan Herald Press, 1970), pp. 32–39.

fascinating, and ravishing Reality who is God. The experience of the *Mysterium Tremendum* suffuses the being of man with awe, a mixed feeling of reverence, fear, and wonder accompanied by an acute, grateful consciousness of one's creatureliness in the presence of an infinitely good Creator. In the experience of the sacred a "shudder" moves the whole person, which, speechless, trembles to the deepest core of its being. The sacred presents God as the *Mysterium Fascinans* before whom the posture of prayer and adoration is the only adequate response called for by the whole of man's being. Thus religion and the sacred always go together. Indeed, religion vanishes with the loss of the sacred, and vice versa. Religion flourishes with growth in the consciousness and love of the sacred. The moment the sense of the sacred diminishes in a people, it is a sure sign that the faithful are becoming secularized, materialized, paganized. For then they have lost an awareness of the presence of God and of His Kingdom that descends from above.[320]

The sacred applies not only to God but to all beings and things that have a special connection with Him—angels, saints, miracles, churches, sacraments, etc. Moreover, there are sacred places and times. The Holy Land where Christ lived, died, and redeemed man is a sacred place. Then, too, sacred time reenacts, relives historically events, e.g., the daily Mass liturgy and especially Holy Week, which relives the events of man's salvation. But in all sacred instances, eternity is not pulled down to the level of time, rather time soars into eternity. For the sacred is above time, though inserted in time and capable of ransoming time. Thus, the sacred, as essentially related to religion can redeem and blot

---

[320] Rudolf Otto, *The Idea of the Holy* (New York: Oxford University Press, 1923), p. 6.

our man's faults committed in time. By transcending and transforming time through a life and liturgy of faith in the true religion, the sacred does not obliterate time, but saves and sanctifies it. The Source of the Sacred embraced man and his history when the Son of God forever embraced in His divinity the sacred humanity he received from Mary, His Mother.

Man, therefore, is capable of transforming his domain of the nonsacred, of the profane, with the sense of the sacred or of degrading that domain and himself by obliterating in himself his love for the sacred. Man attacks the sacred when he rejects God and the true religion. The Antichrist will be the hater and destroyer of the sacred par excellence. For he will promote himself and his affairs on this earth as his only and ultimate concerns—and those will be the destruction of the image of Christ in the souls of men and the branding of those same souls with his own and Satan's seal. Thus the Antichrist would find modern times much to his liking. For in our generation a social climate charged with hatred of God has produced what even the atheist men of culture have sardonically referred to as the "Savage Sixties" and the "Sick Seventies." For once man rejects God, man becomes what Kierkegaard calls "the eternal zero." This is logical and necessary for, since his awareness of himself is founded on his awareness of God, the godless man, rootless and directionless, is at sea in an absurd world. Of course, he has an identity crisis. And with his animus against God and the sacred, he becomes a menace and a plague to the faith and holiness of his fellowmen. For when he breaks the sacred chains of love that bind him to God, he ends up breaking even the chains of civility and decency that should bind him to his fellowmen. Moreover, it is not surprising that the man who has rejected God and the sacred continues to talk about God, religion, liturgy, and the

Church. Now, however, he speaks of these realities as being "interesting phenomena" in the ascent of man from infancy to maturity. Now he experiments with these sacred realities as if he were tinkering with toys or automobiles. Now this "uncommitted interest," this neutrality toward divine, sacred realities is a typical game of ridicule played by the spiritually defeated and exhausted "playboys," choosing to be smart and clever rather than sacred and serious. These atheistic, intellectual snobs refuse to realize that God, religion, the liturgy, and the Church can never be merely interesting or amusing myths. The sphere of the sacred is really uninteresting in the shallow, cute sense of that term. For the sacred sector demands one's total self-donation to God, one's eternal salvation being jeopardized if one refuses to say "yes" to God. Trivial things and affairs can be the subject of interest and cleverness. But adherence to the sacred realm is a tremendously serious, ultimate, tragic affair. It is the awful, shuddering one thing necessary for which all else must eventually be put aside, even temporal life itself. When one jokes about the sacred, one is well on the way to participating in the sacrilegious.

For the rejection of the sacred as revealed in the dynamics of ridicule or in the cult of the clever always degenerates into the dynamics of hate and the cult of self, both of which lead to hatred of God, of the Church, of others, and finally of oneself. Thus, in our times a social climate charged with hatred of God, poisoned with irreducible religious-moral-political tensions and with hourly seditious preachments bereft of all truth, of all objectivity, of all love is the logical, violent result of the loss of the sense of the sacred. A society sickened from its rejection of God and the sacred necessarily produces a sick culture. In a modern play, *Prometheus Unbound*, Prometheus, the Titan who stole fire from Zeus, the god of the gods, is confronted by the foul furies

and asks them wonderingly: "Can anyone exult in his own deformity?" Dostoevsky's Underground Man answers with a soul-
searing affirmation: "I am a sick man.... I am a spiteful man. I
am an unpleasant man." Underground Man then adds that he
finds his only enjoyment "in the hyper-consciousness of his own
degradation."[321] Today the Christian and post-Christian savage is
idealized in philosophical, political, ethical, literary, and theological works as the authentic man-come-of-age—the Rebel Hero
of *Paradise Lost*, the Promethean Savior of a Cosmos Regained.
From the heights of this hateful, overweening pride such a man
has created a culture in which he defines his fellowman as "that
most precious capital," "that useless passion," "that walking bag
of sea water." This is the spirit of the Antichrist who will hate
everyone made in the image and likeness of God. For as sacrilegious man he will hurl these slogans against his fellowman from
a rhetoric of hatred that takes satanic joy in destroying the dignity, sacredness, and divinity with which God has endowed men
created and redeemed by His Son.

Much of the new liturgy has been drained of the numinous
and the sacred. The new forms are without splendor, flattened,
undifferentiated. Why was kneeling replaced by standing? Jesus
Himself fell on his knees and on his face as He prayed to His
heavenly Father. Satan too knows the meaning of worship and
man's need for it. He tried to get Jesus to fall down and worship
him. Why has the liturgical year and the Mass been so unfortunately mutilated against the wishes of the faithful? In fact, the
faithful are now confused about the Mass, the feasts of the saints,
the holy seasons. Why was the *Gloria*, that prayer of total concentration on God's Majesty and Goodness, restricted practically to

[321] Williams, op. cit., p. 57.

Sundays alone, and only to those Sundays outside of Lent? More-over, is the Faith really renewed and vivified by obscuring our sense of community with the Christians of apostolic and ancient times? The new liturgy no longer draws us into the true experi-ence of reliving the Life of Christ. We are deprived of this experi-ence through the elimination of the hierarchy of feasts and the at random changing of the dates of famous feasts.[322] Then, too, the new forms are the result of experimentation. But one experi-ments with things, with objects that one wants to analyze. Experi-mentation is the method of science. The wretched idolatry and vulgarity of tinkering with sacred realities has, unfortunately, penetrated the Church and produced a mediocrity-ridden liturgy, a show for spectators that distracts from the holy, frustrates inti-mate communion with God, and trivializes, where it does not suppress, sacred actions, symbols, music, and words. In reality such diminished liturgies have renewed nothing. Rather these innovations have emptied churches, dried up vocations to the priesthood and sisterhood, driven off converts, and opened the doors wide to a flood of renegades. Even though valid in its es-sence, such a new liturgy cannot inspire for it is colorless, artifi-cial, banal, without the odor and flavor of sanctity. A humanized and popularized, man-oriented liturgy will never produce saints. Only a divinized, God-oriented liturgy can accomplish that mira-cle. One suspects that many priests realize the banality of the new liturgy. That is why they often become, during the Mass and other ceremonies, actors and entertainers. They put on a show in order to gain the attention of the congregation. These come-dians in chasubles preach a utopian Christianity rather than the

---

[322] Dietrich von Hildebrand, *The Devastated Vineyard* (Chicago: Fran-ciscan Herald Press, 1973), pp. 70ff.

true Christianity. Their treasure is man rather than God; their emphasis this-worldly rather than other-worldly; their goal progress rather than sanctity; their apostolate is immanent rather than transcendent; their means to their goal is the way of revolution rather than the way of the cross; they preach a secular Church instead of the Sacred Church founded by Christ; the essence of their morality is self-assertion rather than self-denial; the Christ they present to the congregation is the humanist Christ rather than the God-Man crucified Christ; they speak in tongues of protest rather than in tongues of fire, the fire of love flaming forth from the Holy Spirit; they genuflect before the world and stand before Christ; they work for a democratic Church instead of a hierarchic Church; they are moved by resentment and envy instead of radiating the joy of Christ.

In our times, then, it is not any longer a secret that the enemies within and outside the Church want to destroy belief in the divinity of Christ. Once the liturgy is humanized, Christ the center and Object of it becomes the humanist par excellence, the liberator, the revolutionary, the Marxist ushering in the millennium; he ceases to be the Divine Redeemer. We must be alerted to these shadows of the Antichrist who plan, by convincing us to abandon our sacred forms, at length to seduce us into denying the Christian Faith altogether. The Church is attacked by these children of Satan in and outside her fold, because she is a living form, "the sacrament—the sign and instrument—of communion with God and of unity among all men"; because she is the visible body of religion. Hence these shrewd masters of sedition know that when her sacred forms go, religion will go also. Violate the *lex orandi* and you must inevitably destroy the *lex credendi*. That is why they rail against so many devotions as superstitions; why they propose so many alterations and changes, a tactic cleverly calculated to shake the foundations of the Faith. We must never forget, then, that forms apparently indifferent in themselves become most important to us when we are used to using them to nurture our lives in holiness.

Places consecrated to God's honor, clergy carefully set apart for His service, the Lord's Day piously observed, the public forms of prayer, the decencies of worship, these things, viewed as a whole, are sacred relatively to the whole body of the faithful and they are divinely sanctioned. Rites sanctified by the Church through ages of holy experience cannot be disused without harm to souls. Moreover, in the words of Newman, "Liturgical reform-ists must ever be aware of the following truth; Even in the least binding of sacred forms, it continually happens that a speculative improvement becomes a practical folly, and the wise are tripped up by their own illusions."[323]

Bishops would be wise to follow Newman's conclusions in this war on the sacred liturgy:

> Therefore, when profane persons scoff at our forms, let us argue with ourselves thus—and it is an argument which all men, learned and unlearned, can enter into: "These forms, even were they of mere human origin (which learned men say is *not* the case, but even if they were), are at least of a spiritual and edifying character as the rites of Judaism. And yet Christ and his Apostles did not even suffer these latter to be irreverently treated or suddenly discarded. Much less may we suffer it in the case of our own; lest stripping off from us the badges of our profession, we forget that there is a faith to maintain and a world of sinners to be eschewed."[324]

[323] Newman, op. cit., p. 78.
[324] Newman, op. cit., pp. 78, 79.

The Fathers of the Church emphasize the corruption of the liturgy that will prevail at the last days. As the end draws near, the Church will be subjected to a fiercer, more diabolical persecution than any previously suffered. There will be a cessation of all religious worship. "They shall take away the daily sacrifice." Some Fathers interpret these words to mean that the Antichrist will suppress for three and a half years all public religious worship. Others remind us that the Antichrist will set up his throne within the Temple of God and demand worship of himself from his depraved followers. We are living in times so wicked that many nations will not allow innocent, defenseless human beings natural birth much less the opportunity to receive the grace of supernatural birth. St. Augustine wondered whether in the days of the Antichrist Baptism would be administered to infants of Christian parents. The reign of the Antichrist will be supported with a galaxy of miracles, such as the magicians of Egypt effected before Moses and Simon the Sorcerer displayed before Peter and John. St. Cyril writes: "I fear the wars of the nations; I fear divisions among Christians; I fear hatred among brethren. But enough! God forbid that it should be fulfilled in our day! However, let us be prepared."[325] Unfortunately, it has happened in our day; the liturgy is a sign of contradiction among Christians today; the Holy Mass that once united Christians now, with the new liturgy, fiercely divides Christians. Many Catholics, because of the dilution of the sacred in the new liturgy, and the breezy manner in which many radical priests celebrate it, cannot attend such liturgies;

---

[325] John Henry Newman, *Discussions and Arguments on Various Subjects* (London: Longmans, Green, 1888), p. 102. Newman quotes St. Cyril's Catechism, XV, pp. 16, 17.

they find it morally impossible to have to endure the desacralized antics allowed by the liturgical storm troopers. Hence they stay away. Thus we see that, over and above the persecution of blood and death, there is even today a persecution of craftiness and subversion. The precursors of the Man of Sin are very effective in splitting up and dividing Christians. They are successful in dislodging many from the rock of salvation, in driving many into heresy and schism, depriving them of their Christian liberty, strength, peace, and their household in Christ.

How do we recall a sacrilegiously sick society that functions on the fashionable fallacy that murder is the best therapy for the world's problems to the sanity and sanctity of the sublime? We, especially all true followers of Christ, must help man return to the nature and deep significance of the sacred. Only when men grasp and appreciate the nature, meaning, and value of the sacred will they be equipped and willing to understand and courageously confront the moral disvalues of their dying society. Truly an awareness of the sense of the sacred is a barometer that accurately indicates the vitality of the religion, morals, and culture of a people. A blindness to the nature of the sacred is a sure preparation of society and mankind for the coming of the Antichrist. On the other hand, a clear vision and love of the sacred will enable mankind to see the unearthly beauty of the holy and to fall in love with God who is Holiness itself.

Detente as Dialogue: A Boon for Antichrists

Back in the days of the "great thaw" between the atheistic forces of Russia and the West, the incurably optimistic oracles among the ruling classes began chanting a song of peace. A spirit of buoyant euphoria swept through the West. Good Pope John XXIII was embracing Communist journalists; Red

Russia released to the West some political and religious prisoners to demonstrate its good will. The golden glow of detente
rose with every sunburst from the East. Hope about uniting
our broken world gave birth to a theory of convergence between the free nations of the West and the Soviet Union with
its satellites. It was a tranquilizing, drowsy theory that induced
in the West loss of contact with and moral insensibility to the
harsh truths of reality.

Even the Catholic Church, gathered in a mighty General
Council at the Vatican, caught this spirit of universal convergence. When 450 of its Fathers from 86 countries petitioned to
have the Council produce a special document in which, for the
benefit of the whole world, "the Catholic social doctrine would
be set forth with great clarity, and the errors of Marxism, Socialism and Communism would be refuted on philosophical, socio-
logical and economic grounds," the petition was rejected as
being too divisive. And the tactic used to defeat the petition
was the device of the devious lie. What happened to the 450
signed interventions to have "a solemn reaffirmation by the
Council on the long-standing doctrine of the Church on this
matter?" Father Ralph M. Wiltgen, S.V.D., in his book *The
Rhine Flows into the Tiber* writes: "From four different sources I
learned that the person who withheld the intervention from
the members of the joint commission was the commission's
secretary, Monsignor Achille Glorieux of Lille, France ... the
French prelate had acted as a 'red light' for the interventions
on Communism.... Archbishop Garrone of Toulouse was
obliged by the Council to make a public admission of negli-
gence.... He stated that the interventions on Communism had
reached the office of the commission within the proper time,
but were not examined when they should have been, because,

unintentionally, they had not been transmitted to the commission members."[326]

Thus, clerical intrigue, motivated no doubt by the genuine desire to achieve some sort of peaceful convergence with the Communist world, thwarted the opportunity of the Church in General Council to break an embarrassing silence on the intrinsic evil of Communism, the greatest social evil in the world preparing the ground for the coming of the Antichrist. To this very day, because of this failure to face forthrightly the greatest threat of all times to the Catholic Church, the Church herself is being publicly reprimanded by her own faithful within and friends without for a silence on Communism that is taken, however unjustly, as a sign of cowardice and connivance.

With the defeat of the conciliar try for a special schema on Communism, Pope Paul VI called for a policy of dialogue with atheistic Communism. This posture of concession was further developed into a policy of *la mano tesa*, the extended hand of friendship, and further developed politically as the policy of *ost-politik*, that eagerly tolerant attempt to deal with the Communists in order to gain certain rights for religion and the Church in their Iron-Curtain countries. Unfortunately, this led to a certain permissiveness and trust on the part of many clergy in Communist humanism. And this naive trust further led to damaging political compromises between Church persons and Communist states. What have been the results of this difficult dialogue? They have been nearly all bad for the Church, nearly all good for the Communist world.

(1) The dialogue has succeeded in seducing many Catholic leaders away from the sole purpose of the Catholic Church's

---

[326] Ralph M. Wiltgen, *The Rhine Flows into the Tiber* (New York: Hawthorn Books, 1967), pp. 272–278.

existence — its mission to bring all men to salvation in Christ. Through the dialogue many Church leaders have been cleverly maneuvered into substituting a utopian Christianity whose purpose is to bring all men to natural happiness. (2) The ecclesiastical warmth demonstrated in the policy of "the extended hand" has brought about a fatal kiss of peace between Catholics and Communists, for it has produced thousands of Catholics, many of them priests, nuns, and intellectuals, adherents to Christian Marxism, Christian Socialism, and an army of Catholic Dissidents from their Church's teaching on many essential dogmatic and moral matters. (3) The policy of Catholic detente through dialogue is succeeding in secularizing Christian nations, e.g., France, Italy, Spain, and now Portugal. Moreover, it has so strengthened their Communist parties that Communist candidates have won much regional governing power and are on the threshold of winning national power. (4) The policy of *ost-politik* has led to the legitimizing in the eyes of the world of many Red dictatorships that dominate Christian countries behind the Iron Curtain and even in the West, e.g., Cuba. The agonizing question the captive Catholics have gnawing at their morale is: "Has the Catholic Church abandoned us to these powers of Hell?" (5) These daily accommodations, some say surrenders, to the myth of a possible peaceful coexistence with the godless hegemony of Communism have demonstrated to the enemy that the West has lost its faith in the truths and ideals of Christianity. For a decline in Christian courage is always a certain sign of a prior abandonment of Christian convictions. Aleksandr I. Solzhenitsyn, in his commencement address at Harvard University on June 8, 1978, analyzed accurately and profoundly the spiritual malaise from which the West is dying:

A decline in courage may be the most striking feature an outside observer notices in the West in our days. The Western world has lost its civil courage, both as a whole and separately, in each country, each government, each political party and, of course, in the United Nations. Such a decline in courage is particularly noticeable among the ruling classes and the intellectual elite, causing an impression of loss of courage by the entire society. Of course, there are many courageous individuals, but they have no determining influence on public life. Political and intellectual bureaucrats show depression, passivity and perplexity in their actions and their statements, and even more so in theoretical reflections to explain how realistic, reasonable as well as intellectually and even morally warranted it is to base State policy on weakness and cowardice. A decline in courage is ironically emphasized by occasional explosions of anger and inflexibility on the part of the same bureaucrats when dealing with weak governments and weak countries not supported by anyone, or with currents which cannot offer any resistance. But they get tongue-tied and paralyzed when they deal with powerful governments and threatening forces, with aggressors and international terrorists.[327]

(6) In the face of Western concessions, accommodations, and surrender, the diligent, zealous, united enthusiasm of the Communists for their cause has led some to become bolder, fiercer, more arrogantly violent in their attacks on Christian society and civilization everywhere. (7) The folly of attempting a "historical

---

[327] Aleksandr I. Solzhenitsyn, "A World Split Apart," Commencement Address delivered at Harvard University, June 8, 1978, reprinted fully in *National Review*, July 7, 1978.

compromise" with Communism has led to a further Western self-deception, the belief that a type of "European Communism" is compatible with a system of Christian democracy. But massive, continued violence alone can transform one of these systems into the other. (8) Despite all the friendly endeavors to domesticate Communism, international intrigue and violence have escalated in frequency and ferocity; national wars of liberation have increased the number of countries that disappeared into the Communist darkness. Africa has been allowed to become an uncontested Communist continent of conquest, while all the time the West is being reduced to naked feebleness. What a dismal preparation for the coming of the Antichrist!

How to explain the naive belief of too many Catholic leaders that some common good for mankind will issue from dialoguing, handshaking, and kissing with Communist leaders? Why is it that Catholic leaders express an artless belief in the good intentions of Communist tyrants? Even great minds have fallen for this rose-tinted fantasy. Jean Cardinal Danielou had written: "She (the Church) shares with all men without exception, hence even with Communists, a concern for the material advancement of civilization." But are the Communist leaders really concerned with the material, spiritual, or even cultural advancement of mankind? The testimony of Eugene Lyons, once a youthful enthusiast for the Communist cause and a sympathetic American journalist for many years in Moscow, dissolves the roseate myths of a humane Communism and cuts to the cruel core of Marxist barbarity. In his *Workers' Paradise Lost*, we read:

> By 1934 when I departed from Russia, nothing was left
> of the high mood of dedication, traces of which I had
> still found among Communists six years earlier. The very

vocabulary of idealism had been outlawed. "Equality" was lampooned as bourgeois romanticism. Excessive concern for the needs and sensibilities of ordinary people was punished as "rotten liberalism." Terror was no longer explained away as a sad necessity. It was used starkly and glorified as "human engineering." Means had blotted out ends and have held this priority ever since. The Marxist theory of permanent class struggle rules out compromise, reform, truce, common humanity, mutual respect, family loyalties.[328]

But long before Eugene Lyons wrote his testimony in 1967, two great popes had already warned the world against yielding to made-in-the-Kremlin myths of Communist mellowization. In 1937 Pope Pius XI wrote in his encyclical *Atheistic Communism*:

See to it, Veneral Brethren, that the Faithful do not allow themselves to be deceived: Communism is intrinsically evil, and no one who would save Christian civilization may collaborate with it in any undertaking whatsoever. Those who permit themselves to be deceived into lending their aid towards the triumph of Communism in their own country, will be the first to fall victims of its error. And the greater the antiquity and grandeur of the Christian civilization in the regions where Communism successfully penetrates, so much more devastating will be the hatred displayed by the godless.[329]

[328] Eugene Lyons, *Workers' Paradise Lost* (New York: Paperback Library, 1967), p. 380.
[329] Pope Pius XI, Encyclical *Atheistic Communism* (London: Catholic Truth Society, 1937), par. 82, p. 44.

In a Christmas message, "The Contradiction of Our Age," to the whole world in 1956, the year of the shocking slaughter of the Hungarian people by Russian Communists, Pope Pius XII had to warn Catholics again not to go into orgies of optimism over the supposed evolvement of Khrushchev's Communism into an open society welcoming political dissent:

> We must with deepest sadness mourn the help given by some Catholics, both ecclesiastical and lay, to the tactics of obfuscation, calculated to bring about a result that they themselves did not intend. How can they fail to see that such is the aim of all that insincere activity which hides under the name of "talks" and "meetings"? Why enter a discussion, for that matter, without a common language, or how is it possible to meet if the paths are divergent, that is, if one party rejects or denies the common absolute values, thereby making all "coexistence in truth" unattainable?
>
> Out of respect for the very name of Christian, compliance with such tactics should cease, for as the Apostle warns, "It is inconsistent to wish to sit at the table of God and at that of His enemies."
>
> And if there be still any vacillating spirits, not withstanding the black testimony of ten years of cruelty, the blood just shed and the immolation of many lives sacrificed by a martyred people should finally convince them.[330]

The example of Aldo Moro, president of the Christian Democratic Party in Italy and architect of years of compromises with

---

[330] Pope Pius XII, Christmas Allocution, "The Contradiction of Our Age," December 23, 1956, in *The Pope Speaks*, Spring 1957, Washington, D.C., pp. 331–346.

the Italian Communist Party, is the latest example of the futility of collaborating with this godless party. Moro was a model family man, an excellent Catholic, at Mass and Communion almost daily. An upright man of great talent, professor of law, he was an intimate friend of Pope Paul VI. Moro, the practicing and maneuvering politician, was perhaps the perfect incarnation of Vatican II's policy of accommodation with the Communists. Unfortunately, his whole political career was based on such compromise. He had stated shortly before his death that Communist participation in the Christian Democratic government was "inevitable," ignoring the fact that the convergence of the two in governing would inevitably mean that the Christian Democratic Party would have to accept many of the evil ideals and programs of the Communist Party. He thus engineered the convergency of a special nature whereby the New Italian government would function as a parliamentary coalition between Christian Democratics and Communists. He thereby tied the state's power to rule to Communist approval and control, in effect betraying this power to the enemy of the Italian state.

In working for and justifying his policies of accommodation, Moro calculatedly created ambiguous slogans. He described cooperation between Christian Democrats and left-wing groups as the effecting of "parallel convergencies," a paradoxical, if not contradictory, impossible, mental and political gymnastic bound to end in catastrophic failure. Under the slogan of "creative flexibility" he disarmed the nation's healthy fear of Red Communism and lulled it to sleep over the enormity of left-wing violence. For him the only real national enemy seemed to have been neo-Fascism; there were no enemies to the Left. His antics in semantics showed that he never seemed to realize the depth or seriousness of the spiritual agony through which Italy and the whole of

Europe was passing. He never realized that compromise with the Red national and international menace meant an abandonment of Italy's democratic institutions. For when one plays with baffling figures of speech, with fuzzy formulas calculated to obfuscate real dangers, one in effect dethrones the truth, which alone can make and keep men free. One fosters an ambiguity that psychologically prepares citizens for slavery. Moro seems never to have realized that ideas have consequences and that the violent ideas of the Communists would beget an army of terrorists. Unfortunately, Moro was a lawyer and not a metaphysician. He viewed the art of governing men from the legal aspect. As long as legalistic rapport between parties was proper and on paper and in agreed compromises, he believed the nation could preserve its free institutions. But to base the structure of political life primarily on legalistic relationships is to build a nation on the sand of moral mediocrity, indeed of moral ambiguity. Without the foundation of God and conscience, there are no moral nor civil rights. For a state based solely on such a foundation must necessarily crumble before the onslaughts of Marxist tyrants.

Yet Moro was too intelligent not to have known that it was the Communist Party in Italy that for over thirty years has been vilifying the state, advocating class warfare against hierarchical society, had captured and radicalized the major labor unions, had polarized Church and state on education, divorce, abortion, the Lateran Treaty, etc. Moro also cooperated with the Communist Party in dismantling the Italian Secret Service to such a degree that the government was no longer able to track down native spy groups, terrorists, and foreign infiltrators. Witness the dismal failure of the police forces to track down his own kidnappers and assassins. Moro also knew that the Red Brigades and the other numerous left-wing terrorist groups were the ideological offspring of a Communist Party whose leading saints are Lenin, Stalin, Castro, Che Guevara. Yet he constantly compromised with this monstrous parent of these broods of assassins. He was willing to accept in Italy Euro-Communism's crocodile tears over the violent extremism of these contemptible terrorists. What Moro, lawyer and political practitioner, failed to see in depth is that the roots of Communist terrorism are nourished in the soil of man's rejection of God, of his own creaturehood, and of Being itself. It seems never to have dawned on Mr. Moro that the See of Moscow took him as an Archenemy because of his attempts to seduce Italian Communism into becoming a schismatic branch, cut off from its tree and going its own, heretical, unfaithful way, with ideals and customs opposed to those of its messianic pope and party in Moscow. For this attempt to corrupt Communism in Italy by wedding it to the rottenness of a dying Christian bourgeois society, Moro was ruthlessly tortured and assassinated by Moscow's trained zealots for Marxist orthodoxy. And as a warning to Italian Communist leader Enrico Berlinguer, lest he stray too far in the direction of the bourgeois paradise, the bullet-riddled body of Mr. Moro was delivered close to Italian Communist headquarters, close enough, too, to Christian Democratic headquarters to cause any leader there thinking of creating a national Communism of the Tito-type, to pause and reflect seriously on the grisly consequences that could be the wages of such a sin against the party.

The terrible irony of Moro's fate left the whole world in a state of shock. Here was the president of the Christian Democratic Party in Italy, the *maestro* over the years of seemingly successful compromises for his party with the Communist Party, now a kidnapped prisoner in the hands of the Red Brigades. As a hostage of Red ideological fanatics, Moro attempted to persuade his own party to enter another compromise—to liberate the thirteen Brigade leaders on trial in Turin in exchange for his own liberation. In all justice and charity, one may suppose that Mr. Moro was far less than himself in making this proposal, no doubt depressed, frightened, tortured, and drugged. But the moment of truth had finally arrived for his political confreres. Such a compromise was both morally and politically unthinkable. To turn loose upon fifty-five million Italians, upon all Europe, upon the world such ideological criminals in order to save one politico's life would have been a disgraceful injustice. Moreover, it would have ended the Christian Democratic Party's rule and promoted the Communists to national power. By a sort of Grecian, tragic fate, Moro, the Great Compromiser, designated to be the almost sure next president of Italy for his accommodation with the Communists, was assassinated by the Red Brigades, Communist purists trained by the KGB. Moreover, he was assassinated because his own Christian Democratic Party was forced to realize finally that compromise with the Communists eventually becomes a crime of craven surrender, a cowardly abandonment of the state. As Solzhenitsyn said in his Harvard speech: "To defend oneself one must also be ready to die; there is little such readiness in a society raised in the cult of material well-being. Nothing is left then, but concessions, attempts to gain time and betrayal."

Catholics, especially ecclesiastical leaders, should read reflectively the works of ex-Communist friends of the Church who are experts on Communist tactics that they learned from the Party itself when they held high positions of responsibility therein. One such friend of the Church, who fought and broke with Stalin early, was Bertram Wolfe, scholar, writer, and one of America's foremost experts on Communism. He died on February 21, 1977. In 1919, Professor Wolfe was a founder of the Communist Party in the United States. He edited left-wing labor publications as well as the party organ, *Communist*, and was a delegate to the Red Trade Union International headquarters in Moscow. His disillusionment with the party came in 1929 when he served on the executive committee of the Comintern and met the revolutionary leaders Stalin, Trotsky, Bukahrin, Molotov, and the other greats. He openly opposed Stalin's methods when that stalwart had not yet established himself sole ruler of the Soviet world. For his opposition, Mr. Wolfe was detained in Moscow for two months with Jay Lovestone, who was then the American party's chief, and was excommunicated from the party. From that moment until his death Mr. Wolfe lectured and wrote profusely against Communism. His best known book, *Three Who Made a Revolution*, remains a classic study of Lenin, Trotsky, and Stalin. Published in 1948, it was translated into twenty-eight languages. Other works of his include *Six Keys to the Soviet System*, *Khrushchev and Stalin's Ghost*, and *Marxism: 100 Years in the Life of a Doctrine*. On the death of Professor Wolfe, some of his letters were made available to scholars. Here are his thoughts on Catholic-Communist dialogue expressed in letters to a Catholic priest friend. On March 7, 1967, Professor Wolfe wrote to Father Monihan:[331]

> This brings me to the subject of my gloom. Your Church is now preparing to enter into a "dialogue" with the marxists and the Communists. As men of good will, you are peculiarly eager to deceive yourselves as to those with whom you discourse and concerning what the real subject

---

[331] Copies of these letters were sent to me and I have them in my files.

of discourse is. You (with the exception of an occasional Waldemar Gurian, alas deceased) have not mastered their gospels, but they have mastered yours. They meet your will to be deceived by their ardent will to deceive. Hence to me it seems that the outcome of the dialogue can only be an increase in confusion and the loss of many of your best in the battle for men's spirits.

... I hope you will forgive me this frankness, recognize that my words are well meant and not altogether ill-informed, and accept this at least as my small, if intrusive, attempt to take part in the difficult dialogue which the Church is ill-prepared to take advantage of.

And I ask you to believe that I wish your Church well as one of the bulwarks of sanity in the half-mad contemporary world, as you must have felt when I defended Thomas More and Erasmus against some of your own theologians. I hope I am wrong in my idea of the way that your Church and its spokesmen are preparing for this difficult dialogue with a wily and skillful opponent.

Three years later, October 8, 1970, from his position as a senior fellow at the Hoover Institution on War, Revolution and Peace, Professor Wolfe wrote again to Father Monihan:

I have watched the course of the dialogue anxiously, and now, some three years later, I am compelled to say that it has turned out much worse than I feared. With the exception of the French leader, Roger Garaudy, who may have been moved in part by the dialogue and in part by his distress over the brutal Soviet invasion of Czechoslovakia, I am afraid your Church has won no person of decency and importance. On the other hand, forgive me for saying so, I have noted a growing confusion in the ranks of the Church due, of course, to many things of which dialogue is only one.

I am enclosing a story from a reputable magazine which favors and reports on democracy and freedom in the Americas and the gains and losses suffered from time to time in those fields. It contains a grim story on the murder of the former president of Argentina, and on page 4, you will find a report of the arrest of two Fathers of the Church who joined something called "Movement of Priests," one of whom possessed the typewriter on which the successive missives and pronouncements of the assassins were written and who lent his cassocks for disguise to his fellow conspirators. I am deeply troubled also by the news that comes from a number of lands of dissenting and disintegrating forces within the Catholic Church.

In my letter of three years ago, I wrote: "And I ask you to believe that I wish your Church well as one of the bulwarks of sanity in the half-mad contemporary world...." The bulwark has weakened it seems to me, and I am more troubled than ever.

It is time that Catholic leaders, especially ecclesiastics, abandon their gullible posture before Communist enticements to mutual "meetings," "talks," "coalition governments," and similar exercises in futility. Dialogue in the hands of Communist shadows of the Antichrist is a dagger for destruction; it is an instrument in godless minds and mouths to divide and conquer Catholics, indeed all free men. It has had, and continues to have, tremendous success. The essence of Communist strategy is to attack, attack, attack, even when one is ostensibly engaged in friendly talks. This clever maneuver has trapped Christians on religious, political, economic, and moral fronts into becoming advocates of the cult of softness toward Communism.

A reminder of Khrushchev's crude but frank appraisal of Christian-Communist relationships should shock Christian appeasers into coming to terms with the harsh realities of this age of violence. "We must realize that we cannot coexist eternally (with the Christian countries of the West). One of us must go to the grave. We do not want to go to the grave. They do not want to go to their grave either. But we must push them to their grave." Mr. Moro's bullet-riddled body is bloodcurdling evidence that the Communist precursors of the Antichrist mean business.

Detente as Flight from the Institutional Church

St. John in his first epistle writes: "And every spirit that severs Jesus is not of God, but is of Antichrist of whom you have heard that he is coming, and now is already in the world." There are two ways of severing Jesus. 1) The way the heretic Cerinthus, contemporary of St. John, severed Jesus. He maintained that Christ and Jesus were two distinct persons, that Christ came upon Jesus at baptism and left Him before his Passion. 2) The way of revolution as well as heresy; this is a form of persecution of the Church from within. If Jesus could cry out to Saul, the outside persecutor of His Church, "Saul, Saul, why are you persecuting Me?," how much more bitterly could our Savior cry out to inside Catholic dissenters, "My Children, why are you dividing and severing me?" For we know that Christ identifies Himself with His Church. In October 1976 in the city of Detroit a Catholic "Call to Action" Conference was held as the culmination of the Church's Bicentennial celebration. The conference was sponsored by the U.S. Conference of Catholic Bishops. The purpose of the called-for action was "Liberty and Justice for All." Unfortunately, the theme actually developed by the conference was "A Call to Revolution." And the purpose of the revolution was "A Classless Church for All." At the conference there were 1,340 delegates from 152 dioceses and 1,100 observers from around the nation.

Catholic rebels took over the conference. This became so clear from the outset that John Cardinal Krol could not keep silent about it. In an interview with *The Detroit Free Press*, which printed his remarks in the Saturday October 23, 1977, issue, the archbishop made this complaint: "Rebels have taken over the conference." He then specified thus: "The conference was being manipulated by a few people who had received the support of a naive group of little ladies." Now the few people manipulating the meeting were agitator-priests, Saul Alinsky types. Indeed one of these Monsignori boasts continually that he is a spiritual child of agitator Alinsky. But who is Alinsky?[332]

Saul Alinsky, who died in 1972, is still very much with us as a charismatic leader. He is the author of two very influential books, *Reveille for Radicals* and *Rules for Radicals*. A Marxist humanist and atheist, some brief thoughts and methods of the man will help us understand what went on at the Detroit conference. Alinsky teaches: "Truth is relative and changing; *everything* is relative and changing." And it is on this relativism that the organizer of a movement must thrive. For Alinsky, the enemy is within and the war for change is to be waged within the community to be changed. He writes:

[332] Vincent P. Miceli, "Detroit: A Call to Revolution," *Homiletic and Pastoral Review*, March 1977, pp. 27–32, 47–48.

The first step in community organization is community disorganization.... The organizer, dedicated to changing the life of a particular community must first rub raw the resentments of the people of the community; fan the latent hostilities of many of the people to the point of overt expression. He must search out controversy; people are not concerned enough to act.... Any revolutionary change must be preceded by a passive, affirmative, non-challenging attitude toward change among the mass of our people. They must feel so frustrated, so defeated, so lost, so futureless in the prevailing system that they are willing to let go of the past and chance the future.... The job of the organizer is to maneuver and bait the establishment so that it will publicly attack him as a dangerous enemy. Such a counterattack then puts the organizer on the side of the people.... A revolutionary organizer must shake up the prevailing patterns of the people's lives—agitate, create disenchantment and discontent with the current values to produce a passion for change.

In this system religion becomes politics and politics becomes religion. And this explains why so many priests, infected with the virus of Alinskyism, have become precursors of the Antichrist, enraptured at destroying the traditional Catholic Church.[333]

The priest and nun manipulators of the conference lived up perfectly to the coarse, crude methods of their mentor. Their tactics produced from their audience—delegates and observers—distorted reactions against the Catholic Church, the United States, the First World, business corporations, the white man; all

---

[333] Saul D. Alinsky, *Reveille for Radicals* and *Rules for Radicals*, both Vintage books, New York, the first in 1969, the second in 1973.

these hysterical reactions led to accusations of criminality against these sectors of Western society and to a frenzied cry to bring these sectors to their knees. No injustice, no war, no poverty, no sickness, no difference or restraint, however reasonable, but was used to condemn these sectors as responsible for all the evils in the world. The whole conference was an activity-oriented frenzy and propaganda orgy. Now "the naive group of little ladies" were, though the cardinal was too charitable to specify them, the not-so-naive liberated nuns who responded with emotionally charged outcries, clappings, and vote-acclamations to the wand-waving of their exalted leaders.

The anti-intellectual, anti-rational tone of the proceedings was spiritually suffocating. With a shock it dawned on me, who was a delegate representing the Confraternity of Catholic Clergy, a group counting close to one thousand priests and fifteen bishops, founded in 1975, that I was witnessing a new, alarming, growing phenomenon in the Catholic Church. A movement of Catholic "Know-Nothings" was making a play for power in the Catholic Church. And their first move was to discredit their institutional Church by mounting a witch hunt against her, supposedly to uncover her injustices, her subversive political activity, and her disloyalty to the ideals of her Master. In reality this witch hunt was meant to harass and weaken the entire ecclesiastical structure. These agitated Catholics revealed themselves fully at the conference. They were ignorant of Catholic dogma, morals, canon law, philosophy, culture, and history. But the most dismal aspect of their ignorance was that they did not give a tinker's damn about it. Indeed they gloried in their ignorance! Their contempt for truth was demonstrated every time they tittered against papal teachings and the age-old doctrines of their Church. Their contempt for justice and moral balance was demonstrated when they demanded that the Church change her doctrines on artificial contraception, abortion, the right to national defense, the right to private property, the right to reasonable profit. Their contempt for authority—divine and human—was demonstrated when they shouted against laws reasonably restraining the use of liberty, when they rejected the divine plan for salvation, when they resented such metaphysical and physical differences as God established in the diverse vocations, sexes, and services for the salvation of man. Nor were these exalted souls really interested in "liberty and justice for all." They voted down a resolution presented by an Eastern European group condemning tyranny behind the Iron Curtain. I had to check with a friend to make sure I heard correctly. He assured me I had. The reason given for the rejection of this resolution was that it was decided that "no anti-Communist statements were to be placed in any of the final documents. This would be too negative." Another example of Vatican II's detente? Once again favorite treatment for the anti-christian, universal enemy, the pet of the rascal radicals. Of course, previously it had not been considered too negative to represent the Church, the West, and especially the U.S. as the architects of world tyranny.

The whole conference reeked with the smoke of sulphur. Some years ago Pope Paul VI caused a worldwide commotion by speaking in his Wednesday allocution of the "smoke of Satan seeping into the Church of God through the cracks in the walls" of the faithful. On October 13, eight days before the opening of the Detroit conference, Pope Paul VI told the world in another allocution that "the tail of the devil is functioning in the disintegration of the Catholic world."[334] The allusion is

---

[334] *Corriere della Sera*, October 14, 1977, p. 7.

to the Apocalypse where the tail of the dragon is said "to be dragging along the third part of the stars of heaven and dashing them to earth." Without a doubt there was a demonic dimension at the meeting in Detroit. One need merely relate the dramatic event that occurred near the end. As resolution after resolution opposing the radicals was defeated and things were speeding up to allow participants to catch homeward-bound planes, a group of four or five young men (they seemed to belong to the frustrated Eastern Europeans) quietly walked into the hall carrying a banner before a suddenly silenced and astonished audience. The banner read: "When you leave this city, take our red cardinal with you." A few policemen then went into action. They reached for the banner and were on the point of roughly ushering the young men out of the hall, when cries from the audience mollified their conduct. "Take your violent hands off those men. They have a right to express their opinion." The policemen then restricted themselves to persuading the men to leave quietly. Suddenly the young men shouted in unison: "Judas, Judas. Traitor priests!" They continued this for some minutes as they slowly left the hall. And their voices were heard gradually dying away, with one word returning weaker: "JUDAS, JUDAS, Judas, Judas, judas, judas!" Preparatory work for the coming of the Antichrist was surely accomplished by the Detroit Call for Revolution within the Catholic Church.[335]

In viewing the hysteria of the delegates and observers to the Detroit conference, this writer was reminded of the truth of Dryden's poetic lines: "Great wits are sure to madness near allied.... There is a pleasure, sure, in being mad, which none but madmen know." The following are some of the conference's mad

[335] Miceli, op. cit., pp. 31, 32.

demands that the Catholic Church simply cannot grant without ceasing immediately to be the true Church of Christ. If she granted them she would become a Church of the world, of the Antichrist, a snake pit for demons. She would become a center for doctrinal, moral chaotic disorder and psychoneurotic distress. The Catholic Dissidents demanded: (1) divorced, remarried couples to receive Holy Communion while still living in adulterous unions; (2) ordained women priests and bishops; (3) women given the power to preach the Gospel with authority; (4) a reversal on the doctrine of artificial birth control; (5) a mitigation on the doctrine of abortion; (6) a teaching approving Marxism, Socialism, and pacificism as doctrinally true and morally good practice; (7) a denial of the right to property and to reasonable profit; (8) the creation of a new Church, democratic, nonhierarchical in structure, a classless Church.

The following are some of the demands the Church simply cannot fulfill for that is neither her competence nor her mission: (1) wipe out poverty, ignorance, prejudice, and war; (2) democratize the whole world; (3) stop the sale of arms everywhere; (4) back the E.R.A. as a constitutional amendment. Like her Savior, the Church will not turn stones into bread at the bequest of precursors of the Antichrist, thereby becoming the Mother of godless Socialism or a secularized millennium of this world. Finally here are a few demands the Church will most probably not grant in the interest of her supernatural mission to make converts and saints of all nations: (1) allow married men to be ordained; (2) allow priests to marry; (3) revoke the vow of celibacy of priests and religious; (4) lift the excommunication from divorced remarried Catholics still living in adultery; (5) grant the option to receive Communion in the hand. Of all the demands made by the Detroit Conference, the Holy

See has granted only the last two. She has lifted the excommunication from divorced remarried Catholics still living in adultery, though they may not receive Holy Communion while in that state. She has also granted the option of receiving Holy Communion in the hand.[336]

Christian dissident groups, like those that surfaced at the Detroit conference, which attempt to create a utopian Church, whether it be Marxist, Socialist, or humanist, cannot escape a grave enigma. How will they be able to reconcile the historical Church and the deposit of Faith with their new Church and new theology? There are two possible ways of resolving this problem, and the dissidents have tried both to no avail. The first abandons the Christian Faith and the institutional Church because they are irreconcilable with the utopian Church and its ideology. The second tries to remain within the traditional Church by reinterpreting the corpus of the Christian creed and morality in the keys of Marxist or Socialist or humanist secularism. Those Christians who follow the first procedure have the benefit of being logical. True, they rationalize their departure by accusing the Church of being against the worker, progress, science while being for the rich, the capitalist, the powerful, and the *status quo.* Influenced by the rhetoric of utopian salvation systems, these Christian apostates are incensed at having failed to plunge the Catholic Church into class struggle; they aimed at reducing the Church's apostolate of redeeming men from sin and Satan to an apostolate of liberating men from all forms of personal and social domination. Having failed in this grand adventure, they say goodbye to their Catholic brothers and join the party of their atheistic friends. In the dialectics of friendly detente with the forces of atheism, many Christians

[336] Ibid., pp. 47–48.

have been seduced by the spirit of the world. They opt for a Church with a new philosophy of life, a way of living in harmony with the secularist, materialist vision of history. Calling themselves "Christian Socialists," or "Christian Dissidents," or "Christian Marxists," they proclaim they are liberating the Gospels from the superstructure of a decadent, capitalist society and returning both the gospel message and the Church's mission to their true, original, revolutionary inspiration and vigor. We see here that, with or without the forces of Satan or of his antichristian precursors in time, the infinite capacity of man for self-deception is exploited by the thrill of creating a new humanistic ideology that leads man to the adventure of self-divinization.

But the majority of Christian dissidents attempt to follow the second path. They attempt to remain within the Church in order to convert the Church. This is the modern Teilhardian fashion of being an intellectual Catholic. They too attempt to reinterpret Christianity in humanistic, scientific, up-to-date terms. Hence they too oppose the utopian Church to the institutional Church. They form small Christian communities in more or less open rupture with the institutional Church. But in living this way they fail to solve their problems, for they cannot harmonize Socialist humanism and Catholicism. Thus, since it is impossible to be neutral in the class struggle, they end up on the atheistic side. Thus their communities either try to convince themselves that they are living as part of the universal Church, but then their problem of contestation with the institutional Church festers, becomes inflamed, and they languish in schizophrenic agony. Or these communities are finally convinced that they are outside the Catholic Church, their bonds being broken with the essential structures of the Church. Thus such groups realize in conscience that they no longer belong to the Catholic Church and cease pretending that they remain within her bosom. In the end the dream of the utopian Church is seen to have been bred only in the inflated egos and heads of Catholic rebels, precursors of the Antichrist, who unfortunately prepare a spiritual wasteland in the world for the arrival of the Man of Sin.

Political Defeatism: Fruit of Spiritual Detente

In an age of atheism and general apostasy, what Christian can look for salvation from politics? Hope for peace from a political detente that strives for a balance of powers, a nuclear standoff, an appeasement to the enemy's plan for global conquest is nothing but a form of foolish whistling-in-the-dark. For such political tactics of defection are the inevitable evil fruits of religious forms of disruption that have previously dethroned God, the Church, and the world of sacred values. Peace will never be the result of policies that promote commerce, cultural exchange, and many varieties of communication. Such policies are like cheap cosmetics beautifying a dying body in preparation for its burial. But in the realm of the spirit, fighting for the victory of Truth and Justice is a necessary condition for victory; faith and courage pave the path to peace; fortitude in trials of strength is the guarantee of liberty and life. In the realm of the spirit it is futile to attempt to quarterback a tie, especially against an enemy who will settle for nothing less than one's total destruction. A strategic stalemate between Satan and society, man and mammon, atheism and Christianity, Christ and the Antichrist is an impossibility. We either conquer the forces of evil or they conquer us; we either join the forces of God or the forces of evil; compromise is unacceptable by both sides. Our actions and loyalties in this struggle, though performed in time, are determining our eternal as well as temporal destiny. There is a radical, most important nexus between spiritual health, with its will to win, and the material forces at hand for victory. Without spiritual health, the overwhelming material resources for victory will be dissipated in the feeble hands of a sick nation that draws back because its heart is cowardly, its head confused, its vision blurred, its hearing dulled, its attention flagging, and its feet slipping. Such a nation may rattle its armaments in comic bravado, but it frightens no tyrant. Such a nation plays the international clown, for, though it arms, it is not prepared to draw and, though it draws, it is powerless to shoot.

As the will of the West is inflated by its rebellion against God, that same will is simultaneously vitiated before the technological terror of its own weapons and those it helped create for the world of organized, militant atheism. For the West has lost its transcendent motive for "fighting the good fight," for finishing an honorable course. Not having kept the faith, it is now morally paralyzed, incapable of projecting a cogent politics of peace with dignity. Its politics falters; events are out of control; things fall apart. With the escalation of violence, crime, confusion, wars and rumors of wars are emanating from religious apostasy and political disengagement; the stage is being set for the coming of the Antichrist. Is he waiting in the wings? Will he soon receive his cue from Divine Providence to make his entrance? Will he play out in our time of history the tragedy of the abomination of desolation and the consummation of the universe? True, his name and his time are known only to God. But the portents of his nearness are evident everywhere in the general desertion of the Faith.

No doubt agnostic and atheist sophisticates will smile patronizingly at the prophecy of the Antichrist's coming in a pestilence of heresies, preternatural heroics, and wars. Progressist

Christians will join the intellectual scoffers. It was thus in the days of Noah who was laughed to scorn as he built his ark of salvation. It was thus in the days of Abraham as he pleaded fruitlessly with Sodom and Gomorrah. It was thus in the days of Christ as He wept over the city of Jerusalem. All these skeptics were wiped out violently for their incredulity. It will be thus at the end of time. For the wicked are too proud to accept and understand the ways of God. In those last perilous days men shall be lovers of themselves, covetous, boasters, proud, blasphemers, disobedient to parents, unthankful, unholy, without natural affection, trucebreakers, false-accusers, incontinent, fierce, despisers of those who are good, traitors, heady, highminded, lovers of pleasure instead of lovers of God, scoffers walking after their own lusts and jeering: Where is the promise of His Second Coming? Men will be despisers of government, presumptuous, self-willed, calumniators of civil and religious authorities, promising everyone liberty while subjecting themselves and their fellowmen to the corruption of runaway licentiousness.

Conclusion

The basic issue of detente is not how does mankind domesticate Soviet totalitarian despotism, but rather how does the human race reverse its own conduct of moral perversity? When will men return to a life of sanctifying tensions through a faith that clings to God and a love that serves Him? When will the human race renew its dangerous tensions of war against the world, the flesh, and the devil? When will it cease being unfaithful? When will it reject half measures that temporize in the face of its moral obligations? When will it finally accept God's grace and justification as the only cure for its spiritual exhaustion? Saintly Christians

alone can give the example and inspiration for a universal reconciliation with God. Such Christians never forget that they are
pilgrims without a lasting city here below, but striving forward to
the eternal city that is to come. They reject the temptation to live
in ease and comfort; their first priority is a life of prayer and self-
restraint; they reject the pursuit of money, prestige, and power as
the primary activity of man. Such faithful Christians form "little
islands of holiness" everywhere, but especially in their homes
that will surely but slowly rechristianize the pagan, or rather neo-
pagan world, even as the little band of original disciples christian-
ized the pagan Roman Empire.

"Will I find faith when I come?" asked Christ concerning
those last days. Apparently He doubted He would. St. Pius X at
the beatification of Joan of Arc, December 13, 1908, had his
doubts too. He said on that happy occasion. "In our time more
than ever before the greatest asset of the evilly disposed is the
cowardice and weakness of good men, and all the vigor of Satan's reign is due to the easygoing weakness of Catholics. Oh!
If I might ask the divine Redeemer, as the prophet Zachary did
in spirit: 'What are those wounds in the midst of Your hands?'
the answer would not be doubtful. 'With these I was wounded
in the house of those who loved Me. I was wounded by My
friends who did nothing to defend Me and who, on every occasion, made themselves the accomplices of My adversaries.' And
this reproach can be levelled at the weak and timid Catholics
of all countries."[337]

---

[337] Pope Pius X, Discourse on the Beatification of Joan of Arc, December 13, 1908. Quoted by Denis Fahey in his book *The Mystical
Body of Christ in the Modern World* (Dublin: Regina Publications,
1972), p. 223.

In the Apocalypse, chapter 9, after the fifth angel sounds his trumpet, we read: "And I saw a star which had fallen from heaven to the earth, and there was given to him the key of the bottomless pit, and there went up from the pit a smoke like that of a great furnace; and the sun was darkened and the air, by reason of the smoke of the pit. And out of the smoke locusts went forth upon the earth and they were told—to harm only such men as have not the seal of God upon their forehead."[338]

Now in prophetic symbolism falling stars almost always refer to tepid, weak, wicked, or apostate Catholics—bishops, priests, religious laity. For it is her own children who are the harbingers of grief and disaster to the Church. The key to the shaft of the abyss is an emblem of their apostasy. These traitorous Catholics ally themselves with rebellious angels. Instead of using the keys of the kingdom of God, which they have received through Baptism and the other sacraments, to suppress and defeat satanic forces while advancing the holiness of their confreres, they rather misuse the graces of the Faith to foster and propagate error and evil, to open the abyss and let loose upon the earth the plagues of darkness and wickedness. Today too many fallen stars are misusing the graces of the True Faith to seduce, enslave, and precipitate into damnation vast numbers. The smoke streaming from the pit of darkness blackens the sun of Christ's truth and infects the air with decadent immoral odors. Everything is cast into confusion; darkness infests the world of religion and reason; grace, the life-giving air of the soul and body, is strangled out of the supernatural organisms of the children to God. Moreover, the darkening of the sun and the sky betokens the eclipsing of the teaching authority of the Church, the lowering of men's respect and love for her, their loss of

[338] John, Apoc. 9: 1–5.

reverence for her Master and the demeaning of both Christ and His Church to the level of mere natural beings.

The answer to stars falling from heaven onto the earth, through the pristine betrayal of Lucifer, is stars that stand fixed in the heaven of fidelity to God with the courage and fortitude of the Archangel Michael. The remedy for the tepid is the zealous, for the weak the strong, for the timid the brave, for the wicked the holy, for the apostate the apostle. The Church is sorely in need of Catholics who are men and women of God imbued with the virtue of fortitude, of Catholics who are "valiant in battle."

Fortitude is that virtue which enduringly resists difficulties of mind and body while persistently seeking, defending, and spreading the truth and holiness of the Gospel. St. Thomas reminds us that fortitude is especially concerned with overcoming the fear of performing difficult deeds for the glory of God. This virtue prevents a soldier of Christ, and above all officers in Christ's army, from fleeing the field of battle, from betraying the brethren when real or imaginary obstacles present themselves. The great fault of the pusillanimous is that they succumb easily to irrational fears and leave the field of battle to enemy forces.[339] This moral deformity reveals a lack of faith in the cause of Christ and a distrust of the assurance He gave his followers when He said to His apostles: "Have confidence, I have overcome the world." The defect of irrational fear weakens virtue and renders Christians cowards.

But fortitude is not merely a passive virtue, a patient suffering of assaults of the enemy. Again St. Thomas states that "it is not outside

---

[339] Thomas Aquinas, *Summa Theologica* II, Second Part, trans. the Fathers of the English Dominican Province, Vol. 12, On Fortitude (London: Burns Oates & Washbourne, 1922), pp. 193–214.

the genus of fortitude to go on the offensive for the sovereign good of man and the glory of God." St. Joan of Arc, a mere girl of nineteen unprepared by nature or training to do battle against hardened veteran soldiers, nevertheless, fearlessly followed the will of God and drove foreign infidels out of Catholic France. In the beginning Joan resisted and protested to her heavenly voices: "I am a poor girl; I do not know how to ride or fight." In vain, for the voices only reiterated: "It is God who commands it." Such was her fortitude that she courageously faced all manner of trials, repugnances, humiliations, and finally the ignominious death of being burned at the stake as a witch-heretic in order to remain faithful to the will of God and to fulfill the heroic mission God entrusted to her. At the words: "It is God who commands it," Joan rode forward to certain victory under her banner bearing the words *Jesus, Maria*, with a picture of God the Father, and kneeling angels presenting a *fleur-de-lis*.[340]

We Christians must be the eager heralds of Christ when He comes for the second time. For despite the general apostasy that will be prevalent at that time—for the strong Faith of the Church is what has restrained the coming of the Antichrist so far—the Lord will be welcomed in His Final Coming in power by the remnant of His faithful followers. These will rejoice exceedingly with Him, knowing that this Parousia will put an end forever to the wickedness of Satan and the Antichrist, to the despicable detente of sin, and will gather in His elect to establish eternally that *entente cordiale*, that loving communion with God, known as the beatific vision.

---

[340] Herbert Thurston, "Joan of Arc," in *The Catholic Encyclopedia*, Vol. VIII, ed. Charles George Herbermann (New York: Robert Appleton, 1910), pp. 409–413.

Chapter 11

The Apocalyptic Atmosphere

In the history of mankind, which is God's work for man's creation, re-creation, sanctification, and glorification, events do not happen merely by chance. There are always active, intelligent, visible, and invisible forces at work. Some forces are willingly working to establish a holy harmony between God and men; others are brazenly causing revolutionary upheavals and a universal chaos of astonishing magnitude. Holy Scripture reveals that man is living on a planet that is visited by divine and diabolical persons. God's initial visit in creation crowned man as a king and ruler of this planet. But Scripture also reveals that God has an enemy, Satan. And Satan's visit to the Garden of Eden seduced man to rebel against God, dethroned him from grace, and subjected him and his universe to the humiliation of death and destruction. Satan and his demon forces then became "lords of this world." From the very beginning they have been implementing a vast program to accomplish the total ruination of mankind and his universe.

But after the fall of man, God revisited man's planet in the Incarnation of His Son, Jesus Christ. His program was to liberate man from slavery to Satan and sin, to raise him from death.

St. John in his first letter writes: "To this end the Son of God appeared that He might destroy the works of the devil."[341]

Now it must be understood that Satan could never be a power opposite to God, in the sense of being like God, self-existent from all eternity. For God has no opposite. He is unique. And no being could exist as "perfect wickedness" opposite to perfect goodness. For God can only create what is good; and "perfect badness" is an infinite, impossible absurdity whether conceived as existing from all eternity or as being created. For "perfect badness," which is the absence of all perfection, must necessarily demand also the absence of that most fundamental of all perfections, namely existence. For a being stripped of all perfections to exist is a contradiction and God, Who is Absolute Intelligence, cannot be the author of absolute absurdities. Hence Satan is a creature of God; once he was the most brilliant of all angels, called Lucifer, "the Son of the Morning." He was an extraordinary servant of God, appointed to a place of leadership over myriads upon myriads of angels. He was a prince full of wisdom, holding a high place of honor, privilege, and responsibility in the universe of pure spirits.

But Satan fell in love with his own beauty, rejected God, and led a rebellion among the angels that drew millions of them with him into hell. The prophets Ezekiel and Isaiah tell us what happened as they saw the event by the aid of the Holy Spirit. While prophesying about the evil rulers of their times—Ezekiel about the prince of Tyre, Isaiah about the king of Babylon—both prophets were led by the Holy Spirit to go on from events concerning the local tyrants, to delineate the far greater, universal event of the mysterious fall of Lucifer. Both prophets knew they

[341] 1 John 3:8.

were being projected into revealing an event that took place in eternity. Both knew they were speaking not only their own minds, but also the mind of the Holy Spirit. We have a classic example of this type of prophesying in the life of Christ Himself. When asked by His disciples to narrate the signs that would usher in the fall of Jerusalem and the destruction of the temple, Christ proceeded to indicate those signs and then, moved by His own Holy Spirit, He went on to describe the terrible events that would usher in the end of the world.

In describing Satan's fall, Ezekiel writes:

You were a signet of perfection, full of wisdom and perfect in every beauty.... You were on the holy mountain of God; in the midst of stones of fire you walked. You were blameless in your ways, until iniquity was found in you. In the abundance of your trade you were filled with violence and you sinned. So I cast you as a profane thing from the mountain of God, and the guardian cherub drove you out from the midst of stones of fire. Your heart was proud because of your beauty; you corrupted your wisdom for the sake of your splendor.[342]

In describing Satan's fall, Isaiah writes:

How have you fallen from heaven, O Lucifer, son of the morning! How are you cut down to the ground, you who laid the nations low! You said in your heart, "I will ascend to heaven, above the stars of God; I will set my throne on high.... I will make myself like the Most High." But you are brought down to Sheol, to the depths of the Pit.[343]

[342] Ezek. 28:12–17.
[343] Isa. 14:12–15.

We read also in Scripture that "God draws men through the cords of Adam." Salvation, therefore, is not merely dependent on individual, personal cooperation with God's grace, but it is also a social, human adventure. No one gets saved in a Robinson Crusoe manner. Others must preach the Gospel to us; others must inspire us with good advice, good example, good services. Others pray, suffer, die for us. Man fell as a family; he is to be saved as a family. And the Father of the Redeemed Family, the New Adam, is the God-Man, Jesus Christ Who is man's greatest teacher, preacher, priest, and victim-savior. He founded His Church and sent apostles to continue His work of saving all men.

Aping God's plan of salvation, Satan seduces men through the cords of Adam. Scripture relates that Satan, "the prince of this world," is "at work in the children of disobedience." Sin in man gives Satan the basis on which he can operate in society; it is his fulcrum for toppling man's kingdoms into chaos. To ruin men Satan must gain men's consent to sin, to establish in themselves mindsets and heartburns locked and hardened into evil. To ruin men Satan must gain from among men leaders, generals, false prophets, pseudo-saviors who will, with malice toward God and man, deliver souls and society into his power.

The intention of Satan is to make a physical and spiritual wreckage of all God's creation. He enlists men in that attempt by their lust of the flesh, lust of the eyes, and pride of life. The Bible tells us that Satan will be loosed in the last days and granted permission to accelerate his evil activity greatly until it reaches a crescendo in the appearance of his commander-in-chief of the armies of iniquity—the Antichrist—who will organize and eventually divide society for its final destruction.

We are living in perhaps the most decadent, violent, faithless century in the history of mankind. It is a time of massive negationism of God, of Christ, of His Church. Moreover, the escalating armies of atheists do not, indeed cannot, remain neutral, apathetic, or indifferent to Christ. Rather they zealously declare themselves openly in favor of Satan's program for mankind, maintaining that his false teachings and diabolical deeds are more likely to guarantee man happiness in an earthly utopia than are the teachings and ways of Jesus Christ. That is why the earth is presently filled with activities and conditions that please Satan. He and his legions of demons help to establish spiritual wastelands everywhere with the aid of evil men. More than ever before has Satan become today "the god of the world." The reason is that men, made in the image and likeness of God, have willingly corrupted themselves to resemble more the devils they now follow. They daily engage in strife, treachery, bloodshed, tyranny, violence, terrorism, crime, sexual licentiousness, perversion, abortion, euthanasia, drug addiction, and wars in larger numbers than ever before. God has been supplanted as the center of man's life by foreign gods. Men, in ever-increasing numbers, worship at the shrines of money, property, fame, power, pleasure, success, science. But whatever it is that takes first place in man's life, that is his idol. And behind every idol man prostrates himself before stands Satan the author of idolatry. For whoever worships Mammon and his creaturely satellites, in effect is really worshipping Satan who hides behind all idols. For Satan's main purpose is to oppose God at every point. He does not greatly care what secondary, creaturely objects man worships, for he knows that in practicing such idolatry, man is pledging his chief loyalty to the powers of hell of which he is the king.

Thus there is no realm in which Satan is more active than in religion. A spiritual leader himself, he has used man over the centuries to devise many forms of religion, none of which is able to bring man into a relationship of love and friendship with the living God. Rather all of these religions are certain to bind man ever more securely to the slavery of idolatry and the power of demons. It is small wonder that all false religions, since they come forth from Satan's malicious mind, tend to have certain similarities all over the world, even in vastly different cultures. Such religions are marked by incantations, repetition of magical formulas, idols, protecting charms, ritual orgies. It should not surprise the person alerted to spiritual realities that in an age of atheism diverse forms of the religion of Satanism have sprung up all over the world and are gaining followers at a rapid rate. In these religions often enough Satan sets up as high priests certain evil men or women who boast of having charismatic powers. Such people are more useful to Satan as idols than mere inanimate objects would be. For a living man or woman who is worshipped is able to galvanize more followers to Satan's purposes than dead, gold, silver, or wooden gods. Satan knows only too well the magnetic power of drawing the masses to himself through the charismatic cords of Adam.

Another sign that the modern world is losing its struggle with "the powers and principalities" and hence also its control over its own flesh and blood, is the ease with which it has succumbed to the seduction of the "big lie." St. Paul warned early Christians "to keep Satan from gaining an advantage over us; for we are not ignorant of his designs."[344] Unfortunately, in our day the reverse is true. Men are not alerted to Satan's designs and hence demons

[344] Paul, 2 Cor. 2:11.

have gained a tremendous advantage over this perverse generation. As the father of lies, Satan has succeeded in contradicting Scripture, denying dogma, popularizing immorality. He has demythologized the Bible, reducing its message to naturalistic explanations of events, rinsing the word of God of all the *miribilia et magnalia Dei*, the miracles and mysteries of God. Satan has made use of secular, religious, university scholars who have lost their faith to accomplish this falsification of Scripture. He has used human savants to set up centers of learning where Holy Scripture is mocked and repudiated with contempt, with animus, with so-called objective sophistication, with a false show of scholarship. Thus the allies he has employed among the pseudo-intellectual arrogantly divinize man's intellect while ridiculing the word of God. They reduce the gospel message, the good news, in the minds of their helpless students to being mere superstition. The result is that millions of youth, who must live "not by bread alone but by every word that proceeds from the mouth of God," are spiritually starved to death by the lies that proceed from the mouths of Satan's children. It was for this very falsifying of God's message and refusal to accept the truth He revealed that Christ upbraided the religious leaders of the Jews:

> You are of your father the devil and your will is to do your father's desires. He was a murderer from the beginning and has nothing to do with the truth, because there is no truth in him. When he lies, he speaks according to his own nature, for he is a liar and the father of lies.... He who is of God hears the words of God. The reason why you do not hear them is that you are not of God.[345]

[345] John 8:44–47.

The Antichrist

The Seduction of Youth

Since the early 1960s youth throughout the world has come under the massive invasion and attack of the evil spirits. Living predominantly in his bodily senses, which are highly excitable and have not yet been totally reined in and matured by reason and experience, youth is seduced by Satan through the allurement of limitless sex, pot, the bewilderment about religion, the fascination for the thrills of rebellion, and the joys of unrestrained freedom. One cannot visit a major college campus without being made aware in campus newspapers, posters, leaflets, discussion groups, or magazines of the three-pronged drive to capture youth body and soul. That drive is a mixture of fornication, marijuana, and mysticism. The college bookstores are overflowing with the books and the paraphernalia that foster revolution and promiscuity. McCandlish Phillips, former reporter for the *New York Times*, presents these observations on the situation.

Students clamor to be left alone in dormitory rooms long enough and late enough so they can go to bed together if they wish without prospect of interruption or subsequent reproach. Unlimited opportunity for free love ("the practice of having sexual relations without legal marriage or any continuing obligation") is at the core of the demand. Off campus, students live together as man and woman without any commitment to each other for the future.

Any one of these three—premarital or nonmarital sex, Eastern mysticism, and marijuana or LSD—supplies a basis for direct demonic activity in the lives of those who indulge in them. Thus students are softened up for the push for anarchism, rebellion, insurgency.

As these three things also reach down into the high schools and the junior high schools, similar conditions of disruption and destructiveness will break out there, as they have begun to do. It is the tragic result of the increasing degree of influence and control that demons have gained in the lives of young people through sin.[346]

The Quagmire of the Youth Culture

With the cooperation of worldly men, a youth subculture was created in the 1960s whose spirit is shot through with the ideals of Satan. It has popularized the psychedelic snakepit in which youth—and many not so young—is encouraged to sport long, wild hair, dirty jeans, a laxity of manners, electrified music, screaming noise, wild rhythms, thundering drums with a beat, beat, beat. The Beatles, the Rolling Stones, and many other similar quartets continue to provoke today more than ever, the frenzied gyrations of millions of youth who twist, bend, leap, and swoon to noises amplified to the point of ear-smashing intensity and head-bursting pain. The youth swirl like bats in the whirligig of wildly pulsating neon lights. They are dressed in beads, buttons, scanty clothes with bare feet and bare breasts flashing in the artificial lightning. This whole subculture is meant to be a revolt against the superculture of the bourgeois, a superculture that youth rejects as being fat, sleek, self-serving, and swinish. In an article entitled "Meet the Women in the Revolution," Peter Babcox wrote that "there is a quickening disposition among the young ... that the salvation of our culture is revolution. It is an amorphous, tumultuous phenomenon, both a state of mind and

[346] McCandlish Phillips, *The Bible, the Supernatural and the Jews* (New York: World Publishing Company, 1970), p. 184.

an organized political force, called The Movement." Mr. Babcox spoke with a twenty-seven-year-old woman who writes poems of revolution and he quoted these lines, "I am pregnant with murder. The pains are coming faster now."[347]

That the frenzied dancers are the children of Satan, whether they are aware of this fact or not, is also made clear by the revolutionary, salacious lyrics screamed out in their songs. "The time is ripe for palace revolution ... the time is ripe for fighting in the streets." The Rolling Stones have produced such albums as "Street Fighting Man," "Beggars Banquet," "It's All Over Now," "Let's Spend the Night Together." These last two albums precipitated riots. And Satan himself comes in for special music in such acid rock overtures as "Their Satanic Majesties Request," and "Sympathy for the Devil."[348] Now the media—motion pictures, records, prints, TV, radio—are all plugging this acid rock with great enthusiasm, for there are millions of dollars flowing from those masses of youth jumping and rioting in exalted commotion. One is reminded of the poet Shelley's apt line as he gazes on the tumultuous tempest whipped up in youth by acid rock: "This age shakes like a reed in the unheeding storm." Nor is this a tempest in a teapot. For this quagmire—with its come-ons of easy sex, drugs, LSD, PCP, hallucinations, riots, revolutions, murders, sudden untimely deaths, and violence of all kinds and varieties—is a satanic trap for youth. The kids in the millions go dancing hilariously into this whirlpool of revolution. And many of them never return to sanity, but are ruthlessly cut off by death in their youth. And the Pied Piper behind it all is Satan showing up as an angel of flashing light and of thundering music.

[347] Ibid., p. 269.
[348] Ibid., pp. 271–272.

Barry Farrell, in a *Life* essay on the great Woodstock Music and Art Festival held in August 1969, wrote of "rock dope" as the new "American religion" whose believers massed on the hillside at Bethel, New York, as though for a camp meeting of some "electro-chemical Church."[349] A statement coined in the classical time of the Greeks and Romans concerning the pagan gods—who really never existed but in myth—applies rather perfectly to Satan who hides behind these idols: "Whom the gods would destroy, they first render mad." The actual truth is "Whom the devils would destroy, they first render mad." And so the crazed music of acid rock at times tames, numbs youth by the millions into bovine passivity, leaving the intellectual powers paralyzed. At other times it charges the emotions to such fever pitch that it extinguishes the light of reason, calls up black demons from the subconscious, drives youth to "turn on, tune in, drop out" or arouses them to "groove" with the music in a frenzy of madness. The result is that today millions of youth will "groove" with rock music, but tomorrow they will be passively submissive to the cadences of some demagogue behind whose tyranny will be the controlling power of the puppet masters, Satan and all the forces of hell.[350]

Demons in the Family

Satan, his demons, and their human henchmen know that the fate of mankind depends on the spiritual durability of family relationships. If one splits the atom, the smallest unit of matter, tremendous physical disaster results from the explosive forces released. And if one splits the family, the smallest unit of society,

[349] Ibid., p. 254.
[350] Ibid., p. 254.

tremendous social disaster results from the explosive passions released. There is no law against splitting the atom. But God Himself forbids splitting the family. "What God has joined together, let no man put asunder." From the very beginning the Creator insisted: "A man shall leave his father and mother and cleave to his wife, and the two shall become one flesh."[351] God planned that the peace and holiness of the family should consist in the unity of mind, heart, soul, and body expressed by mutual love and sacrifice. But the forerunners of the Antichrist are destroying the family.

It has been a special scar on the worst pagan cultures and the worst idolatrous religions that they openly attacked the gender identities of the sexes. They celebrated sexual indulgence, sexual experimentation, sexual symbols, fertility rites, temple prostitution, seasonal sex orgies, sexual abuse and enslavement of young women, girls, and boys. Such abominations are back with us in a flood tide and increasing at an alarming rate every day. The heterosexual relationship is under violent attack. Women, in ever growing numbers, are despising and abandoning their femaleness. They thus cripple themselves for the fulfillment of their sublime vocation of mothering children to maturity. Men, frightened by the blazing fury of the women's liberation movement, are surrendering male roles and positions to psychologically desexualized women. Charles Winnick's book *The New People: Desexualization in America* gives shocking descriptions of the evil effects of this movement. Men and women are being considered interchangeable in a vocational sense, even within the family by those who believe that men can be mothers while women can be masculine breadwinners.[352]

---

[351] Matt. 19:4–7.
[352] Dr. Harold M. Voth, "The Family and the Future of America," *The Phyllis Schlafly Report*, October 1978.

But sex is not an accidental characteristic of man and woman. A human person without sex is a monstrous abstraction. Sex entails the very identity of each person; sex plunges to the deepest mystery of each person. Hence the sexes and the vocations pertaining thereto are not interchangeable. Each person is called to serve God and his fellowman, accepting gladly the sex with which one is endowed and the vocation attached to that sex. Explaining the text "man was not created for woman but woman for man," enemies of the Church—and even some sincere Christians—misinterpret the phrase "woman for man." They say there is indicated in this scriptural passage an essential superiority of the male over the female human. Thus they see in the "for man" that woman's role is to be an instrument, a means, an intermediate end for man's aggrandizement. Nothing can be further from the truth. Woman was created for man to save him from social isolation, to be his loving companion, wife, and mother of his family. When He created woman, God had in mind that both man and woman would find their social joy in their mutual surrender in love. The divine dimension of that surrender is found in the surrender Christ made when He became man *for us,* for our salvation, emptying Himself and becoming a slave *for* love of us. Despite His loving surrender Christ always remains infinitely superior to us; for He is our God. So Eve, though man's metaphysical equal, is yet socially man's wife, helper, mother. Thus femininity does not enslave woman to man; rather it enshrines woman in the place of love in the family as sweet counterbalance to the weight of authority emanating from the man.

The Dutch scholar Buijlendijk has expertly unmasked a modern error concerning the sexes. In his book *Woman* he says that it is only at an embryonic state of modern "feminism" that it is naively supposed that equality of women to men means women must do all things men usually do. This error fails to honor women, for it neglects their positive, unique contribution to human society. Indeed, under the guise of advancing women to equality with men, this false principle makes a final attempt to subject women completely to the tyranny of purely masculine criteria.[353] Women cannot be made "copy-cat" men without degrading them by unnaturally robbing them of their femininity. A bogus masculinity does not honor or liberate women. Woman is honored and left free when she is genuinely accepted as an integral woman with all the characteristic charms of femininity. For woman contributes to human society what she alone can contribute with consummate excellence — the mothering, nurturing, and training of the human family through tender love. It is the sin of sham modernity to subject women to the imperialism of the egalitarians. They would destroy the identity, the very humanity, of woman, both of which are linked mysteriously to her femininity. Yet mothering is perhaps the most important social activity for the establishment of sanity and sanctity in the family and society. It is a full-time, demanding vocation, requiring a constant spirit of gentleness, persevering commitment, steadiness, and a limitless capacity to give oneself in self-sacrifice and total love. Hence a woman needs a good man, husband, father by her side to bring out the best in her character, to prevent her from becoming distracted, depressed, or depleted in her dedication to the family. Moreover, true fathering provides for the physical, psychological, and spiritual security of the mother and the family.

[353] Quoted by Rev. Louis C. Bouyer, *Sexuality, Theology, Priesthood*. A scholarly symposium on the ordination of women, published by Concerned Fellow Episcopalians, San Gabriel, California, 535 West Roses Road, p. 3.

Thus a good wife-mother brings out the best in her husband-father and a good husband-father brings out the best in his wife and children. All together they create an integral family, a domestic shrine where persons of great strength are formed, who in their turn create strong societies.

From this ludicrous, unnatural phenomenon—the cancellation of gender identity—the personalities of parents are stunted. Psychological conflicts destroy the natural functions of parents and children. For with the blurring of the clear distinction and meaning of maleness and femaleness, grim social results have developed. Men and women still mate and beget children, but they cannot live in harmony or carry out the responsibilities of mature parenthood. Their children, starved for genuine mothering and fathering, grow up warped, disturbed, incapable of facing the demands of life or of becoming in their turn parents and builders of harmonious, integral, stable families. For disturbed parents, unable to form lasting heterosexual commitments, beget disturbed children who grow up unable to enter lasting matrimonial unions. And thus divorce becomes a chain-reaction phenomenon from one generation to another.

Some Frightening Statistics

Dr. Harold M. Voth, psychiatrist and psychoanalyst at the Menninger Foundation and author of the book *The Castrated Family* gives us some sad statistics on the broken families of our times. The overall divorce rate is now 40 percent, and 59 percent of second marriages end in divorce. More than 50 percent of marriages of young people end in divorce. In California more young people are living together than are formally married. The number of unmarried couples in the United States has doubled between 1970 and 1975. Currently there are 1.3

million such couples. The offspring of these casual unions as well as the millions from broken homes have become the vast liabilities of today and tomorrow's societies. Moreover, the sufferings and psychiatric illnesses these millions endure defy description. Incidentally, the marriages of the young usually break up with the coming of children. The typical picture is for the children to range in ages from six months to six or seven years, exactly when the developing child needs parental input of the highest quality. There are 11 million children being reared by a single parent, usually a woman. Here is another shocking aspect of the gravity of the family situation. One million of these are under three years old. One-half of the nation's annual product of 13.5 million babies who will be born to mothers between eighteen and twenty-four years old will be illegitimate. Unmarried black women of the same age range will bear two-thirds of all the babies, that is to say 78 percent of the black babies of that 13.5 million will not have a father. The nation's overall rate of illegitimacy is around 20 percent. To get an idea of how weak fathers have become in the family circle, a recent poll of ten thousand families revealed that in 70 percent of the families men no longer attended to the family finances. CBS radio recently devoted an entire weekend to the question of what is happening to the American male. It found that he is becoming more emasculated as more women are becoming "liberated." And to make matters worse, as more parents abandon their biologic and primary duties, more children are becoming fugitives from broken homes; they are unable to live in a "house divided" and are forced to shun the unbearable tension of its constant chaos.[354]

[354] Voth, op. cit.

The powers of Satan have succeeded in creating among men a way of life that excludes the making of a home through the formation of a family. Often the militant leaders of the women's liberation movement tend to be psychologically masculinized as a result either of embittered childhood experiences or sufferings under masculine tyranny or from masculine desertion. Some of these women become admittedly overtly homosexual. The negative impact of such perverted development on women and family life is catastrophic. Then, too, the feminist movement is a powerful and persuasive force. It induces women with families to enter professions, to the neglect of their homes and preschool children. The children and society are the losers. Other young women are lured away from marrying by the siren call to make a career, though many of these women would be happier and more maturely developed as family makers. The alarming result is that 54 percent of women with children up to teenage are working and 39 percent of working women have preschool children. The absence of these mothers, particularly those with preschool children, must necessarily have a negative effect of some degree on childhood development. Small babies need object constancy, that is, the continuous input of good mothering by one and the same person. Some of the most severe damage to human development can be done to the human spirit when the child-mother bond is discontinuous or broken during the first three years of life. Volumes of evidence have been written on this. When children are small and the mother is away most of the day, the quality of life in the home changes dramatically; only her presence can fill the void.[355]

More than thirty-five thousand American adolescents killed themselves last year, and the problem of suicide among the

[355] Ibid.

young has reached "epidemic proportions." This was revealed during a conference held on the subject on March 2, 1978, at the New York Hilton Hotel. The conference, sponsored by the National Association of Independent Schools, was called to bring awareness to teachers and school officials that there is a growing problem of adolescent suicide. Indeed, suicide is now the second highest cause of death of the young. And loneliness has become a national symptom. Youngsters are lost, filled with anguish, disoriented, finally overcome with despair, and they terminate the most precious gift of all, their lives. The spiritual disturbances within youngsters are created by crippled family life. Loneliness *is* now a national illness. Many experts attending the conference in New York believe the number of suicides among adolescents far exceeds the thirty-five-thousand figure given by the American Association of Suicidology, a West Point, Pennsylvania, group whose aim is to prevent suicides. Mary Susan Miller, one of the speakers at the conference, said that the true figure of suicidal deaths among the young "may be closer to 100,000" a year.[356] People are lonely because they are empty inside; that comes from not having any meaning in life as children, as members of a family, as children of a loving Creator. Drug usage is a means of escape from psychic pain, from loneliness, from a meaningless life, one that fills one with anxiety and despair. The exalted, excited state produced by some drugs gives youth meaning, courage. Other drugs lull souls into passivity, extinguish intellectual and spiritual alertness. The end result of all drugs is a poisoned human spirit that loses all spiritual effectiveness. Many youthful drug users are the product of broken homes, separated parents, the offspring of absent mothers or of fathers who have deserted

---

[356] Reported in the *Daily News* story for Friday, March 3, 1978, p. 8.

the family. Some twenty-five million Americans smoke pot regularly; laws allowing this self-poisoning have been liberalized. The Presidential Commission on Mental Health estimates that eight million American children need immediate help for psychiatric disorders. Some estimates reach thirty million, and many believe the latter figure is closer to reality. In view of the disintegration in the durability of the male-female bond, the collapse of so many families, and the inability to make a complete bond by those who attempt it, these figures will surely be a mere drop in the bucket in the near future.[357]

As one views the vast wasteland of broken homes, one is not surprised to learn that in one year seventy thousand assaults were made on teachers, one hundred murders were committed in schools, and a billion dollars' worth of property damage was done to schools. Schools in large cities are in advanced stages of decay; students there are four or five years behind the level of achievement of children from smaller cities. Students of large cities have become wrathful radicals as a result of emotional deprivations, lack of authority within the home, lack of guidance from enlightened parents, lack of inner controls that could have come from consciences formed by responsible parents. Uncivilized and undisciplined parents have produced uncivilized and undisciplined children and turn them loose as if they were wild animals on a disintegrating society.[358]

Venereal disease has also reached epidemic levels; ten million cases were reported in the year 1977. Who knows how many more cases were *not* reported. Rational control of the sexual appetite is a must for the salvation of society. In America there has

[357] Voth, op. cit.
[358] Ibid.

been a mad escalation of sexual eroticism. Sexual experiences are in vogue anytime, with anyone, anywhere. The ethics of the day is "do your own thing," which is usually a form of sex experience. Venereal disease, along with millions of illegitimate babies, mostly unwanted, is part of the price for sexual licentiousness. No wonder there are more than one million runaway children each year. Promiscuous cultures rot quickly from within; many a great empire was felled by its unrestrained sexual mores. This is happening today to the whole Christian West.[359]

But we ask, "What happens to those million runaway children from broken homes? Are they cared for by a compassionate society?" Far from it. They fall into the hands of Satan and his evil human allies. They are exploited by wicked adults for prostitution and pornography. Child pornography has become a multimillion-dollar business. That means millions of Americans degrade themselves by paying for and enjoying the viewing of child porno. In Los Angeles alone, thirty thousand boys and girls were exploited for child pornography and child prostitution. In other larger cities the numbers of youth sold into this sexual slavery exceed by far those in Los Angeles. When one realizes that even parents sell their offspring to perform in sexual perversion movies, then one can begin to realize what is happening to the character of the family, to the soul of society.[360]

Then there is the skyrocketing surge of violence within the family. Child abuse has reached epidemic levels. But what is a novel development is the very high incidence of brutality perpetrated by wives against their husbands; an evil fruit, no doubt, of the rebellion led by women's liberation groups. Then, too,

[359] Ibid.
[360] Ibid.

wife-beating is on the upsurge. Centers have been opened in many large cities to aid children, wives, and husbands who are victims of brutality within the family. Just recently within the city of Cleveland a brother and sister, both teenagers, paid another youth sixty dollars to assassinate their father. Leaving the body of their father on the living room floor where he fell shot to death, the young murderers went on a spending spree with the money and checks they robbed from his pockets. When arrested and questioned, the youngsters affirmed that they had their father killed because he would not allow them to smoke pot and do as they pleased. They seemed totally cold-blooded about their heinous crime of patricide. The father was divorced and trying to raise the children as well as work for a living.

Homosexuality and lesbianism are both on the increase. And they too, as abnormal human activities, point up the moral landslide that is burying the family and society. The cause of these perverted activities has been unequivocally traced to childhood experiences within the family. Often it is traced to personalities of the parents and to the warped nature of their relationship. Man's biology is not the cause of this abnormal condition. The increase in this form of psychopathology is directly related to the faulty psychological development of the child within a disturbed family. It is an ominous fact that the gay movement is having its way of life redefined as a simple variant of normal sexuality and woven into the fabric of society. Bills are introduced in Congress and state legislatures to make it illegal to discriminate against anyone because of a different sexual preference. This means gays can "marry" and have access to any and all aspects of society, including teachers' platforms in classrooms of the young.[361] It is

---

[361] Ibid.

said that "the hand that rocks the cradle rules the world." But if the person who rocks the cradle is warped and crippled in personality then the world will not be ruled but ruined. In England gay "marriages" have already been legalized and homosexual couples are allowed to adopt and raise children. In the United States lesbian couples live together and often raise adopted children as a *de facto* situation. A spokeswoman for gays told Mrs. Carter, the president's wife, that there are twenty-five million gays in the United States. Dr. Abram Kardiner, distinguished physician, psychoanalyst, and anthropologist, states that homosexuality reaches pestilential and plague proportions in morally rotting societies during the final stages of total collapse.[362] The cult of softness is perhaps the most pronounced public phenomenon among nations today. It is certainly responsible for the rotting of the moral fiber of Western civilization not only in sex but also, in the erosion of Christian truth, in education, in art and in letters, in the repudiation of personal responsibility, and in the increasing tendency to side with the forces of crime against the forces of law and order.

But perhaps the most reprehensible, shocking attack on sexual morality and the family is the campaign to undermine the ban on incest. *Time* magazine for April 14, 1980, reveals the plans for this campaign in an article entitled "Attacking the Last Taboo." John Money of Johns Hopkins and co-author Gertrude Williams, in their book *Traumatic Abuse and Neglect of Children*, hold that one who commits incest is like "a religious deviant in a one-religion society," the implication being that opposition to incest is quite like religious intolerance. Wardell Pomeroy, co-author of the original Kinsey reports on males and

[362] Ibid.

females, is even more blunt. "It is time to admit that incest need not be a perversion or a symptom of mental illness. Incest between ... children and adults ... can sometimes be beneficial." Anthropologist Seymour Parker of the University of Utah writes: "It is questionable if the costs (of the incest taboo) in guilt and uneasy distancing between intimates are necessary or desirable." Mary Calderone, editor of the *Siecus Report*, depicts the taboo against incest as a mindless prejudice. Author James W. Ramey writes: "We are roughly in the same position today regarding incest as we were a hundred years ago with respect to our fears of masturbation."

In the propaganda campaign to make incest acceptable, words and phrases formerly used to describe incest are undergoing a euphemistic change. "Child abuse" is distinguished from "consensual incest" involving a parent; "abusive incest" is distinguished from "positive incest." Seduced by such antics in semantics, by pseudo-historical and specious anthropological rationalizations, the public interest in incest has increased enormously. The movies too are a good index of the escalation of the public's involvement in incest. In the '20s there were six movies about incest; in the '60s there were seventy-nine. And today the numbers are increasing more rapidly. Recent films on the subject are: *Chinatown*, *Luna*, and the made-for-TV *Flesh and Blood*. Incest has now become a topic for sexual entertainment. Recently a law-enforcing officer from New York City's Police Department told me that the incidents of incest in the city are increasing at an alarming rate and that the number of children fleeing from sex-abusing, pleasure-seeking predatory parents and relatives is approaching astronomical figures. Here is a corrupted, broken society made-to-order for conquest by the Antichrist.

An awesome picture of the logical end product of Satan's plan for society is given by G. H. and Winnifred Whiteley in their book *The Permissive Morality*. After a careful analysis of the present trends toward social chaos, they picture the arrival of a controlling, directing force who guides the Permissive Society as though it were a Termite Society toward its own evil purposes.

> We can imagine that in such a society the issue between chastity and sexual freedom would be settled in favor of freedom, premarital sexual experience would be normal, adultery a triviality, and change of partner no more than change of job. The logical outcome might well be the disappearance of marriage save between those who positively desired children and as much family life as the new society would allow. Fresh techniques of contraception would limit parenthood to the genuine enthusiasts, and with the development of eugenics even these might find themselves submitted to a screening process before they were permitted to breed....
>
> A society of the utmost blandness would ensue.... Training, job, meals, living quarters, medical attention and recreation would be provided by a single public organization so that the ordinary fellow need not worry about these things but could give all his attention to amusing himself. Advertising would easily transform into state propaganda. Individual protest would be ignored unless it became persistent, when it would be treated as symptomatic of an illness to be cured at public expense. If a man proved a reliable worker and socially amenable only when under the influence of drugs, then drugged he would be. Training-in of suitable attitudes would be undertaken at school and later on the job. All of this is the logical outcome of the morally permissive trend; if the ordinary person is to be relieved of responsibility some few persons in authority must undertake it on his behalf.

Thus the need for individual conscience and individual moral struggle would disappear. And so the managements' idea of the greatest happiness of the greatest number could be economically dispensed through the community.[363]

Just such a Confederation of Termite Nations is being moulded today for control and direction by the coming Antichrist. And he will gladly undertake all authority and responsibility for organizing the unthinking, wayward masses that are drifting into this League of Permissive Nations. Indeed the masses will be cheered on to accept their lot patiently by those evil allies who stand to gain most financially or in terms of power and prestige from the establishment of this kingdom of Satan on earth. These will be the people who have rebelled against God's plan of salvation, who would revise or devise man's way of life, who would mould his attitudes and set his fashions to run toward the idols of the kingdom of darkness.

Resurgence of Satanism

In a world of brilliant colored television, of exquisite stereophonic cassettes, of space ships speeding men to the moon, of space explorers speeding back to Earth marvelous photos of Jupiter, its moons, and newly discovered galaxies, in a word, in a world of hundreds of other technological marvels, the addiction to witchcraft and parallel occult phenomenon has escalated everywhere. Mr. George Steiner, Extraordinary Fellow of Churchill College Cambridge University, and professor of English and comparative literature at the University of Geneva, in an essay

[363] G. H. and Winifred Whiteley, *The Permissive Morality* (London: Methuen, 1964), pp. 44, 132–135.

appearing in the *New York Times*, December 9, 1977, entitled "The Lollipopping of the West," writes: "There are three times as many registered astrologers in Europe and the United States as there are chemists and physicists. Charlatans, either giggly or sinister, peddle millions of copies of books about visitants from outer space who, in some Edenic past, left their occult spoors on the deserts of Peru or stone circles of Carnac and Glastonbury. Star Trekkers and galactic warriors drug the imagination. Frightened of future wars and famines, dizzied by models of scientific and technological futurity, a bone-tired human species is looking toward saucers in the sky for solace and surveillance."[364]

What explains the current revival of occultism and witchcraft? It is my strong conviction that the decline of Christian Faith has led to the decline of man's confidence in the powers of human reason to attain reality and truth. Man has concluded today that all truth is relative. There is no real standard of truth nor universally accepted method for its verification. Thus epistemological relativism allows man to assess truth on his own personal experiences, no longer on the endless chain of coherent, logical reasoning. But since reason can no longer support itself, it is not surprising that it no longer can support revelation. Thus faith, too, has come increasingly to rely upon personal dogmatic assertion and experience. In rejecting the permanent authority of truth as founded by God in reality, reason, and revelation, man set himself up as the autonomous source of truth. Yet man is to himself an insoluble dilemma. He admits that some phenomena of experience give him much factual truth. He can even give a certain order to these facts with his intellect, but he cannot

---

[364] George Steiner, "The Lollipopping of the West," *New York Times*, December 9, 1977.

explain their existence nor their intelligibility. Moreover, man must admit that there remain many phenomena that his autonomous intellect cannot explain. This is the realm of mystery, the area of the "not yet known nor experienced." Despairing of his reason or of revelation to make this realm intelligible to him, man has convinced himself that he can get in contact with the mysterious, with the unknown, by means of his emotions and his will. To aid himself in making this contact man has consulted the seer, the fortune teller, the prophet, the sorcerer, the medium. Hence man is no longer a philosopher nor a believer; he has become the atheistic scientist who has gone on a ghost hunt. For without the God of reason and of revelation, man is condemned to dabble at diabolism. Thus to explain the many phenomena that escape rational laws, man has recourse to table tapping, to spiritualists, witches, seance people, yoga people, the Mystical Church of Cosmic Vibrations people. He has become in large numbers the only too willing victim of the swamis, gurus, mahatmas, healers, mumblers, and holy men, many of whom claim they have been chosen by God in miraculous visions granted them on trips made to heroin heaven.[365]

God's Ban on Occultism

Because men have rejected reason and, above all, revelation, they are vulnerable to occult forces. For a religion of modern secular humanism is powerless intellectually to stem the rush to the coves of occultism. Indeed, secular humanism is one of the primary causes of the revival of the religion of Satanism. The Chosen People were protected from occultism by the revelation of God

---

[365] Gary North, *None Dare Call It Witchcraft* (New Rochelle, NY: Arlington House Publishers, 1976), p. 22.

concerning Himself, His relationship to creation as well as by His promise of their ultimate salvation. But doctrines alone are never sufficient to preserve a people from the idolatry of the pagan rituals that surround them. God had also to place explicit prohibitions on His people to avoid dabbling in explicit occult acts. The most comprehensive prohibition appears in Deuteronomy 18:10–12: "There shall not be found among you anyone who burns his son or his daughter as an offering, anyone who practices divination, a soothsayer, or an augur, or a sorcerer, or a charmer, or a medium, or a wizard, or a necromancer. For whoever does these things is an abomination to the Lord." In Exodus 22:18 we read this condemnation against witchcraft or sorcery: "Wizards thou shalt not suffer to live." Against necromancy or spiritualism we read in Leviticus 19:31: "Do not turn to mediums or wizards; do not seek them out, to be defiled by them. I am the Lord, your God." And in chapter 20 verse 6 of the same book: "If a person turns to mediums and wizards, playing the harlot after them, I will set my face against that person, and will cut him off from among people." In Deuteronomy 18:20–22 on the subject of false prophets we read: "But the prophet who presumes to speak a word in My name which I have not commanded him to speak, or who speaks in the name of other gods, that same prophet shall die." Isaiah 47:13 announces God's condemnation against astrology thus: "Thou hast failed in the multitutde of thy counsels; let now the astrologers stand and save thee, that they gazed at the stars, and counted the months, that from them they might tell the things that shall come to thee. Behold they are as stubble, fire hath burnt them, they shall not deliver themselves from the power of the flames." And St. John the Evangelist in his first letter, 1 John 4:1, writes: "Beloved, do not believe every spirit, but test the spirits to see whether they are of God; for many false prophets have gone out into the world." And Ezekiel the prophet relates God's scorn against divination 21:21: "For the king of Babylon stands at the parting of the way, at the head of the two ways; he shakes the arrows, he consults the teraphim, he looks at the liver." Isaiah also explains that Israel's punishments are due to its fascination with enchantments, 47:9–12: "Stand fast in your enchantments and your many sorceries ... perhaps you may be able to succeed.... All things have befallen you because of the multitude of your sorceries, and for the great hardness of your enchanters." In Jeremiah 10:2 the Lord condemns the practice of the idolatrous nations who seek truth in omens: "Learn not the way of the nations, nor be dismayed at the signs of the heavens because the nations are dismayed at them, for the customs of the peoples are false."

The Devil's Ambassadors

The witch of the biblical world was more accurately a "sorcerer," one who used diabolical power over people to break their covenantal faithfulness to God and to lead them into a ritual relationship with demons. Despite Walt Disney's charming creation of the traditional witch image—a skinny, old, midnight hag with broomstick, black hat, black cat, terrifying children—a witch is never an amusing character in the Bible. And so today twentieth-century witches are deadly serious; they are not all a piece of arcane flummery. Their chants, swords, music, symbols, herbs, and incense are pretty much what they were in pre-Christian times in the use of bizarre nature cults. The witch of the classical world was an expert in potions, rather known as a poisoner.

Now God prohibited the practice of sorcery to preserve mankind from becoming the slave or advocate of the devil. Other gods were always necessarily false gods, and sacrifice to them not only poisoned man's relationship to the true God, but brought on spiritual death and, often enough, even physical death. Once man's hunger and quest for personal transcendence ceases to be a religious ascent to the true God, it degenerates into being an impetus toward false gods, a descent into occultism. Thus occult liturgies are too often the means of fleeing the monotony and torture of self-divination; they seek a promised escape beyond the self, a self-transcendence to foreign gods. Today in the last quarter of the twentieth century, Baudelaire's frequently quoted dictum, "The devil's cleverest wile is persuading us that he does not exist," seems belied. Much as he would prefer to remain unknown and to work his evil unnoticed, a faithless and perverse generation has gone in search of Satan and called up his fiends and spectres from the yawning abyss. Even the insomniac, so-called Christian West is up late peering into the black night to read the stars. There is thriving also a multibillion-dollar industry of Satanism in movies, on television, in magazines, in novels. It breathes and feeds on man's ignorance, fears, isolation, bewilderments, faithlessness, and rebellions.[366] The Church of Satan, founded in 1966 by Anton Szandor La Vey, Exarch of Hell, now numbers some twenty thousand members, grouped in many "daughter grottoes" around the United States. Complete with newsletter, creed, ceremonies, and its own biblical books, this contemporary Satanist movement is a growing, popular religion. Recently a United Press International newswire carried this story from San Francisco on a wedding rite of La Vey's witchcraft cult:

> Asking the blessings of Lucifer for a union "conceived in hell," Beelzebub, a priest of Satan, performed a marriage ceremony last night using a naked woman as an altar....

---

[366] Richard Woods, O.P., "Satanism Today," in *Soundings in Satanism*, ed. F. J. Sheed (New York: Sheed and Ward, 1972), pp. 92–104.

The dark rite was performed in the small icon-filled, black-walled living room of Anton La Vey, 32 ... who bills himself as the first priest of the Satanic church. It was conducted before a stone fireplace, by the light of candles stuck in human skulls. (Of the nude woman) La Vey explained that the altar shouldn't be a "cold, unyielding slab of sterile stone or wood. It should be a symbol of enthusiastic lust and indulgence." The bridegroom, 35, had been married twice before.... La Vey said it was the first time ever for the diabolical ceremony which he said he concocted from his fifteen-year study of witchcraft, sorcery and Satanism. The rite consisted of bells, gongs, chanting in magic language from an old book, *The Equinox*, and some play with a sword and chalice.... Stuffed ravens, wolves, owls and rats looked down from shelves everywhere.[367]

Also emphasizing the recent upsurge of fashionable and pathological diabolism are the activities of the Long Island cult headed by Lady Rowen and her husband Rabat to give them their cultist names. They are white witches who have accumulated quite a library of occult books. The couple dropped out of the Church of England and became disciples of Dr. Gerald Gardner who was considered the grand old Master of British witchcraft. Their expedient philosophy is found in *The Book of Shadows*, which contains all the rites, spells, charms, cures, and chants. "Once a month," the book advises, "... gather in some secret place and adore me who am the Queen of all witcheries." The Long Island Coven holds its rituals in Rabat's basement. On Halloween, the major festival of the eight holidays of every witch's calendar, the witches,

[367] Phillips, op. cit., p. 202.

all nude, sing and dance. Lady Rowen has often brewed potions that cured minor ills of children. All these witches share a common faith in reincarnation.[368] Hell's Angels, that band of black-jacketed, motorcycled ruffians, hold Satan as their patron, a sort of totemic symbol of their revolutionary power and independence. The Manson Family slayings gave clear signs of the influence of Satanism on Manson and his bewitched girls.[369] The ritual suicide of Vineland, New Jersey, also demonstrates the power of the Satanist cult that has led to devil worship. *Mademoiselle* magazine made witchcraft the theme of a "Special Magical Mystery Issue" whose cover promised: "Sorcery and Sex: A terrific tour of spells, charms, witchcraft and the mysterious East … Yoga … India's exciting Tantric art. Chilling occult novel complete in this issue." The same issue reported an interview with Dr. Harry E. Wedeck, a college professor with an extensive knowledge of the history of witchcraft. The interviewer remarked to Dr. Wedeck that whenever he read about witches, especially in the book *Rosemary's Baby*, there always seemed to be strong links between sorcery and sex—and a very sick sex at that. Dr. Wedeck replied: "Well, witchcraft often attracted people of unbridled or frustrated sex appetites. And even if you were possessed of neither, you couldn't be a witch unless you gave yourself completely to it. Which meant involving yourself with your coven—twelve disciples and the devil and the Sabbat (defined as 'a secret rendezvous of witches and sorcerers for worshipping the devil, characterized by orgiastic rites, dances, feasting, etc.') The Sabbat always had a ceremonial orgy, ending in a kind of communion, but sexual in nature, with the devil."[370]

[368] Ibid., pp. 201–202.
[369] Woods, op. cit., p. 99.
[370] Phillips, op. cit., pp. 202–203.

Satanic rites today, probably more than ever because of the almost complete loss of the sense of the sacred, often include the ritual of the black Mass. Basically this liturgy is the inversion of the Catholic Mass. The black Mass employs black candles, reversed symbols and gestures, a conscious profanation of the Host, which in former times was to have been consecrated by a defrocked priest or stolen from a Catholic Church. Such sacrilegious rites, when employed for magical purposes, often develop into truly hideous proportions, including ritual murder and varieties of sexual pathology.[371]

From what we have seen so far of satanic rites, contemporary diabolism cannot be dismissed by sophisticated, atheistic intellectuals or updated theologians as a "lot of harmless fun-and-sex games." There is evidence which proves that sadomasochistic rites have led all too often to serious injury and death among the California cultists. These brutalities and deaths reflect the undeniable morbid aspect of occult revolution. Voodoo is becoming increasingly noticeable in many Southern and Southwestern states, as well as in New York City, Los Angeles, Chicago, and New Orleans. It took the Tate–La Bianca murder court proceedings, which went for more than a year in 1970 and 1971, to shock and frighten the world into a realization of the extent of the diabolical influences characteristic of a modern society that produced the Manson Family. The grim combination of sex, violence, drugs, witchcraft, and Satanism that led to the horrible slaughter of seven persons in a ritual sacrifice clearly indicated that a wave of wickedness was engulfing modern society. The mood of revulsion and terror following the Manson slayings was heightened even more when Dr. Victor Ohta and his family were

[371] Woods, op. cit., p. 95.

murdered less than a year later by a young occultist with ecological paranoia. Then followed the tragic ritual slaying of a teenage Vineland, New Jersey, Satanist. Believing that he would return at the head of a legion of devils, Patrick Newell was pushed to his death by two friends, after performing a satanic ritual. The cult of Satan had already spread to as many as seventy young Vinelanders before the killing took place. A month later an elderly man was stabbed to death in Miami by a twenty-two-year-old Satanist who believed that she had seen the devil in person. Daily the grim episodes of violent diabolism can be found in increasing numbers in newspapers and magazines. This massive publicity may be a possible factor in the faddish popularity of pathological occultism. In May 1972 the suburban community of Waukegan, six miles north of Chicago, was shaken by lurid accounts of diabolical rites performed by groups of drug-drenched teenagers and adults. Night-time revels in local cemeteries with satanic invocations, animal torture, and even human sacrifice rounded out these bizarre liturgies. Well-organized satanic groups are mushrooming all over the Western world, not only in America.[372] Satan is starring today in almost as many movie and TV programs as the most beauteous damsels and the most famous godfather chieftains. The growing corps of devil's advocates are preparing today a world that will be ready and eager to accept the ideals and rule of the Antichrist when he comes. This will be a world saturated with witchcraft and occultism, a world that has demolished the temples and altars of God and set up altars to demons in Houses of Idolatry. That world will be one vast supermarket peddling objects of magic, idolatrous statues, trinkets of superstition; in that world daily libations of human blood and

[372] Ibid., pp. 98–100.

bodies will be offered to placate the Antichrist and his master Satan. In an atmosphere of violence, rebellions, wars, international intrigues, and the creeping advancement of politically and militarily organized atheism, contemporary man already fearfully feels that Armageddon is in the very air he breathes, in the chemicals and foods that sustain his body. A sense of doom pervades the universe under Satan's malevolent, fierce rule over the nations of the earth. Despite the myths establishing the twentieth century as the most enlightened, the herald of eternal progress, the Dark Ages and the Renaissance were not as black as our present era. Medieval ideals were far superior to those of the present age. For in those times man was inspired by faith and lived coherently with truth and virtue, despite his faults. Today, however, man is oppressed and wearied by the loss of faith, the barbarism of politics, the autocracy of technology and the collapse of organized religions. As a result, he lives in a world that has become a witches' cauldron, a weird brew of sex, flowers, drugs, incense, tear gas, acid rock, rhetoric, bombs, and blood.[373] Enter the Antichrist, ruler of the Moloch World?

The Revival of the Moloch State

We have seen so far that when the true God is banished from man's society, new gods rush in to replace Him. But perhaps what has not been clearly seen today is that when man accepts new gods in his practice of the occult, he also necessarily brings about a revival of the politics of ancient paganism. A normal development of the worship of pagan gods was the creation of a divine state that rested on a theology of continuity, that is, on the denial of the Creator-creature distinction. The pagan theocratic

---

[373] Ibid., p. 102.

state could take the lives of its children, or any members, as a sacrifice to the god of the state. The worshippers of Moloch ordered their sons and daughters to pass through fire as a form of sacrifice and testing. Thus God's prohibitions to the Chosen People against occult worship were not only a means of protecting people's lives morally from perverse practices, but also a means of restricting the power of the omnipotent political rulers who were theoretically unbounded by the restraint of limited, reasonable men and could take human life indiscriminately in the name of the god Moloch. Rousas Rushdoony gives a description of what he calls the "Moloch state":

> While relatively little is known of Moloch, much more is known of the concept of divine kingship, the king as god, and the god as king, as the divine-human link between heaven and earth. The god-king represented man on a higher scale, man ascended, and the worship of such a god, i.e., of such a *Baal*, was the assertion of the *continuity* of heaven and earth. It was the belief that all being was one being, and the god therefore was an ascended man on that scale of being. The power manifested in the political order was thus a manifestation or apprehension and seizure of divine power. It represented the triumph of a man and of his people. Moloch worship was thus a political religion.... Moloch worship was thus state worship. The state was the true and ultimate order, and religion was a department of the state. The state claimed *total jurisdiction* over man; it was therefore entitled to *total sacrifice*.[374]

---

[374] R.J. Rushdoony, *The Institute of Biblical Law* (Nutley, NJ: Craig Press, 1973), p. 32.

Now a religious, pagan state that claims total jurisdiction over man is a state directed by demons through the actions of rulers who justify their tyranny by having recourse to their Moloch god. Such a state provides its subjects not with law and justice, but with order—a man-centered, oppressive, demonic order. It begets the totalitarian state. The modern world everywhere is succumbing to the power of such a Moloch state. For secular, rational, and occult humanism denies that there is any really transcendent, higher-than-human voice or authority that cares for man. Secular and occult humanists are at one in denying the true God. They are at one in divinizing man, the secularist through science, the occultist through demonic powers. Both seek power. The secularist seeks political power in the name of humanity; the occultist seeks the power of the underworld in the name of humanity. But both seek power for their own benefit. And both eventually come together to create the super-instrument of power, the modern omnicompetent state that claims absolute authority over the life and death of each citizen. Rushdoony expertly unmasks the nature of this state:

> The Moloch state simply represents the supreme effort of man to command the future, to predestine the world, and to be as God. Lesser efforts, divination, spirit-questing, magic and witchcraft are equally anathema to God. All represent efforts to have the future on other than God's terms, to have a future apart from and in defiance of God. They are assertions that the world is not of God but of brute factuality, and that man can somehow master the world and the future by going directly to the raw materials thereof.[375]

[375] Ibid., p. 33.

Somewhere George Santayana emphasizes man's "brute necessity of believing something as long as life lasts." But a disembodied creed cannot inflame hearts. A revelation must pour forth from the soul of a Messiah if it is to win men's adherence. We read that "God draws men through the cords of Adam." Not to be outdone, Satan seduces men through the wiles of pseudo-saviors. And in our day liberation is in the air. Thus the many Moloch states of our age have their redeemers, prophets, emancipators. Ronald Knox tells us that "when strong currents of spiritual emotion, aroused by some religious crisis, sweep through a multitude of human hearts, physical (and spiritual) reactions of an abnormal kind are liable to occur as their byproduct."[376] Now just such a frenzied phenomenon caused the rise and sudden, bloodcurdling fall of Jonestown and the Peoples' Temple in Guyana. For Jonestown, Guyana, is a classic case of the modern revival of the Moloch state. Let us analyze briefly its rise and fall.

The Peoples' Temple arose in an era when magnetic preachers and prophets are sweeping huge audiences out of their minds by the whirlwind of their utopian oratory and projecting them into an apocalyptic golden or ghastly age, depending on the mood of the prophet. What were the spiritual influences that unleashed the floodgates and fostered the mass suicides and murders in Jonestown? By way of preparing the social milieu for the creation of the Peoples' Temple, one of the most basic causes must be the massive apostasy by Christians in the West from faith in the Judaeo-Christian God of revelation. Because of this apostasy the relentless advance of the icecap of

<hr/>

[376] Ronald Knox, *Enthusiasm* (New York: Oxford University Press, 1950), p. 110.

secularism in America has produced a heartless, affectless society in which nobody tends to care for anyone but himself, for anything but instant self-gratification. In a society that seeks sex without love, violence for the thrill of it, drugs for the get-away-from-it-all trip, the sensibilities of citizens are blunted. An Auschwitz is attained in which the slaughter mills of abortion and euthanasia are legalized.[377] The Center for Disease Control in Atlanta, Georgia, gives us a statistic which proves incontrovertibly that the United States has become a Moloch state. It states that for the two years 1976, 1977 in the United States 3.1 million babies were born and 1.2 million were legally aborted. *Newsweek* for August 1978 gives even higher figures. Indeed the figures given must be rather conservative, for there is no penalty imposed for not reporting abortions. Here is a nation that has usurped the power of God over life and death. In the name of its new secular gods, Progress and Liberty, titles that are false fronts for Rebellion and Licentiousness, many formerly Christian nations are driving their sons and daughters through the demonic fires of sacrificial murder. Thus France, England, Italy, and other so-called Christian nations, having legalized abortion and while preparing to legalize euthanasia, have become Moloch states. Such brutalized states, with their corrupted institutions, abandon citizens to the scourges of drugs, street terrors, broken homes, schools of scandals, and, in general, to a coarse, venal, profligate quality of life, a life of fear and loneliness.

Now today false christs on the prowl for lost sheep (and the Rev. Jim Jones was one of these par excellence) fully realize that the established religions are in deep crisis. They see Churches

[377] Arnold Lunn and Garth Lean, *Christian Counter-Attack* (London: Blandford Press, 1969), pp. 47–56.

genuflecting before the world, substituting the City of Progress for the City of God. They hear churchmen trafficking for souls by offering them security and riches instead of challenging them to attain sanctity through a life of loving self-sacrifice and service. In place of the virtues of faith, hope and charity, the updated preacher urges souls to practice the art of self-awareness, self-assertion, self-fulfillment. Self-watchers are engaged in the most boring, futile activity imaginable. They become mental and moral midgets. Perhaps this explains in part the mass exodus of clerics, religious, teachers, and youth among the disenchanted faithful.

The prophet Jim Jones and his wandering flock first sought to better the heartless society at home by filling the spiritual vacuum they encountered with humanitarian activities. Under the facade of effusive affection, understanding, and a flood of welfare services, they recruited hundreds of neglected souls. But their sect was doomed to failure for it was founded on the lie that religious Socialism can save men. Jones himself was always a liberal, or rather, a zealous Communist posing as a liberal; to keep up appearances he preached the gospel of social salvation camouflaging it with a thin veneer of Christianity; his faith was a false and cruel caricature of Christianity.

On the verge of being revealed as an evil, false prophet, Jones led his flock into the promised land of the lush Guyana jungle. There he founded his charismatic community, the Peoples' Temple. There, free from the prying eyes, ears, and mass media of a hostile world, Messiah Jones, by now permanently exalted and sick with paranoid utopian fantasies, ascended the throne of God. Formerly, while doling out liberally social goodies, he claimed to be the reincarnation of Jesus. Now he demanded the service of adoration from his faithful. For in the wake of his tremendous political, social, and monetary successes in collusion with liberal, humanistic politicians, the savior Jones enthroned himself as the sole idol of his kingdom. The Moloch Jones began to devour his subjects. His megalomania having soared to infinite proportions, Jones now claimed to be the very God who made the heavens and earth. His picture became a necessary relic for subjects to ward off evil. He ruled his slaves with the use of physical and psychological torture; he imposed on the community regular mass-suicide drills. He was the peoples' political, social, religious, and even phallic god, compelling his subjects to serve his most unnatural egotistical, monetary, and sexual lusts. Having totally controlled their lives, he brainwashed and drilled them to deliver, sheep-like, into his hands the power to decide the time and the manner in which he would deal out to them their deaths.

Jonestown, the Marxist-liberal-socialist caricature of a Christian Church, conferred on its faithful but one sacrament—the sacrament of death, of suicide. Of old, Moloch asked his sons and daughters to pass through fire as a holocaust to himself. Modern Moloch in the Peoples' Temple—in a liturgy reminiscent of stoical heroics—asked his children to gather in community and drink the cup of cyanide together. Thus a church of naive, hoodwinked, simple folk was led astray by an evil, militant Communist, posing as a God-man liberal do-gooder. For the devil and the emperor Jones sacrificed their high priest and his followers on the altar of the inflated ego of the revived, modern Moloch state. When they had all drained the chalice of cyanide, the Peoples' Temple became a Church of the dead. The modern Moloch state was left a city of suicides-murders, a city of 911 rotting corpses.

There is a warning and somber lesson to be learned from the carnage exacted by the modern Moloch state, whether that takes place in the jungle of Jonestown or in the abortion mills of Western cities. The warning is that established forms of Christian religions have lost their hold on and power to attract most people—especially the educated middle class and even the masses of the poor. Why is this so? Because such religions have secularized the Christian message. They teach in favor of the Christ of Karl Marx instead of the Christ of the Gospels. Even so-called Christian universities no longer teach a love of truth nor the skill in attaining, defending, and sharing it. They are teaching the American, Molochian gospel of power and wealth. In the consequent metaphysical and spiritual darkness these universities have so diluted revealed truth that their graduates enter the professional world either as bemused agnostics, enraged atheists, or "chicken Catholics." These malformed Catholics, when they are not attacking and misrepresenting the Faith, are unable and unwilling to speak up in its defense, much less suffer and die for it. So too have the Churches adjusted and distorted the original deposit of the Faith, the process being rationalized, of course, by the desire to clarify and update the Christian message. But the end product is always the same, a teaching conformed to the spirit of the world that prefers Jesus to be a revolutionary leader, a social reformer. A world, too, that wants God's Church to be a kingdom of this earth, tailoring everlasting truths to the exigencies of man's temporal convenience.

The millions who turn away from such utopian Christianity are preyed upon by pseudo-saviors and captured as lost sheep by the many prophets like Jones who hunt in the savage wilderness that lies at the fringes of the cult desert. We have now further evidence that the Christian facade of the Peoples' Temple was a phony front for a so-called Communist utopia. Letters have been found testifying that the cult leaders were planning to bequeath more than 7 million dollars to the Communist Party that rules the Moloch state known as the Soviet Union. One letter, read at the coroner's jury in Matthews Ridge, Guyana, December 17, explained that the Peoples' Temple was turning over "all our assets" to the Soviet Union "because we, as Communists, want our money to be of benefit for help to all oppressed peoples all over the world, or in any way that your decision-making body sees fit." This letter and four others were addressed to Fyodor Timofeyev, the consul for the Soviet Union in Georgetown, the Guyanese capital.

The somber lesson to be learned is that a religion that promises progress in liberty, science, education, economic, and social welfare, without belief in a transcendent God, cannot produce a secular utopia in which all will be content to live in peace. The starry-eyed men of the Enlightenment produced a Moloch state that ruled with a Reign of Terror and plunged Europe into nationalist wars that led to the apotheosis of the emperor-god, Napoleon. The incurable optimist-rationalists of the nineteenth century produced the secular gods and architects of totalitarian Molochs—Marx, Lenin, Stalin, Mao—the imperialistic tyrannies of Communist Russia and China. The Moloch states of race and blood were engendered by the Nazi-Fascist tyrants, Hitler and Mussolini. The tragic truth is that the gods of modern Moloch states have been the architects of such worlds of depravity as Auschwitz, the Kremlin, Cuba, Vietnam, China, Jonestown, and others. But the Moloch states of the West are no better than those of the East. Besides devouring their children on the one hand supposedly for humanistic reasons, Western Moloch states on the other hand have gone in for creating babies "by mechanizing the generative act." In legalizing the production of test-tube babies, they are playing God according to secular standards. For laboratory fertilization severs the inherently God-given intelligible relationship between the unitive and procreative meaning of sexual union. The Moloch states of the West have replaced the God of love who creates and resides in the heavens, with the god of technocracy who experiments and flouts the law of love in the laboratory. Nor will the facade of religious adornments hide for long the atheistic steel and concrete that enslaves, tortures, and murders millions in these Moloch states. If there is any lesson for men in the massacres of Jonestown and all modern Moloch states, it is this: "It is a terrifying experience to attempt to escape from the Divine Lover. Every flight from him leads down the road to serfdom and violent self-destruction."

The inspired Psalmist gave mankind this lesson long ago in terse, clear, dogmatic language. "Unless the Lord builds the house, they labor in vain who build it."[378] This truth holds for the building of families, societies, nations, international communities, and, above all, of Churches. Jonestown and all Moloch states tragically specify the meaning of the vanity of building without the Lord. For they demonstrate that building without the Lord is equivalent to building with the aid of Satan. And any city that rises from Satan's blueprints can only end up a City of Hatred and violent death. Moreover, in testifying that Satan is not dead, Jonestown and every Moloch state, also witnesses to the truth that neither is God. If the world is not to be destroyed by that final pseudo-savior, the Antichrist, whom the present world seems bent on welcoming and who, at his coming will orchestrate all evil, revolutionary sects so expertly that the very framework of society will shatter into pieces under his wicked wand, it will have to come to terms humbly and lovingly with the Word and Law of the Living God.

[378] Psalm 126.

Chapter 12

Mary and the Antichrist

With the arrival of the 1980s, a dense fog of fear has descended upon the world. There is an awesome feeling abroad that mankind is finally about to keep its inevitable appointment with the end of the world. Inflation and terrorism, the energy crisis and the resurgence of religious wars, the evidence and advance of militant atheism in Africa and Afghanistan, the moral decadence and paralysis of the West, the satanic zeal and envy of the East—all these currents of woe and wickedness, coming to a climax simultaneously, have created a chaotic social concoction that is highly explosive. Dread increases as man witnesses this new escalation of evil, as yet not even understood by him. From religion to politics, from runaway economies to human-engineering biologics, strange phenomena, never before experienced, press heavily on man's heart. In the fields of communication, consciousness, production, survival man encounters nothing but events that aggravate his anxieties. Thus, today, mankind, horror-stricken at these appalling happenings, is asking itself this frightening question: "Are we at the closing end of the 'big bang,' the one that will destroy the universe with fire?" Let there be no doubt about it, the events of the '80s will decide whether man will arrive at the year 2000, still an image of God growing in truth and enjoying liberty or whether he will arrive as a member of a human race that is "collectivized," "robotized," frozen in a servitude developed and imposed through the ideological formulas thought up by the godless technocrats of a secularized, progressive humanism.

Thirty or forty years ago, when the children of the present world leaders were not yet born or were mere tots, the human race was afflicted with tragic historical events. Today the tragedies of those times, intensified to unimaginable proportions, are again threatening mankind. In the far-off days of 1945 the whole world suffered together. There was the vast, global destruction that remained at the end of the Second World War. There was the cold-blooded massacre of innumerable thousands of war prisoners. There was the betrayal of Europe, divided by the Russians and the Americans at the infamous Yalta Conference. The first atomic bomb had already been exploded; the United Nations was coming into existence. The world shuddered at the complete destruction of Hiroshima, Dresden, Berlin, Stalingrad, Belgium, and most of Europe. The youth of those days, today's matured middle-aged, remember what they had for their daily viaticum—hatred, defeat, misery, and, for their future, there loomed on the horizon the spectre of atomic disintegration. History recorded for them that nine million persons were killed in World War I, and they lived through World War II, which exacted fifty-four million lives. And now they stare into a future that unhinges the mind at the thought of the frightful efficiency man has attained in the art of weaponry, an efficiency capable of reducing himself and his earth to a cloud of atomic ashes lost and floating in endless space.

The Pope's Solicitude for the Future

On January 1, 1980 Pope John Paul II celebrated Holy Mass at St. Peter's Basilica before more than twenty thousand of the faithful.

His homily was dedicated to the attainment of world peace through man's adherence to truth, his practice of prayer, and attainment of mutual trust. He warned that if man refused to work for these spiritual goals, he would have to face the pulverization of civilized Christian society in the fires of atomic annihilation. Here are his words:

> I have recently received from some scientists a concise forecast of the immediate and terrible consequences of a nuclear war. Here are the principal ones:
>
> - Death, by direct or delayed action of the explosions, of a population that might range from 50 to 200 million persons.
>
> - A drastic reduction of food resources, caused by residual radio-activity over a wide extent of arable land.
>
> - Dangerous genetic mutations occurring in human beings, fauna and flora.
>
> - Considerable changes in the ozone layer in the atmosphere, which would expose man to major risks harmful for life.
>
> - In a city stricken by a nuclear explosion the destruction of all urban services and the terror caused by the disaster would make it impossible to offer the inhabitants the slightest aid, creating a nightmarish apocalypse.
>
> - Just two hundred of the fifty thousand nuclear bombs which it is estimated already exist, would be enough to destroy most of the large cities in the world. It is urgent, those scientists say, that the peoples should not close their eyes to what an atomic war can represent for mankind.[379]

[379] *L'Osservatore Romano*, English edition, January 21, 1980.

Mary versus Lucifer

Pope Pius XII said about our times: "The human race today is involved in a supreme crisis, which will end in its salvation by Christ, or its dire destruction."[380] Now from the very beginning of salvation history, Mary was foreseen and predicted to be "the woman whose seed shall crush the serpent's head."[381] By the power of the Holy Spirit, she conceived and gave birth to the Creator of the universe, Christ the God-Man, Who died to redeem the world from the power of Satan and restore mankind, in even greater holiness, to the family of the Blessed Trinity. Faith, not ignorance or superstition, leads Christians to recognize Mary's prayerfully omnipotent role in God's economy of salvation. Thus, Christians honor and love Mary in imitation of the infinite love and honor the Holy Trinity bestowed upon her in choosing her to be the Mother of the Son of God Who assumed His human nature in the virginal womb of Mary. Unfortunately, in our era of apostasy some pretentious theologians, secularized intellectuals, and demythologizing exegetes have attempted to downgrade the sublime role of Mary in the false hope that only thus can they win over their separated brethren. But, as if to counteract this reductionist Mariology, Christ has sent His Mother in modern times in many marvelous apparitions to various nations to remind men that Mary, who is the Mother of the Second Person of the Blessed Trinity, exalted as she is beyond all creatures in her closeness to God, is nevertheless the Mother of all men as well as of God. And we poor humans do well never to forget this wondrous truth, but to ponder on it and savour it.

[380] Pope Pius XII, Evangelii Praecones, 1951.
[381] Gen. 3:15.

Though silent and hidden through most of her life on earth, Mary, Mother of the Church, has, during the last three hundred years and notably in our times of crisis and turmoil, made many public visits to our earth and spoken out eloquently so as to convert and save mankind from the judgments of a much-offended God. It is clear, then, that in these last days of the history of salvation, Mary is exercising quite frequently the role the ancient Hebrew prophets performed to the Chosen People. As Queen of Prophets, Mary comes among Christians today warning them, and indeed the whole world, of the terrible catastrophes advancing upon us all, unless we return to her Son.

Now according to St. Thomas Aquinas, "apparitions do not bring us new doctrines, but new graces."[382] Hence Mary's apparitions are part of private, not public, revelation; they do not constitute part of the deposit of the Faith. As apparitions they do not have to be believed as if they were truths necessary for salvation. But once the Teaching Church has declared any private revelations "worthy of credence," and allows religious devotions to be practiced under their inspirations, reputable authorities in the Church declare that it would be rash and temerarious to contest openly what the Church has approved, particularly if these revelations are supported by authentic miracles. Needless to say, the Church adopts a policy of utmost reserve and caution in dealing with private revelations. After long, careful, painful examination—almost always while watching the seers involved (usually innocent children) run the gauntlet of criticism, ridicule, persecution from both religious and civil authorities not to mention from family and friends—the Church, I say, after years of intense study of the entire question, only then approves such apparitions as

[382] St. Thomas, *Summa Theologica* II, II, q. 175, art. 6.

369

worthy of credence, if they contain nothing against the deposit of the Faith and their authenticated miracles shower graces upon souls, leading them and the whole Christian community to a closer union with God in holiness.

Apparitions of Mary

In Mary's visits to this valley of tears, there are two themes she emphasizes to her children. First, she consoles and brings them the spiritual peace of Christ her Son. Second, she warns them of impending evils—of spiritual evils that will sweep all nations into the vortex of physical catastrophes, world wars, famines, earthquakes, plagues, and finally into hell, all of which are God's chastisements for nations addicted to and unrepentant over their sins. In Paris at Rue de Bac in 1830, at Lourdes in 1858, and at Fatima in 1917, her message was a warning and a pleading: "Come back to my Son through prayer and penance. Pray for sinners, make sacrifices for them, for many go to hell because no one is willing to pray and make sacrifices for them."[383] At La Salette in 1846 the Virgin in sorrow was seen sitting and weeping before two peasant children over a world that had plunged into desperate, moral chaos through its rejection of God and His Church. The ultimatum she announced from the throne of Divine Mercy to a laicized France and a world following the allurements of Satan echoed the threats of the Divine Savior: "Unless you do penance, you shall all likewise perish."[384] Lourdes continues to demonstrate Mary's dramatic efforts to save the unfaithful Christian West from the powers of darkness. The Virgin urges all

[383] John Ireland Gallery, *Mary vs. Lucifer* (Milwaukee: Bruce Publishing Company, 1960), p. 126.
[384] Luke 13:3.

to pray and do penance. And she continues to pour forth a flood of miracles, curing thousands of petitioners of the ills of both soul and body.

Since 1660 twenty popes have issued decrees favoring the divine image of Our Lady of Guadalupe. In 1754, upon viewing a copy of the image, Pope Benedict XIV was deeply moved and exclaimed: "*Non fecit taliter omni nationi.*"[385] God and Mary have not performed such a marvelous deed for any other nation. When the Blessed Virgin appeared to Juan Diego in Mexico in 1531, a handful of Spanish Franciscan missionaries had been laboring with great zeal for six years, trying to convert the Aztec Indians. But they had little success and were becoming greatly disheartened. For they were attempting what was certainly impossible for men—the rescue of the Mexican nations from two thousand years of servitude to Satan. The Aztecs unknowingly worshipped Satan as their Serpent-God in whose honor they sacrificed twenty thousand human persons yearly and feasted on their flesh.[386] The darkness and cruelty of this demonic paganism seemed unconquerable. For the Indians fought the Spaniards savagely to preserve their idolatrous religion, a religion of the Serpent-God that was rampant in all Latin American countries.

But within seven years of the apparition of the Virgin on the rocky hill of Tepeyac, the precious image of the Virgin stamped out, abolished, eradicated the religion of the stone Serpent and converted eight million Indians to the Catholic Faith. Mary had

---

[385] Helen Behrens, *The Virgin and the Serpent-God* (Mexico City: Editorial Progreso, 1963), quoted p. 204.

[386] Ibid., pp. 78, 79. At the inauguration of the reign of Ahuizotl, the most warlike of the Aztec leaders, eighty thousand prisoners were sacrificed, their hearts placed before the sun, their limbs served at ritual banquets and their mutilated bodies thrown to wild beasts. *Encyclopedia Britannica*, Vol. 2 (London: William Benton, 1768), pp. 938-939.

predicted this victory over Satan in her visits to Juan Diego and Juan Bernardino. She fulfilled her prophecy within the lifetime of Juan Diego upon whose mantle she had stamped her beautiful, overwhelmingly tender image.[387] This divine image was the heavenly instrument that obliterated the pagan gods of the Aztecs and their human sacrifices. To this day the faith of the Mexicans is nurtured and strengthened by the presence of the Virgin's miraculous image. Even those modern forerunners of the Antichrist, the Masonic and Communist rulers of Mexico, have failed to diminish or extinguish this faith.

At the turn of the century these champions of atheism strove by every possible means to destroy the Mexican religion and civilization. They isolated the youth from their Church in an attempt to educate them as militant atheists; they exiled bishops and priests, hunting them down like criminals; they shot and killed many in an inhuman fashion; they vexed, persecuted, dragged off to mock trials whoever courageously witnessed to the Faith.[388] But the Virgin Conqueror of the stone Serpent kept drawing millions of Indians to her shrine where her love as their Mother consoled, strengthened, protected, and sanctified them. In the last days the same Virgin will crush the head of the Serpent-God who will be present in the idolatrous worship that will be demanded from all men by the Antichrist for himself and for his master, Satan. The Mother of God and of all men will destroy this would-be murderer of God and of all men, this emissary of Satan, the Antichrist. But perhaps the apparitions and miracles at Fatima, since they are events much closer to our own times, will demonstrate more dramatically how essential a person the

[387] Ibid., p. 163.
[388] Pope Pius XI, Encyclical *Atheistic Communism*, 1937.

Mother of God is in a Christian's heritage and salvation, how necessary Mary is in the Church's struggle against the Antichrist and how the whole of mankind is every moment in need of her influence and intercession.

The Story of Fatima

The events of Fatima have a basis in Holy Scripture. The terrible tragedy that overtook the Chosen People who refused to listen to God's prophets has a message for all men today. Will modern man decide to become the descendants of Cain or the spiritual off-spring of Abel and Abraham? There are many stunning analogies between appearances of the great prophets who came to warn the Jews of approaching destruction from the Babylonians, Assyrians, Egyptians, Canaanites under the heels of their antichrists and the appearances of the Queen of the Prophets who came to Fatima to warn the Christian world of its ultimate destruction under the heels of the Russians, Chinese, Cubans, or Western atheists led by their godless leader the Super-Antichrist.

Jeremiah pleaded in vain for the Chosen People to return to their God. He sent Baruch to read to the king a roll of a book containing the punishments God threatened to inflict upon His people if they did not repent and return to Him with contrite hearts. After listening to the first four pages, the king seized the document, hacked it to pieces, and threw it into the fire. The ensuing events demonstrate what a terrible thing it is to reject the warnings of God sent through His prophets and confirmed by miracles. The ferocious Nebuchadnezzar, considered by many of the Fathers a sure forerunner and shadow of the Antichrist, acting as an instrument of God's justice, besieged the city of Jerusalem. For eighteen months the Jews were trapped within the city walls. Then a plague decimated their numbers drastically. Finally the Babylonians entered the city, pillaged it, burned it to the ground, utterly destroyed it, and killed the inhabitants at random. With his own hands Nebuchadnezzar put out the eyes of the king and dragged him into exile. The enraged Babylonians burned the wonderful Temple of God built by Solomon, destroyed the Ark of the Covenant and carried off to Babylon and into captivity the rich and better-educated Hebrews.[389]

The history of Jeremiah outlines the traditional method of God in dealing with His Chosen People, indeed with all nations. He is accustomed to warn and rebuke them, to point out the road back to His graces through the mouths of His judges and prophets. Nations are free to obey His commands or to reject them, but they are not free to undergo the consequences of their decision. If they are contumacious in their rebellion against God, then all manner of disasters will fall upon them. We need only read the warnings given by Noah, Abraham, Moses, Daniel, Jonas, and so many other prophets to find the story of Fatima long ago prefigured many, many times in salvation history. Fatima is merely an updated, modernized course in God's dealings with His Chosen People. To Fatima, God sent His Mother, the most divinely honored of all His messengers, after her own Son, the Queen of Prophets herself, to warn mankind to live by her message or suffer unspeakable consequences. God will surely not suffer the words and person of His Mother to be despised. For all we know, God may be presently raising up the Antichrist as "My servant," the name he gave Nebuchadnezzar, to be the instrument, just as that wicked king was, for punishing the obstinate apostasy of His Christian People. Mary, Queen of the Prophets, was sent by God to repeat, in all her splendor and dignity as Mother of God, the

---

[389] Jer. 36:23; 39:6–10.

age-old message: "Return to the Lord and be saved; refuse God the homage that is His due and you must suffer the divine wrath that will inevitably follow."[390]

The Great Red Dragon

"And a great sign appeared in heaven," wrote St. John in the twelfth chapter of his Apocalypse. "A woman clothed in the sun, and the moon under her feet, having on her head a crown of twelve stars ... and I heard a voice in heaven saying: 'Now is come salvation and strength and the kingdom of God and the power of His Christ.' ... And another sign was seen in the heaven, and behold, a great red dragon having seven heads and ten horns, and upon his head seven diadems. And his tail was dragging along the third part of the stars of heaven and he dashed them to the earth."[391]

Most Scripture scholars agree that the sign of the Woman in heaven has a double symbolism, referring to Mary and to the Church. The sign of the red dragon and the beast, who comes up from the abyss to wage war against the camp of the saints, refers to Satan and the Antichrist. Earlier in chapter 9, St. John depicts the confusion and division, through heresy and schism, that these two agents of evil will bring upon the Church and the whole world in the last days.

Once again it is profitable to apply St. John's vision of falling stars, but this time with special application to the relationship between Mary and her priests. In her many apparitions Mary constantly requests prayers, reparation, and compensation for the

[390] Robert Bergin, *This Apocalyptic Age* (Coconut Grove, FL: Fatima International Press, 1972), p. 125.
[391] St. John, Apoc. 12:1–4.

sins of priests. As the most valiant of all women, indeed, of all saints, she wants to bestow on all who have been ordained into the holy priesthood of her Son a high degree of her own heroic faith, fidelity, and zeal. For she knows how necessary these virtues are for priests if they are to dedicate their lives wholeheartedly to attaining the glory of God and the salvation of souls. Mary knows, too, that priests are the special target of Satan's malice who would destroy her Son's Church through the corruption of His priests. St. John, using striking dramatic metaphors, reveals the destructive tactics of Satan and the Antichrist.

"And I saw a star which had fallen from heaven to the earth, and there was given to him the key of the bottomless pit, and there went up from the pit a smoke like that of a furnace; and the sun was darkened and the air, by reason of the smoke of the pit. And out of the smoke locusts went forth upon the earth and they were told … to harm only such men as have not the seal of God upon their forehead."[392]

Now in prophetic symbolism falling stars almost always refer to tepid, weak, or apostate bishops and priests who are harbingers of grief and disaster to the whole world. The key to the shaft of the abyss is an emblem of their apostasy. Such traitorous religious leaders and teachers ally themselves with the rebellious angels. Instead of using the keys of the kingdom of God, which they have received from the Church through their priesthood and the mission of teaching the Gospel so as to suppress and defeat the satanic forces incarnate in wicked men while advancing the holiness of the faithful, they rather abuse their powers to foster and propagate error and evil. They opt to open the abyss and let loose upon the earth the plagues of darkness

[392] Ibid., 9:1–4.

and wickedness. Today too many fallen stars—rebellious bishops, priests, theologians, philosophers, nuns, and Catholic intellectuals—are abusing their sacerdotal powers and intellectual gifts to seduce, enslave, and precipitate into hell vast numbers of wayward sheep. Out of the darkness of the pit they have loosed the forces of error, evil, and scandal. The smoke streaming from the pit darkens the sun of Christ's truth and obliterates the splendor of His holiness; it infects the air with decadent, immoral odors. Everything is cast into confusion; gloom infests the world of religion and reason; grace, the life-giving oxygen of the soul and body, is strangled out of the supernatural organisms of the children of God. Moreover, the darkening sun and sky betoken the eclipse of the Teaching Authority of the Church, the lowering of men's respect and love for her, their loss of reverence for her Master and the demeaning of both Christ and His Church to the level of being mere natural, defective organs of society lusting after domination over men's souls and bodies through the accumulation of material riches and political power.

The answer to the stars falling from heaven onto the earth, through participation in the pre-Adamite betrayal of Lucifer, is the appearance in splendor of the Virgin of Fatima, fixed in the heaven of fidelity to God. She is the one who is arrayed in the jewels of the universe—clothed with the sun, the moon as her pedestal, the stars her crown. Moreover, she exercises power over hell and heaven.

In the apparition of July 13, 1917, Mary demonstrated her power over demons. After asking for prayers and sacrifice for the salvation of sinners, the Lady of Fatima opened her hands and their radiance seemed to penetrate the earth. The three children saw a great sea of fire. Plunged in that ocean of flames were demons and human beings in appearance like red hot coals, transparent, black, bronze-colored. They floated amid clouds of smoke. The fire lifted them up but they fell back without weight or equilibrium, shrieking and groaning in despair. The demons were distinguishable in the form of strange animals, horribly loathsome and repulsive. Our Lady of Fatima spoke in part this message to the children petrified with fear:

> The war is going to end (World War I). But if men do not stop offending God, another even worse (war) will begin in the reign of Pius XI. When you see a night illumined by an unknown light, know that this is the great sign that God gives you that He is going to punish the world for its crimes by means of hunger, war and the persecutions of the Church and the Holy Father.... If they listen to my requests, Russia will be converted and there will be peace. If not, she will scatter her errors throughout the world, provoking wars and persecutions of the Church. The good will be martyred; the Holy Father will have much to suffer and various nations will be annihilated.[393]

Unfortunately, history is the implacable witness that the nations did not heed Mary's plea and give up their sinful ways. The strange light prophesied by Mary, later known to astronomers as the Aurora Borealis, appeared on the night of January 25, 1938. Seen all over Europe, it was given wide coverage in national papers the next day.[394] In its wake followed the heightened atrocities of the Spanish Civil War and soon after the Second World War. Thus the

[393] Damien Walne and Joan Flory, *Oh, What a Beautiful Lady* (South View, London: Augustine Publishing Company, 1976), pp. 43, 44.
[394] Ibid., p. 119.

results predicted by Mary are with us today. Communist Russia is spreading its errors most successfully throughout the world; she is promoting wars in Asia, Africa, the Middle East, Central and South America; she has stepped up her persecutions everywhere. All has happened just as the Virgin predicted in 1917, the very year in which at St. Petersburg a handful of God-hating conspirators planned and launched the most satanic totalitarian atheism ever conceived by evil men. Since 1917 its advance has been dramatically successful; its power and influence has never been stronger and is growing hourly. It is slowly but surely enveloping a decadent West by its singleness of purpose, its demonic zeal, and the incarnation of its evil doctrines and deeds into vast armies, into the steel and atoms of the most efficiently sophisticated weaponry ever devised by advanced technocracy. And the faithless West stands paralyzed before this evil monster, fascinated by its own approaching destruction. The question must be pondered today by the spiritually alert: "Is God going to allow godless Communism to become the instrument the Antichrist will perfect and use to punish and purge a decadent Christian world?" The fact that such an all-conquering flood of evil is gaining in power and influence is in itself a barometer that is measuring the mounting wrath of God.

In the apparition of October 13, 1917, the Virgin of Fatima demonstrated her power over the forces of heaven by causing the Miracle of the Sun. This great sign in the heavens was witnessed by some seventy thousand pilgrims. Our Lady was literally clothed in the sun. In the words of Lucy: "The Lady was not just a bright figure, but she seemed to be made of light." Mary again opened her hands as she was taking leave of the children. The light streaming from her hands shot straight up to the sun, which darkened a bit so that all could easily look at it with the naked eye. At once the heavy rain stopped and the clouds rolled back, allowing the sun to appear fully in a cloudless sky. "Look at the sun!" cried Lucy. It was then that the vast audience of pilgrims saw the sign promised by the Virgin to authenticate the veracity of her prophecy.[395] Ages before, Isaiah the prophet had predicted that in the last days "the sun will be darkened ... and the powers of heaven shall be moved."[396] Then without any warning the sun did darken; it cast different colors—yellow, blue, white. Radiant as a silver pearl, it began to rotate, whirling at an ever-increasing speed. From this violent dancing different colors spun off its circumference, until it resembled a giant wheel of fire, its hues dramatically lighting up the earth below. When it became a jaundiced yellow, it shook itself off its axis with a tremendous force, gyrating furiously in a zigzag fashion. Then decreasing its momentum, it tantalizingly hovered for a short time in space, and finally plunged madly toward the earth, increasing in menacing size until, as a giant explosive fireball, it obliterated all else.[397]

Overcome with terror, the people cried out: "Miracle, miracle!" "Marvel, marvel!" But as the sun kept plummeting toward them, they threw themselves on the ground, begging God's mercy and forgiveness, quite convinced that they were witnessing the end of the world. Thousands prayed the Creed and the Hail Mary, frightened to death that the planets were on a collision course and that the world would end in a fiery cataclysm, as St. Peter had predicted. Then the sun, as if drawn by some mighty hand, suddenly returned to its rightful place in the heavens where it functioned normally again. And the thousands who had been drenched by rain ten minutes before, suddenly found their

[395] Gallery, op. cit., pp. 135–137.
[396] Isa. 13:10.
[397] Gallery, op. cit., pp. 134–137.

clothes perfectly dry, as they returned home mingling laughter and joy with their tears.[398]

Truly a great sign appeared in the heavens at Fatima signaling the last and final round of the struggle with Satan and the Antichrist. But the seventy thousand persons never saw the majestic tableaux that the children saw during the gyrations of the sun. The children saw Our Lady and St. Joseph carrying the divine Child with the sun between them. Then they saw the divine Infant blessing the world. Finally they saw Our Lady both as Mother of Sorrows and Our Lady of Mt. Carmel.[399] St. John's mystical allusion to the encounter between the Woman and her Child and the great red dragon possesses real meaning in the worldwide struggle that rages today as mankind prepares for the coming of the beast, the man of sin, the lawless one, the Antichrist.

The Antichrist in Poland

"And the great dragon was cast down," wrote St. John, "the ancient serpent who is called the devil and Satan who leads astray the whole world."[400] This prophecy is verified today even within the strongholds of Communist countries. Mary in Poland, venerated as the Black Madonna, is a revered Byzantine icon before which millions upon millions of Polish Catholics have worshipped for 598 years. When Pope John Paul II visited there recently 4.4 million pilgrims participated in twelve great religious ceremonies, including three days of Masses presided over by the pope himself. And the Communist mini-antichrists stood by helpless, paralyzed by the faith and fidelity of the Virgin's army

[398] Ibid., p. 136.
[399] Bergin, op. cit., p. 132.
[400] St. John, Apoc. 12:9.

of saints. Even the godless government reluctantly admits that between 5 and 6 million people made pilgrimages to the Madonna of Czestochowa in the year before the pope's visit. Of course, the godless agents of Satan refer to these pilgrims as "tourists." On the feast of the Assumption of the Virgin, August 15, thousands walked all the way from Warsaw. They prayed before the stations of the cross in the adjoining park and approached through the courtyard on their knees before gazing at the Virgin of Jasna Gora, which is worshipped in a resplendent gold chapel, hung with votive offerings.[401] Ninety percent of Poland's 35 million citizens are Catholics who are devotedly attached to the Black Madonna as their Mother, Protectress, and Guide to holiness in Christ through the practice of their Catholic Faith. Thus before the power and holiness of the Virgin in Poland the twentieth-century red dragon with its militant mini-antichrists has been rendered helpless in its efforts to lead that nation astray into the slough of apostasy and wickedness. In Poland, perhaps more than in any other country in the world, the victorious cry of the Church is verified: *Christus vincit, Christus imperat, Christus regnat!* Christ conquers, Christ commands, Christ rules!

Mary, the Antichrist, and the World of Islam

In its latest move to conquer the world for Satan, the Juggernaut red dragon of Russia, on the wheels of massive tanks, on the wings of giant planes and on the marching feet of thousands of Red soldiers, has invaded the world of Islam. Already the nation of Afghanistan, comprising some seven million Moslems, has

[401] John Darnton, "Poland's Catholics Win a Battle ... ," *New York Times*, February 11, 1980, p. A10.

been taken. And the neighboring nations of Iran, Pakistan, Kuwait, Saudi Arabia, Yemen, not to mention Yugoslavia—where Tito, a rebel Red leader, died in 1980—are all trembling over the very threat of an invasion by Russia. The Mother of God has predicted that if her requests were not granted by men, the red dragon would spread his errors throughout the whole world and many nations would be annihilated. And now a "Christian" West that has been faithless to Christ is raising the lament: "There goes the whole Middle East into the vast concentration camp of organized, messianic atheism!"

In reaction to this new militant wave of atheistic aggression, a revived Islam has rediscovered the power and zeal of its religion. Muslim fundamentalism has become once again exhilarated, self-confident, and seriously spiritual. It is determined to prevent the atheistic "scorched earth policy" of spiritual surrender to secularistic progress whereby nation after nation of the decadent Christian West has succumbed to a soft, gutless materialism. Islam is returning to its religious roots and traditional beliefs. Indeed to the average Muslim his faith is much more in evidence in everyday life than is the Christian Faith to citizens of Western nations.[402] The Muslim prays publicly three times a day. Moreover, religious Muslims are revolting in disgust against Western—and especially American—commercialism and moral decadence. They disdain Western values so dominated by greed and the lust for pleasure and power. Not that the Muslims are perfect, far from it, but they do still maintain high moral values for women and the family. Recently an American theatre in Iran was burned to the ground by angry Iranian youths because it was showing filthy American movies,

---

[402] "The World of Islam: The Militant Revival," *Time*, April 16, 1979.

movies calculated to destroy the sacrosanct family structure through their advocacy of easy divorce, pleasurable infidelity, the flight from parental responsibility by means of abortion, and the enticement of all viewers to sexual promiscuity.

The resurgence of religion in the Islamic world is being used also as an instrument for striking back at the materialistic, unbelieving West.[403] It is important to recall that the Muslims believe in the Virgin birth, something that is, sad to say, denied by certain notorious "Catholic" theologians in religious circles today. Mary has always claimed the love and reverence of countless millions not of the Catholic Faith. The Pilgrim Statue of Our Lady of Fatima has traveled all over the world and was received with deep reverence and honor among the Muslims. There have been spontaneous demonstrations of Muslim enthusiasm and affection for this statue in Asia and Africa. Moreover, it is frequently pointed out that Muslims are particularly attracted to the Virgin of Fatima because Mohammd had a daughter named Fatima whom he placed first in paradise after Maryam as the Muslims called Our Lady.[404] Robert Bergin in his book *This Apocalyptic Age* has this to say of Mary's religious influence in the Muslim world:

> It is well recognized that the best meeting ground for Christians and Muslims is the common affection they have for Mary. An eminent Franciscan scholar Father John Avd-El-Jalil, a convert, states that Muslim devotion to Mary is deep and dogmatic, that there is in Islam a "rudimentary form of Mariology." There is in the Qur'an at least a hint of the Immaculate Conception in the lines:

[403] Ibid.
[404] Bergin, op. cit., p. 102.

O Mary, God has chosen you
and purified you
He has chosen you above
All the women of the world.[405]

From a cursory glance at the teaching of the Qur'an as compared with Christianity, it will be seen that the differences between the doctrine of these two religions lie rather in what Islam denies than in what it affirms. Both Islamism and Catholicism agree that God is the Creator of the universe, that Jesus was miraculously born of a pure virgin, and that He ascended into heaven. They agree that there is a holy spirit, that God will forgive men's sins and grant them eternal life.[406] With the negations we are not here concerned.

No doubt the attack of the Russian red dragon with his godless armies of mini-antichrists against the Muslim world is being used by God to bring Muslims and Christians willy-nilly together against the combined forces of Satan. It seems clear that traditional religions are tottering and collapsing before the subversive and ferocious attacks of the armies of atheism put in the field by the red dragon and his beast, the Antichrist. Confucianism, Taoism, Buddhism, Anglicanism, indeed all forms of Protestantism, Christianity, and even Islamism have wilted under the fires of hatred emanating from godless Communism.[407] The potential is there that God in his goodness, through the prayerful omnipotence of the Holy Virgin, may attract all these religions to the Cross, to the Crucified, and to the Catholic Church.

[405] Ibid., pp. 102, 103.
[406] Alfred Guillaume, *Islam* (Middlesex, UK: Penguin Books, 1978), pp. 198, 199.
[407] Bergin, op. cit., p. 103.

No doubt, the East and the world is being purified again for a resurgence of the sublime idealism and mysticism of Christianity. In the crucible of war, sparked by the stark hatred of the legions of the Antichrist, the nations may again begin to realize that not the power of politics, not oil wealth, not technological progress, not the affluent materialism of the West, nor the militant materialism of the East are the final goals of man that will insure his happiness. Rather a life of holiness with God and man is the absolutely irreplaceable purpose of each human being and unless he strives for that goal there will never be any true peace, justice, fraternity, or happiness among men.

What the Islamic East resents about the Christian West is that the West has abandoned its Christian way of life, its faith in Christ the Redeemer. It then has the arrogant gall to tell other nations how to live, what their goals should be, how they should imitate the West. But the mentality of the West has been corrupted. It is preoccupied with living life for the purpose of getting and having instead of living life for the purpose of being, of becoming more God-like, more Christ-like. An affluent lust has blinded the West to the importance of religion in the whole life of the Muslim faithful. Purse-pride over the highest standard of living has rendered the West insensitive to the moral ideals of the Muslim world. What can God be telling the morally worthless West through the angry, inflammatory rising of the East? Is it that the West is down to its last chance? That unless the West has a change of heart, the jig is up? Is it that the red dragon will finally produce his Antichrist from the corrupt social womb of the West and that both will carry everything down to destruction?

Mary against the Antichrist

Salvation history, the only history that can adequately depict the actions of man in the concrete, that is, man created in a supernatural order, fallen and then redeemed by Christ, begins and ends in the vision of Mary. The Antichrist is sure to come on earth in the last days. He will make a final, useless assault on God and his saints. He will attempt to rip the very idea of God from the consciousness of men. It seems indicated in Scripture that he will have great success in seducing the vast majority of believers away from Christ and into his own ranks of idolators. Christian fantasy has not created the fable of the Antichrist, nor playfully painted him in the fiery hues of hell. The Antichrist, as we hope we have shown at this point, is not a product of theology-fiction. He is really foretold and confirmed by the prophets, the evangelists, the apostles, all of them bearers, preachers, and writers of the infallible revelations of God from Genesis to the Apocalypse.[408] And then, too, the whole living tradition of Christianity, guided by the Holy Spirit, has witnessed to the reality of the Antichrist.

The power of the Antichrist will be vast, his skill at persuasion so great that he would fain suck into error many of the elect. The miracles performed by him will be so thrilling and spectacular that he will be followed and adored by many as a god. Yet the Antichrist will be the greatest threat and adversary the Church has ever encountered. Who will save the Church from the power and "lying wonders" of the Antichrist? Mary, Mother of the Church, will be her omnicompetent protectress. For from the beginning in the Garden of Eden, the Serpent-Dragon lay in waiting for the coming of the Woman who would crush his head.

---

[408] Paolo Calliari, *Maria Vincitrice di Tutte le Eresie* (Torino: Editrice Lanteriana, 1976), pp. 143, 144.

The final days, the end of the world, according to the Gospels, will produce a terrifying bloodcurdling spectacular closing to the drama of salvation. The scene boggles the mind and escapes the wildest efforts of the imagination to depict it. Indeed all the terrors, all the wars, all the horrors, all the famines, earthquakes, and tragedies up to the present will be but pallid, anticipatory rehearsals of Time's chaotic, curtain-closing demolition of the universe. Let those who will be participators in that cosmic smash-up be prepared to shed tears. Certainly they deserve the compassionate condolences of whoever is spared that nightmare.

But in those days, even worse than the physical cataclysms with their millions of victims, will be the deluge of moral evils. Everywhere confusing ideological heresies, the babel of misleading tongues, the escalating immorality in all sectors of human activity will create clouds of doubt, an atmosphere of fear and uncertainty, a sense of nausea from which no one will be able to liberate mankind. Then when all material and moral, personal and social, political and religious evils have converged and reached their climax, the Antichrist, scourge of all holy persons and things, will be allowed by God to appear on the scene and to teach and do the very opposite of the teachings and deeds of Jesus Christ. Then will night have descended upon the history of mankind—the last, blackest night destined never to be dissipated by another sunrise. That longest night in history will torture unhappy man with innumerable terrors emanating from evil spirits. "Men will be withering away for fear of what shall come upon the world."[409] For all the biblical seers agree that the Antichrist will possess supreme power to wreak his vengeful havoc upon mankind for three and one-half years.

[409] Luke 21:26.

The arrival of the Antichrist in history, according to St. John in his Apocalypse,[410] will signal the final phase of the war between the Woman and the Serpent, a war to which all persons have been called from the beginning of the world. The sign in the heavens reveals that the Woman is ready to give birth to a Son and the red dragon stands eager to devour the Child at its birth. The Archangel Michael and his angelic forces rout the Serpent-Dragon in defense of the Woman and the Child. Then the battlefield changes as the dragon is cast down upon the earth. But on earth the dragon pursues the Woman again bent on destroying her, now that her Child has eluded his grasp by being snatched up into heaven. However, on earth the Woman is rescued and given asylum in the desert. But the Serpent, breathing revenge, attempts to trap the Woman by belching forth a river that he sends speedily after her to drown her. But earth swallows up the river, again aiding the Woman to safety. Then the Serpent-Dragon, enraged to the point of madness against the Woman, declares war against men and the Woman's offspring, the camp of the saints. He sends his highest general, his supreme human ambassador of evil, the Antichrist to defeat the armies of the saints and to capture and destroy their fortress—the Church founded by Jesus Christ, the Child who had escaped to heaven, but who had left behind him for his followers this fortress of salvation.

Mary, the Woman whom Satan attacks but can never conquer, was always well known to the world of demons. Indeed they came to know her from the beginning of time. After their seduction of Adam and Eve, Lucifer and his demons were sentenced by God to grovel in fear in the dust, awaiting the Woman's heel that would crush their heads. Some Catholic theologians speculate that

[410] St. John, Apoc. 12:10.

Lucifer and his angels, together with all the angels, were given a special trial so that they could prove their own love of preference for God, even as God had demonstrated His own love of preference for them by freely creating them all from nothing. According to this theory, the vision of the Holy Virgin with her Child was presented to all the angels who were then invited to adore the Child as their God and to accept the Mother as their Queen. It was revealed to them that both Mother and Child would figure mightily in the redemption, sanctification, and glorification of a race of rational beings a little less in dignity than the angels themselves, namely men. But Lucifer and his rebel angels refused to trust God, to adore His Incarnate Son, to venerate the Holy Mother of God. They rejected the loving Providence of God for mankind. And in an envious rage they declared war on the Woman, her Son, and on their children found in the Church as the communion of saints. But they waged war on all men because the Woman and her Son, Who died to save all men, were working to bring all men to salvation. Today Satan's human minions, mini-antichrists all of them, do not wait for the birth of the children of men before attacking them. They have outdone their Master's techniques for murder; they attack mothers and children simultaneously by killing children in the sanctuary of the womb.

The history of salvation closes with Mary as Mother with Child even as it began with Mary as Mother with Child. The circle of salvation history will close with Christ and His Mother as it opened with the Mother of God and her Son. The Woman, the Mother of God, and Christ and His Church, which is the camp of the saints, have all been foreseen and rightly considered from the beginning of time, the great and fearsome adversaries of the Serpent-Dragon, his mini-antichrists and his supreme Antichrist. And so when many Modernist priests and intellectual

Catholics downgrade devotion to Christ through Mary, when they cut off the spiritual life line of zealous love for the hearts of Jesus and Mary, it is small wonder they lose a sense of their own identity, of the meaning of being a Christian. It is small wonder that they become tepid, confused, and fall victims to Satan's snares. For the devil and his Antichrist are conquered by men and women of God, men and women of Mary.

Today Mary's war continues to be waged victoriously against the Antichrist and against all who imitate and follow him. But victory over these forces of evil depends on man's fidelity to the Holy Mother and her divine Child. Mary, who was never for an instant a slave of Satan, is doing and will continue to do her prayerfully omnipotent utmost to assure victory over the Serpent-Dragon and his Antichrist. But the peace and joy of that victory will be tasted eternally only by those who never cease to trust and follow her guidance.

Appendix:
Dark Pieces on the Antichrist

Things fall apart; the center cannot hold;
Mere anarchy is loosed upon the world,
The blood-dimmed tide is loosed, and everywhere
The ceremony of innocence is drowned;
The best lack all conviction, while the worst
Are full of passionate intensity.

Surely some revelation is at hand;
Surely the Second Coming is at hand.

Yeats, *The Second Coming*

* * * * *

Make haste, Satan, make haste, you who are calumniated by the priests and rulers; hasten that I may press you to my heart; we have known each other for a long time. Your works, O cherished one of my heart, are not always good and pleasing, but they give tone to the universe and save it from being absurd. What would justice be without you? An instinct. What would reason be? A routine. What would man be? A beast. You alone do impart prosperity to all; by you riches are enobled. *You are an excuse for all authority* and the seal of virtue. Hope on, proscribed one! The only arm that I can wield in your service is my pen, but that is worth millions of bulletins!

Proudhon, quoted by Bishop Dechamps in his *The Christ and the Antichrists*

* * * * *

The smoke of Satan is seeping up into the Church.

The tail of the devil is functioning in the disintegration of the Catholic world.

Pope Paul VI

* * * * *

They will deliver you up to tribulation and will put you to death; and you will be hated by all nations for my name's sake. And then many will fall away and will betray one another, and will hate one another. And many false prophets will arise, and will lead many astray. And because iniquity will abound, the charity of many will grow cold. But whoever perseveres to the end, he shall be saved. And the Gospel of the kingdom shall be preached in the whole world for a witness to all nations; and then will come the end.

Therefore, when you see the abomination of desolation, which was spoken of by Daniel the prophet, standing in the holy place—let him who reads understand—then let those who are in Judea flee to the mountains.... Then if anyone say to you, "Behold, here is the Christ" or "There he is," do not believe it. For false christs and false prophets will arise, and will show great signs and wonders, so as to lead astray, if possible, even the elect.

Matthew, Chapter 24: 9–24

* * * * *

The split in today's world is perceptible even at a hasty glance.... The truth is that the split is a much profounder and more alienating one (than a mere political one), that the rifts are more than one can see at first glance. This deep, manifold split bears the danger of manifold disaster for all of us, in accordance with the ancient truth that a Kingdom—in this case, our Earth—divided against itself cannot stand....

A decline in courage may be the most striking feature which an outside observer notices in the West in our days. The Western world has lost its civic courage, both as a whole and separately, in each country, in each government, each political party, and, of course, in the United Nations. Such a decline in courage is particularly noticeable among the ruling groups and the intellectual elite, causing an impression that the loss of courage extends to the entire society....

Destructive and irresponsible freedom has been granted boundless space. Society appears to have little defense against the abyss of human decadence, such as, for example, the misuse of liberty for moral violence against young people, motion pictures full of pornography, crime and horror. This is considered to be part of freedom, and theoretically counterbalanced by the young peoples' right not to look or not to accept. Life organized legalistically has thus shown its inability to defend itself against the corrosion of evil.

> Aleksandr Solzhenitsyn, "A World Split Apart,"
> Commencement Address at Harvard University,
> June 8, 1978, reprinted in *National Review*,
> July 7, 1978

* * * * *

Jones: So my opinion is that you be kind to children, and
            be kind to seniors, and take the potion like they
            used to take it in Ancient Greece, and step over
            quietly; because we are not committing suicide — it's
            a revolutionary act. We can't go back; they won't
            leave us alone. They're now going back to tell more
            lies, which means more Congressmen. And there's
            no way, no way we can survive....

Woman: Damndest thing. So many people.

Jones: I saved them. I saved them, but I made my example. I
            made my expression. I made my manifestation and the
            world was ready, not ready for me. Paul said I was a
            man born out of due season. I've been born out of due
            season, just like all we are — and the best testimony we
            can make is to leave this goddamn world. (Applause)

Woman: You must prepare to die....

Jones: Lay down your burdens. I'm gonna lay down my
            burden. Down by the riverside. Shall we lay them
            down here by the side of Guyana? No man didn't
            take our lives. Right now. They haven't taken them.
            But when they start parachuting out of the air,
            they'll see some of our innocent babies. I'm not — I
            don't want.... They've got to shoot me to get
            through to some of these people. I'm not letting
            them take your child. Can you let them take your
            child? (Voices: No, No, No.) ...

Jones: I don't know how in the world they're ever going to
            write about us. It's just too late. It's too late. The
            Congressman's dead. The ... Many of our ... are
            dead. They're all laying out there dead....

Woman: I just want to say something for everyone that I see standing around or crying. This is nothing to cry about. This is something we could all rejoice about. We could be happy about this. They always told us we could cry when you're coming into this world. So we're leaving it, and we're leaving it peaceful.... I don't see nothing that I should cry about. We should be happy. At least I am. (Applause)

Excerpts from the Transcript of a Tape of the Final Moments
at Jonestown. *New York Times*, March 15, 1979, p. B8.

* * * * *

The devil has always managed to get rid of the Mass by means of the heretics, making them the precursors of the Antichrist who, above all else, will manage to abolish, and in fact will succeed in abolishing, as a punishment for the sins of men, the Holy Sacrifice of the altar, precisely as Daniel had predicted.

St. Alphonsus Liguori, "La Messa e l'Officio Strapazzati" in *Opere Ascetiche*

* * * * *

Once humanity to a man renounces God (and I believe that period, analogous with the geological periods, will come to pass) the old outlook on life will collapse by itself without cannibalism and, above all, the old morality too, and a new era will dawn. Men will unite to get everything life can give, but only for joy and happiness in this world alone. Man will be exalted with a spirit of divine, titanic pride, and the man-god will make his appearance. Extending his conquest over nature infinitely every hour by his will and science, man will every hour by that very fact feel so lofty a joy that it will make up for his old hopes of the joys of heaven. Everyone will know that he is mortal, that there is no resurrection, and he will accept death serenely and proudly like a god. His pride will make him realize that it's no use protesting that life lasts only for a fleeting moment, and he will love his brother without expecting any reward. Love will satisfy only a moment of life, but the very consciousness of its momentary nature will intensify its fire to the same extent as it is now dissipated in the hopes of eternal life beyond the grave.

Dostoevsky in *The Brothers Karamazov*, Penguin
Classics, Vol. 2, pp. 763-764.

* * * * *

Well, then, listen. We (The Cardinal Grand Inquisitor and the other cardinals of the Catholic Church) are not with you but with *him* (Satan). That is our secret! It's a long time—eight centuries—since we left you and went over to *him*.... Why did you reject that last gift (Satan's world and his offer to you of all his kingdoms)? By accepting the world and Caesar's purple, you would have founded a world state and given universal peace. For who is to wield dominion over men if not those who have taken possession of their consciences and in whose hands is their bread? And so we have taken the sword of Caesar and, having taken it, we of course rejected you and followed *him*.... But then the beast will come crawling up to us and will lick our feet and will bespatter them with tears of blood from its eyes. And we shall sit upon the beast and raise the cup, and on it will be written "Mystery!" And then, and only then, will the reign of peace and happiness come to men.... Then we shall give them quiet, humble happiness, the happiness of weak creatures, such as they were created.... Oh, we shall permit them to sin too, for they are weak and helpless, and they will love us like children for allowing them to sin. We shall tell them that every sin can be expiated, if committed with our permission; that we allow them to sin because we love them all and, as for punishment for their sins—oh well, we can take it upon ourselves, and they will adore us as benefactors who have taken their sins upon ourselves before God.... It is said that the whore, who sits upon the beast and holds in her hands the *mystery*, will be put to shame, that the weak will rise up again, that they will rend her purple and strip naked her "vile" body.... And we who, for their happiness, have taken their sins upon ourselves, we shall stand before you and say: "Judge us if you can and if you dare. Know that I (the Cardinal Grand Inquisitor of Seville, Spain) am not afraid of you. Know that I too was in the wilderness, that I too fed upon locusts and roots, that I too blessed freedom, with which you have blessed men, and that I too was preparing to stand among your chosen ones, among the strong and the mighty, thirsting to 'make myself of the number.' But I woke up and refused to serve madness. I went back and joined the hosts of those who have *corrected your work*. I went away from the proud and returned to the meek for the happiness of the meek. What I say to you will come to pass and our kingdom will be established. I repeat, tomorrow you will behold the obedient flock which at a mere sign from me will rush to heap up the hot coals against the stake at which I shall burn you because you come to meddle with us. For if anyone ever deserved our fire, it is you. Tomorrow I shall burn you. *Dixi*! I have declared it!"

Dostoevsky in *The Brothers Karamazov*, Penguin
Classics, Vol. 1, pp. 302–305

* * * * *

The medium through whom Satan was beginning to overthrow all norms of law and morality, which had hitherto, in-
spite of progressive dechristianization, been generally re-
spected, this medium was Adolf Hitler. There is no shorter,
apter, clearer definition of Hitler's character than the comprehensive epithet: *medium of Satan*. If it is characteristic, without
exception, of all mediums that they are of low moral calibre,
both in character and personality, this is *a fortiori* true for a
medium of the devil. No one who is not a prey to phantasma-
goria can consider Hitler a great personality. At the Nurem-
burg trials General Jodl said of him: "He was a great man, but
an infernal great man."

Dom Alois Mager in his Satan

* * * * *

Lying and Homicide: We find both these characteristics fully
developed in the career of a man like Hitler. Could we not say
the same, or even more, of his rival, Stalin?

The presence of Satan in our age and time, and the collective
possession of whole peoples, can hardly be doubted on the evidence of *Nazism*, which was fortunately ephemeral in Germany,
and more formidably because more lasting, menacing and arrogant, on the evidence of *Communism* in immense countries such
as Russia and the People's Republic of China.

Leon Cristiani in Evidence of Satan in the Modern World

* * * * *

Power from above was thus eliminated from the universe, in both its Christian and its pagan versions. Moreover, in looking at *the power in man*, it became apparent that mind, in terms of evolution, had to be ruled as a shallow-rooted late comer. The older and more basic forces in man lay below the surface, and Freud located them, as did others, in the unconscious, in the subterranean within man. There followed what Dr. Cornelius Van Til has described as integration downward into the void: man was re-interpreted in terms of the child, the child in terms of primitive man, primitive man in terms of a mythological animal past, and so on. Culture began to seek vitality in the subterranean, in what lay below modern civilized man. Primitivism in the arts became synonymous with vitality. A jungle beat in music with an abandonment of reason became a symbol of power, and, in every area, the downward quest for power was held to be the only means of escape from sterility and impotence. The perverted, lawless, primitive and chaotic became equated with power....

It (power from below) also means a greater stress on mindless religion, as witness the so-called charismatic movement, an emphasis on mindless experience as power. The charismatic who learns to babble insanely in what is no tongue at all has no answer therein to moral and intellectual problems, but he "witnesses" eloquently to others of the feeling of "power in the Spirit," power which is in essence a cultivation of what is mindless and subterranean....

The world is thus in crisis. *Power from below* is a faith which insures the triumph of mindlessness and violence. No calls for law and order can stem this intense faith of the new pagans. The so-called religious revivals of recent years have only been part of the same ugly faith. Instead of "turning on" with narcotics, the call is for "turning on with Jesus." Instead of the narcotic "trip", the "trip" with Jesus and the "great Trip" (the Rapture) are offered so that religion is made a part of the same tradition as the pagan creed, and mindlessness is not challenged.

Rousas John Rushdoony in "Power from Below,"
reproduced by Gary North in his book
None Dare Call It Witchcraft, pp. 222–224

* * * * *

My Dear Wormwood,

... We are really faced with a cruel dilemma. When the humans disbelieve in our existence we lose all the pleasing results of direct terrorism and we make no magicians. On the other hand, when they believe in us, we cannot make them materialists and skeptics. At least, not yet. I have great hopes that we shall learn in due time how to emotionalize and mythologize their science to such an extent that what is, in effect a belief in us, (though not under that name) will creep in while the human mind remains closed to belief in the Enemy. The "Life Force," the worship of sex, and some aspects of Psychoanalysis, may here prove useful....

Once you have made the world an end, and faith a means, you have almost won your man, and it makes very little difference what kind of worldly end he is pursuing. Provided that meetings, pamphlets, policies, movements, causes and crusades, matter more to him than prayers and sacraments and charity, he is ours.

Your affectionate uncle, *Screwtape*
C. S. Lewis in *The Screwtape Letters*, Letter VII, pp. 39–43

* * * * *

Banks complain that the millions of checks passing through their facilities and the Federal Reserve System are becoming an impossibility. A new system must be found. And it is actually in use today. It has been named "The Beast." This giant computer takes up three floors at the Administration building of the Common Market Confederacy in Brussels. Here is the way it is described. This monster is a self-programing unit that has over 100 sensing input sources. Computer experts have been working on a plan to computerize all world trade. This master plan involves a digital numbering system for every human on earth. The computer would assign each citizen of the world a number to use for all buying and selling to avoid the problem of ordinary credit cards. The number would be invisibly "laser-tattooed" on the forehead or the back of the hand. It would provide a walking credit card system. The number would show up under infra-red scanners to be placed at all check-out counters and places of business. Dr. Eldeman suggests that by using three six-digital units the entire world could be assigned a working credit card number. Other Common Market officials believe that the present chaos and disorder caused by the "mystery," points to the need of a world currency—perhaps an international mark that would do away with all currency and coin. Instead, credit notes would be exchanged through a world bank clearing center. No member could buy or sell without having an assignment of a digital mark.

From *On Target*, weekly magazine, Flesherton, Ontario, June 1975

* * * * *

We have not been able to check out a report said to be from a magazine called *Die Betschaft Von Reich*, but if it is correct, it brings the age of financial domination very close. It is claimed that a Christian working at the UNO in Switzerland reported a speaker as saying that plans were already in hand for a World Tribunal to replace the UN. Each individual would receive a number and a certain amount of money which was already printed. The project provided for a single form of worship and the unification of Church and state. Everyone with a number would be employed in some area. Asked what would happen to the minority who refused to be involved, a questioner is said to have been told that their number would be cancelled; they would be deprived of the right to buy or sell and thus be forced to destruction.

Whether this is true or a piece of imaginative reporting is not known here. The interesting point, however, is that this is what is envisaged by serious students of the New Testament, including the Rev. Webber. In his article *The Checkless, Cashless Society* (Network of Patriotic Letter Writers—U.S.A.) he quotes Revelation 13:16-18:

"And he causes all, both great and small, rich and poor, free and bond, to receive a mark in their right hand, or in their foreheads:

"And that no man might buy or sell, save he that had the mark, or the name of the beast, or the number of his name.

"Here is wisdom. Let him that has understanding count the number of the beast: for it is the number of man; and his number is Six hundred threescore and six."

The Rev. Webber then wonders if the number 666 could turn out to be the computer code for a world dictator, the Antichrist as a person.

From *Ladies Line*, monthly magazine,
Australia, September 1974

The Dragon is clearly Satan. Then comes the battle of Michael and his angels against the dragon, whereby the dragon is vanquished and falls. From the deep he (the dragon) calls up a terrible creature, the first apocalyptical beast.... Here is the antithesis (of Christ): revelation of the Antichrist. He will be a man of stupendous talents and spiritual force, of great knowledge and might. He will also be filled with religious power. Indeed, he will even have a certain resemblance to Christ, for it will be said also of him that he is mortally wounded and yet alive, in other words, that he has sacrificed himself and vanquished, so that there will be something perversely redemptory about him that is directed against the living God and His Christ. This beast defies God, blaspheming against Him and his name. All men save those registered in the book of the Lamb submit to its power. Then a second beast arises, coming up out of the land. Outwardly, it resembles a Lamb, but it speaks like a dragon. It proclaims the Antichrist, erects his image, performs miracles, and persuades men to worship him. Perhaps we are meant to see in this beast the evil counterpart of him who proclaimed the Savior, the Precursor, John the Baptist. From all sides, from all races, this beast summons men, leading them to the Enemy of God.

Romano Guardini, *The Lord*, p. 510.

One day the Antichrist will come: a human being who introduces an order of things in which rebellion against God will attain its ultimate power. He will be filled with enlightenment and strength. The ultimate aim of all aims will be to prove that existence without Christ is possible—nay rather, that Christ is the enemy of existence, which can be fully realized only when all Christian values have been destroyed. His arguments will be so impressive, supported by means of such tremendous power—violent and diplomatic, material and intellectual—that to reject them will result in almost insurmountable scandal, and everyone whose eyes are not opened by grace will be lost. Then it will be clear what the Christian essence really is: that which stems not from the world, but from the heart of God; victory of grace over the world; redemption of the world, for her true essence is not to be found in herself, but in God, from whom she has received it. When God becomes all in all, the world will finally burst into flower.

Romano Guardini, The Lord, p. 513

Selected Bibliography

Alinsky, Saul D. *Reveille for Radicals*. New York: Vintage Books, 1969.

———. *Rules for Radicals*. New York: Vintage Books, 1971.

Aquinas, St. Thomas. *Summa Contra Gentiles*, Vol. 1. Translated by English Dominican Fathers. London: Oates Burns & Washbourne, 1924.

Augustine, St. *The City of God*. Translated by Marcus Dods. New York: Modern Library, 1950.

Baumiller, R. C. Director of *The Human Sexual Response-Ability*, Washington, D.C., Georgetown University, 1972.

Behrens, Helen. *The Virgin and the Serpent-God*. Mexico City: Editorial Progreso, 1963.

Belloc, Hilaire. *The Crisis of Civilization*. New York: Fordham University Press, 1937.

Benda, Julien. *The Treason of the Intellectuals*. New York: William Morrow, 1928.

Benson, Robert Hugh. *The Lord of the World*. Hawthorne, CA: Christian Book Club of America, 1976.

Bergin, Robert. *This Apocalyptic Age*. Coconut Grove, FL: Fatima International Press, 1972.

Blamires, Harry. *The Christian Mind*. London: SPCK, 1963.

Bousset, Wilhelm. *The Antichrist Legend*. London: Hutchinson, 1896.

Brochado, Costa. *Fatima in the Light of History*. Milwaukee: Bruce Publishing Company, 1955.

Butterfield, Herbert. *Christianity and History*. New York: Charles Scribner's Sons, 1950.

———. *Writings on Christianity and History*. Edited by C. T. McIntire. New York: Oxford University Press, 1979.

Calliari, Paolo. *Maria Vincitrice di Tutte le Eresie*. Torino: Editrice Lanteriana, 1976.

Calvez, J. Y. *La Pensée de Karl Marx*. Paris: Éditions du Seuil, 1956.

Campanella, Tommaso. *De Anticristo*. Roma: Centro Internazionale Di Studi Umanistici, Edizioni Rinascimento, 1965.

Campbell, James Marshall. *The Greek Fathers*. New York: Longmans, Green, 1925.

Chamberlin, E. R. *Antichrist and the Millennium*. New York: E.P. Dutton, 1952.

Clement, Marcel. *Christ and Revolution*. New Rochelle, NY: Arlington House Publishers, 1974.

Coakley, Mary Lewis. *Rated X: The Moral Case against TV*. New Rochelle, NY: Arlington House Publishers, 1977.

Conquest, Robert. *The Great Terror*. NY: Macmillan, 1969.

Costanzo, Joseph F. *This Nation under God*. NY: Herder and Herder, 1963.

Cox, Michael J. *Rain for These Roots*. Milwaukee: Bruce Publishing Company, 1956.

Cristiani, Leon. *Evidence of Satan in the Modern World*. NY: Macmillan, 1962.

Culleton, R. Gerald. *The Prophets of Our Times*. Rockford, IL: TAN Books and Publishers, 1974.

———. *The Reign of the Antichrist*. Rockford, IL: TAN Books and Publishers, 1974.

Cyril of Jerusalem. *The Catechetical Lectures*. In *Nicene and Post-Nicene Fathers*, Vol. 7, Cyril of Jerusalem and Gregory Nazianzen. Edinburgh: T & T Clark, 1994.

Dawson, Christopher. *The Gods of Revolution*. New York: New York University Press, 1972.

Dechamps, V. *Le Christ et les Antechrists dans les Écritures, L'Histoire et la Conscience*. Paris: Librairie de P. Lethielleux, 1958.

De Gaulle, Charles. *Memoires of the War*, Vol. 3, 1944–46. Translated by Richard Howard. New York: Simon & Schuster, 1960.

Dostoevsky, Fyodor. *The Brothers Karamazov*, 2 Vols. Harmondsworth, UK: Penguin Books, 1969.

Eberhardt, C. M., and C. Newman. *A Summary of Catholic History*, Vol. 1. St Louis: B. Herder Book Company, 1961.

Elar, J. J. *The Apocalypse, the Antichrist and the End*. London: Burns & Oates, 1906.

Ellul, Jacques. *The New Demons*. New York: Seabury Press, 1975.

Eppstein, John. *The Cult of Revolution in the Church*. New Rochelle, NY: Arlington House Publishers, 1974.

———. *Has the Catholic Church Gone Mad?* London: Tom Stacey, 1971.

Fahey, Denis. *The Mystical Body of Christ in the Modern World*. Dublin: Regina Publishers, 1972.

Farrer, Austin. *Light on C.S. Lewis*. London: Geoffrey Bles, 1965.

Feret, Henri Marie. *The Apocalypse of St. John*. Westminister, MD: Newman Press, 1958.

Feuerbach, Ludwig. *The Essence of Religion*. Translated by George Eliot. New York: Harper Torchbooks, 1957.

Gallery, John Ireland. *Mary vs. Lucifer*. Milwaukee: Bruce Publishing Company, 1960.

Gannon, Robert I. *The Cardinal Spellman Story*. New York: Doubleday, 1962.

Greg, W. W. *The Play of Antichrist*. London: Oxford University Press, 1935.

Gregory the Great. *Moralia*. Translated by John Henry Parker. London: J.G.F. & J. Rivington, 1844.

Grillo, Francesco. *Tommaso Campanella in America*. New York: S.F. Vanni, 1954.

Guillaume, Alfred. *Islam*. Middlesex, UK: Penguin Books, 1978.

Higgins, Marguerite. *Our Vietnam Nightmare*. New York: Harper and Row, 1965.

Hippolytus in *Ante-Nicene Fathers*, Vol. 5. Edited by A. Roberts and J. Donaldson. New York: Scribner's Sons, 1903.

Hitchcock, James. *The Decline and Fall of Radical Catholicism*. New York: Herder and Herder, 1971.

Houghton, Bryan. *Mitre and Crook*. New Rochelle, NY: Arlington House Publishers, 1979.

Huchede, P. *History of Antichrist*. Rockford, IL: TAN Books and Publishers, 1969.

Hughes, Philip. *A History of the Church*, Vol. 1. New York: Sheed and Ward, 1934.

Hyde, Douglas. "Medieval Account of Antichrist." In Gertrude Schoepperle Loomis, *Medieval Studies in Memory of Gertrude S. Loomis*. New York: Columbia University Press, 1927.

Irenaeus, St. *Against Heresies*, 3 vols. Translated by Rev. Alexander Roberts and Rev. W. H. Rambaut. Edinburgh: T & T Clark, 1884.

Knox, Ronald. *Enthusiasm*. New York: Oxford University Press, 1950.

Kramer, Herman Bernard. *The Book of Destiny*. Rockford, IL: TAN Books and Publishers, 1975.

Lewis, C.S. *The Screwtape Letters*. New York: Macmillan, 1943.

Lilienthal, Alfred M. *There Goes the Middle East*. New York: Devin-Adair, 1957.

———. *What Price Israel*. Chicago: Henry Regnery, 1953.

Lucken, Linus Urban. "Antichrist and the Prophets of Antichrist in the Chester Cycle." Ph.D. Diss., Catholic University, 1940.

Lunn, Arnold, and Garth Lean. *Christian Counter-Attack*. London: Blanford, 1969.

———. *The Cult of Softness*. London: Blanford, 1965.

———. *The New Morality*. London: Blanford, 1967.

Lyons, Eugene. *Workers' Paradise Lost*. New York: Paperback Library, 1967.

Mager, Dom Alois. *Satan*. Paris: Desclée, 1948.

Maida, Adam J. *Ownership, Control and Sponsorship of Catholic Institutions*. Harrisburg, PA: Pennsylvania Catholic Conference, 1975.

Malvenda, Thomas. *De Antichristo Libri Undecim*. Roma, 1604.

Marcel, Gabriel. *The Decline of Wisdom*. Translated by Manya Harari. London: Harvill Press, 1954.———. *Le Signe de la Croix*. In *Vers un Autre Royaume*. Paris: Plon, 1949.

———. *Man against Humanity*. Translated by G.S. Fraser. Chicago: Regnery, 1952.

———. *Man against Mass Society*. Translated by G.S. Fraser. Chicago: Henry Regnery, 1952.

Marcuse, Herbert. *Eros and Civilization*. Boston: Beacon Press, 1955.

Martin, Malachi. *Hostage to the Devil*. New York: Reader's Digest Press, 1976.

Mascall, E. L. *The Secularization of Christianity*. New York: Holt, Rinehart and Winston, 1965.

———.*Theology and the Gospel of Christ*. London: SPCK, 1977.

McCallum, Scott. *Goodbye Beloved World*. Oadby, UK: Fintra Publications, 1978.

Miceli, Vincent P. *The Gods of Atheism*. New Rochelle, New York: Arlington House Publishers, 1971.

Muggeridge, Malcolm. *Christ and the Media*. Grand Rapids, MI: William B. Eerdmans, 1977.

Newman, John Henry. *Discussions and Arguments on Various Subjects*. London: Longmans, Green, 1888.

———. *Parochial and Plain Sermons*, Vol. 2. Westminister, MD: Christian Classics, 1966.

———. *Tracts for the Times*, Vol. 5. London: J.G.F. & J. Rivington, 1840.

———. *Via Media or the Anglican Church*, Vol. 1. London: Longmans, Green, 1885.

Nietzsche, Friedrich. *The Antichrist*. In *The Portable Nietzsche*. Translated by Walter Kaufmann. New York: Viking Press, 1954.

Otto, Rudolf. *The Idea of the Holy*. New York: Oxford University Press, 1923.

Phillips, McCandlish. *The Bible, the Supernatural and the Jews*. Cleveland: World Publishing, 1970.

Pius X. Encyclical *Suprema Apostolatus*. 1903.

Pius XI. Encyclical *Atheistic Communism*. London: Catholic Truth Society, 1937.

Proudhon, Joseph. *La Justice dans la Revolution et dans L'Eglise*, Vol. 3. Paris: Garnier, 1858.

Rice, Charles. *Authority and Rebellion*. New York: Doubleday, 1971.

Roche, Anne. *The Gates of Hell*. Toronto: McClelland and Stewart, 1974.

Roth, Joseph. *Antichrist*. New York: Viking Press, 1935.

Rousseau, J. J. *Complete Works*. Paris: Éditions Dalibon, 1824.

Rushdoony, R. J. *The Institutes of Biblical Law*. Nutley, NJ: Craig Press, 1973.

Santayana, George. *Winds of Doctrine*. Gloucester, MA: Peter Smith, 1971.

Senior, John. *The Death of Christian Culture.* New Rochelle, NY: Arlington House Publishers, 1978.

Sheed, F.J., ed. *Soundings in Satanism.* NY: Sheed & Ward, 1972.

Smith, Gary V., ed. *Zionism: The Dream and the Reality.* London: David & Charles, 1974.

Tombler, John W., and Hubert J. Funk. *The Raptured.* East Orange, NJ: Trumpet Press, 1977.

von Dollinger, John J. *Prophecies and the Prophetic Spirit in the Christian Era.* Translated by Alfred Plummer. London: Rivingtons, 1873.

Von Hildebrand, Alice. *Introduction to the Philosophy of Religion.* Chicago: Franciscan Herald Press, 1970.

Von Hildebrand, Dietrich. *The Devastated Vineyard.* Chicago: Franciscan Herald Press, 1973.

———, *The New Tower of Babel.* New York: P.J. Kenedy & Sons, 1953.

Walne, Damien, and Joan Flory. *Oh, What a Beautiful Lady.* South View, London: Augustine Publishing Company, 1976.Walsh, Edmund. *Total Power.* New York: Doubleday & Company, 1948.

Whiteley, G.H. and Whiteley, Winifred, *The Permissive Morality.* London: Methuen, 1964.

Williams, Duncan. *Trousered Apes.* New Rochelle, NY: Arlington House Publishers, 1971.

Wiltgen, Ralph M. *The Rhine Flows into the Tiber.* New York: Hawthorn Books, 1967.

Articles on the Antichrist and Cognate Subjects

Arendt, Hannah. "The Jewish State: Fifty Years After—Where Have Herzl's Politics Led?" In *Zionism: The Dream and the Reality*, edited by Gary V. Smith, pp. 67–80.

Baker, Kenneth, ed. "The New Christianity." *Homiletic and Pastoral Review*, November 1976, pp. 54-61.

Barry, William. "John Henry Newman." In *The Catholic Encyclopedia*, Vol. X, edited by Charles George Herbermann. New York: Gilmary Society, 1913, pp. 794-800.

Selected Bibliography

Boland, John. "Liberation Theologists." *The Mindszenty Report*, June 1977.

Bousset, Wilhelm. "On the Antichrist." In *The Encyclopedia Britannica*, 14th ed., Vol. 2, p. 60ff.

Bucke, Emory Stevens, ed. "Babylonian or Persian Chaos Myths." In *The Interpreter's Dictionary of the Bible*, Vol. 1, A--D. New York: Abingdon Press, 1962, pp. 141ff.

Cales, Jean. "Prophecy, Prophet and Prophetess." In *The Catholic Encyclopedia*, Vol. XII, edited by Charles George Herbermann. New York: Robert Appleton, 1911, pp. 433-476.

Chapman, John. "The Fathers of the Church." In *The Catholic Encyclopedia*, Vol. VI, edited by Charles George Herbermann. New York: Gilmary Society, 1913, pp. 1-18.

Cortes, Donoso. "Ensayo Sobre el Catolicismo, el Liberalismo y el Socialismo." *Editorial Americales*, Buenos Aires, 1943, pp. 23ff.

Costanzo, Joseph F. "Academic Dissent: An Original Ecclesiology." In *The Thomist*, XXXIV, October 4, 1970, pp. 636-653.

------. "Academic Freedom and the Intellectual." Cork University Press publication as a pamphlet, 1960.

Divine, Arthur. "Prophecy." In *The Catholic Encyclopedia*, Vol. XII, edited by Charles George Herbermann. New York: Robert Appleton, 1911, pp. 473-476.

Hudleston, G. Roger. "St. Gregory the Great." In *The Catholic Encyclopedia*, Vol. VI, edited by Charles George Herbermann. New York: Gilmary Society, pp. 780-787.

Hyde, Douglas. "Medieval Account of Antichrist." In Gertrude Schoeperle Loomis,*Medieval Studies in Memory of Gertrude S. Loomis* New York: Columbia University Press, 1927, pp. 393ff.

Lunn, Arnold. "Apologetics without Apology." *Triumph*, November 1966, pp. 15-19.

Miceli, Vincent P. "Detroit: A Call to Revolution." In *Homiletic and Pastoral Review*, March 1977, pp. 27ff.

Ousset, Jean. "Dark Disorder within the Church." In *Christian Order*, January 1974, pp. 19-33.

Plummer, Alfred. "Introduction on Antichrist." In John J. von Dollinger, *Prophecies and the Prophetic Spirit in the Christian Era*, pp. xix–xx.

Pope John Paul II. "Valedictory Address in U.S.A." *Wall Street Journal*, November 9, 1978.

Pope Pius X. "Discourse on the Beatification of Joan of Arc." December 13, 1908.I In Denis Fahey, *The Mystical Body of Christ in the Modern World*, pp. 233ff.

Pope Pius XII. "The Contradiction of Our Age." Christmas Allocution, December 23, 1956. *The Pope Speaks*, Spring 1957 [March 1977], pp. 331–346.

Solzhenitsyn, Aleksandr I. "A World Split Apart." Commencement Address at Harvard University, June 8, 1978. *National Review*, July 7, 1978.

Steiner, George. "The Lollipopping of the West." *New York Times*, December 9, 1977.

Thurston, Herbert. "Joan of Arc." In *The Catholic Encyclopedia*, Vol. VIII, edited by Charles George Herbermann. New York: Robert Appleton, 1910, pp. 409–413.

Vermeesch, A. "Modernism." In *The Catholic Encyclopedia*, Vol. X, edited by Charles George Herbermann. New York: Gilmary Society, 1913, pp. 415–421.

Voth, Harold M. "The Family and the Future of America." *The Phyllis Schlafly Report*, October 1978.

Woods, Richard. "Satanism Today." In *Soundings in Satanism*, edited by F. J. Sheed, pp. 92–104.

Acknowledgment

The research for this study of the prophecy concerning the Antichrist and its relationship to modern times was sparked by an article I wrote for the journal of Christendom College, *Faith & Reason*: "Detente Reconsidered: Prelude to Antichrist." The article aroused the interest of many readers. Two of them, Neil McCaffrey, Sr., at the time president of Arlington House Publishers, and his son, Roger, a direct mail fund-raising expert, persuaded me that the hour had arrived to expand this subject into a book. For the editorial help of these extraordinary friends and of Richard Band, also a former Arlington House editor, I am glad to render many thanks.

To the students of many colleges throughout the nation and to the audiences of many Catholic organizations before whom each chapter was delivered as a conference, I express my gratitude for their stimulating questions and observations. Their concerns helped in the spiritual clarification and formation of this work. An accolade is here tendered to Clifford Forster, of Fitelson, Lasky & Aslan law firm, for his generous and expeditious unraveling of a legal knot that threatened the birth of this book.

The jacket of the book, so beautifully adorned with a detail of Luca Signorelli's (1499–1504) forceful masterpiece "The Sermon of the Antichrist," found in the splendid Cathedral of Orvieto (Italy), is due to the generosity of Dr. Arcadi Nebolsine, guardian of Christian art and architecture. I thank him for putting his excellent reproductions of Signorelli's frescoes at my disposal. Robert E. Ward, artist and friend, is here offered grateful praise for the symbolic graphics he wrought in the title of the book. In his generosity he contributed a splendid touch of his art to this volume, especially as he is deeply interested in its theme.

Two gracious scholars and friends, the Rev. James H. Reid, S.J., Professor of Classics, and the Rev. James A. Sadowsky, S.J., Professor of Philosophy, both of Fordham University, studied the manuscript and by their wise suggestions helped raise the work to a higher degree of cogency and scholarship. While I thank them for their expert cooperation, I, nevertheless, take sole responsibility for the work's limitations. I am also most grateful to Margaret McNamara who produced correct, clean copies of the manuscript with great efficiency.

Finally, I am cordially grateful to Malcolm Muggeridge, world-renowned author, journalist, and prophetic critic of the world's dying civilizations, for his kindness in honoring this study with a foreword of brilliant insights. As an international neo-Socratic nomad, he has appeared frequently in academic, journalistic, and electronic media milieux good-naturedly goading the moulders of the modern world to return from the intellectual chaos and moral madness of their lost, liberal utopias to the sanity and sanctity of the Christian vision. His presence in these pages is a great personal honor, for Malcolm Muggeridge, besides being a person of warm charm and scintillating wit, is also one who in his personal life transcends the excellence of his many writings.

About the Author

The late Rev. Vincent P. Miceli, S. J. earned his doctoral degree in contemporary philosophy from Fordham University while studying under Dietrich von Hildebrand. He taught at Spring Hill College, Loyola University in New Orleans, the Pontifical Gregorian University and the Pontifical University of St. Thomas, both in Rome, and at St. John's University in New York City. He is the author of *Ascent to Being*, a study of the philosophy of communion in the writings of Gabriel Marcel, the noted French philosopher, dramatist, and essayist. He is also the author of *The Gods of Atheism*, a study of modern atheism as it developed among philosophers and some theologians from the eighteenth century to present times. Dedicated to Pope Paul VI with his approval and enhanced with a laudatory preface by John Cardinal Wright, this work had great success. He published many articles in journals and magazines—*L'Osservatore Romano, Thought, The New Scholasticism, National Review, Homiletic and Pastoral Review*, the *New York Times, Triumph, Human Events, Christian Order, Social Digest, National Catholic Register, Men of the South*, et al. He died in 1991.

Fr. Miceli also made appearances on countless national TV and radio programs to promote the Catholic Faith and to defend Church moral teachings.

Sophia Institute

Sophia Institute is a nonprofit institution that seeks to nurture the spiritual, moral, and cultural life of souls and to spread the gospel of Christ in conformity with the authentic teachings of the Roman Catholic Church.

Sophia Institute Press fulfills this mission by offering translations, reprints, and new publications that afford readers a rich source of the enduring wisdom of mankind.

Sophia Institute also operates the popular online resource CatholicExchange.com. *Catholic Exchange* provides world news from a Catholic perspective as well as daily devotionals and articles that will help readers to grow in holiness and live a life consistent with the teachings of the Church.

In 2013, Sophia Institute launched Sophia Institute for Teachers to renew and rebuild Catholic culture through service to Catholic education. With the goal of nurturing the spiritual, moral, and cultural life of souls, and an abiding respect for the role and work of teachers, we strive to provide materials and programs that are at once enlightening to the mind and ennobling to the heart; faithful and complete, as well as useful and practical.

Sophia Institute gratefully recognizes the Solidarity Association for preserving and encouraging the growth of our apostolate over the course of many years. Without their generous and timely support, this book would not be in your hands.

www.SophiaInstitute.com
www.CatholicExchange.com
www.SophiaInstituteforTeachers.org

Sophia Institute Press® is a registered trademark of Sophia Institute.
Sophia Institute is a tax-exempt institution as defined by the
Internal Revenue Code, Section 501(c)(3). Tax ID 22-2548708.